ALSO BY TED WILLIAMS

Don't Blame the Indians—Native Americans and the Mechanized Destruction
of Fish and Wildlife

The Insightful Sportsman: Thoughts on Fish, Wildlife, and What Ails
the Earth Wild Moments

inal publication credits listed on page 415–416.
skyhorsepublishing.com

ry of Congress Cataloging-in-Publication Data
7 6 5 4 3 2 1

ms, Ted, 1946-
hing's fishy : an angler's look at how we've distressed gamefish and
aters, and how we can protect and preserve both/Ted Williams;
rd by Paul Guernsey.

cm.
-13: 978-1-60239-130-7 (alk. paper)
-10: 1-60239-130-0 (alk. paper)
hing—United States. 2. Fishes—Conservation—United States.
hing. 4. Fishes—Conservation. I. Title.

569 2007
—dc22

2007020067

the United States of America

SOMETHING'S FISHY

An Angler's Look at Our Distresse
Gamefish and Their Waters—and Ho
Can Preserve Both

Ted Williams
Foreword by Paul Guernsey

Skyhorse Publishi

CONTENTS

FOREWORD

So here we stand at the dawn of the twenty-first century, and for people who love wild fish and the places they inhabit, the future looks murky at best. The one piece of unambiguously good news has been that, in the wake of the federal Clean Water Act, water quality in U.S. rivers and major lake systems is generally better than it's been in 100 years. But the Clean Water Act was amended into its current, highly effective, form in 1977, and that was a long time ago. Since then, a host of other man-made problems, both large and extra-large, have been giving us plenty of cause for concern.

Take, for instance, the fact that mechanized commercial fishing is decimating our ocean fish stocks on a scale matched only by the Great (so-called) Buffalo Hunt of the late 1800s—and seems on the verge of producing an equally tragic result.

Consider as well the grim irony surrounding the hydropower dams that choke most of our country's large to medium-size rivers: Built in the twentieth century to produce cheap, "clean" energy, they have impoverished our aquatic world by reducing native salmon and steelhead populations in the Pacific Northwest to shadows of their former selves and, on the East Coast, snuffing out all but the final handful of Atlantic salmon.

In addition, we face rapacious forestry practices that have been destroying fish spawning areas across North America, rampant watershed development of all types that has been chewing up vast stretches of irreplaceable fish habitat everywhere, and a daunting array of exotic diseases, parasites, pests, and invasive fish species showing up in waters worldwide.

Now, I don't intend any of this to mean that we who want to protect wild fish should be discouraged. Far from it; we need to keep our sleeves rolled up and work even harder and, most importantly, we need to start speaking with one clear, consistent and rational voice to the government and to a public that is showing signs of finally being ready to hear what we have to say. ("Green" is "in" again, in case you haven't heard; let's hope it never goes "out" again.)

In America, in recent decades, the two groups most interested in preserving fish and other wildlife unfortunately have often viewed one another with mutual suspicion. One group has been made up of the traditional "conservationists," people who hunt and fish and supposedly are interested only in the well-being of species they can kill or catch—the more the better, and the hell with everything else.

In the other camp are people who would describe themselves as "environmentalists." These are the stereotypical "tree huggers," folks who would never harm a fly, much less a fish, who love nature for her own self, and who, many sportsmen assume, turn up their noses at such "consumptive" pursuits as hunting and fishing. Many of them have perhaps never handled a fishing rod; most, we are led to believe, would sooner cut off their own hands than touch a firearm.

Of course, there is often some truth in stereotypes, and I've met plenty of both "granolas" and "rednecks" who fit these respective tickets to a "T." Some anglers do indeed believe that "the greens" are linked with PETA in an unholy alliance to outlaw all fishing and hunting. And plenty of enviros suspect that most anglers and hunters are in thrall to industry, the gun lobby, and anti-environmental politicians, and would as soon eliminate any non-game endangered species that might eat a game fish or animal.

Most people, however, whether they call themselves "conservationists" or "environmentalists," while perhaps not completely understanding or appreciating others who logically should be their allies in protecting fish and wildlife, stand nowhere near either of these extremes. And that's good, because if the fish are to survive, the people who care about them need to talk to one another, and to work together.

One of the greatest values of Ted Williams and his writings for *Audubon* magazine and *Fly Rod & Reel* magazine—in which most of the essays in *Something's Fishy* were originally published—and many other places, is that he provides a strong bridge between the "conservationist" and "environmentalist" points of view. In fact, he loudly insists that any important differences exist mainly in our overly fearful imaginations.

In his private life, Ted embodies the unity of sportsman and environmentalist. He is an enthusiastic and successful hunter, as well as a ferocious and relentless fisherman—something I've witnessed with great awe on a number of occasions. And, unlike many fly fishermen, he often eats what he catches. Many of his exciting and red-blooded fishing adventures—"Essence of Patagonia," "Bluefin Summer," "How it is at South Andros," to name a few—are found among the more conservation-oriented pieces in this superbly written and meticulously researched collection.

On the other hand, Ted is every bit as passionate about the parts of nature that he enjoys with his eyes and ears rather than his palate. He has written even the most environmentally hardcore of these essays with a lyricism and a sense of delight that will leave any nature lover with a powerful sense of yearning.

Some of the pieces in *Something's Fishy* deal directly with the aforementioned problem of sportsmen and environmentalists singing from different pages and thereby losing important opportunities to conserve fish and other wildlife. Ted Williams is a tough man and a hardnosed journalist, and he's not afraid to name names and to point out the errors of either sportsmen or "enviros," especially when those errors jeopardize fish or fish habitat. For instance, you will discover in these pages that he's got no patience for anglers who would sacrifice native species of any sort in order to benefit an introduced game fish. And he has plenty of sharp words for misguided environmental "chemophobes" who object to the use of chemical piscicides for clearing out streams overrun by alien fish in order to give dwindling natives a much-deserved second shot at survival.

Sure, Ted's tone is harsh on occasion, but the threats are growing and our living natural resources are in great peril. Someone needs to speak up and lead the way, and that someone is Ted Williams. He's an environmental journalist—or conservation writer, if you prefer—like no other in our country. As so many *Fly Rod & Reel* readers have pointed out over the years, he is a national treasure.

Paul Guernsey, Editor
Fly Rod & Reel Magazine
May 2007

INTRODUCTION

What I've tried hardest to do in my writing is get anglers and environmentalists to work together toward common goals and to perceive fish as wildlife. It has been a major challenge, but it would have been impossible had I not been blessed with editors possessed of integrity and courage. Investigative reporters referred to as "gutsy" are much less so than the people who publish their copy. The latter, after all, have much more to lose when their magazines contain facts certain readers and advertisers don't want to know.

Finding such editors has been only slightly less difficult than catching coelacanths. Most outdoor publications are uncomfortable with real investigative reporting. As a general rule, editors are afraid of it and advertisers don't want it. Investigative reporters who write for outdoor publications are frequently told not to name names unless they say nice things. My friend and mentor Mike Frome—fired from *American Forests* in 1971 for "writing critically about the U.S. Forest Service [and] the forest industry" and fired from *Field & Stream* in 1974 for exposing anti-fish-and-wildlife voting records of powerful congressmen—taught me that staying hired is easy. What takes talent, effort and spine is getting fired—or, rather, choosing to get fired when principles are at stake.

I expect to be congratulated by Frome for accomplishing a feat I'm certain is a first in hook-and-bullet journalism—getting hired and fired as conservation editor of one of the nation's biggest fishing magazines all in the same day. The editor, who was new, young and idealistic, called about 9:00 a.m. and welcomed me to the staff. I asked him if he was sure the publisher wanted the kind of stuff I write.

"Definitely," he said. So I faxed a sample contract, stipulating that the magazine defend me in case of a lawsuit. This I explained was a non-negotiable ground rule for any serious investigative reporter. You can imagine what kind of Watergate coverage we would have had if

The Washington Post had given the following pep talk to Woodward and Bernstein: "Go out and get the goods on Nixon and his people, leave no stone unturned and, by the way, if you get into any legal hassles, you're on your own. You can swing in the wind." I asked the editor of the big fishing magazine to make sure he showed the sample contract to the publisher.

"Don't worry, there won't be a problem," intoned the editor. He called back that afternoon. "Gulp," he said. "I showed the contract to the publisher. He said, 'You mean we could get sued? Forget it!' "

But whenever doors have closed others have opened. The editors I have found and who have found me don't bow and scrape for advertisers, and they believe in telling readers what they need to know instead of what they want to hear. I can't think of a better demonstration of editorial integrity and courage than the reaction of *Fly Rod & Reel* editor Paul Guernsey when I queried him about doing a piece advocating lethal trout control on the Colorado River. The trout, I explained, were alien invaders and threatened the existence of an endangered native chub—you know, the "trash fish" anglers over 40 were taught to squeeze and toss into the bushes. He groaned, but before he said anything I told him about a conversation I'd just had with our mutual pal Charles Gauvin—Trout Unlimited's national president and the man who converted TU from a top-heavy, directionless social club to the nation's most effective force for the protection and restoration of native salmonids. "Go for it!" said Guernsey.

In the piece I quoted Gauvin as follows: "If we fight this, what will we say to Walleyes Unlimited when they complain about some coho recovery program in Oregon? Let's grow up. This is a problem we have to live with in these altered habitats where trout are a mitigation species. If the science is good, what business have we to be complaining about efforts to save a native species?" I then challenged my readers as follows: "What good is the humpback chub? If you have to ask, you won't comprehend the answer, which is this: It is good not because it is beautiful, not because it is interesting, not because it reaches 18 inches and is every bit as exciting to catch on a dry fly or nymph as any trout, not because it is anything, only because it is. And it needs to be saved because, to borrow the words of naturalist/explorer William Beebe, 'when the last individual of a race of living things breathes no more, another heaven and another earth must pass before such a one can be again.'"

Fly Rod & Reel subscribers tend to be better educated than those of most hook-and-bullet magazines. But few had thought of native fish as wildlife or vital parts of aquatic and terrestrial ecosystems. Typical of the verbal lashings we received was this: "So let me get this straight, a paid writer for *Audubon* wants to wipe out a thriving wild fishery? I'll bet he has alternative motives, like let's end sport fishing altogether. If you allow this type of thinking to guide the decisions about what stays and what goes, maybe Manhattan will be given back to the natives?"

But a few subscribers expressed support and, after a lengthy and acrimonious exchange on our Internet bulletin board, others came around. In the end, almost as many readers supported trout control on the Colorado as opposed it, and the piece helped provide the public support needed by the National Park Service to sustain the project.

Attempting to educate environmentalists has been no less challenging, but because I'm an environmental activist myself and write two columns for each issue of *Audubon* magazine I'm a more credible critic than other fish writers. My editors at *Audubon* have also been courageous, allowing—in fact, encouraging—me to expose the stupidity and arrogance of the environmental community (including an Audubon chapter) in its blind opposition to chemical piscicides—the only tool we have for saving imperiled fish from being hybridized and/or competed off the planet.

When I wrote in *Audubon* about how Audubon members had helped block a second effort to remove alien pike from California's Lake Davis the outraged editor of the Plumas Audubon Chapter newsletter wrote us about how, during the first effort, he had observed "bald eagles, white pelicans, and other birds and mammals as they scavenged poisoned carcasses that lined the shores." He had indeed, but he didn't mention that not one of them was killed or sickened. The reason for this is that rotenone—a safe, organic piscicide that has been used by fish managers for 75 years—does not harm birds or mammals, humans included. I told him in the letters section that I wished he and his fellow chemophobes would express as much (or even some) concern for the endangered races of Chinook salmon and steelhead trout that cling to existence in the San Joaquin and Sacramento River systems and which may be ushered into oblivion by the illegally introduced pike.

Fish are every bit as beautiful and colorful as birds, but few environmentalists ever see them because few are anglers. For instance, when you log onto the website of the Adirondack Council you hear the vocalization of a common loon—the symbol of wilderness. The council sees and hears loons, but it doesn't see or hear the brook trout that sustain loons and that are also symbols of wilderness. Wild brook trout in the Adirondacks have declined by roughly 97 percent. Today only about three percent of the park's brook-trout habitat still sustains brook trout, and the figure would be only .5 percent had not the state used rotenone to reclaim ponds infested with alien fish. But the council, which chooses not to learn about rotenone, has basically blocked its use in park wilderness.

Other vanishing icons of American wilderness include westslope and Rio Grande cutthroat trout and Gila trout. But a group called Wilderness Watch, which doesn't see them as such or see them at all, is perfectly willing to sacrifice these beautiful creatures by blocking use of rotenone and the equally safe and even shorter-lived organic piscicide, antimycin. "Poison has no place in wilderness stewardship," proclaims Wilderness Watch. But fish and plant poisons are essential to wilderness management. Without them all hope of restoring native ecosystems takes wing. According to Wilderness Watch, restoration of imperiled salmonids is only about sport: "The purpose [of Gila trout restoration] is to remove stocked trout and replace them with the listed Gila trout, in an effort to boost the population to a level that will allow delisting and resumed sport fishing of the species." That's like saying that the recovery program for the California condor is only about bird watching.

Every now and then sportsmen and environmentalists do forge alliances, and some of their accomplishments have been stunning. But nothing is more discouraging than when these alliances destroy rather than restore biodiversity. In many cases environmentalists would not have succeeded in blocking restoration of imperiled fish without help from sportsmen. In California sportsmen and environmentalists conspired to nix recovery of the Paiute cutthroat, rarest salmonid in the world. The environmentalists hadn't bothered to learn about rotenone and therefore didn't like it; sportsmen wanted their mongrels even though, in a year or two, they'd be able to fish for pure Paiutes.

One of my more angry and persistent critics at *Fly Rod & Reel* wrote us as follows: "I am a mongrel of sorts myself and delight in my diversity … We Americans abhor those who seek human genetic purity! American military men and women have died and continue to die for the freedom of others oppressed by those who wish to impose the same limitations on man as you are seeking to impose on trout. One could argue that what you champion is an environmental form of 'ethnic cleansing' or the Nazi equivalent of racial purity. 'Purity.' I am uncomfortable with that word! 'Purity' is a word often used by racists, Nazis and bigots. 'Purity'–that word is very much part of the argument to restore the Paiute cutthroat trout."

Our correspondent was an accomplished fly fisher, a fly shop owner, and a fly casting instructor. But he had never thought of fish as wildlife. To him they were merely game, and their entire purpose on earth was to titillate him by bending his rod. For him—and, alas, many anglers across the nation—a trout is a trout, and genetics are irrelevant. To borrow the words of Tom McGuane in the foreword to Dr. Robert Behnke's magnum opus, *Trout and Salmon of North America*, "A mind thus festooned with ignorance is unlikely to inform itself." But such minds must not be allowed to dictate fisheries management, as they have in the past and, too often, still do.

I have a more positive outlook than some of these essays might indicate. Whenever I get discouraged I think back to what it was like in 1970, when I signed on as wildlife journalist with the Massachusetts Division of Fisheries and Wildlife. There was no Clean Water Act, no Clean Air Act, no National Environmental Policy Act, no effective Endangered Species Act. DDT and its evil sisters had not been banned. I had never seen an eastern bluebird. The big river down the street from me, the Blackstone—birthplace of America's industrial revolution—sustained one fish species, the white sucker. When my insurance agent's dog frolicked in the Blackstone, it died as a result. Today the river sustains 33 fish species, and when my dog frolics in it he only stinks. As I write these words I am watching two pairs of bluebirds eating mealworms ten feet from my office window, and one of those pairs is incubating five eggs in my field.

I have lived to see striped bass and redfish essentially wiped out, then rebuilt to an abundance never before seen by any living human being.

In 1970 releasing fish was considered wasteful, the equivalent of not cleaning your plate. In our first and most beloved national park, grizzlies had been converted to circus bears; grandstands were being built around dumps; and the most common item in garbage cans by weight were uncleaned Yellowstone cutthroats.

Within a few months a biologist named John Varley was to lead a campaign to require largely no-kill fishing in Yellowstone. Fisheries managers across the nation upbraided him, parroting the management establishment's cherished and fallacious bromide that "you can't stockpile fish." But Varley and his colleagues persisted in a crusade that was to prove more contentious than wolf reintroduction in the 1990s (which Varley also led).

In the 1960s no Yellowstone grizzly was seen taking a spawning cutthroat. Today grizzlies have no access to garbage, and cutthroats have replaced garbage as their main spring-time diet. Cutthroats are now the sockeye salmon of the greater Yellowstone ecosystem, fueling vast food chains that also include pelicans, ospreys, eagles, herons, kingfishers, and otters.

In 1980, on my first assignment for *Audubon*, I reported on major fishing tournaments around the country. In Florida I attended the Marathon Tarpon Tournament where these magnificent, basically inedible fish were gut-hooked, bashed on the head, strung up, weighed, photographed, and dumped off the Bahia Honda Bridge. On Long Island I observed the Bay Shore Mako Tournament in which hundreds of large sharks representing at least a dozen species were strewn, whole and eviscerated, across a large cement pier. Before they could be slung onto garbage trucks, Japanese restaurateurs with buckets and large knives would dash from the shadows of buildings to slice off a fin or two, then dash back—always to derisive jeers of the crowd. But they were the only ones who were using the resource.

Today, of course, such behavior is unheard of. You'd be safer and more popular shooting raptors at Hawk Mountain among birders than slaughtering tarpon in the keys among fly fishers. Catch and release is such an institution that it's almost a conditioned reflex. Sometimes it's even carried to ridiculous extremes, as in several Rocky Mountain National Park streams in which brook trout have somehow survived the rotenone treatments that have restored native greenback cutthroats, once believed extinct. Although anglers are encouraged to kill the alien invaders, fully 80 percent of the park's brook trout have been released at least once.

Today there is much hand-wringing in fly-fishing literature about the morality of catch-and-release—"torturing" fish merely for our amusement. Considering what we used to do to them and considering all the real and pressing threats they face, I suggest that this amounts to contemplating our navels and that people thus occupied don't have enough to do. They need to go fishing.

In fact, everyone needs to go fishing. Anglers—at least the ones with open minds—eventually become advocates of native fishes and the aquatic and terrestrial ecosystems fish are part of.

I do believe we are making progress, and I devoutly hope that this book contributes to it.

Ted Williams
June 2007

I
TROUT MATTERS

ESSENCE OF PATAGONIA

<(-)->-

Patagonia—the arid, wind-swept plateau in the south of Argentina—has all the beauty and diversity of the Rocky Mountain West with almost none of the land abusers. Only about two million people live there, yet it is a quarter the size of Argentina, which itself is two-thirds the size of our contiguous states. Basically it is Montana upside down, backward and before Norman Maclean's brother first looked through the bottom of a wet whiskey glass.

There are vast, rolling steppes so dry that cows can't make a living and sheep stay lanky as poodles. There are forests and deserts, arroyos blasted by snowmelt, green river valleys raucous with lapwings and ibises, spring-nourished wetlands dappled with waterfowl, meadows indigo with lupine, perennial ice fields that flow between ragged peaks and cling to high slopes like candle wax. In our summer, native pumas move down from the high country. In our winter, condors and their lesser cousins, jotes, rise on mid-day thermals. Best of all, there are hundreds of emerald-tinted trout streams born in the high Andes and cleansed and stabilized by deep, alpine lakes that filter out glacier-milled rock flour and, even in heavy runoff, keep the channels intact and the trout feeding. As my photographer wife Donna and I discovered last December, Patagonia is a grand thing to wrap up in when your friends have put away their tackle and the Great Bear comes down to walk across the frozen spine of North America.

So there we were at midnight, December 5, 1995, on the lawn of Hosteria el Trebol in the tiny village of Cholila where Ursa Major has never set paw, sipping a superb Argentine whisky called Breeder's Choice, listening to a pair of lapwings scream into each other's faces, and staring up at strange constellations undefiled by air pollution or ambient light. What was the one between Taurus and the Southern Cross, we asked Martin Johnson, an optometrist from New Mexico. It was Orion, he said. We hadn't recognized it because it was upside down.

These blazing, oddly positioned stars, it seemed to me, might be the essence of Patagonia. Donna, on the other hand, opted for the lupine fields she had been clicking her shutter at all afternoon. We went to bed that first night with our bearings still not right, sleeping fitfully and dreaming of wildflowers and waggling dorsal fins. At 3:00 a.m. I realized that for the first time in my life I was not rejoicing in birdsong. Accordingly, I walked out onto the cold, wet grass to evict the lapwings who screamed even louder than before and, spluttering like beer-soaked teenagers, sculled out over Mosquito Lake toward the cloud-washed, moon-washed Andes.

At breakfast we learned that we were bound for everyone's favorite river—Rio Rivadavia, named for Argentina's first president. It flows through Parque Nacional Los Alerces (named for South America's only redwood), connecting Lake Rivadavia with Lake Verde. As with so much water we fished in Patagonia, trout may not be killed and barbless hooks are mandatory.

After 40 minutes on a winding, dusty dirt road, it was good to stand beside the lake and inhale the crisp alpine air. Rowing our raft was Greg Vincent, a young Welshman newly arrived from Jackson Hole, Wyoming. In the other raft—guiding Ron Scott of West Hartford, Connecticut, and John Nolen of Dallas, Texas—was our host, Jorge Graziosi, owner/founder of Safaris Acuaticos. As we moved down the lake and into the river, the day's first breeze stirred the locust-like trees on the near shore, sending yellow seed pods out into the green, clean water. All around us were snow-capped peaks. And under us trout shadows shot over sand and gravel.

A quarter mile downstream Greg and Jorge tossed their anchors onto a gravel bar, and we slogged shoreward. With Greg at her side, Donna cast a bead-head caddis pupa into a pocket along the high bank, and I moved up to a downed tree that lay across the bar. Behind the tree the current had sculpted a trough, and in it—holding tight against the trunk and vectoring nervously in the fast flow—were at least a dozen fine rainbows. Two seconds of drift and the fly was past them. They glanced at the Elk-Hair Caddis; they scorned the Parachute Adams and the Quill Gordon; they swilled the Turkey-Wing Caddis.

Whenever I managed to drop the fly an inch or two from the tree, a fish would swing down with it, then sip it, just breaking the surface and showing me the white of its mouth. It would hang there in the current until it figured out it was hooked, then dash into the tree's branches and break me off, or slice out into the main channel, leaping and making me dance down the bar. Downstream, I could see Donna's rod high and bent.

When the sun cut through the rain clouds I couldn't make out the fly anymore, but each time I saw the flash of a white mouth I would set and feel the pulse of wild trout flowing through the nine-foot wisp of graphite into my wrist, arm, heart and soul. When all the fish behind the tree had been educated I cast out into a deep channel and took a heavy, brilliantly spotted brown of about 19 inches. I would have stayed there all day, but there were four more miles of river to see, and 100 yards downstream Jorge was standing by his raft, waving us on.

Jorge—pronounced "Hor (as if you were clearing your throat) Hay"— is an unofficial ambassador to the United States, a raconteur, humorist and connoisseur of wine, food, sport and life. He has skied for Argentina's national team, served as a commissioner for the Argentine National Parks Service, operated a 7,000-acre ranch, hunted, fished and guided over two continents. Currently, he is president of the Argentina's Guides Association and directs the year-old Fundacion-Challhua Co. ("Good Fishing Waters"), his nation's version of Trout Unlimited. Working with Washington State's Wild Salmon Center, three universities in Patagonia and two in America, the fundacion raises money for scientific research aimed at preserving the nation's spectacular trout resource. And, toward this end, it agitates against hurtful development schemes. For example, it recently organized a 5,000-person march against a hydro dam that would choke off Rio Limay, spawning habitat for the salmon-sized rainbows and browns of Lago Nahuel Huapi. Shrewdly, Jorge's group scheduled the event to coincide with a pow-wow of all South America's presidents and the King of Spain at Bariloche. Argentines aren't used to this sort of thing, and the demonstration shocked the nation.

Ten years ago, when outfitters started assigning "beats" on some of the rivers north of Bariloche made famous in the 1950s by Joe Brooks, Jorge fled south to explore the remote, largely unknown water around

Cholila and Esquel. He found (and is finding still because his exploration is ongoing) better fishing on wilder rivers, most of which are so clear you can choose the fish you want to cast to. In an entire week Donna and I encountered only two other parties—a couple of shore-based Belgians and a raft we never saw till we were taking out.

The best feature of the south, and one of the reasons for Jorge's 50-percent repeat business, has been flexibility. When a river in the north isn't fishing well, you stand a good chance of getting stuck on it. In the south, your guide straps a raft to his truck and moves you to where the fish are cooperating. In 1995 Jorge started offering a package of six days on these southern rivers and four days at the bottom of the continent, fishing for the giant sea-run browns of Tierra del Fuego.

I knew that the white mouths flashing behind the blowdown would be what I'd remember most about Rio Rivadavia. Could they be part of the essence of Patagonia, I wondered as we floated down to the next bar? No, I finally decided. Trout, as lovely as they are, don't belong here. The yellow lupine, if not the blue, is native to Argentina. But salmonids are alien species, unleashed on the nation's aquatic ecosystems at the dawn of the twentieth century. They came on ships as eyed eggs, packed in moss and cooled by chunks of iceberg—the browns from Germany, the rainbows from California, the landlocks and brookies from Maine. It was, I've heard it said, one of those rare cases when humanity's obsession for playing musical chairs with flora and fauna produced a happy result. But happy for whom?

Certainly not the smallmouth perch I saw hanging in a feeder stream. Smallmouths are bigger than largemouth perch, sometimes reaching twelve pounds. Like their European and North American namesakes, they are splendid table fare but not too titillating to fly-rod-wielding naked apes from the far north. This one weighed maybe six pounds. It was a drab brown with none of the quickness or nervousness of the gaudy invaders who had overwhelmed its habitat and suppressed its tribe. It hugged its native gravel with what seemed resignation—a sad, slow vestige but an expression of the tenacity of life and the toughness of nature.

At Rio Rivadavia's first major tributary we encountered the two Belgians—nice guys but not so nice that we needed to tell them they had stumbled onto a spring creek teaming with robust trout. They'd even managed to catch a couple on grotesque, split-shot-weighted streamers. Now they eyeballed the soft-mud bottom and asked if there was a way across so they could continue along the main river. "Yes," said Jorge honestly enough, "but very far to walk and not really worth it." Pretending that we had disembarked only for a coffee break, the rest of us sipped air from empty cups while the Belgians talked incessantly to Jorge. Just when I had become convinced that they'd be with us for the afternoon they hooked their flies to their keep rings, cranked their reels, and trudged into the woods.

We fished the spring creek from the rafts with tiny nymphs hung motionless from buoyant strike indicators, as if we were after bluegills. Each of us took a fish, all fat and strong. Mine—a rainbow—jumped half a dozen times.

Nant Y Fall, named by the Welsh who settled around it, is not a spring creek; but it has all the characteristics of one. Lake-fed, it backtracks and dawdles through a broad meadow on a private estancia south of Esquel; and if you plan to fish there, better get permission because the owner wears a six-shooter and has a thing about trespassers. We arrived about noon on a day so hot we had left our neoprene waders at the La Chacra lodge, our new base outside Esquel. Riseforms bloomed and faded all over the glassy run. On the far side a flock of ibises flapped over the wide, green meadow. A harrier soared and dipped, and, far upstream, flamingos stepped across the lake's marshy floodplain.

Lunches with Safaris Acuaticos are splendid affairs with folding tables, cloth napkins, homemade cheese and bread, cooked meats, salads, desserts, and fine Argentine wines, including 1988 Malbeck. Last season Jorge bought 2,360 bottles. Throughout the long meal I was tormented by the rises. Hatches are few and fleeting in Argentina, and this one could run its course while I engaged in the cardinal sin of gluttony, something I could attend to anywhere, even in the sludgy bowels of Massachusetts. When I could stand it no longer I took a last long pull of wine, hauled on my flyweights and bolted for the river where, with mixed emotions, I discovered that all the fish were pejerreys. It was nice to see a native holding its own with the trout, but after my twentieth pejerrey the naturalist side of me gave way to Yankee prejudice and I yearned for an alien rainbow. Pejerreys are vaguely reminiscent of our mountain whitefish but more slender, with even tinier mouths and two dorsal fins.

Maybe because of the heat Nant Y Fall was being niggardly with her trout. Late in the afternoon I lost my last Turkey-Wing Caddis to a beaten one-pound rainbow thrashing at my feet. I took another decent fish on a skated Elk-Hair Caddis; and then in the twilight with white caddises billowing out of the reeds I slogged back toward the trucks. The parent of the nutria that bit the tip of Greg Vincent's fly rod cut a silver wake across a wide pool, and something moved against the near bank. As I drew closer I could make out half a dozen spotted tails waving in the evening, the smallest five inches across.

Trying to stay calm, I skated the little caddis into the tails. It vanished in a slurp, and I missed the strike, launching six torpedoes into mid-current. For 15 minutes I skated the caddis across the wide, pink and black pool. And then an enormous trout porpoised behind it, the pink of her flank and back made pinker by the dying sun. At the sting of the hook she jumped once, cartwheeling like a salmon, then ran and sounded. Four feet out from the bank and two feet under the surface was a mud lip protruding over deep water. Each time I'd work her up to the lip she'd dive under it, tearing out line, shaking her head and changing directions. The contest went on and on until it seemed she'd hang in deep water all night. I could hear someone splashing over the floodplain a hundred yards upstream, so at least I wasn't holding up our departure.

Finally, the great fish came up and over the lip, and, rod low, I skidded her onto the wet reeds. There was more than two feet of her, and, even if she didn't belong in Patagonia, she was the most beautiful thing I had seen there—the essence of the trip, if not the place. I needed two hands to hold her while she caught her breath.

The Rio Grande—not to be confused with the river of the same name in the island province of Tierra del Fuego—is a huge spring creek, 200 yards wide in some places, that gushes out of the bottom of Futaleufu Dam on the southern boundary of Parque Nacional Los Alerces, flowing west into Chile and the Pacific. For most of our day there Donna thought she had found the essence of Patagonia in the sunlit formation of thirty-six black-necked swans that flew down the river, framed against forested mountains. Jorge, half a mile behind us, had flushed them and worried that Donna had missed the shot. "Not a chance," she told him when he caught up to us for lunch.

Safaris Acuaticos has developed a fly called "Pancora," after the native freshwater crab on which Argentine trout glut themselves. You fish these flies dry on a sink-tip line because real pancoras have a habit of rising to the surface, gazing around, then dropping back to the bottom. Often, fish take just as the sink-tip drags your fly under. So, with guide Andres Muller at my side, I stood in a shallow channel in back of an island, and fed the trout of Rio Grande Jorge's floating-sinking Pancoras. They inhaled them just below the surface, leaving lusty swirls. Again, I wanted to stay there all afternoon, but there was a lot more river to see.

Casting from the raft in the late afternoon, I hooked a rainbow about a foot long—a good fish in any of my Yankee rills. As I was bringing it in, a big brown appeared and clamped down on it like a cigar. I counted to ten-Mississippi, set hard, and fought both fish to the raft where they wallowed on the surface, eliciting laughter from Andres, Greg and Donna. What was connecting me to the big brown was not my hook but his greed. After Donna had fired off a roll of film and I had the brown close enough to grab by the tail, he grudgingly released his prize. A second later the fly pulled out of the rainbow; the brown circled us like a stinger missile and walloped it again, this time seizing it by the head.

Less than two hours east of Rio Rivadavia, which flows into the Pacific, is Rio Chubut, a willow-fringed freestone stream that curls across 600 miles of steppes to the Atlantic. We headed out to it with Marcos Jaeger, part owner of Hosteria el Trebol. The ubiquitous brown hawks called chimangos perched on the fence posts along the 300,000-acre Bennetton sheep ranch. Beside green hills and yellow plains that merged with a hazy horizon, Marcos braked his Suburban and dug out a pair of field glasses. Orbiting over this endless, semi-desert was an Andean condor, the white tops of its wings flashing in the sunlight each time it banked. "Look," cried Donna, "there are two others with it." For a long while we stood in the warm, dry morning, watching these ice-age relics soaring over the endless steppes of Patagonia. Soft Argentine music was playing on

Marcos's tape deck, and never once did I feel impatience. "If this isn't the essence of the Patagonia, what is?" I asked.

The Chubut fished very well that day, with rainbows to eighteen inches sucking greased pancoras a reel-width from the cut banks.

The biggest trout in Jorge's new stomping grounds inhabit the remote mountain lakes of Rio Pico south of Esquel. Getting there over the high, rough roads is a major undertaking, so you spend at least one night in a generator-lit log cabin on a grassy hill overlooking Lago Number 3 (the best of the five lakes).

I hadn't been euphoric about the prospect of sitting on stillwater, slinging grackle-sized streamers on 2X tippets and high-grain sink tips. But my pretensions quickly evaporated. While Marcos muscled the raft into a hard wind I dropped some kind of a green-tailed, bead-head bugger I'd pilfered from his fly box up against the vast field of reeds that nearly circles the lake. "Bottom," I grunted, feeling brief resistance. But on the next cast bottom belted back and tore out line. Far out in the lake a rainbow the size of a summer steelhead launched itself into the air and hung across the grey-green mountainscape. I lost it, but that afternoon and the next day I landed nine others up to five pounds and got the best out of one of at least seven.

The wind fell away at night; and, into the whisky again, Donna and I stretched out on the grass in the sweet Argentine springtime. The lapwings were calling, but somehow they sounded more melodious now—like Pavarotti yelling at his kids. As we lay there all the images of Patagonia merged into an essence as hard to catch on paper or film as the woodsmoke from Marcos's freshly kindled fire that swirled around us and up into the infinite southern night. Now we had our bearings; and with our heads toward the lake, Orion flopped back to its familiar position.

ROLE REVERSAL ON THE COLORADO

⤙ ⤚

For about 210 miles in Arizona, the Colorado River below Glen Canyon Dam is infested with alien fish that threaten natives. So, to control the aliens and thereby test the feasibility of recovering the natives, the U.S. Department of Interior has approved a two-year experiment. At Glen Canyon Dam, the Bureau of Reclamation (BuRec) will fluctuate flows in order to expose redds and kill eggs. In a 9.4-mile stretch above and below the mouth of the Little Colorado River (which enters the mainstem 76 miles downstream of the dam) the U.S. Geological Survey's Grand Canyon Monitoring and Research Center (GCMRC) will lead an effort to remove the aliens with electro-fishing gear, euthanize them with an anesthetic, then hand out the carcasses to local Indians to use as fertilizer. At Bright Angel Creek, 103 miles below the dam, the National Park Service installed a weir on November 18, 2002 that has been interdicting aliens as they enter what is believed to be their most important spawning tributary.

The aliens are wild, self-sustaining trout—virtually all rainbows in the 15 miles below the dam known as the Lees Ferry reach, virtually all browns at Bright Angel Creek and a mix, top-heavy with rainbows, near the Little Colorado River. The natives are chubs; you know, the "trash fish" your grandfather taught you to squeeze and toss into the bushes— in this case "humpback chubs," federally listed as endangered. The feds weren't always so protective of humpbacks. For example, 40 years ago, above what is now Lake Powell, they tried to eradicate them (along with bonytail chubs, razorback suckers and Colorado squawfish—all currently endangered) by applying 20,000 gallons of emulsified rotenone to 445 miles of the Green River and its tributaries. As one angler later told the Fish and Wildlife Service: "Everybody was tickled to death. There was so much chub and trash fish, [but] there was no trout."

Trout control on the Colorado outrages some sportsmen. "We cannot go back to the Garden of Eden," writes Mike Miller of the

Colorado Fishing Federation in an action alert entitled Endangered Species Threaten Sportfishing. "You can poison all of the sportfish in the basin, and the evidence suggests it would have very little impact on recovery of the endangered species ... Millions of sportsmen's dollars are used on endangered species protection. This is a fact short-sighted, narrow-minded environmentalists never seem to consider. In the end, the alienation and disenfranchising of anglers will have a much greater negative impact on endangered species protection."

A more thoughtful and dispassionate analysis is offered by Terry Gunn, a dedicated conservationist entering his twenty-first year guiding fly fishermen at Lees Ferry and one of the best guides I've fished with. Not that Gunn is happy about the plan.

"I really have to question the science," he told me. "It's a shot in the dark, a supposition at best. I think the [rainbow] trout are getting a bad rap here; the predation rate on humpbacks is only .07 percent [of trout stomachs checked]. And there are so many other things affecting the humpback chub. Now they've got an Asian tapeworm."

Dave Foster, another highly respected Lees Ferry guide and conservationist, has worked here since 1988, fished here since 1966. Like Gunn, Foster does his homework and never shoots from the hip. "We're mixing our science," he declares. "We've got a flow regime aimed at reducing spawning trout and at the same time a very expensive program to eradicate trout at the mouth of the Little Colorado River. A few years down the road you're not going to be able to tease out which was the most effective method. I've always felt that what's good for the trout is good for the chubs." He agrees with Gunn that the fluctuations aren't going to hurt the trout at Lees Ferry, but that doesn't mean they won't hurt the fishing. "Anglers will do great in the morning," he says. "But then when the water rises in the afternoon [during peak demand] they'll be standing up to their nipples and casting to gravel bars that were dry the day before."

There are a few humpback populations above Lake Powell, but only about 2,000 adults survive in the lower basin, mostly in the Little Colorado River. Like the other seven native fish species once abundant in the 277-mile Grand Canyon stretch of the main Colorado, the humpback is a big-river fish adapted to flows that could vary between 2,000 and 200,000 cubic feet per second. Large fins allow it to sail through fierce currents. Small eyes protect it from swirling silt. So adept is it at sensing vibrations that it can pick off floating insects in water turbid enough to obscure your rod tip an inch below the surface. It has silver flanks, a long snout, a pencil-thin "wrist" before the tail, and the hump of a male pink salmon in spawning condition. When humpback fry, sweeping down from the Little Colorado, hit their traditional habitat in the dam-chilled mainstream they go into thermal shock and are easy pickings for predators. About 10 percent of brown-trout stomachs checked contain humpbacks; and, while humpbacks are found in the stomachs of only one half to one percent of rainbow trout, there are so many rainbows that this could mean between 125,000 and 250,000 rainbows.

The Colorado squawfish (or "pikeminnow" as the PC police have renamed it), the bonytail chub, the razorback sucker and the roundtail chub have been extirpated from the park (though they still occur above Lake Powell). If trout predation continues at its current rate, the U.S. Department of the Interior reckons the population of adult humpbacks could fall to 500 within the decade. Extirpation would likely follow shortly thereafter.

Angry sportsmen didn't get very far when they bitched to Trout Unlimited's national president Charles Gauvin, who—more than any angler I know—has dedicated himself to imbuing the public with what Aldo Leopold called an "ecological conscience."

"I backed Babbitt's [1996] flood to restore beaches," says Gauvin, "and I got nasty mail from TU members, proclaiming that I wouldn't be happy 'til every trout in the Colorado was flushed into the Sea of Cortez. If we fight this, what will we say to Walleyes Unlimited when they complain about some coho recovery program in Oregon? Let's grow up. This is a problem we have to live with in these altered habitats where trout are a mitigation species. If the science is good, what business have we to be complaining about efforts to save a native species?"

Critics, including Gunn, Foster and a large element of the environmental community, say the science is bad. But the science hasn't happened yet. What is underway on the Colorado is called "adaptive management"—you try something, collect and analyze data, then see if you got results; if you didn't get results, you try something else. Basically, you do the best you can with the information you have. In 1991 adaptive management called for the stabilization of flows. This, reasoned managers, would be good for trout and chubs. Unfortunately, it was good for neither. According to best estimates, it quadrupled the number of trout (which is not the same as benefiting them). Concurrently, the humpback population started to fall off. Before 1991—when flows fluctuated wildly—the trout fishery at Lees Ferry depended on stocking. Now it's self-sustaining.

The fishery is world famous, the pride of the Arizona Game and Fish Department. I knew I could count on the department for a strong opinion about federal trout control, and fisheries biologist Bill Persons didn't disappoint me. Was he outraged? Well, no. In fact, just the opposite.

"From the lower end of Lees Ferry and the rest of the river we'd like to manage for our four remaining native fish—that's humpback chub, flannelmouth sucker, bluehead sucker and speckled dace," he said. "In the first 15 miles below the dam we're trying to maintain a quality tailwater trout fishery. The condition and average size of those trout is way down. Growth is very poor. There just aren't enough groceries to go around." The fish sampled by the department's electro-fishing crews average eight inches. Foster reports that fish caught by his anglers average better than that—about thirteen inches—but that the trophy fishing days at Lees Ferry are definitely over. With flow fluctuations Persons and his colleagues expect the size and condition of Lees Ferry trout to dramatically improve. Moreover, because the flow fluctuations won't be as severe or as sustained as they were previously, the trout will probably be able to sustain themselves. But Persons says this: "I think if we lost three year classes in a row, we'd want to go in with a stocking of fingerlings so we didn't have a big hole in the fishery."

What I find astonishing is that precisely the same reservations articulated by Gunn and Foster are being articulated by biologists who advocate trout control. Sometimes the biologists even use the same words. "A shot in the dark," for example, is also how University of British Columbia fisheries professor Dr. Carl Walters describes trout removal in the vicinity of the Little Colorado. For the past six years Walters has worked as a consultant to the Grand Canyon Monitoring and Research Center; and, being from Canada, he doesn't carry any of the bureaucratic baggage that might cloud his objectivity. Sometimes, he explains, you have to take shots in the dark because once a native ecosystem has been nuked by a dam, there aren't lots of options. "We don't know why the chub population is declining," he says. "We think it has something to do with too many predators at the mouth of the Little Colorado. But we're not absolutely sure. And we're not sure that, if those trout are taken out, the chubs can survive."

What's more, both Persons and Walters share Foster's opinion that "what's good for the trout is good for the chubs." Here's how Walters describes the mutually beneficial influence of fluctuating flows: "At Lees Ferry we went from a trophy fishery to your standard jillions of twelve-inch rainbows. I've worked on rainbow trout for fifty years, and I've never seen densities this high. For twelve miles they're lined up like cordwood. The first time I walked down there I thought I was back in one of those California fish hatcheries I grew up in. That's exactly how it smelled. [He's not sure what he was smelling—maybe the fish themselves, maybe their excrement, maybe both.] Even if there weren't a native-fish issue, I think we'd recommend fluctuating flows to kill some of the eggs and try to get better sizes of fish. The river can grow lots of little trout or a few big ones. Gunn and Foster understand this. But some of the other guys keep thinking more fish, more eggs, more fish ... That's just wrong; it's a rat race that has been played out in tailwaters all over the United States, and it always backfires."

But what about the browns at Bright Angel Creek? It's clear that they're eating lots of chubs; and, once they get out into the Colorado, they have no problem growing.

Fisheries consultant and former Fish and Wildlife Service biologist Dr. Richard Valdez, who has conducted extensive studies on humpbacks and other native Colorado River fish, reports seeing ten- and twelve-pound browns in and around Bright Angel. "They swim from there up to the Little Colorado; that's a big [twenty-seven-mile] migration, but browns will do that," he told me. "I suspect that there are some guys who know that this is one of the best-kept secrets for big browns and that they're not pleased about this effort [to eliminate them]."

But managers don't have a choice—morally or legally. First, the Endangered Species Act mandates the action. Second, while the river from Lees Ferry to the dam is managed by the Park Service as part of the Glen Canyon National Recreational Area, the next 277 miles are managed as part of Grand Canyon National Park. Above Lees Ferry the agency's mission is recreation (although this mission is trumped by the Endangered Species Act whenever it conflicts with the welfare of a listed species). Below Lees Ferry the mission is to protect and restore all the natural parts and, within reason, allow "natural processes to proceed unimpeded."

One reason trout are so prolific in the Colorado is that the squawfish—the only large predator fish that evolved in the stretch managed by the Park Service—has been eliminated. This minnow, which can attain weights of eighty pounds or more, is a salmonid-eating machine in other systems, frequently to the dismay of managers. There has been talk about re-introducing squawfish; but they wouldn't spawn in the cold tailwater, and the idea of put-grow-and-eat-trout management turns off biologists. "There's concern about fiddling too much," says Randall Peterson, BuRec's rep on the Adaptive Management Work Group (a diverse collection of stakeholders including government agencies, Indian tribes, power companies, sportsmen and environmentalists that advises the U.S. Department of the Interior on how to operate the dam). "When we saw the unexpected outcome of the exploding trout population it taught us all to go slow and careful."

More serious thought has been given to reintroducing river otters, a project that by no means fits the definition of "fiddling." Otters may have been extirpated when the first dam releases drowned kits in their dens and when the Glen Canyon Dam and the Hoover Dam downstream blocked gene flow. "Without its top aquatic predator the Colorado River ecosystem is just as out-of-whack as Yellowstone used to be without wolves," comments park biologist Elaine Leslie. "We should be looking at native species restoration wherever possible, and the restoration of ecosystems. The problem at Grand Canyon is that there doesn't appear to be a viable population of Sonoran river otters [the subspecies that belongs in the park] anywhere in the Southwest. So, if we were to reintroduce otters, we'd want to get the closest possible relative to the

Sonoran otter. The issue of most concern with otter reintroduction is the potential impact on the highly endangered humpback chub, which is slower moving than brown or rainbow trout." But otters target whatever fish is most abundant—i.e., trout—and Leslie believes that, unless otters took up residency on the Little Colorado River (in which case they could be relocated because they'd be wearing radio collars), the impact would be insignificant.

Carl Walters says this: "I don't think otters would hurt the chubs; they'd be well adapted to this kind of predation. The biggest threat to the chubs, beside the trout and the warmwater fish, is each other. They're pretty fierce cannibals. I wouldn't worry about adding otters."

What good is the humpback chub? If you have to ask, you won't comprehend the answer, which is this: It is good not because it is beautiful, not because it is interesting, not because it reaches eighteen inches and is every bit as exciting to catch on a dry fly or nymph as any trout, not because it is anything, only because it is. And it needs to be saved because, to borrow the words of naturalist/explorer William Beebe, "when the last individual of a race of living things breathes no more, another heaven and another earth must pass before such a one can be again." The framers of the Endangered Species Act understood this.

So do Gunn and Foster, despite their grave reservations about the current experiment. Both stress that they want to see humpback chubs do well. And both have it right when they say that trout should not get all or even most of the blame for the chub's predicament. But trout are one of the few things adaptive managers can do something about.

Everyone who loves the wild, self-sustaining trout of the Colorado had better hope that the current experiment works. If it doesn't, the next experiment the Department of the Interior is almost sure to try is warming the river by releasing water from higher up on the dam. This could, as Walters puts it, "unleash vampires from the basement," bringing more alien predators such as stripers, largemouths, brown trout and channel cats up from Lake Mead and the lower river. On the other hand, the enormous amount of restored habitat in the main river might bring on an explosion of humpbacks sufficient to overwhelm the increased predation.

The vampire that frightens Walters most is the brown trout. "They wouldn't just eat chubs," he says. "Right now the brown population is small and mostly restricted to Bright Angel Creek. We think that the reason browns haven't been able to spread out very far is that the water's too cold. If they move up to Lees Ferry, they're going to eat the rainbows and ruin the fishing. And the brown trout fishery would never replace it. Big rivers and brown trout fishing don't go together very well."

That doesn't mean that Walters—or anyone else with an ecological conscience—will fight temperature control on the Colorado if it really has to come to that. It means only that the current rainbow fishery is a nationally important mitigation resource that should be retained if it doesn't mean sacrificing the humpback chub.

Much of the environmental community doesn't agree. It is pushing hard for temperature control right now. The Grand Canyon Trust—which has announced that it will sue the Fish and Wildlife Service over a humpback recovery goal that's "a feel-good fairy tale based not on sound science, but political expediency and the desires of powerful special interests"—proclaims that "the Colorado River must be warmed in order to improve recruitment of the humpback chub." Eight other groups, including the frenetically litigious Center for Biological Diversity, have sent a letter to BuRec charging that one of the goals of its strategic plan—maintaining naturally reproducing rainbows around Lees Ferry "to the extent practicable and consistent with the maintenance of viable populations of native fish"—is not supported by law, contrary to the needs of native fish, and should be eliminated. Maybe they're right.

But maybe the adaptive managers will prove that humpbacks can be saved just with flow fluctuations and localized trout removal. And maybe the Lees Ferry reach will again produce big rainbows. Meanwhile, sportsmen need to support the professionals they've trained and hired with their tax and license dollars, forget everything their grandfathers taught them about "trash fish," and remember how they reacted most everywhere else—where the natives harmed by aliens are trout.

DIXIE TROUT

⊰⊱

On a warm March morning I crouched beside a stream high in Great Smoky Mountains National Park, cradling a brook trout in the icy current. In sunlight, muted by the kind of cloud bank that gave these mountains their name, the belly of the little fish glowed with impossible shades of orange. The Yankee trout I knew had two or three rows of red spots along their chestnut flanks, but this one had seven. The dorsal fin was broader and marked with strange but lovely black stripes. Underfins, with the familiar cream trim, seemed larger.

In the water two Park Service biologists, Matt Kulp and Joe Beeler, slogged around, stunning fish with 600 volts from gasoline-powered backpack generators. They were looking for rainbow trout and happy not to be finding them. Apparently rainbows had never been stocked here, and a downstream waterfall was keeping them out. In previous summers Kulp, Beeler and their colleagues had sorted out the rainbows from other park streams, releasing them below natural barriers. Why would they do such a thing when rainbows grow bigger, fight harder, and when the Park Service had gone to all the trouble and expense to plant them?

Well, values change. These days the mission of the Park Service, unique among state and federal agencies, is to preserve and restore "naturally functioning native ecosystems." Rainbow trout, which the park quit stocking in 1975, don't belong here. They evolved in the Pacific Northwest.

The slice of mountain sunrise I was holding in my hand quickly revived and darted back into the flow. At seven inches it was a giant among southern Appalachian brook trout—a subspecies isolated these past three million years in the high country of Virginia, Georgia, the Carolinas and Tennessee. Because of competition from the stronger, larger rainbows, this unique fish, the South's only native trout, is now confined to high-elevation streams where it is particularly vulnerable to acid rain. In Great Smoky Mountains National Park only about 15 percent of the brook trout are pure southerners because before 1975 the park also polluted its waters with brook trout of the northern race.

The restoration process has been arduous—a tough sell to anglers who lack what Aldo Leopold called an "ecological conscience." To many of them a trout is a trout, and "bigger" and "better" are synonyms. But a trout is no more a trout than a tree is a tree. In fact, a brook trout isn't a trout at all; it's a char descended from an Arctic char prototype landlocked by ancient glaciers. That's why it seeks out frigid water and why its generic name, Salvelinus fontinalis, means "dweller of springs." The vanishing southern subspecies is a national treasure, no less valuable than California's redwoods or Minnesota's timber wolves.

So far the park has restored 11.1 miles of brook trout habitat on nine streams. "We already had about 121 miles of brook trout water, and we're shooting to restore another 40 miles," says project leader Steve Moore. "Restoration of the rest of the original habitat [629 miles] just isn't practical." Among the reasons: lack of natural barriers and the proliferation of brown trout, aliens from Europe that can leap over waterfalls rainbows can't negotiate.

Sam's Creek, scene of the latest and most spectacular success, was too big to restore with just electroshocking. But when the park proposed to kill the rainbows with a selective, short-lived, utterly safe fish poison called antimycin, some anglers were outraged. Last fall, after a painstaking environmental-review and public-comment process, the park completed the job, but not before shocking and evacuating most of the native brook trout and opening the stream to unrestricted rainbow fishing. Patient and intelligent public education, by the park and a private outfit aptly called Trout Unlimited, has turned attitudes around. When all comments were in, the approval rate for the first antimycin treatment was 81 percent.

Now anglers with new values are contributing money and time to save their native trout. Not because it is a better game fish than the aliens that suppress it (it is smaller and weaker), not because it is more beautiful (although it is), but because it is part of the South's purple, cloud-wrapped mountains and of the Earth's genetic wealth—because it belongs.

Bringing Back the Giants

--- ⇠⟨ ⟩⇢ ---

We called them "coasters" and "salmon trout" because they patrolled the coastlines of Lakes Superior, Huron, Michigan and Nipigon, and because they were the size of salmon. Then, before we had a chance to learn much about how they lived and reproduced, we essentially wiped them out. We caught and killed a lot of these giant brook trout—but that doesn't mean there had been a lot of them. Few if any species are as vulnerable to angling pressure. As with so many brook trout extirpations, this one was also accomplished by ripping up landscapes so silt and sand buried streambed spawning gravel, and by razing tree cover that shaded, cooled and slowed runoff.

Today there are only three recognized strains of wild coasters in the United States, all in Lake Superior and all in Michigan: the two stream-spawning populations of the Upper Peninsula's Salmon Trout River and Isle Royale's Big and Little Siskiwit rivers, and the shoal-spawners of Isle Royale's Tobin Harbor. There are countless rills in Minnesota that funnel brook trout into the lake at which point, by definition, they become coasters. Most of these fish aren't much over a pound and a half. Ontario provides eggs from its Lake Nipigon coaster strain to Ojibwa Indian and state managers around the Superior Basin.

Attempts at coaster rehabilitation began in 1890. It was going to be easy—just cluster-bomb the lake with hatchery brook trout. During the next 100 years Wisconsin alone stocked about 23 million fry, fingerlings and adults. Despite those efforts, the state is apparently without wild coasters. And the populations that persist in Michigan's, Ontario's, and Minnesota's Lake Superior shorelines are tiny remnants. In Ontario's Lake Nipigon (sixty miles long and forty miles wide) recovery is well underway.

Whether coasters can be restored to lakes Huron and Michigan is questionable, but there is reason for much optimism in Lake Superior. Since I last reported on coasters (in the July 2001 *Fly Rod & Reel*) Superior's

Canadian and American partners—twenty-seven governmental, tribal, university and non—profit organizations-have pooled coaster research and coordinated management. At this writing working groups are about to publish papers that will answer some of our many questions about stream habitat, lake habitat, ecology, populations and genetics.

In 2001 it grieved me to report that Wisconsin and Michigan were thumbing their noses at coaster rehabilitation by permitting Lake Superior anglers to kill three fish a day, which only had to measure fifteen inches in Wisconsin and ten inches in Michigan. But now all partners have implemented strict lake-wide harvest regulations—one fish over twenty inches per day in the states; and one fish over twenty-two inches in Ontario. The tribes are doing even better, having basically committed to no-kill and, as has been their traditional practice, refusing to stock exotic species. Although Wisconsin and Michigan still allow the mass slaughter of potential coasters in most of their tributaries, Minnesota and Ontario have applied their one-fish limit in every stream at least up to the first migration barrier. The new state and provincial regs, which went into effect in 2005, are by far the best news coaster advocates have ever received. Minnesota and Ontario anglers report more and bigger coasters already, though it will probably be at least five years before they see dramatic results.

The only good coaster data we have comes from Lake Nipigon, but it is applicable to Superior because growth and maturity rates are identical. The previous limit on Lake Nipigon (in place from 1990 through 2004) of two coasters over eighteen inches protected only 22 percent of the fish on South Bay Shoal, a major spawning bed. The year-old limit of one fish over twenty-two inches (also in effect in Ontario's Lake Superior waters) is protecting 87 percent. Rob Swainson of the Ontario Ministry of Natural Resources, the godfather of North American coaster rehabilitation, predicts a "huge" and speedy improvement in the Nipigon population and a slower but still impressive one in Superior's. When he took over coaster management in 1988 the fish were presumed extirpated from the Nipigon River (which meets Lake Superior north of Thunder Bay). When he asked his colleagues for coaster data they told him there weren't any.

Destroying brook trout habitat has long been a criminal offense in Ontario, but because managers assumed there was none left they'd been allowing Ontario Power Generation to flush and fill the river as if it were a toilet bowl, stranding eggs, fry and invertebrate prey in the process. Swainson got that stopped two years after he arrived, then set about the Herculean task of convincing the angling community that you can catch lots of brook trout or eat lots of brook trout, but that if you do the latter, you won't do either for long.

In 1989, despite an ugly confrontation with the fillet-and-release crowd—namely the Ontario Federation of Anglers and Hunters (OFAH)—he implemented a limit of two fish over eighteen inches in Lake Nipigon and the Nipigon River. Seven years later—after another ugly confrontation with OFAH—he implemented a one-fish, twenty-inch limit in the Nipigon River and Superior's Nipigon Bay. A year ago, when he proposed the one-fish, twenty-two-inch limit for all Canadian coaster waters including Superior's tributaries to the first migration barrier, OFAH shrieked louder than ever, claiming that such a limit at the bottom of the tribs was anti-sportsmen and anti-father-and-son. So Swainson and his colleagues suggested that perhaps the trib limit could be one fish over twenty-two inches or one fish under ten inches. This time, however, there was so much support for coasters among enlightened anglers that they shouted the proposal down.

Some coasters—the Tobin Harbor and Lake Nipigon strains, for example—are known to spawn in the lake (on shoals at the mouths of rivers or over upwellings of groundwater). But others—maybe most—spawn in feeder streams. In order to shut down the slaughter, not just in Canada but in Minnesota as well, managers had to show doubters such as OFAH that coasters need tributaries. Providing the evidence was graduate student Silvia D'Amelio of Trent University in Peterborough, Ontario. D'Amelio compared the DNA of trout captured in the tribs to that of trout captured in the lake and found that fish from both habitats were part of the same population, thereby dismantling the widespread superstition that coasters depend only on the lake. "My research showed that not all tributaries within Lake Superior contribute to the coaster presence within the lake," she writes me. "However, all the tributaries I looked at seem to have the potential to do so. Because coasters are not unique unto themselves, it is not possible to create a coaster broodstock. You can, however, create a broodstock with the potential to produce coasters. The key is in finding the trigger(s) that cause some brook trout to make the switch from resident to coaster. The most important point to remember for rehabilitative stocking is that to maintain the long-term integrity of these populations, closely related populations should be used to rehabilitate each individual tributary. Using a single source for the whole lake could greatly hamper the long-term survival of these fish."

One of the environmental triggers is obviously weather. Many of the small North Shore rills that ripple with brookies in May dry up in July. The fish don't have a choice; they have to go out into the lake, at which point they become coasters even if they're two inches long. In some cases fish above the barriers are genetically distinct from fish below, but when they get swept over the falls they apparently migrate to the lake also. There's a coldwater trickle collected by Superior near Swainson's house that produces no trout of its own; yet every spring it is full of young of the year brookies. In summer they're gone. "Brook trout have very plastic life histories," observes Trout Unlimited's watershed programs director Laura Hewitt. "Full siblings can be two inches and living under an ice shelf and two feet and living in open water."

So does all this vindicate Wisconsin trout manager Dennis Pratt and his colleagues who don't even like to use the word "coaster" and who have been criticized by a host of fisheries professionals (including salmonid guru Dr. Robert Behnke) for arguing that, in their opinion at least, "a brook trout is a brook trout"? In a way it does—if, as I suspect, what they meant to say is "all brook trout with access to Lake Superior are probably potential coasters."

Still, each of the recognized coaster strains has distinctive genetic markers that allow managers to ID them from tissue samples. And there are measurable genetic differences between the coasters of the Salmon Trout River and resident brook trout farther upstream. Whether or not there's a genetic trigger to migratory behavior is not known. And while D'Amelio's research was hugely important in that it showed the link between stream and lake habitat, she has never pretended that it tells us anything about possible genetic triggers or even genetic differences between coasters and resident brookies. After all, if the trout she sampled in the tribs were the progeny of coasters, you'd expect them to share DNA.

Pratt makes an excellent point when he observes that Wisconsin's brook trout habitat has been so grievously damaged by logging, agriculture and development that there may no longer be sufficient competition to force trout out into the lake or sufficient food base for them to grow large enough to want to move out into the lake; and that, in any case, most of the wild trout are far upstream because the low-gradient river mouths are clogged with silt and sand. "We have extremely good groundwater flow," he told me, "with some streams influenced all the way to the lakeshore. But flow and velocity are so great that survival of eggs and fry is poor. Most Minnesota brook trout populations, on the other hand, are in fairly close association with the shoreline because of barrier falls."

To its credit Wisconsin is doing something about its habitat problem. It is controlling beavers, smoothing banks to stop sloughing, engineering logjams, flushing sand and silt off gravel by removing tag alder and woody debris, then letting the systems recover on their own (a process which, once the gravel is re-exposed, includes natural accumulation of woody debris).

Some of the most promising work is occurring on Whittlesey Creek, Graveyard Creek, and the Bark River—all subject to no-kill regs. In cooperation with the Fish and Wildlife Service, Whittlesey is being stocked with both strains of Isle Royale coasters. Seventy-six adults, about a third of them radio-tagged, were released in August 2003. Fertilized eggs and yearlings are scheduled in even-numbered years, fry in odd-numbered years. There will be four more years of stocking, then assessments for about five years. Graveyard Creek and the Bark River aren't being stocked in the hope that their native fish will become coasters.

In Michigan the Upper Peninsula's only viable coaster producer, the Salmon Trout River, is threatened by a massive metallic sulfide mine proposed by Kennecott Minerals Corporation. No mineral extraction is nastier: Target metals are bound in ores along with sulfur, and when the ore is removed and exposed to air and water it produces sulfuric acid and heavy metals, both of which can foul surface and ground water. Partly due to pollution from Kennecott's sulfide mine in Flambeau, Wisconsin, that state has essentially banned sulfide mining. Michigan has done about all it can by enacting a decent law, and at this writing a working group comprised of all interests is hashing out specific regulations. But regulations are only as good as enforcement; and there are few places in the nation where mining companies are much bothered by strict enforcement. Trout Unlimited is particularly worried about the footprint. "For us the biggest concern is the relatively remote location of the mine means that all the ore has to be hauled by truck," says Rich Bowman, director of the Michigan TU Council. "You're talking forty trucks per day moving thirty miles from the site to the railhead."

In cooperation with the Fish and Wildlife Service, the Michigan DNR had been stocking Tobin Harbor coasters in three streams in Pictured Rocks National Lakeshore. But the Park Service has wisely nixed the program because researchers using radio tags have found that the streams are producing little coasters of their own. Not messing with native genes is just common sense; and, what's more, the agency is mandated to "let natural processes proceed unimpeded within reason." Although spawning runs have yet to be seen, coaster stocking continues on the Keweenaw Peninsula in the Gratiot and Little Carp rivers.

Minnesota managers, who see silvery brookies in the mouths of essentially fishless tribs at spawning time, have shied away from stocking because they want to preserve the genes of the coasters they obviously have. "Our goal is to see if we can rehabilitate some of our own stocks with the restrictive regulation," comments Don Schreiner, the state DNR's Lake Superior fisheries supervisor. "Grand Portage [Ojibwa tribe] has been stocking for ten years like there's no tomorrow. So we see no reason to reinvent the wheel. Let's watch them and see how it works." Schreiner and his colleagues would like to see that tribe and others make better efforts at assessment.

The one major disappointment I had in these most recent conversations with my coaster contacts was learning that the stocking of splake (artificially concocted lake trout-brookie hybrids) is still going hot and heavy in Wisconsin and Michigan. (Minnesota and Ontario mess around with these Frankenstein fish on inland lakes but have never polluted Lake Superior with them.) In 2001, when I suggested to Michigan DNR's Lake Superior Basin coordinator Steve Scott that his agency drop its Lake Superior splake program, he reported that he and his colleagues saw an opportunity to "replace splake with planted coasters." At that time the DNR was stocking about 80,000 splake a year. Now it stocks between 100,000 and 150,000. Wisconsin stocks about 60,000 (down from about 180,000 five years ago, but mostly because there was poor survival in Chequamegon Bay).

Splake were supposed to have been sterile; but, like the monsters of *Jurassic Park*, they've found a way to reproduce. And in some parts of Lake Superior they're apparently mixing their warped genes with those of lake trout and brook trout. Not only do they compete with brook trout, they eat them—so voraciously, in fact, that managers actually use splake to control stunting when brookies become superabundant in Western lakes. Finally, the average angler can't tell the difference between a splake and a coaster. A confirmed Minnesota state record brook trout turned out to be a splake after someone decided to thaw it out and perform an autopsy. And in a recent court case a Michigan angler contested a citation he'd received for illegal possession of a coaster, contending that any reasonable person would have thought it was a splake. The judge agreed.

Wisconsin DNR's Stephen Schram submits that because lake trout spawning reefs are far off shore and splake haven't been seen on them, and because brook trout don't appear to be utilizing nearshore areas, splake stocking is "a nonissue." Other biologists disagree.

Dr. Casey Huckins, who teaches biological sciences at Michigan Technological University, told me this: "I don't believe it's a good idea to stock a hybrid of two species you're trying to rehabilitate. There's the potential for interbreeding, and I also question it on ecological grounds. Splake could potentially compete and predate; and there's angler confusion as to what they have when they catch one." Henry Quinlan, the Fish and Wildlife Service biologist working on coaster rehabilitation at Whittlesey Creek, and Ed Baker, a research biologist with the Michigan DNR, heartily agree with Huckins.

Schram vows that if coaster recovery starts to happen in Wisconsin, his agency will abandon its splake program. But this is easier said than done. When I asked Baker why Michigan, which has three self-sustaining coaster populations, hasn't been able to do this he said: "Because anglers want splake." To me (and doubtless to Baker, who used the word "unfortunately" when he told me splake stocking was still underway) that's not an answer. Leading the public toward an ecological conscience and a refined taste in natural objects is, after all, why state resource agencies have information-and-education sections. But if you start giving anglers something, even something as offensive as splake, you have to be a lot tougher than your average DNR director to take it away from them. Michigan's internal review of its splake program has already spawned splake-defense groups. One, in Copper Harbor, is passing out caps bearing the shibboleth "I'd rather be splake fishing." And Doug Miron, president of the Alger County Fish and Game Alliance, is quoted by the Associated Press as intoning: "Do whatever you want with your coasters, just don't take away our splake."

We're still making major mistakes with coaster management. Unleashing splake in Lake Superior is pure insanity, as is killing generous limits of potential coasters in the feeder streams of Michigan and Wisconsin. And while the new lake-wide U.S. regulation of one coaster over twenty inches (and the Ontario reg of one fish over twenty-two inches everywhere) is frankly better than most anyone had dared hope for, it should be remembered that in order to kill a trophy of this size one has to release a few dozen under that size. So a single, barbless-hook regulation like the one that exists in Lake Nipigon is desperately needed in Superior. So is a bait ban. Also, I remain unconvinced that you can kill any brook trout—even one a day—and expect a truly healthy population over the long term.

Still, at this writing coaster rehabilitation looks as if it's going to happen in Lake Superior—provided anglers don't get impatient (as they have with Atlantic salmon restoration in New England, for example). And it's easier to be patient if one is realistic in one's expectations. Coaster rehabilitation in the biggest char habitat on earth—now seething with exotic species and charter boats—doesn't mean a return to the days when businessman were checking into the posh Chequamegon Hotel on Friday, catching and killing 100 coasters over four pounds, then taking the train back to Chicago on Sunday night.

But it does mean that coasters can again be a significant part of the big lake's biota. And it means that, if everyone keeps on track, you will have an excellent chance of going out with a big streamer or a mayfly pattern in still or moving water and landing a truly giant brook trout—on purpose instead of by mistake.

TWILIGHT OF THE YANKEE TROUT

‹‹⟨ ⟩›

The ancient cedar raft hovered over Secret Pond's air-clear spring hole; Maine's endless, silent forest and its reflection above, below and all around; in my hand, a wild brook trout. The fish, perhaps three quarters of a pound, was immense by our standards. The markings on the green back resembled grub trails on the inside of dead elm bark. Chestnut flanks were spattered with scarlet flecks, each ringed with an azure halo, bottom fins trimmed with ivory, belly brighter than a New England sunset. It was the most beautiful fish or, for that matter, creature I had ever seen. I ran my thumb up through the gills and lanced the spine, then held the quivering carcass aloft for my Colby College roommate, Robert J. "No-Birds" Daviau of Waterville, Maine who was brought up to believe that the Pine Tree State rides atop a giant tortoise and that her borders fall away into primal chaos. "Eeee Tabernac," he shouted from the other raft. The year was 1966.

No-Birds, who himself knows of nothing more beautiful than wild brook trout (unless possibly ruffed grouse, whose aerial acrobatics gave him his name) had taught me that there is also no food more succulent when fried in bacon fat over dry popple and eaten with your fingers to the mad, discordant strains of loonsong. In Maine throwing back a perfectly good trout was and is seen as sinful, akin to not cleaning your plate. In the words of life-long Mainer Bill Vail, who worked his way through the Warden Service to the helm of the state Department of Inland Fisheries and Wildlife, "Catch and release to an awful lot of people in Maine is an elitist, yuppy idea that comes from somewhere outside and that ought to be fought at all costs. If they're not successful at defeating us at the public hearings, they go to the legislature." A case in point is the repeal last year of the lures-only law for the Kennebec River from Harris Dam to Skowhegan.

The regulation, if not quite catch-and-release, was seen as the next worst thing. It had been proposed in 1991 by Maine Trout, an 80-member group then led by chemistry professor Sam Butcher of Bowdoin College (an institution technically in Maine but so far south as to be considered "out-a-state"). The idea was to save all the wild brook trout that would be released now that the length limit on the river has been extended from six to ten inches and the bag limit reduced from five to two—also at the behest of Maine Trout.

Fisheries and Wildlife liked the lures-only notion, mostly because it unsnarled a morass of complicated rules. Locals had little to say one way or another, and the measure sailed through. But when they read the lures-only notices in 1992 they bawled like mired Herefords. The kids (always it was "the kids") couldn't go worming like their fathers and grandfathers. Local culture was being flung down and danced upon by snotty, tweedy, fly-casting intellectuals probably born in Massachusetts. A phone-book-size petition was flung at the feet of the legislature, and Vail was required to hold another hearing. "I was reluctant to do it because once you start jumping through hoops on these things you can very quickly have to change the whole damn law book," he told me. "It was one of the few public hearings where I lost my temper. I pounded the table to the point where my fist hurt, trying to get order. The only proponents for the original change were the people from Maine Trout. There were two or three of them there, and I still admire their courage. They were from 'away,' didn't even talk like Mainers." Bait was reinstated.

Maine has the only significant populations of decent-sized wild brook trout remaining in the eastern United States and 97 percent of all native brook trout ponds in the nation. With the exception of a few major streams, especially those connected to lakes, the biggest fish abide in stillwater. Three hundred and five of Maine's brook-trout ponds never have been defiled by hatchery fish and therefore contain a priceless reservoir of genes. Each spring in these and other Maine ponds there are an estimated 1.7 million wild trout over the general six-inch minimum size limit of which about 365,156—with a mean length of eleven inches—are caught and killed during the open-water season. Yet few people who reside in Maine—least of all the politicians—understand the significance of this resource. On those rare occasions when they look past their borders into the primal chaos, they see lots and lots of big "trout." But they need to look harder and deeper into the warm, silted water—at the gill covers that don't fit, the pinched caudal peduncles, the rounded pout tails, the matted dorsals, the pectoral fins abraded by concrete to fleshy stumps. If they did so, they might realize that there are wild trout, and there are "rubber trout"—i.e., those tame, sallow, inbred imitations mass-produced in hatcheries. And they would realize that they are entrusted with a national treasure every bit as valuable as Alaska's grizzlies or California's redwoods.

But they don't realize. So every year Maine's wild squaretails get smaller and scarcer. Slap-dash logging and farming have heated and choked spawning streams, but Maine is unique among states in that her trout woes are not primarily habitat related. The managers will tell you that the problem is one of "access." Traditionally, the public could not use its rivers because they were reserved for paper companies to choke with logs and poison with yellow bile that had the bouquet of New England boiled dinner gone bad and that—especially on those wet, still mornings when the grouse were in the apples—you could almost taste thirty miles back from the river. When the log drives were banned in 1976 the paper companies hacked up the north woods with a web of high-speed, permanent haul roads. The fate of Secret Pond (which, of course, is not its real name) was typical. It used to take No-Birds and me two hours to hike in and then only after we had jeeped ten miles of rock-strewn, beaver-flooded tote roads and a rickety bridge swaying across a deep gorge. Now you can drive a Cadillac to the shore.

But access is only the facilitator of the problem, not the problem itself. One can, after all, drive a Cadillac to the shore of Yellowstone Lake, populated by Yellowstone cutthroats—arguably the one freshwater game fish even less selective and more suicidal than brook trout. Yes, I have fished for and sworn at the troutlings, venerated by the late John Voelker, who thumb their noses with their tails from Frenchman's Pond; but these are the exception. When Yankee brook trout go on the feed, they eat like Vikings. If you live in Maine, chances are you know when these orgies happen, and because you and your buddies don't want the pond fished out by strangers, you do it yourselves. You may even obey the law. The general, any-gear-goes regulations don't work. Never have.

If you follow tradition, you will not obey the law. "You go to the barber shop in Greenville," says Vail, "and the old fellows are complaining because they used to go to Horseshoe Pond and fill a canoe, and now you can only get half a dozen or so. 'What's the problem? What are you guys doing wrong?' Well, the problem is that they used to go there and fill a canoe." Maybe, as the old saw goes, a few rotten apples spoil the barrel, but we're talking here about a hogshead of fermented cider mash.

"I hardly fish brook trout in Maine anymore," says Harry Vanderweide, editor of *The Maine Sportsman*. "I can't stand it. I go to Quebec. The brook trout is an anachronism; and the state of Maine is an anachronism. Time has passed them by. You want to have wild brook trout, it's really pretty simple. You can't kill them. I do not believe a naturally-reproducing brook trout fishery can withstand any significant level of exploitation. Forty years ago—when everybody had a job in the mill and worked six or seven days a week, didn't have money to travel, didn't have equipment—it was different."

Certainly, there are some fine, dedicated brook-trout fishermen/conservationists still extant in the Pine Tree State. One such is Warden Sergeant Dan Tourtelotte. Like all wildlife law-enforcement personnel I have worked with on stories, Tourtelotte is smart, tough and highly motivated. You don't last long in the business if you're otherwise because no line of police work is more underfunded, none more undercut in the courts and none, including drug interdiction, more dangerous. Tourtelotte, who has lived all his thirty-nine years in Maine, likes and respects his neighbors; he tries not to wax cynical. Some days are harder than others.

"One weekend in 1992 I worked with two different district wardens," he told me, "Eighty-five percent of the trout fishermen we checked were breaking the law. We worked one pond and got nine. Eight boats on the water, and all eight in violation. Lures-only regs, and all were fishing worms; some were over the limit. The next day I went to a different area. I got one guy over the limit, two for littering—tossing beer cans along the trail and the case in bushes—one guy for operating a boat under the influence. On this fly-fishing-only pond there was a fellow dressed right out of the Orvis catalog, and he was catching a few trout. 'Finally,' I said to myself, 'a guy doing it right.' He was a good fly caster, having a good time. It was kind of nice to see, so I sat down on the shore and had my lunch. I hadn't even finished it when he got into his pack and brought out a canister of worms. When he was done with it he threw it in the water, so I wrote him for littering too. You get days like that."

They weren't filling any canoes at Horseshoe Pond when Tourtelotte and I staked it out last Memorial Day weekend, and the trout we did check were runts, the sort you encounter more and more in Maine these days. We were hoping to apprehend the highly skilled "Mort," who, according to a reliable informer, had killed forty fish the previous Saturday, thereby exceeding his bag and possession limits by thirty-five. But low pressure had settled in. There had been heavy, cold rain, and more was on the way. Even Mort couldn't kill five trout.

"This weather's saving a lot of fish," Tourtelotte declared. He'd catch Mort later. Perhaps, as he had done the previous winter with another suspect, he would knock on his door late into Happy Hour and say, "Word is you got four hundred trout in your freezer." And, as the other guy had done, Mort would bellow, "Waahden, what the hell you talkin' about? Look heah!" and whip open the freezer door, proving that he had no more than fifty.

At the lovely fly-fishing-only section of West Branch Stream we encountered a party from Winterport angling with chartreuse and orange closed-faced spinning outfits terminally rigged with bobbers, spinners, radish-sized sinkers and bass hooks baited with freshwater mussels. A deep-sea rod reposed against the dirty camper, an open can of corn teetered on the edge of the wooden bridge. One guy didn't even have a license.

We pressed on to Second West Branch Pond, now easily accessible by logging road. At the landing I counted twenty-six metal boats. Later we stopped in at Little Lyford Pond Camps, the oldest and nicest in Maine, to see our pal Bud Fackelman, the horse doctor turned trout outfitter. Alas, his famous goat (more about it directly) had gone to its reward, albeit after a long and lavish life. Because the two Little Lyford ponds, restricted to fly fishing, are well off the road and Fackelman fiercely patrols them and imposes a slot limit on his guests, the fishing has held up. We met him on the path, flyrod in hand and toting litter—snelled-hook wrappers from the latest poaching, committed the previous day when he'd been in town.

Back at the Fisheries and Wildlife office in Greenville on the south shore of wind-tattered Moosehead Lake, I met Warden Sergeant Pat Dorian—41, thick black hair, clipped Maine humor with matching accent, an 18-year veteran of the service and another ardent advocate of wild brook trout. Recently he had checked four anglers with 110 trout over the limit. Another party of three were only 83 over. "You should have seen the look on their faces when they saw me standing behind them as they were stooped over the brook, cleaning the fish," he said.

There were five other wardens in the office, drinking coffee and coordinating the evening patrols. The subject of conversation was the new logging road—yet another—being cut within a cast and a half of one of the area's most productive trout ponds. "Kiss 'er goodbye," lamented one. They spoke of other denuded troutwater. Carpenter Pond, for instance—the 160-acre jewel up north of Chamberlain Lake that had produced what may have been the state's finest trouting. Dorian said he knew of two seven-and-a-half pounders that had come out of it—"squaretails, not togue"—and he had checked five-pounders each spring until the haul road went in. "They killed Carpenter in one season," he said.

Having closely observed Maine game wardens at work over the past thirty years, I have but one major complaint about them—they are too few. In other states, and especially on the federal level, wildlife law enforcement gets scant support from the public or politicians. Even the environmental community which obsesses, with excellent cause, over "habitat issues" ignores the importance of law enforcement, this to the peril of the very creatures whose habitat it seeks to defend. Because ponded troutwater in Maine is largely intact, the state has much to gain from aggressive enforcement. Yet, because it has no conception of the significance or value of its wild brook trout, no state more rashly underfunds its warden service.

Today Maine sells roughly 300,000 fishing licenses per year, an 85 percent increase from 1950. Yet there now are fewer wardens than at any time since 1950. Airplanes have been reduced from five to three. They call it "austerity" and "budget protection," but it is as sensible as trying to save federal tax money by laying off the IRS.

"Not only do we have fewer wardens in the field," comments Al Meister, erstwhile Chief Biologist for the Maine Atlantic Sea Run Salmon Commission, "their quality time in the field has been reduced. They're enforcing snowmobile laws; they're enforcing ATV laws, boating laws. If a fisherman is stupid enough to go get drunk and drown, that's his problem. I don't consider it the state's problem. Back when snowmobiles and ATVs weren't invented Maine wardens got out on snowshoes and checked ice fishermen; they got out and put a canoe in and traveled up and down some of those streams. They're not doing it now; they don't have time, and they're [generally] limited to about forty-one hours a week [by budget restrictions and the federal Fair Labor Standards Act]."

One warden I met is responsible for 100 trout ponds. And biologists are stretched even thinner.

Fisheries scientist Forrest Bonney puts it this way: "We used to have two research biologists working on brook trout. Through attrition we've lost those positions, and now I as a regular management biologist am trying to manage the brook trout population in Maine, too. It's not getting the attention it should. We haven't done the work on wild trout some states have because we lack the resources." Yet Maine is the one state in the East that does have the resources, if by "resources" you mean what money-spending tourists go there to fish for.

Like most state fish and wildlife agencies, Maine's operates on dedicated revenue—i.e., funds derived from sale of hunting and fishing licenses and special taxes on sporting equipment. And like most state politicians, Maine governors and legislators regularly raid this dedicated revenue for such sustenance to the human spirit as road widening. Fending off these raids goes with the territory of any decent, competent fish and wildlife commissioner, such as Bill Vail. There came a point, however, when even Vail couldn't fend off the raids. So last February he quit in protest. "To some extent the administration saw our dollars as a way to help balance the budget," he says. "I'd just been in the department too long, and the sportsmen had been too good to me to be a party to that. So rather than be the director at my department's funeral I resigned … All we've been able to do is keep existing programs going, sometimes with just a skeleton crew. But I have always felt strongly that there should be general-fund support for fish and wildlife management. At some point there's got to be a recognition of the value of fish and wildlife to Maine's economy."

The positive note in all of this is that the trout ponds are still there and, for the most part, physically undefiled. The spur roads into them are not unattractive—narrow, untarred and shrouded in greenery. Moreover, the recuperative power of a wild brook trout population is astonishing. I have seen Maine ponds heal themselves in two seasons when gated off or protected with special regulations.

Although the Piscataquis Chapter of Trout Unlimited is pushing catch-and-release for five ponds and a major tributary of Moosehead Lake, returning a perfectly good Maine brook trout to its element still is an idea whose time has not come. Meanwhile, the state is experimenting with what may prove to be the next best thing—two-fish limits on 137 trout ponds. The results, in the few places they've been monitored, are heartening. One of the first two-fish waters—protected in 1988—was 9,500-acre Big Eagle Lake, source of the Allagash. A 1992 study reveals that "brook trout catch rates increased dramatically compared with the previous survey in 1987 from .23 to .43 trout per angler" and that the percentage of anglers catching at least one fish rose in the five years from 18 to 28 percent.

When the two-fish ponds are scattered among general, five-fish water the public shuns them. Pat Dorian will not be pleased to read here that Tourtelotte inadvertently disclosed to me the location of the two-fish pond they both haunt during the five-week green drake hatch. But, then, Tourtelotte had shown it to him. "I happen to fish there quite a lot," said Dorian when he thought I didn't know which pond he meant, "and there was hardly anybody in there last year. Now we're starting to get a lot of fish back fifteen and sixteen inches. Last year I'd average eight to ten trout, but that's only fishing like an hour in the evening. One night I landed 22. Biggest was eighteen and a half inches."

I promised more about Fackelman's goat. The previous owner had hauled it into Tufts University Vet School to be put down for no apparent reason other than he'd discovered what goats are really like. But anyone, especially Fackelman, could see that it was a perfectly good goat, if such an adjective can properly modify such a noun. Accordingly, the kindly doctor had rescued it from death row, keeping it chained in his yard down the street from me in Grafton, Massachusetts. Thus confined, it had chomped perfect circles in the grass around its stake. (Norman Mortimer Taft maintained that the circles had been inscribed by flying saucers.)

When Fackelman moved from traffic-choked Grafton to the wilds of Maine there no longer was need for the chain, so he unleashed his goat in the lush meadows around Little Lyford Pond Camps. But the goat was bound by tradition; it had developed a certain way of doing things, and still it chomped perfect circles in the grass.

The story of Fackelman's goat strikes me as a parable for Maine brook-trout fishermen who won't change even when there is every good reason to do so, even when they could let the resource recover and grow and make them rich as Montana springcreek owners. Even when, in the long run, they and the rest of us could have more of something most rare and beautiful.

Environmentalists vs. Native Trout

⤙ ⤚

Having been an environmental activist for most of my life and having worked for and with national environmental organizations for thirty years, it grieves me to report that the biggest and, in many cases, only impediment to recovery of vanishing native trout is the environmental community.

That's not to say that most environmental outfits actively oppose trout-restoration projects. And that's not to say that the few who do wouldn't back off if they'd stop talking long enough to listen to biologists.

Enviros tend not to see, handle or understand fish and to distrust the motives of agencies dedicated to their recovery. Thus, in announcing a lawsuit to halt use of TFM, a remarkably safe and selective chemical used since the 1950s to kill sea lampreys, a splendid organization like the Vermont Public Interest Research Group can advance the argument that Atlantic salmon—native predators every bit as ecologically important to Lake Champlain and its basin as wolves to greater Yellowstone—are being restored "strictly for sport fishing."

Without two naturally derived piscicides—rotenone (from derris root) and antimycin (from bacteria)—most native fish restoration simply cannot happen. Rotenone has been used to kill fish for centuries on two continents; modern fish managers have used it for the last seventy-five years. In all that time there has never been a documented human injury. There's no record of antimycin, introduced for fish control in the mid-1970s, harming anyone either. Both rotenone and antimycin are easily neutralized with potassium permanganate, and both break down fast in the environment. In fact, one of antimycin's few drawbacks is that it sometimes breaks down too fast; under some conditions its half life is less than an hour. Antimycin's great advantage is that the recommended dosage is usually between 8 and 12 parts per billion, so you can strap a bottle on a pack horse and treat a whole chain of high-country lakes. And, unlike rotenone, fish can't smell it and therefore don't take evasive action.

But enviros tend to fear all pesticides. Moreover, they frequently reject as spin all data that proves a pesticide safe even as they spin data themselves to depict it as dangerous. For example, the environmental community parrots the fiction that rotenone, applied to fish habitat at 0.5 to 4 parts per million, has been "linked to Parkinson's disease." It conjured this from an unrelated study in which Emory University researchers induced Parkinson's-disease-like symptoms (not Parkinson's disease) in lab rats by mainlining concentrated rotenone into their brains.

Although rotenone and, to a much lesser extent, antimycin kill a very few non-target gill breathers such as insect larvae, these organisms bounce back within weeks; and, with their alien fish predators removed, they are far more prolific.

One of the most effective environmental outfits I know is the Center for Biological Diversity. I work closely with it in my environmental reporting, and I have helped raise thousands of dollars for it through my work on a major charitable foundation. As its name implies, it exists solely to protect "biological diversity." Except that the threatened Paiute cutthroat, probably the rarest trout in the world, doesn't count with the center.

Citing wives' tales and spewing pseudo science, the center has derailed Paiute recovery by suing the U.S. Forest Service and thereby frightening away the California Department of Fish and Game, which has jurisdiction over native fauna and doesn't need the Forest Service anyway. About 11 stream-miles of California's Silver King Creek watershed in the Carson-Iceberg Wilderness of the Toiyabe-Humboldt National Forest comprise the entire native range of the Paiute cutthroat. In 1912, before bucket biologists made mongrels of all the fish in all their natural habitat, another bucket biologist—tending sheep in the area—inadvertently saved the Paiute by transporting a few trout to a fishless stretch above impassable Llewellyn Falls.

Had the Forest Service proceeded in the fall of 2003 as planned, it would have accomplished a first in salmonid management—restoring a native to 100 percent of its historical range. Then the Fish and Wildlife Service would have removed the Paiute from the Endangered Species List, another first. But could delisting have been an unwelcome development for the litigious center, reducing its arsenal of legal weapons? Yes, according to one professional trout advocate who worked hard for the project, and whose colleagues helped evacuate some of the mongrels to a different watershed in order to placate local sportsmen: "When an organism loses its Endangered Species Act protection it's no longer any use to groups like the Center for Biological Diversity."

"If you're attempting to fix an expensive watch, you don't reach first for the sledgehammer; neither should the state necessarily be poisoning streams in a wilderness area without looking at other options," proclaims the center. Had it read the literature, it would have understood that there are no other options. The stream's too big for effective electro-shocking. And, while antimycin (classified by EPA under "no threat to human health") would be great, it's no longer registered in California because the only manufacturers (Nick and Mary Romeo, working out of their home) can't finance the endless lab tests required by the state's new pesticide code.

"This watershed," continued the center, "is historic habitat for the mountain yellow-legged frog, a species in serious decline." Had it read the literature, it would have understood that yellow-legged frogs don't occur in the proposed treatment area.

As part of a legal settlement with the center, the Forest Service is currently engaged in more National Environmental Policy Act review, re-studying everything the state has already studied and everything the scientific community already knows about rotenone and fish reclamation. The agency had hoped to resume work in 2004, but pressure from an ill-informed public has shut down the project again.

The Pacific Rivers Council, with which I also work closely and for which I also have helped raise thousands of dollars, does all sorts of fabulous work, too. Yet it swallowed the BS about rotenone hook, line, boat and motor. It filed a scathing critique of the project's first environmental assessment; and it issued an "action alert" in which it recycled the misinformation about the yellow-legged frog and made the astonishing claim that "neither the Silver King Creek nor Tamarack Lake drainages historically supported the threatened Paiute cutthroat" when these were the only habitats that had supported it.

The National Audubon Society is making progress. For example, its magazine recently condemned "chemophobes" and defended piscicides in a piece entitled "Trout Are Wildlife, Too." But the society is routinely embarrassed by its affiliates. Seven years ago the California Department of Fish and Game rotenoned alien pike in 4,000-acre Lake Davis in order to protect endangered steelhead trout and chinook salmon of the Sacramento and San Joaquin river systems. But, instead of helping fight a real threat to biodiversity, local Audubon members and other enviros attacked an imaginary threat to water quality. They mounted vicious protests, held all-night candlelight vigils, chained themselves to buoys, cursed, wept, marched around the lake with placards that said things like "Burn in Hell, Fish & Game!" For crowd control the state deployed 270 uniformed officers, including a SWAT team. Currently, on the National Audubon Society's Web site, Harry Reeves, editor of the Plumas Audubon Chapter's newsletter, goes on and on about the alleged evils of rotenone and laments: "Bald eagles, white pelicans, and other birds and mammals scavenged poisoned carcasses that lined the shores." They did indeed, and not one was sickened because rotenone-killed fish don't harm wildlife.

Also weighing in on the Web site is one Ann McCampbell of Santa Fe, New Mexico—the nation's busiest piscicide protestor, who rarely misses a chance to spread bogeyman stories about rotenone and antimycin and who professes to be so allergic to all chemicals that she can participate in public hearings only by phone—a tedious, time-consuming process that tests the patience of everyone involved. The rotenone used in Lake Davis, writes McCampbell, who also claims to be a medical doctor, "made residents sick." It did not.

Concern for people and scavengers is admirable even when based on hogwash. But now that pike are back in Lake Davis (possibly because of sabotage) and now that Fish and Game is too frightened to eliminate them, I wish the environmental community would express as much (or even some) concern for the endangered salmon and steelhead, which surely will be ushered into oblivion unless rotenone is used again.

To save Montana's state fish, the westslope cutthroat trout, the Montana Department of Fish, Wildlife, and Parks proposes to kill introgressed Yellowstone cutts dribbling alien genes into the South Fork of the Flathead River. To do this it must apply antimycin and rotenone to eleven high-elevation ponds in the Bob Marshall Wilderness. The westslope cutt, named for Lewis and Clark (*Oncorhynchus clarki lewisi*), is as much an icon of American wilderness as the grizzly. So you'd think that any group advocating wilderness would rally to the defense of this magnificent, vanishing creature.

But Wilderness Watch is doing its best to kill the project, making absurd and untruthful pronouncements such as "Poison has no place in wilderness stewardship." (Piscicides are essential to wilderness stewardship.) And: "Both poisons have adverse effects on aquatic biota." (They do not.) Wilderness Watch expresses outrage that managers would have to make some noise with motorboats and helicopters. And while it correctly observes that the ponds were originally fishless, and might even make a case that they should remain so, it claims that the westslopes (to be stocked as eyed eggs) have been diminished by domestication and therefore threaten the natives. Considering the gross genetic pollution now underway and the group's ongoing attempt to block removal of the mongrels, I can't imagine a more hypocritical and disingenuous argument.

In New Mexico's Gila National Forest, Wilderness Watch has been agitating against the use of antimycin in the ongoing recovery of the endangered Gila trout. It's all about sport, according to Wilderness Watch: "The purpose is to remove stocked trout and replace them with the listed Gila trout, in an effort to boost the population to a level that will allow delisting and resumed sport fishing of the species." Other untruths include: "It is not known whether antimycin is a carcinogen." (It is known that it's not.) And: "It is highly likely that the poison will adversely impact the endangered Chiricahua leopard frog that inhabits the area." 1) The Chiricahua leopard frog is threatened, not endangered; 2) Antimycin is very easy on juvenile amphibians, and has no effect on adults, and the Forest Service evacuates tadpoles from target streams anyway. And, 3) "The poison antimycin will kill ... all the native macroinvertebrates and amphibians in the streams." (Most likely it will kill none of the amphibians, and it will kill very few macroinvertebrates. Researchers from the University of Wyoming's Department of Zoology and Physiology, reporting on their stream studies, write: "Antimycin alone seemed to have little to no effect on invertebrates, with drift rates not substantially different than control sites during the antimycin addition.")

Wilderness Watch is also trying to derail restoration of New Mexico's state fish—the Rio Grande cutthroat, endangered in fact if not by fiat. It upbraids the state's Water Quality Commission for ignoring the rantings of Ann McCampbell who, for example, testifies that the antimycin label carries "a skull and crossbones … warning that it is fatal in humans if swallowed." (I'd agree that the public shouldn't drink it from the bottle.) Here, too, the alleged motive is frivolity and greed: For no purpose other than to amuse anglers and generate license revenue, the U.S. Forest Service, the New Mexico Department of Game and Fish, and the U.S. Fish and Wildlife Service are conspiring to "dump poison in 30 miles of Animas Creek and 21 miles of the Gila River to kill introduced non-native trout and then re-stock the streams with native Rio Grande Cutthroat trout. … The Rio Grande Cutthroat is not an endangered species, but is a popular sport species among fishermen. … It is both sad and ironic that it was Aldo Leopold who convinced the Forest Service to protect the Gila as our nation's first wilderness in the 1930's—now, it is in danger of being converted to a fish farm for recreationists."

I see a different irony: It was Aldo Leopold who wrote the following in his essay "Wilderness": "If education really educates, there will, in time, be more nad more citizens who understand that relics of the old West add meaning and value to the new."

Acid rain is not the main threat to brook trout in New York State's Adirondacks. In fact, compared with alien fish introductions, it's unimportant. Perch, sunfish, white suckers, bass, pike, bullheads, etc. got flung around so long ago that there's not even a record of what used to be trout water; and these aliens are still being flung around. Thus defiled, ponds and lakes in this country simply cannot sustain wild brook trout.

But since the early 1970s the New York Department of Environmental Conservation (DEC) has been guided by the State Land Master Plan. This far-sighted document prescribes specific management for various land classifications. For each wilderness area it requires the department to formulate a plan and, for that plan, to inventory all plants, fish and animals. While it forbids permanent structures in wilderness, it provides a few exceptions essential to wilderness management—such as fish-barrier dams. It forbids helicopters and other motorized vehicles in wilderness except in "extraordinary conditions"—such as rescuing people from disaster or brook trout from alien fish. It establishes that the single most important thing managers must do for wilderness is to preserve and restore native flora and fauna.

Following the mandates of the State Land Master Plan, DEC fish managers have identified what they call "heritage trout"—pure strains of brook trout that evolved in the Adirondacks and that, apparently, have never been contaminated by hatchery genes. Mostly, DEC has been working with three of these strains, named for the lakes from which they were collected in the nick of time—Windfall (where they've since been lost to alien fish), Little Tupper (where they're in the process of being lost to alien fish), and Horn Lake (where they've been lost to acid rain). In the last fifteen years managers have restored heritage trout to about fifty remote ponds. Domestic brook trout live about three years, but heritage trout live six or seven; so they grow lots bigger. Four-pounders are now common. "When I was in the office our single most requested piece of literature was the reclaimed pond list," says Larry Strait, DEC's regional fish manager who retired in 2001. "That was no accident."

The Adirondack Council, another environmental group that does great work and for which I have raised lots of money, exists, in its words, to "sustain the natural and human communities of the region." Log onto its Web site, and you'll get hollered at by a loon. Loons are a symbol of wilderness, but the wild brook trout loons depend on aren't—at least not to the council, which doesn't see or hear them. Nor do wild brook trout count as part of the "natural community" the council is pledged to defend. The council rails against helicopter and motorboat use by DEC trout managers and says it wants them "to follow the same wilderness rules as the public." It says it finds the practice of reclaiming ponds with rotenone "offensive" and wants it banned.

When I interviewed communications director, John Sheehan, he repeated all the standard wives' tales. For example: "There appears to be a relationship between rotenone use and Parkinson's disease." And: "Rotenone essentially kills everything that breathes with gills." It was clear that the council hadn't bothered to learn the first thing about fish restoration or wild brook trout. "The trout they're putting back generally exist in another place or several other places or are the same acid-resistant strain of Little Tupper trout that they've been stocking," Sheehan declared.

But Little Tupper trout are natives, not the supposedly acid-resistant Canadian-domestic hybrids DEC used to play around with. Heritage trout recovery is all about sport, he explained: "The problem we've had is that rotenone is generally used to create sporting opportunities, not as a means of preserving specific species necessarily. Generally we're not thrilled about killing off entire ponds and replacing them with monocultures." Yet Adirondack brook trout evolved in monocultures; in fact, they can't survive without them.

Armed with all this misinformation, the council urged DEC to adopt a rule that forbids managers to fly or drive into wilderness except in "off-peak seasons," i.e., before Memorial Day and after Labor Day. DEC—increasingly staffed by young enviros who don't see, handle or understand fish and who fear all pesticides—complied in November 2003.

The only time you can check to see if ponds are thermally suited for brook trout is when they're stratified, and they're stratified only in summer. You can't reclaim ponds when everything is iced up. And because brook trout are fall spawners and rotenone doesn't kill trout eggs, you can't eliminate domestic and introgressed fish much after Labor Day. So the new rule effectively ends heritage trout recovery in wilderness.

"The department has made it impossible for resource managers to engage in meaningful debate," says Strait. "Trout Unlimited [pushing heroically and lonesomely for virtually every native trout restoration project across America] was denied the opportunity for a public hearing, and their comments were given short shrift. The Adirondack Council has rejected science. That's a shame because they could be great allies if they'd look at what we were able to accomplish over the last 15 years."

In Montana's upper Missouri River system, where westslope cutthroats have been extirpated from all but two percent of their historic range, the state Department of Fish, Wildlife and Parks is using a total of twenty gallons of antimycin and ten gallons of rotenone to make a westslope sanctuary from seventy-seven miles of upper Cherry Creek, now infested with brook trout and introgressed rainbows and Yellowstone cutts. You've heard the old saw that just one concerned environmentalist can "make a difference." Well, it's true but not always good. For four years the Cherry Creek project, arguably the most ambitious riverine piscicide treatment ever attempted in North America, was placed on hold purely because of a lay person's fantasies about antimycin, rotenone and even the potassium permanganate with which they are neutralized at downstream stations. William Fairhurst of Three Forks, Montana, sued in state court on grounds that the department was "polluting" a public water supply. The utterly meritless action was finally dismissed, but while it was underway, and for much of the time Fairhurst was threatening a federal suit, the department's legal advisors made managers sit on their hands.

The first phase—treatment of 105-acre Cherry Lake and about eleven miles of stream with 10 parts per billion antimycin—was completed with superb results in August 2003. "We had sentinel fish posted in net bags throughout each treatment site every day; and we got 100 percent mortality," reports project leader Pat Clancey. "After a second treatment next year, we'll seed this stretch with westslope eggs, and we'll stock catchable adults in Cherry Lake just for the recreational fishery."

But Fairhurst isn't finished. Now he's filed his federal suit on grounds that "the Federal Insecticide, Fungicide and Rodenticide Act requires the Environmental Protection Agency to prevent unreasonably adverse effects on the environment."

During the alleged pollution of upper Cherry Creek in the summer of 2003 Clancey and his team observed the most sensitive invertebrate in the watershed, a species of caddis, happily scavenging poisoned trout.

Trout Are Wildlife, Too

⤛⤜

On August 6, 2002, the PMDs started coming off Armstrong Spring Creek at 10:00 a.m. PMDs (pale morning duns) are delicate yellow mayflies that shuck their larval skins on the surface and, if they don't vanish into the maws of trout, dance around like garden fairies, with sunlight flashing on translucent wings. A spring creek leaps full grown from rocks or wet earth. Armstrong, the most famous spring creek in the world, is collected by the Yellowstone River in Montana's Paradise Valley.

As I stood in the icy flow, nighthawks and swallows dipped from the cloudless, mountain-rimmed sky, picking off emerging PMDs, while all around me large trout were finding plenty of their own, bulging through the surface and wagging flaglike dorsal fins. These were browns and rainbows that, at the sting of my hook, somersaulted into the air and raced off on long runs, most of which ended with a sickening snap because my fluorocarbon "tippet" was so fine it broke at 1.5 pounds of pressure. Anything heavier and the trout would refuse my PMD imitation. As an angler I've been trained to measure the quality of game fish by this kind of strength and selective feeding behavior. But as a naturalist I'm conflicted. Browns evolved in Europe, rainbows in the Pacific Northwest. Both were unleashed decades ago in the interior West by managers blind to the beauty and importance of native ecosystems.

The trout that belong here are cutthroats. Rainbows hybridize with them, swamping their genes. Browns displace them, as do brook trout (imported from the East). Of the fourteen named and unnamed cutthroat subspecies, two are already extinct, and the rest are in desperate trouble, pushed into river tops where they're protected from alien invaders by waterfalls or manmade barriers but where they're also genetically isolated.

Late in the day, when the PMDs were gone, I was delighted and astonished to catch a Yellowstone cutthroat, the native subspecies of this river system. It slurped my beetle pattern on a sloppy drift, and it came in easily, shaking its head and rolling. All wild trout are beautiful, but cutthroats mesmerize me. This one glowed with the gold of autumn aspens and the pinks of a Big Sky sunset. Its flanks were flecked with obsidian spots that got bigger and more profuse toward the tail, and under its jaw were the two scarlet slashes that give the species its name. Cutthroats are hardwired: They're not selective, because they evolved in sterile water where they couldn't afford to let something drift by that might have been a bug; and they never developed the kind of energy-draining musculature of other trout. When the state of Idaho sought to restore Yellowstone cutts to Island Park Reservoir, one prominent guide—an educator of local anglers—declared: "They're stupid, and they fight like slugs." So fierce was public opposition that the project was abandoned.

In the Yellowstone drainage, however, cutthroats are making a comeback, because trout managers of the Montana Department of Fish, Wildlife and Parks are the most progressive in the nation. They've leased water rights on tributaries dewatered by irrigators. Now native trout are spawning in these rivers again.

Montana has learned that hatcheries, which the angling public underwrites with license fees and a federal tax on fishing tackle, are among the greatest threats to wild (stream-bred) trout, whether naturalized or native. Genetic diversity, by which trout adapt to different habitats in large river systems, is bred out of hatchery trout. They are selected for domesticity, warped by inbreeding. They survive in the real world only long enough to suppress and displace wild trout. Moreover, hatcheries spread pathogens such as whirling disease, imported from Europe with frozen pike and to which North American trout lack natural immunity. But when game and fish departments try to phase out hatcheries, anglers—unwilling to learn the truth—scream to their legislators, who threaten budget cuts. "If you cross a sacred cow with a military base, you get a fish hatchery," says Bernard Shanks, the gutsy former director of the Washington Fish and Wildlife Department, who tried to de-emphasize hatchery production.

In 1970 Montana stopped stocking hatchery fish (browns and rainbows) in a section of the Madison River where these species had long been established and which is far too big for native trout restoration. Four years later large fish (three years and older) were up 942 percent. The study horrified anglers and hatchery bureaucrats, who wanted to believe that stocking was the key to trout abundance. In apparent sabotage, the study area was stocked in 1972 (presumably with trout purchased at a private hatchery) and the towing hitch on the department's truck was loosened so that boat and trailer parted company on the highway. The illegal stocking only corroborated the earlier data, because immediately the brown trout biomass dipped by 24 percent, then, with two more years of no stocking, jumped back to where it had been. The study convinced Montana to cease all trout stocking in moving water. As a result it is now the number-one trout-fishing destination in the nation.

In most habitats, trout are not easily seen. Except where they are conditioned with pellets, they don't come to feeders. While they're every bit as colorful as birds, they're cold and slimy, and most of the public remains unmoved by their plight. Groups such as Trout Unlimited and the Federation of Fly Fishers are winning important battles for native-trout restoration, but they're outnumbered and outshouted by the gull-like masses for whom trout genes (and even trout fins, abraded into fleshy stumps by the sides of hatchery raceways) have no relevance, for whom a trout is not part of a native ecosystem but a slab of meat.

Anyone seeking the answer to "What good is a native trout?" need not look beyond Yellowstone National Park. Eighty percent of the world's remaining pure Yellowstone cutthroats abide in 87,000-acre Yellowstone Lake, spawning in at least fifty-nine feeder streams. Today Yellowstone cutts fuel aquatic and terrestrial ecosystems in and around the park the way sockeye salmon fuel ecosystems in southern Alaska. But it wasn't always this way. Thirty years ago the park's native trout had been pretty much wiped out. Dead cutthroats—caught, killed, and discarded by tourists—comprised the main item in park garbage cans. Grizzlies, sustained by this and other garbage, had been reduced to circus bears. Then, in the early 1970s, a smart, tough biologist named John Varley (who now directs the park's Center for Resources) led a successful effort to require anglers to release most of their trout. The initiative was far more contentious than wolf reintroduction (which Varley also led). Outfitters charged the park with plotting to "put them out of business." Outdoor writers reported that the feds planned to end all sportfishing. Fisheries managers parroted the old wives' tale that "you can't stockpile trout."

When the Craighead brothers were studying grizzlies in the 1960s, they never saw a bear take a fish. By 1975 bear activity was being observed on seventeen of the lake's fifty-nine cutthroat-spawning streams. Now bears work at least fifty-five of those streams, and one research team has observed a sow with cubs averaging 100 fish a day for ten days. In 1988 there were 66 nesting pairs of ospreys in the park; by 1993 there were 100. While in the park, white pelicans get almost all their nourishment from cutthroats, consuming an estimated 300,000 pounds a season. In all, Yellowstone cutts provide an important food source for at least twenty-eight species of birds and mammals.

Last July 18, I stood in the swollen Yellowstone River in the park's Hayden Valley with the current piling up around the top of my chest waders. I fish here not to "fight" native trout but to connect with them and their world. Sometimes the insect hatches are so prolific that the fish don't bother to rise; they just hold in the current with their heads out of water and, like drunks under wine spigots, let the river's richness fill their bellies. The nutrient flow starts with the sulfurous fumes that bubble white and pungent from underwater vents; cycles skyward with squalls of caddises and mayflies; drops back to the trout; then out onto the banks with the otters and minks; up and south with the eagles and ospreys; seaward with the loons and pelicans; high into the stream-etched Absarokas with the massive spawning run; and, finally, into the gullets of grizzlies.

The cutthroats of Yellowstone Lake, restored by the no-kill fishing regs that were going to ruin the outfitters, now generate about $36 million a year for them and other local businesses, and the figure doubles when you include other restored park waters. But now Yellowstone's trout-based ecosystem and trout-based economy may collapse again. Lake trout, unavailable to wildlife because they live and spawn in deep water, have been illegally stocked in the lake, and wherever these large, voracious predators have been superimposed on native cutthroats, the cutthroats have been eliminated.

When a fisherman caught the first lake trout on July 30, 1994, the news made Varley physically ill. Unless the park can permanently suppress the aliens (elimination is out of the question), Yellowstone cutthroats are doomed in the lake and probably the world. In a never-ending project that leaves virtually no money for other trout restoration, crews on two large boats set gill nets at depths favored by lake trout. They're getting good at it; in 2001 they killed 15,000 lake trout with an accidental cutthroat bycatch of only 600. But there are alarming indicators. On Clear Creek the cutthroat spawning run has declined from about 12,000 to 8,000 fish; there's a corresponding decline at sample stations in the lake.

Particularly discouraging is the ignorance of sportsmen. Facing a future no less bleak than the Yellowstone cutthroat is the westslope cutthroat. Ambitious restoration projects are under way in Montana, where pure westslopes have been driven out of something like 75 percent of their historic range. But the most ambitious westslope-restoration project ever proposed has been derailed for the past three years by a sportsmen-endorsed property-rights group called the Public Lands Access Association. The group's president, Bill Fairhurst, threatened to sue the state in federal court on the grounds that it would "pollute" public water with the safe, selective, short-lived fish poisons with which it plans to remove the brook trout, rainbows, and hybrid cutthroats that infest seventy-seven miles of Upper Cherry Creek, in southwest Montana. What's really bugging the association and its allies is that 85 percent of the project area is owned by media mogul and native-ecosystem champion Ted Turner, who has offered to pick up $343,350 of the $475,000 cost. Like the previous owner, Turner doesn't invite the public onto his land, although the Montana access law permits anglers to wade Cherry Creek.

In January 2002 *Fly Rod & Reel* magazine, where I serve as conservation editor, recognized Turner's commitment to native trout by making him its Angler of the Year, thereby eliciting the biggest blizzard of nastygrams we've seen in our twenty-three-year history. I had "a political agenda," I'd done it for money, I was a "snot nose," a "moron," a "nasty bully," a "nature Nazi," an acolyte of "Hanoi Jane," an espouser of "vitriolic leftist environmentalism." "I see your magazine is lining up lock-step with the wild-animal-rights fly-fishing crowd that Left Wing Ted [Turner] leads and which appears to be taking over the leadership of Trout Unlimited and the Federation of Fly Fishers ..." wrote Bruce Cox of Springdale, Pennsylvania. "I am completely opposed to the wild-at-any-cost perspective of this left-wing animal-rights crowd and to wit will ... politically align myself with anti-wild-fish groups and politicians."

Preserving Cherry Creek's alien and mongrel trout was the priority of most readers we heard from. The fishing was already good—why change species? Anglers had been programmed by the mass-circulation hook-and-bullet press, particularly *Outdoor Life* magazine, which had attacked the project with an article rife with misinformation entitled "Playing God on Cherry Creek." When the editors invited readers to vote for or against making Cherry Creek a sanctuary for westslope cutthroats, 98 percent voiced opposition.

In the late 1980s the Idaho Department of Fish and Game announced that it would cease polluting the Big Wood River with hatchery trout. But to appease the masses, which had threatened legislative intervention, the department kept stocking a few token fish. Idaho also went to wild-trout management on the Teton River but found it necessary to buy a four-acre gravel pit—safely isolated from the river—into whose seepage it poured a gravy train of hatchery fish. This direct dump-and-catch approach proved so popular that the department now does it all over the state.

On Henrys Lake, an important sanctuary for Yellowstone cutts, Idaho Fish and Game had been stocking rainbow-cutthroat hybrids because they fight harder. But in 1976, when managers announced they would stop stocking the lake with manmade mongrels, anglers threw a hissy fit and got the legislature to hold hostage the department's budget. So today the stocking of Henrys Lake continues, but with sterile "triploid" rainbows, which have three sets of chromosomes instead of the normal two and which hatchery technicians produce by heat-shocking the eggs. Despite the wastefulness and tastelessness of this strategy, native cutthroats in Henrys Lake and elsewhere are much safer than they used to be. Idaho is more progressive than most states; still, it was only in 2001 that it fully implemented a policy of not stocking viable hatchery fish on top of wild populations.

In Lake Superior, restoration of coasters—a race of giant brook trout—is finally getting under way. Ontario is doing great work. So are the Chippewa Indians. Minnesota and Michigan are making reasonable efforts, but Wisconsin is resisting. When I asked Wisconsin managers why they weren't doing more for coasters, I was told that the state has decided there's nothing special about them, that "a brook trout is a brook trout."

Such talk infuriates Robert Behnke of Colorado State University, the world's leading authority on trout and the man who rediscovered Lahontan and Bonneville cutthroats after they'd been declared extinct. "A grape is also a grape," Behnke wrote me. "One species of grape (*Vitus vinifera*) is used in virtually all wine made in the world—reds, whites, best and worst. The grape-is-a-grape point of view is the most simplistic and would save money for wine drinkers, because the cheapest wines would be the same quality as the most expensive wines. I wouldn't want some of the managers [you] quote selecting wine for me or, for that matter, being in charge of fisheries programs where subtle genetic differences that may not show up in genetic analysis can be important."

Managers have achieved a stunning success with the Gila trout of New Mexico. I'd given up on the species when I inspected its habitat in 1994. In Black Canyon Creek, one of two perennial streams in the Aldo Leopold Wilderness, I encountered cattle in the water, knocking down the banks and defecating. So tolerant of cattle was the local Forest Service ranger that when I stopped in to see her I found cow pies on her office steps. When I asked Brub Stone, then a director of the Gila Fish and Gun Club, why his group opposed Gila trout restoration in Mineral and Willow creeks, he said: "They're using some kind of a fancy-name poison [antimycin]. ... Years ago they said the breast implant would not hurt women. My God, it's killing them, isn't it?"

In 1998, as the U.S. Fish and Wildlife Service and the state of New Mexico were preparing to reintroduce pure Gilas to Black Canyon Creek, they found rainbows, browns, and cutthroats (alien to the region and of undetermined race). The project had been sabotaged. Another stream, also cleansed of aliens, was apparently sabotaged. Grant County tried to kill the project—by preventing the use of antimycin—with what it called the Pollution Nuisance Ordinance Act. Because of this ordinance (as well as the fact that managers wanted to avoid the hassle of evacuating, holding, then restocking rare dace and suckers) a twenty-man crew equipped with backpack shockers removed 376 alien trout from Black Canyon Creek over the course of eighty-eight days, a job that would have taken minutes with antimycin. The reintroduced Gilas have been reproducing. The Forest Service has kicked out the cows, and streambanks are healing. In 1970 Gila trout survived in about twelve miles of stream in four drainages; now they inhabit about eighty miles in thirteen drainages.

There's enough momentum in native trout restoration that it might succeed nationwide if the environmental community gets behind it. The old-guard managers who flung trout around the country like Johnny Appleseed on applejack are dead, and, with only a few exceptions, their replacements are fiercely committed to natives. But most of these young scientists lack communication skills. For instance, they attempt to generate excitement for their work by pointing out that native trout are "indicator species," thereby implying that their worth is right up their with, say, a $200 water-sampling kit.

Managers need to quit trying to figure out what native trout can do for us and attempt a new approach. Maybe it starts with a simple statement that these fish are priceless works of art that need to be protected for themselves, for the species that need them, and for people who cherish them for what they are and because they are.

WESTERN WATER CURE

—‹‹· ·››—

One of the missions of our national forests is to provide water for human use. In the arid West, where the demand on rivers frequently has exceeded their flows, the diverter or diverters who arrived earliest got the water—sometimes all of it. In such cases everyone and everything else got dry creekbed. "First in time, first in right," as western water law proclaims.

For most of its history the U.S. Forest Service handed out unconditional "special-use" permits for water to anyone who wanted one. Then about forty years ago Congress got to thinking that maybe this wasn't always such a great idea, that there were other important uses and missions for the National Forest System such as sustaining fish and wildlife and providing human recreation, and that these were precluded by giving away all instead of just most of a river. If the American public was going to hand out its water to irrigators, power companies, cities and the like, maybe the gift should have a few strings attached such as the requirement that receivers leave a trickle to preserve at least a part of the aquatic ecosystem. So Congress passed laws like the Multiple Use and Sustained Yield Act, the National Forest Management Act and the Federal Land Policy Management Act (FLPMA), all of which clearly require the Forest Service to manage for fish, wildlife and recreation as well as for timber and water. Under FLPMA, for example, the Forest Service must "minimize damage to scenic and aesthetic values and fish and wildlife habitat and otherwise protect the environment."

The agency really didn't need any of these laws to protect the rivers to which we've entrusted it. The Property Clause of the Constitution provides the United States unlimited authority to control use of land belonging to it. To wit: "Congress shall have power to dispose of and make all needful rules and regulations respecting the territory or other property belonging to the United States." Moreover, the Supreme Court has ruled that the

Property Clause includes authority to protect public lands "from trespass and injury and to prescribe conditions upon which others may obtain rights to them" and that, like any other property owner, the United States "should be expected to allow uses of and access to its lands only on conditions that are consistent with its land management objectives."

Following the law, the Forest Service began requiring "bypass flows" for new projects or when permits came up for renewal every fifteen years. It didn't ask to retain much of our water—not enough, in fact. On the Big Thompson River in northern Colorado, for instance, it required a hydro facility that dewaters the river by pipe for about five miles to leave but 7 percent of a flow that averages roughly 150 cubic feet per second. FLPMA and the other laws requiring bypass flows on rivers issuing from national forests have worked like the Endangered Species Act (which is one of those laws). That is, they provide a motive for cooperation on the part of water users and therefore are hardly ever enforced. At last count the Forest Service had imposed bypass flows on only fifteen active special-use permits. The remaining 8,285 water users agreed on their own to provide flows that satisfied the Forest Service's painfully modest goals. "I think the fact that the bypass-flow requirement has rarely been used is a reflection that it has worked," declares Colorado TU director David Nickum. "It's a club, so the users work to find reasonable solutions."

The current trouble—centered in Colorado but seen throughout the West—started in 1990 when the Forest Service went to trial in an effort to win legal recognition to what it claimed was a reserved right to water on the Arapaho-Roosevelt National Forest that almost surrounds Rocky Mountain National Park in north-central Colorado. The court found that the agency didn't have a reserved water right and that it didn't need one because it could adequately protect streams with its own regulatory authority—i.e., bypass flows. This sent water users, especially the cities of Boulder and Greeley, into full cry because they'd never had to think about bypass flows and now their permits were up for renewal. On August 12, 1992, Wayne Allard, then a U.S. Representative from the district, Senator Hank Brown (R-CO) and nine other western Republicans wrote a spleenful letter to U.S. Secretary of Agriculture Ed Madigan: "This position violates the law, injures vested property rights, destroys established management practices. ... If the Forest Service is allowed to proceed in this manner, this administration will have taken private property rights, interfered with the development and use of state and interstate water allocations and replaced state water administration systems with a federal permit system."

Madigan folded up in the hot west wind like a paper parasol. "New bypass flow requirements will not be imposed on existing water supply facilities," he replied. He further stated that permits would accommodate resource goals of the Forest Service only "to the extent feasible without diminishing the water yield or substantially increasing the cost of the water yield from the existing facility." The Madigan Policy, as western water users and their allies fondly refer to it, was patently illegal, and less than two years later was rescinded by President Bill Clinton's secretary of agriculture, Michael Espy. Allard (now a senator) and Brown then embarked on an unsuccessful bid to do away with the bypass-flow requirement through an amendment attached to the 1996 Farm Bill called the "Salvage Rider for Western Water."

Forest Service personnel on the ground—men and women who get their feet wet and dirty—generally understand what fish and wildlife need and try to do the right thing by them. But they only make recommendations, and even in environmentally enlightened administrations their recommendations tend to get overruled by bureaucrats. "Water issues are a big deal on this forest," says Carl Chambers, the Arapaho-Roosevelt's hydrologist. "Any time we start talking about water rights we start getting calls from the secretary's office and from Congressional delegations. And any time we talk to permittees about water rights we end up talking to lawyers. We believe that if you use national forest lands, the Forest Service has the right to condition that use to protect national forest resources." The Constitution, among other laws, makes it clear that Chambers is entirely right. The courts have consistently ruled that he is right. But any time the agencies do something to modestly reduce the yield of a project, water users—the most deficient of all self-proclaimed constitutional scholars—start screaming "Taking."

In 1993 seven water projects on the Arapaho-Roosevelt National Forest were coming up for permit renewal, and the Forest Service chose to take them on all at once. At the time, the forest plan called for preserving 40 percent of a diverted river's habitat, a figure basically pulled out of a hat. Saving 40 percent of a river's habitat doesn't mean keeping 40 percent of the water—more like 10 percent. Three of the four reservoirs that feed Cache la Poudre River, Colorado's only Wild and Scenic River, were subject to permitting. In a tradeoff, the forest agreed to let the users (the cities of Fort Collins and Greeley and the Water Supply and Storage Company) release a little more water into the upper mainstem and Joe Wright Creek, a tributary, if they could continue to release nothing at Long Draw Reservoir that feeds another tributary, La Poudre Pass Creek.

Rising in Rocky Mountain National Park near the Continental Divide and hurrying down through the big, boulder-strewn woods along the Comanche Peaks Wilderness Area, this mountain stream had been a national treasure, providing habitat for the federally threatened greenback cutthroat trout—the only salmonid native to the drainage and which had been considered extinct until 1969 when it was rediscovered by Dr. Robert Behnke of Colorado State University above an impassable waterfall on a nameless little rill which had to have been stocked by pioneers.

There was no reason other than timidity to sacrifice La Poudre Pass Creek. With a bit more resolve the Forest Service could have required a bypass flow because it had the law on its side. Instead, the users were allowed to keep sucking two miles of the creek dry. This hadn't been the way Chambers had wanted it, nor the way the interdisciplinary Forest Service study team on which he served had wanted it. The team—which also consisted of an ecologist, a fisheries biologist, a wildlife biologist, a public affairs specialist, and an expert in land management—had recommended minimum bypass flows to mimic the creek's natural cycles and had reported that this was "the only alternative which achieves a reasonable degree of resource protection." What's more, in a biological opinion, the Fish and Wildlife Service had declared that continued operation of Long Draw Reservoir without a bypass flow into La Poudre Pass Creek "is likely to jeopardize the continued existence of the [endangered] whooping crane, [endangered] least tern, [threatened] piping plover ... and may adversely affect the [threatened] greenback

cutthroat trout and the [threatened] western prairie white fringed orchid."
The Forest Service's final EIS correctly stated that without bypass flows
there would be "zero habitat potential ... conditions [that] preclude the
maintenance of self-sustaining fish populations immediately downstream
of Long Draw Dam."

Despite all this, the forest supervisor at the time, Skip Underwood,
elected to impose no bypass flow for La Poudre Pass Creek. "I considered
that responsibility [under FLPMA], and I conclude that I have the authority
to impose winter bypass flows below the dam to protect the park," he
wrote in his record of decision. "However, in my discretion, I have
balanced the public's interest in water facilities and the environment."
But the law did not provide him with any such "discretion." So, after
an unsuccessful administrative appeal, Trout Unlimited sued. The case
got delayed by a bogus, Republican-dominated commission hatched
by Allard and Brown that supposedly was to "study" whether or not
the Forest Service really had bypass flow authority. Then the case got
bumped to a Wyoming judge who didn't want to deal with it and hoped
it would just go away. Seven years later there's still no decision and still
no water for La Poudre Pass Creek.

Last year the Forest Service, then under the inspired leadership of
Mike Dombeck, issued guidance strategies for stream protection in the
form of a white paper. Ten alternatives—including mandatory bypass
flow requirements as a last resort—were offered. The document was a
summary of existing policy, a reaffirmation. But western Republicans
and their shrill property-rights constituents perfidiously seized upon
it as a radical Clinton administration policy shift secretly imposed in
smoke-filled rooms. "The policy allows the Forest Service to extort water
rights from Colorado's citizens," puffed Sen. Allard. "If you've lived in
Colorado for any period of time at all, you know that, in this great state,
water is sacrosanct. It's our lifeblood. When outsiders start meddling
with our water resources—whether it's Los Angeles, Las Vegas or the
federal government—they can and should expect a fight."

On May 22, 2001, Rep. Scott McInnis (R-CO), who took Allard's place
in the House and who chairs the Subcommittee on Forests and Forest
Health, called a joint oversight hearing with the Subcommittee on Water

and Power regarding this alleged policy shift. "I believe that the Forest Service's coercive practice of tying bypass flow restrictions to land-use authorizations for existing water facilities represents the single largest threat to water users in Colorado and indeed throughout the West," he said in his opening remarks. "In my mind, the policy looks an awful lot like federal blackmail."

Performing at McInnis's dog-and-pony show was one Kent Holsinger, assistant director of the Colorado DNR. One might suppose that a state department of natural resources would come out against the squandering of natural resources such as wild trout. But no. "The U.S. Forest Service must abandon the illfounded, and we believe, illegal, practice of imposing bypass flows on water providers," proclaimed Holsinger. "State instream flow programs may provide the best avenue towards real environmental protection on forest lands. Today, we have a program that effectively balances the needs of people and the environment. This program is particularly well suited to protecting instream values on national forest lands."

But, as Holsinger and his colleagues well know, Colorado's instream-flow program is next to worthless because the state's water claim is junior to most others. Not until 1973 did Colorado get the radical notion that fish and the aquatic invertebrates they eat need water and that, therefore, there is, as the legislature declared that year when it implemented instream flow, a "need to correlate the activities of mankind with some reasonable preservation of the natural environment." Other water users had been diverting rivers for decades or, in some cases, a century. In fact, white men had exhausted Colorado's east slope water thirty years after they got there and in 1880 had started piping it in from the sunset side of the Continental Divide. So when the users line up in dry years there's not a drop for the state's youthful instream-flow program.

One gets a perspective on the effectiveness of western-state instream-flow programs (some states, like New Mexico, don't even have them) by examining the demise of the lower Dolores River, tailing out of McPhee Reservoir on the San Juan National Forest in southwestern Colorado. The river had provided a world-class fishery for browns, rainbows and a few cutts until 1993 when there was a severe drought. Flows plummeted, temperatures soared, diverters diverted and trout went belly up. Since then diverters have allowed no recovery. The Forest Service can't impose a bypass flow because there's no special-use permit; the reservoir is operated by the Bureau of Reclamation.

Speaking for the diverters is rancher Chester Tozer of Cortez, president of the Southwest Colorado Landowners Association, an outfit that begrudges the public's trout even the public water they're not getting. "There's no limit to what TU wants," Tozer told me. "They're working with the Sierra Club and Wildlands Project and all of those environmental groups. But their real purpose is to get the farmers and ranchers off the land. And this Endangered Species Act and Clean Water Act and Animal Feeding Operations Act are going to run the farmers and ranchers out of business. The Forest Service is trying to take water away from farmers and ranchers. It's a violation of property rights. They want water for the boaters. They want water for the endangered species. They want water for the sucker fish they tried to kill for years, you know; now they're calling them endangered species. They know they can't do it in court, so they're trying to do it by negotiations and having kind of secret meetings with Trout Unlimited and the Southwest Water Conservancy District."

At last May's oversight hearing the Forest Service's deputy chief, Randy Phillips, was reported by *The Denver Post* to have "reversed" the Clinton administration's bypass flow policy: "Pleasing Colorado's Republican lawmakers and water utilities, the administration has decided that the Forest Service will no longer make such demands on water users seeking renewal of their permits to use federal land." But apparently *The Post* had gotten its information from Rep. McInnis, who had publicly declared victory. I read Phillips' testimony and didn't hear him say anything about a reversal. Though, given the George W. Bush administration's extraordinary deference to western Republicans, that's what I fully expect.

What I did hear Phillips say was that the administration had received another screed from "members of Congress" who are demanding a return to the Madigan policy (illegally imposed by Dubya's dad) and that "the administration is reviewing the direction that this letter suggested and will consider the benefits and costs of a change from current policy." That in itself is plenty disturbing.

Meanwhile, the two-year-old draft plan for the White River National Forest (just southwest of Rocky Mountain National Park) sets a goal for leaving 10 percent of the water in streams given to diverters. The public should be outraged that Forest managers have proposed so little; but instead, water users are outraged that they get to keep only 90 percent. They're confident that the 10 percent figure won't be in the final document, and they're probably right. The plan was due out in May and hasn't appeared as of this writing (early October).

"What we're hearing from sources inside the Bush administration is not good at all," comments Melinda Kassen, who runs TU's Colorado Western Water Project.

But Carl Chambers, the hydrologist who tried to save La Poudre Pass Creek, says this: "The Forest Service is an extremely large agency—35,000 employees. We manage millions of acres of land. One of the things about a bureaucracy that big is that changing course is like steering the Titanic. What I find is that as administrations change you hear a lot about shifts in policy and related discussion at The White House and the Department of Agriculture in Washington. As it all drifts down through the agency it just causes minor course corrections here and there. Often, particularly for administrations that last only four years, the changes have barely begun to be apparent at ground level when the administration is gone and we've got a new one."

Whether or not he's right, it's going to be a very long three years. And of all possible symbols for George W. Bush's ship of state—at least the part supposedly tending the precious resources of our National Forest System—the *Titanic* seems most apt.

II
MORE THAN A TOUCH OF SALT

BLUEFIN SUMMER

—‹‹·››—

The warm, overcast morning of September 11, 2004, has become a reference point in my life. Alone at daybreak, two miles out of Chatham, Massachusetts, in my twenty-one-foot Contender, *Assignment*, I'd seen a cloud of birds over busting fish. I assumed they were bluefish, but just to make sure they weren't stripers, I grabbed the spinning rod and fired out a hookless torpedo plug. As it landed a gleaming bluefin tuna of perhaps eighty pounds pounced on it like a mousing coyote.

Attacking the ancient, overfilled Fin-Nor reel verbally and with a screwdriver, I excavated the leader, set up my 12-weight Sage, and tied on a Jellyfish—the white, wing-flapping concoction of legendary Montauk guide and raconteur David Blinken. For the next three hours I chased tight pods of tuna. They didn't race around like albies but, save for rare breaches, rolled lazily or cruised just below the surface like sluiced pulp logs. The sweet, fruity scent of sand eels whole and chopped hung on the soft south wind. Finally three beasts about the size of the first one I'd seen appeared under my fly just as it hit the water. The middle one sucked it in.

I could beat the fish on this gear, given generous measures of luck and knowledge—neither of which I possessed on that day. The first mistake I made was to follow—steering, reeling, hauling down the radio antenna and extra fly rods, reaching over the high side to flip the line off a lobster buoy. When tuna swim they oxygenate, and if you follow before you have to, they'll go on forever. My second mistake was trying to herd the fish away from a cluster of lobster pots. It worked the first time, not the second. Now, an hour after hookup and nine miles seaward, the fish doubled back, creating so much slack I couldn't keep the backing out of the prop when I plunged the rod into the water. They could hear me in Chatham.

Cut to August 2005. I receive a phone call from Richard Reagan—creator of the famed Albie Whore (similar to the Jellyfish, but with wings plastered to the sides with hot glue) and, in his lesser role, president and fellow board member of the Norcross Wildlife Foundation. Richard Reagan—the man who until this very minute had defined flyrodding for bluefins as "a boat ride," but who guided by Blinken, had just landed seven off Rhode Island. "No one lands seven tuna in one day," I informed him. But he insisted it was true; and from across the room, barely audible over the clinking ice in their single malts, Blinken backed him up. For most of the day they'd been surrounded by vast schools that churned the water white. I ordered Reagan and his able assistant, Capt. John McMurray (a saltwater flyrod guide on weekends), to appear at my house the next evening. Reagan offered the lame excuse of work.

But at 5:30 a.m. on August 9 McMurray and I splashed *Assignment* at Galilee, Rhode Island. The fog that had worried us all the way down lifted a hundred yards from the ramp. Two miles out McMurray yelled, "Tuna!" I wasn't convinced. Then tuna erupted all around us, sending up showers of one-inch peanut bunker. Nothing lazy about these fish. They didn't roll or cruise; they slashed and leapt, frequently clearing the water. We could see their geysers a mile away. I eased *Assignment* to the edge of the nearest school, and McMurray laid down one of the Albie Whores Reagan had tied for us.

"There he is," he shouted after his third strip. Backing poured out of his reel, but I resisted the temptation to follow; and when I had to follow, the fish shot toward us. Three other boats arrived. Blinken hailed us on the radio. New schools popped up at all compass points, and the brightening sun turned the peanut bunker into welding sparks. McMurray, using a reel with no anti-reverse, switched hands, holding his 9-weight briefly with his bloody left and shaking his right.

These were two-year-old tuna—twenty to thirty-five pounds—and most likely progeny of the big 1994 year class. Every flyrodder wants to tangle with an older fish, as I had the previous year, but they'll tie up the boat for three hours and the chances they'll survive aren't great. Even to target bluefins a boat owner/operator needs a "highly migratory" permit available for $22 from the highly unfriendly Web site of the National Marine Fisheries Service (www.nmfspermits.com) or by phoning 888-872-8862. Guests fish free. Size and bag limits (which apply to boat, not individual anglers) change according to harvest, so keep checking the Web site. During most of the summer of 2005 a boat was allowed to kill one fish per day between twenty-seven and seventy-two inches fork length. You must report every tuna landed at the same number (press 1 to avoid an endless stream of BS). Even if you don't have a tuna in your boat when you're checked, you're going to have to do some fancy talking if you don't have a permit and someone has been casting a tarpon rod with a big, anti-reverse reel.

Fifty minutes after McMurray struck his fish I hoisted it by the leader and hard tail and laid it on the gunwale tape. It measured thirty-three inches from lip to fork. Calico flanks were hard and cold, seemingly scaleless and with barely any slime. Horizontal stabilizers jutted from the caudal peduncle. Fins folded into grooves that facilitated speed bursts of at least 55 mph. Double-hinged jaws swung the mouth out as well as open. Gills were immense. Instead of pumping water through their gills like lesser fish, tuna reverse the process, pushing their gills through the water, mouths agape, supercharging their warm, blood-rich muscles like ramjets. Bluefin tuna lack air bladders, so they must swim every minute of their lives; restrained, they suffocate and drown. When you run your hand over their brows you can sometimes feel the light-sensing window used for navigation. Paired arteries and veins with opposite directions of flow act as heat exchangers and barriers to heat loss.

When I bled this fish its enormous heart shot thick pulses of blood into a five-gallon bucket, and when I gutted it I could feel the body heat. You don't kill one of these highly advanced wanderers of our planet casually, but you don't need to don ashes and sackcloth if you do. These are the babies; and, even before predation by humans, very few make it to spawning age.

McMurray's fish taught us two lessons: 1) Anything under a 12-weight is going to hurt you and the fish; and 2) do your best not to let any object, even the tape measure, touch a tuna; the scaleless appearance is an illusion. Scales come off easily, leaving a gel of gray dust on anything they contact.

With our daily limit iced down, I manned the bow while McMurray steered us into another school and phoned his young wife, Danielle, a gourmet chef, instructing her to relay recipes for tuna rolls and sushi to my wife, Donna. I missed four strikes before I hooked up. With the

12-weight I had the fish, a clone of our first, to the boat in 30 minutes. It seemed in good shape, and McMurray held it high by the tail and dropped it into the water, giving it a jump-start and a quick charge of oxygen. That fish taught us that you need the thickest of hooks. The seemingly stout one on the Albie Whore was badly bent.

More boats appeared, but we still had fish to ourselves, and with the quiet four-stroke we could cruise into the middle of them without putting any down. I have always envied the willpower that, in these situations, allows McMurray to rack his rod and pick up his camera. And I envy his results. When he resumed casting a bluefin provided a particularly painful lesson, especially for McMurray—i.e., that improved clinch knots tied (at least by me) on 25-pound flurocarbon come unwrapped. Use a loop knot.

After each of us had landed another fish, we were no longer intimidated. You just have to accept the fact that you will always lose 200 yards of backing in the first fifteen seconds.

As we moved east we encountered larger schools and fewer boats. "God, look at that blitz," yelled McMurray, spinning the wheel and swatting the throttle. I pooh-poohed him when he suggested trying the little crease flies we use for albies in low light. But tuna devoured them on their way down from arcing vaults.

At 5:00, with eleven fish to the boat, McMurray inquired if I thought we should "call it a day."

"Are you crazy?" I demanded. "You and I may never live to see this again." But the action faded with the light, and we were driven off the water by darkness. We filleted our fish in my barn and saved every scrap. Donna had the sushi and tuna rolls ready by 11:00—by far the best we'd ever had. The stuff you order at restaurants is flash-frozen, the better to kill parasites (virtually non-existent in small bluefins); and the minimum commercial limit is 72 inches.

"To hell with any assignment that doesn't float," I told McMurray. "I'm on these fish twice a week till they leave. So how about Thursday?" It was the easiest sell I ever made. But Richard Reagan had an important commitment that day and needed McMurray to fill in at the office.

So there I was at 5:30 a.m. on August 11, 2005, alone on a fog-shrouded Rhode Island Sound, listening for birds and fish, eyes glued to the GPS. Finally, I made out whitewater close by my starboard beam and promptly hooked and landed a fine fish. I steamed due south, searching for an opening. Then halfway to Block Island, I passed abruptly into bright sunlight and glassy water broken in a dozen spots by schools of bunker-gorging bluefins. I saw flying fish, storm petrels dancing on the water and small tunoids racing west—almost certainly green bonito.

"Hey Ted," came a clear voice on the radio. "Are you in fog?" It was Capt. Amanda Switzer, the famous Montauk guide and movie star (at least on the ESPN series *Guide House*).

"Only figuratively," I replied. "Head straight for Block." And in ten minutes her white Parker broke into the sunlight like the slow-motion TV ad footage of the passenger jet nosing out of the cloud layer. In the bow, wearing his trademark orange fleece and flailing his right arm like the drowned Ahab, was Richard Reagan. "Haar, Teddy," he called. "I seek the bluefin tuna." At noon Amanda radioed to tell me he'd blown up a rod.

It was the best fifteen hours of fishing I've ever had. I try not to count fish, but you can't help it with tuna—fourteen hooked, twelve landed. I learned a lot about bluefins that day: that their little teeth can make your thumb and forefinger look like you used them to stop the wire brush on an electric grinder, that unhooking them is infinitely harder with no one to hold them for you, that when they get under your boat (as they always do after fifteen or twenty minutes) you need to raise your motor (and then remember to lower it before you start it again), that it is absolutely impossible to land a bluefin alone unless you slack off, throw down your rod, and grab the leader. And, finally, I learned what it must feel like to play sixty minutes of tackle football with no pads.

McMurray, a patron of the fly-fishing forum www.reeltime.com, wrote up our adventure, eliciting an immediate e-mail to me from the Socrates of Yankee striper guides, Capt. Doug Jowett. "Get down here fast," I ordered. "You and I may never live to see this again." We had a good day on Rhode Island Sound durring which Jowett blew up a 14-weight rod 200 yards from shore but landed the fish handily with the butt section. And we had an epic day on Cape Cod Bay in lightning and driving rain, amid whales, lunging sheerwaters and huge, frothing schools of tuna which, more often than not, stayed with us all the time we were hooked up, then vanished like summer love. We learned that 20-pound tippets aren't enough because bluefins can bust them with zero rod pressure merely by dragging line and backing at warp speed.

After Jowett sacrificed his shoulder to a fifty-pounder, which he beat despite the pain and which proved the best fish of the summer, I took *Assignment*'s bow for the rest of the day, mumbling a brief and feeble protest. When fish spurned my Jellyfish, Jowett passed me one of his Bunny Flies, and I was tight on the first cast. But it was the next school that taught us the lesson because it spurned the Bunny Fly and jumped all over the Jellyfish.

The tuna stayed around till November, but we encountered only lazy rollers. Jowett's clients had a few to the boat, but no one aboard *Assignment* hooked up again.

There are all kinds of plausible theories for the tuna invasion of 2005, none of which is good management. A law—written by and for the commercial fishermen of the East Coast Tuna Association—mandates that U.S. tuna regs can't be more restrictive than international ones. And the fishmongers and politicians who run the international management body (the International Commission for the Conservation of Atlantic Tunas) have looked after the species like nineteenth century bison hunters. In 2005, when the East Coast Tuna Association failed to kill its quota of giants in Cape Cod Bay (despite its "gentleman's agreement" not to go there), it sought and received permission from the National Marine Fisheries Service to plunder the fish off North Carolina. There have been no good year classes since 1994, and none coming along from before. The 2001 bluefin biomass (the last measured) was 13 percent of what it was in 1975.

I wish I could be more sanguine, but my theory is that lots of bait blew into Rhode Island Sound. As for Cape Cod Bay, you can find a few bluefins there most every summer, and perhaps Jowett and I, for once, hit it right. Finally, what I believe most fervently—not a theory but a postulate—is the mantra we chanted all summer: "We may never live to see this again." That, of course, could apply equally to the sunrise. So if the tuna show up next year, get your priorities straight and chase them.

How It Is at South Andros

About the third day of our first trip to South Andros Island I realized that my wife, Donna, and I would be coming back at least once a year for as long as it or we remained in operation. That was eight springs ago, and as I read through the entries in my fishing journal, it occurs to me that certain experiences at this magical place have become reference points in our lives. As in: "Yes, that was the year we saw the hawksbill turtle at Cowhorn Key" or "That was the year the Hausners were at Bair Bahamas and you won the land crab races." Never let anyone tell you that fishing is unimportant.

But I have learned that, while nothing in fishing is more important than fish, they can't make fishing important by themselves. As an outdoor writer, I get to fish free all over the world; and while I've enjoyed a lot of great bonefish destinations including Christmas Island, North Andros, Belize, and Venezuela, I find myself turning down these "freebies" in order to preserve time for Bair Bahamas. I know that Andy Bair and his wife, Stanley (who occasionally argues on the phone with officious bureaucrats who tell her she's a man), would offer me a freebie if I asked, and they know I would never ask. For us, as for so many of the good people we meet here, Bair Bahamas Guest House has ceased to be a "lodge" and has become instead our friends' house. This is the year's one serious expedition, for which everything—not discounting weddings, magazine assignments and family functions—must give way.

There are days at South Andros, as there are days at Christmas Island, when you will catch few fish or no fish. This is a reality of bonefish fishing that doesn't get written about. It's never that the fish aren't there. But clouds will hide them; cold fronts will drive them to deep water; gales will muddy the flats and send your line coiling around your neck like a milk snake on a rat. There aren't many such days at South Andros, but you will experience them. That's when "accommodations"—far more important to Donna than to me—save the day. There is the indelible vision of Andy the quintessential southern gentleman from Atlanta, standing on the conch-shell-and-concrete seawall, greeting each returning boat with a smile, wading out to take the rods. He knows better than to ask us how we did.

The progression of sounds and facial expressions from the wet, cold anglers is fascinating and funny. After warm showers (not in the vile brew of mud, salt and sulfur you get in other Bahamian bonefish lodges, but in filtered freshwater you can drink straight from the tap) grunts evolve to phrases, and a few stillborn smiles appear. Several half smiles as the guests pour their drinks (no nickel and diming with chit sheets here). Full smiles when the plate of hot conch fritters arrives. At supper—always a memorable affair and commonly featuring fish or conch or lobsters caught that day—laughter flows with the fine wine, and grand plans are made for the morrow.

The front is supposed to pass through, but Andy will tell you that only if you ask. Better to expect the worst and not be disappointed. Don't look at the sky at 5:00 a.m. It will always deceive you, toying with your hopes and fears. The wind is up a bit. There are black clouds backlit by lightning. But there are also blazing stars undefiled by smog or ambient light. At breakfast the fierce Bahamian sun already has muscled the storm clouds to the horizon. The wind has dropped with the tide. "We gonna rip lips," says our guide as we climb into the skiff.

Today we are going to the West Side through a bight where key-flecked lagoons, miles wide, collect and disgorge mangrove-lined creeks. Don't even try to remember the way. Green, iridescent needlefish tail dance from the skiff's wake and from barracudas that burst out of the shallows. Suddenly we're directly over a blacktip shark that bolts in a puff of mud. An osprey dives, scattering a school of shad like welding sparks. Roseate spoonbills, snowy egrets, great egrets, tri-colored herons, great blues and little blues stalk coral shoals or billow from mangrove tops. The guide points to a green turtle sculling over a flat faster than any wide receiver can run. No buildings, no roads, no people. This side of the island is every bit as wild as Alaska. And, along with North Andros, it's the largest unexplored land mass in the western hemisphere.

After seven miles our guide, Nat Adams, slows the engine, props up the shaft with a chunk of two-by-four, and "bubbles" through a long thoroughfare. I sit on the deck, dragging my boot-baked feet in the deliciously cool water and peering into coral grottos where crabs wave and mangrove snappers hang and turn as if suspended from mobiles. More creeks. More lagoons. Finally, Nat swings the boat toward a golden beach, kills the engine, and throws out the anchor.

The sun and wind are at our backs. The bottom is firm, clean sand. We wade for half a mile without seeing an aquatic life form. Then a ray, then a nurse shark, then a school of shad. Something is changing; the flat is coming alive. "Big school coming," says Nat with not much excitement in his voice. How can he possibly see them? We've done this so much that we like to think we're good at spotting fish, and in this transparent water with the perfect lighting it seems that nothing could escape our gaze. But there is no hint of a fish anywhere.

Then, 200 yards out, I see faint ripples in the lee of mangroves, as if a light breeze had just kissed the surface. The ripples are headed straight for us. At last we see the pollywog shadows on the sand—more than a hundred fish in tight formation, still moving towards us. You don't need to be a good caster to succeed at South Andros. My brother-in-law, Barry Reed, was catching fish here the first day he picked up a fly rod. Because South Andros bonefish see so few flies they are very forgiving. I've caught them by accident when I was wading and my flyline was trailing behind me. What's more, there are so many keys and creeks that you can almost always get out of the wind or put it behind you where it will actually help.

We cast our Gotchas when the fish are still 100 feet away. (Fifty percent of the bonefish at South Andros are caught on Gotchas because anglers who fish South Andros use Gotchas half the time.) "Leave it. Leave it," whispers Nat, finally excited. "Okay. Short strips. Short strips." A dozen fish rush my fly. A dozen fish rush Donna's. Tails up, snouts down, pectorals flared, they pause and hover. We strip. They rush again, pause and hover again. (Sometimes when the guide says "Strip" you have to ignore him or you'll run out of line.) I feel a take, and set with the line only—lightly so as not to spook the fish if I miss. I do miss. I strip again and miss again. Now I am out of line and am desperately double hauling. I can hear line peeling from Donna's reel. Now fish, slightly spooked, are streaming past my feet. I cast and miss two more fish. I turn into the sun and wind, cast again, and I'm on.

Big schools don't contain big fish. But, at about three pounds each, these are plenty big enough to make me happy. Our lines hiss through the water, kicking up spray. I hold my rod high so Donna can duck underneath. No other three-pound fish on earth can take you into the backing almost every time. We get our flylines back, then lose them again.

Finally, our fish circle us a cast out, satellites in decaying orbits. We turn with them, pumping and cranking. Once you force their heads above the surface, you have them beat; but they know this too, and will resist to the limit of your tackle. At last my fish splashes at my feet. It is good to hold one again, to admire the large obsidian eyes, the green, faintly barred back, the silver flanks, the azure-tinged tail. The Bahamians get it. They allow no commercial plunder or even take of bonefish. There's even a bonefish on their dime. How uplifting to fish in a place you know will be just as good in a year or a decade!

We find another school, and another, and another, and another. We don't count our fish, but the guides do because they love to compete. "How many is that for you, Ted?" shouts Nat, whom I've left with Donna. I make up a number that is probably accurate within five: "Thirty," I shout back. Donna catches a twelve-incher and asks if that counts. It does. "We don't make 'em; we just take 'em," Nat declares.

The fair-weather days aren't always this easy, of course. Sometimes— especially when there's no breeze or "they feel a cold front coming," as the guides theorize—you have to work for your fish. You add four feet of tippet and change flies a lot. But if you have sun, rare are the afternoons you'll come in fish hungry.

Sometimes the flats are so silent we hear the crackle of insect wings in the mangroves and the caroling of redwings and warblers that we'll meet again a month later in Yankee Land. Nat points out a three-foot iguana on a mangrove. "Where in relation to the dead branch?" I ask.

"That's not a dead branch; that's the iguana," says Nat. We stop and watch a pair of porpoises herding shad in shallow water. One year a mother and her calf, overcome with curiosity, raced toward the boat from at least a mile away. For a full minute we watched the unidentifiable black specks getting bigger. The mother held her distance, but the baby kept coming, circling the boat ten feet out and tilting back so he could eyeball us.

If you've caught your fill of bonefish or if they're not cooperating, try the barracudas. There are some monsters close to the lodge, and they're always in the mood. If you have some wire tippet material, you can take them on long, green flies and poppers, but (dare I say it?) you'll do much better slinging tube lures with a light spinning rod; and, in a way, it's more exciting. You drop the lure thirty feet ahead of the fish and crank as fast as you can. He'll turn and streak after it, inhale it, then make a blazing fifty-yard run capped with a high, twisting leap. There is no shortage of barracudas, so it's a nice gesture to kill a couple for your guide. The lodge will even cook one up for you. The cudas you catch on the flats are delicious and always safe to eat.

The tide birds—a species of rail that shouts raucously from deep in the mangroves whenever the tide turns—make me laugh; but they make me a little sad, too. They remind me how fast our week passes and that time and tide wait for no man, or woman either. For years I didn't believe in tide birds. I thought the guides were kidding. But they exist, and I have seen them, albeit fleetingly. I ask every guide if the tide birds shout because they're mad or happy. Only one, Carl Moxey, professed to know: "Well, mon, when the tide come in and cover up all dem flats dey shout 'cause dey're mahd. But when the tide go out dey see all dese nice crahbs and worms and shrimps, and dey shout 'cause dey're happy."

On our last day we always ask to be put off on the sandbar half a mile out from the lodge. About seventy-five acres are exposed at low tide. With each step you raise clouds of pure white sand, fine and dry as powdered sugar. At the highest points you can see the perfect impressions of the rays that buried themselves six hours earlier. It's the sort of place the beautiful, elegantly dressed ladies in the paintings on the Bair Bahamas Guest House's walls must have walked, carrying their parasols and towing their little black dogs. At night Neptune stands here and empties his purse of perfect sand dollars. (They don't make good tips, but Stanley—who belongs in one of those paintings herself—will show you how to break one apart and pick out five tiny doves.)

The sandbar is the one place on South Andros where time slows for us. But even here it passes too quickly. Soon our hats are full of sand dollars, and we're back in the skiff. Even from here we can see Andy on the seawall.

THE EXHAUSTED SEA

━━━━━━━ ⤛ ⤜ ━━━━━━━

The year is 1965, circa July 4. Rocked by gentle swells on a glassy sea, Robbie Troup and I are fishing from a wooden lobster boat off Rye, New Hampshire. Five miles seaward the gray backs of the Isles of Shoals breach through the morning haze like humpback whales. The dawdling offshore breeze carries the fragrance of salt marsh, clam flat, and kelp. "It's amazing what you can do with monofilament and sea worms," announces Ken, our skipper, while we boat haddock. Most of the forty or so fish already onboard weigh more than eight pounds.

We let the cod go unless we've brought them up too fast and their air bladders stick out their throats like cadaverous thumbs. We club the mini sharks called dogfish and toss them overboard because we've been taught that there are "too many" and that they are "trash fish." Whenever they get too thick, we haul anchor and move.

Suddenly it is June 23, 2002. I am standing on the fish pier at Chatham, Massachusetts, as the commercial fishing fleet unloads its catch. Every fish from every boat is a dogfish. Gray and skinny, they lie tangled together in wooden crates, staring with dead, reptilian eyes. Almost three decades of litigation, legislation, planning, and media flap about the worst debacle in the history of American fish management—the demise of fourteen bottom species collectively called "groundfish"—hasn't fixed anything. Nine years earlier the National Marine Fisheries Service (NMFS), a tentacle of the Department of Commerce, had declared haddock commercially extinct in the Gulf of Maine. The cod population has collapsed, too. Still, in its twenty-seven-year history, there has never been a time that the New England Fisheries Management Council—which, with NMFS oversight and approval, sets quotas for cod, haddock, and other groundfish—has not allowed gross overfishing.

When groundfish disappeared, dogfish expanded, feasting on the rich shoals of baitfish that were suddenly available. The response of state and federal managers and seafood promoters in the New England and mid-Atlantic states was to encourage an unsustainable fishery for dogfish, which they called an "underutilized species" and to which they assigned the consumer-friendly name "cape shark." But unlike cod, dogfish don't start spewing millions of eggs at age two. It takes females as long as humans to reach sexual maturity, and dogfish bear their young alive, producing dog-size litters of six to ten pups after two-year pregnancies.

The fishery, directed at females because they're larger, got under way in the late 1980s. By 1996 annual landings had increased from about 9.9 million pounds to 60 million pounds. Four years later mature females had declined by 80 percent.

The New England and Mid-Atlantic Fishery Management Councils, which manage federal waters (from 3 to 200 miles out), didn't even hatch a dogfish plan until 2000. And the Atlantic States Marine Fisheries Commission (ASMFC), which manages state waters (out to three miles), procrastinated until 2002. But the states' plan had been in place only three months when, in February 2003, commission members effectively deep-sixed it after Massachusetts flimflammed them with bogus data. Despite the fact that 80 percent of the mature females had been killed off and virtually no new pups had been born during any of the past seven years, the commission rejected the recommendation of its own scientists and increased the annual dogfish quota from 4 million pounds to 8.8 million pounds. Still, there would be a chance to amend that at the commission's June 10, 2003, meeting in Crystal City, Virginia.

For four months the environmental community—led by Sonja Fordham, the Ocean Conservancy's fish conservation project manager, and Merry Camhi, assistant director of Audubon's Living Oceans Program and president of the American Elasmobranch Society—blitzed the ASMFC with letters pleading for sanity.

At the June 10 meeting the scientists on the dogfish technical team objected to the increase. Still, the motion to lower the quota failed. "And this was after the commission had watered down the amendment to have the right quota but a high limit on the number of trips," declared Fordham, who testified for the Ocean Conservancy, Audubon, and Environmental Defense.

"The New England states wouldn't even vote for their own compromise. It was the worst day for marine fish management I can remember. What an embarrassment! The U.S. blew it at a time when we're running around to international meetings and telling the world how vulnerable sharks are and how we need to protect them." No sooner had the Atlantic states more than doubled their dogfish quota than Canadian fishermen, who had been leaning toward responsible management, announced that they wanted to double theirs as well.

In the Northeast and elsewhere in U.S. marine waters, at least 40 percent of the species that managers have information on are overfished (meaning the population is too low to produce maximum sustainable yield) or are experiencing overfishing (meaning they're being caught at a rate that exceeds maximum sustainable yield). Such is American marine fisheries management in action.

With a few notable exceptions (Alaska being one), the situation is no better in the Pacific or the Gulf of Mexico. And it's even worse in foreign waters. Canada has depleted its cod to the point that commercial fishing is basically over for the foreseeable future. Recovery may not be possible. The journal *Nature* reports that the planet has lost 90 percent of its high-level marine predator fish, such as cod, flounder, and tuna. "I still believe the cod fishery ... and probably all the great sea-fisheries are inexhaustible; that is to say that nothing we can do seriously affects the number of fish," proclaimed the great British biologist Thomas Huxley.

Since he made that comment, 140 years ago, marine biologists have learned better. Managers, politicians, and commercial fishermen have not. The United States has no discernible policy for the oceans. Management decisions are made by special interests or court rulings, and they are implemented in three geographical jurisdictions under 140 statutes by six frequently feuding departments.

If any entity can convince Congress, the administration, and the public to do better, it is the Pew Charitable Trusts. On June 4, 2003, amid a perfect storm of professionally generated fanfare, the eighteen-member Pew Ocean Commission unveiled a three-year, $3.5 million study that offered the first comprehensive review of U.S. ocean policy together with recommendations for reform. It was everything Audubon, the

Ocean Conservancy, the Natural Resources Defense Council (NRDC), and other environmental outfits have been saying for thirty years, but it was said all at once, in a flashy, easily understood way and by people who have lots more credibility with this administration and Congress. The commission included New York governor George Pataki, former Kansas governor Mike Hayden, philanthropist David Rockefeller, and Kathryn Sullivan, a former astronaut and onetime chief scientist at the National Ocean and Atmospheric Administration.

What I was seeing at the Chatham fish pier is called "fishing down the food chain." As you destroy each descending link, you reduce biodiversity, until you literally hit jellyfish. In the early 1990s, when marine activist Carl Safina, then director of Audubon's Living Oceans Program and a member of the Mid-Atlantic Fisheries Management Council, suggested a management plan for tautog, he elicited incredulous stares. "There are plenty of tautog," exclaimed one member. "That's the whole point," Safina said. "Let's keep it that way."

"Next you'll be asking for a management plan for jellyfish," remarked someone else. The following year mid-Atlantic fishermen, desperately seeking "underutilized species," started netting jellyfish and shipping them to the Japanese, who had decided they liked them in salads.

Fishing down the food chain is dangerous, because recovery of a depleted species may not be possible. It may be permanently suppressed by species that have moved into its niche. Also, survivors may be spread so thinly over the continental shelf that they have difficulty finding one another. Consider the Atlantic halibut—a giant, predacious flounder that doesn't spawn until it's three feet long and that is capable of attaining weights of 700 pounds. It was fished to commercial extinction in the nineteenth century. But despite the fact that there has been virtually no directed fishery ever since, it hasn't recovered. When Atlantic halibut are caught today, it's almost always by accident. They're rugged fish and lack air bladders, so they can be safely released even when brought up from great depths. But incredibly, the NMFS allows commercial fishermen to kill one per trip. "We have fishery management regimes but not ecosystem regimes," comments Steve Murawski of the NMFS's Woods Hole Science Center.

In those rare cases where scientists are allowed to set quotas, marine fish management isn't an oxymoron. Sometimes, however, even the scientists are reluctant to cut the public out of decision making. It's just not PC. "We rely heavily on the regionalization of the process and a lot of public input," says Murawski. "Ours is an exercise in Jeffersonian democracy." But there are places where Jeffersonian democracy doesn't work—such as in cardiovascular-surgery units and carrier battle groups. Americans have never understood this. In 1976, after watching vessels from the Soviet bloc wipe out Atlantic groundfish, Congress passed the Magnuson Fishery Conservation and Management Act, thereby creating the 200-mile limit, setting up eight regional councils on all three coasts to manage fish in federal waters (supposedly under the paternal gaze of the NMFS), and providing sufficient financial aid to the U.S. fishing fleet to double it by 1983.

The Magnuson Act was a grand experiment in Jeffersonian democracy in that it ensconced user-group representatives on the councils, thus giving people who profited directly or indirectly from commercial fishing "a stake in their own future." It sounded wonderful and very American. But when regulations are made by those requiring regulation, nothing good ever seems to happen. The public pays to educate fisheries professionals, pays for their salaries and benefits, pays for their equipment, then tells them how to take care of fish. So the guiding principle of American fish management has become: "Strict dieting, except in cases of hunger."

By 1989 it was clear that we had saved our marine fish from foreigners in order to wipe them out ourselves. With record low catches that year, the New England council declared groundfish "overfished." When scientists recommended a 50 percent reduction in catch, the council refused. In 1991 a lawsuit by the Conservation Law Foundation and the Massachusetts Audubon Society forced the council to write a new groundfish plan, a process it dragged out for three years. Congress tried to fix things in 1996 with the Sustainable Fisheries Act, which finally defined and forbade overfishing and mandated the fast recovery of overfished stocks. But there has been scant enforcement.

Despite the new law, the NMFS allowed the New England council to implement groundfish quotas four times those deemed safe by scientists on the technical committee. So in 2000 the Conservation Law Foundation, Audubon, the Ocean Conservancy, and the NRDC sued. On April 26, 2002, U.S. District Judge Gladys Kessler ordered prompt, tough restrictions needed for groundfish recovery. But after hearing arguments from states, cities, fishermen, and the NMFS, Judge Kessler amended her original decision and substantially weakened protections. "We won hands down, and we now have weaker groundfish restrictions than we did before," laments Fordham.

"We have to separate the scientific aspects of fisheries management from the allocation," Camhi told me. "You can't have them both done under the same roof by the same people." Consider the Cape Cod Commercial Hook Fishermen's Association (CCCHFA), represented on the Joint Dogfish Committee of the New England and mid-Atlantic councils by John Pappalardo, who fishes out of Chatham, Massachusetts. Hook fishing by longline (at least for dogfish and groundfish) is promoted by the environmental community as "habitat-friendly," because it doesn't bulldoze the seabed like mobile net gear, or drown seabirds and turtles like pelagic longlines. Along with Audubon, the CCCHFA is a member of the Marine Fish Conservation Network. It is funded by the Pew Charitable Trusts and other conservation-minded foundations. It's a good group in lots of ways, but it's conflicted because 80 percent of the dogfish quota for the New England and mid-Atlantic management regions is taken by Massachusetts, and 65 percent of that is landed at Chatham. Moreover, most of the dogfish are caught by hook fishermen. When Massachusetts proposed doubling the quota, Pappalardo and the other five members of the Joint Dogfish Committee cast yes votes. To its credit, the NMFS overrode the committee, insisting on a sustainable quota. But this didn't ease the slaughter in state waters.

It is difficult to understand the thinking of your typical commercial fisherman, who is outraged by all quotas and who invariably gets politicians to increase them. Essentially, the argument is this: "We need fish for our livelihoods, so let us eradicate them." I have heard more than one commercial fisherman utter words to this effect: "When the law of diminishing returns kicks in, we back off, and the fish recover." Their apologists even have a name for it: "pulse fishing." Left to regulate themselves, commercial fishermen will continue to strip-mine the sea, fish down the food chain, and spew pseudo science to justify whatever seems profitable at the moment.

Where they have been regulated by scientists, commercial fishermen have profited from healthy fish stocks. Good fish managers, like good parents, eventually learn that one of the kindest words they can utter is "no." There aren't a lot of happy endings, but an examination of successes (or near successes) illuminates the reasons for failures. Fordham and Camhi don't agree with the NMFS's Murawski that summer flounder management is a "success," but they acknowledge that it's close. A good reason for this is that the Ocean Conservancy, Audubon, Environmental Defense, and the NRDC won a lawsuit against the NMFS four years ago, forcing it to impose quotas that had a decent chance of helping the stock recover. But another reason is that the Mid-Atlantic Council, in charge of summer flounder (even though the fish's range extends well into New England), has behaved aberrantly—that is, it has accepted quotas for a decade. The New England council seems allergic to quotas. Instead, it seeks painless diets, vainly trying to make things right by restricting gear and limiting days at sea.

Swordfish are recovering, despite the dereliction of the International Commission for the Conservation of Atlantic Tunas (ICCAT), a sorry congregation of fishmongers and politicians that tends "highly migratory species" (tuna, sharks, and billfish) beyond our federal waters. In 1990, under intense lobbying by commercial swordfishermen, Congress enjoined the NMFS, which tends highly migratory species in federal waters, from setting regulations that were stricter than ICCAT's. As a result swordfish collapsed. Average weight dropped from 115 to 60 pounds, and 25-pounders were being sold at Manhattan's Fulton Fish Market as "pups."

The NMFS, which was doing nothing to stop gross longline bycatch of sublegal swordfish, needed to be shaken by the lapels, and in 1998 the NRDC and SeaWeb (a Pew offshoot) did just that by organizing the "Give Swordfish a Break" campaign, which convinced twenty-seven leading East Coast restaurants to remove swordfish from their menus. This got the attention of the feds. Meanwhile, Audubon and its allies went to court and forced the NMFS to close large areas to fishing. Today North Atlantic swordfish have recovered to 94 percent of the biomass scientists consider "healthy." But most of the fish are still juveniles, and now the industry is pushing a plan to open up swordfish sanctuaries in the guise of "scientific research."

Although the ASMFC recently punted on an opportunity to recover the age and size structure of the Atlantic Coast striped bass population, the management of "stripers," as they are affectionately known by anglers, is about as close to pure success as fish management gets. As with virtually all species of marine fish, however, we had to nearly wipe them out before we managed them. Despite effort that I'd call prodigious (others, "obsessive"), I went whole seasons in the mid-1980s without catching a single striper, contenting myself instead with the giant bluefish that had surged into the inshore niche. Today a dozen stripers, caught and released, is a slow day. Striper recovery has come about because Congress got fed up with the individual states' inability to say no, and in 1986 passed the Atlantic Striped Bass Conservation Act, which transformed the ASMFC from a sideline adviser to an enforcement power. Now the agency can shut down fishing if a state doesn't manage stripers scientifically.

But there's another reason for success. Stripers are caught (and were depleted) mostly by recreational fishermen. And recreational fishermen were willing to accept—in fact demanded—draconian quotas: one-fish daily limits at first. Now, for most states, it's two fish. "Stripers are a success," remarks Camhi, "because we got the commercial guys off the fish, and the recreational guys were willing to do what it took."

Largely responsible for the consistent excellence of the fisheries sections of the recent Pew report was Pew oceans commissioner Mike Hayden—trained biologist; ardent angler and conservationist; former Republican governor of Kansas; former Assistant Secretary for Fish, Wildlife, and Parks under George H. W. Bush; former president of the American Sportfishing Association; and now secretary of the Kansas Department of Wildlife and Parks. When Hayden talks fish, his friend George W. Bush listens.

The President himself is an ardent angler. So is the Vice-President. So is Commerce Secretary Donald Evans, who presides over the NMFS.

On April 25, 2003, the administration took a strong stand for marine fish when Evans blasted ICCAT for consistently setting unsustainable quotas against the advice of its own scientists. In a letter to Pascal Lamy, European Union Commissioner for Trade, Evans wrote: "I am urging you to take prompt action to improve EU compliance with existing ICCAT obligations and to reconsider accepting science-based conservation measures to guarantee a sustainable future for species like the Atlantic bluefin tuna and white marlin."

Congress is in far greater need of education than the administration. For example, Richard Pombo (R-CA), chair of the House Resources Committee, which has primary jurisdiction over the oceans, calls the Pew report "a $5 million coffee-table picture book." And Senate Appropriations chair Ted Stevens (R-AK), who co-wrote the Sustainable Fisheries Act provisions that kept commercial fishermen regulating themselves, proclaims that the document "is tainted by the millions of dollars [the Pew Charitable Trusts] spend on environmental litigation aimed at stopping commercial fishing."

Pew released its report at precisely the right time. As of this writing, an even more ambitious study by the U.S. Commission on Ocean Policy, established and funded under the Oceans Act of 2000, is expected out in draft form in October. The governors of each state, all of whom have received the Pew report, will get thirty days to comment on the federal study. Probably in November the final draft will go to the administration, which will have ninety days to formulate an oceans policy, and to Congress.

If enough people who care about marine ecosystems make themselves heard, the result could be the nation's first cogent, cohesive oceans policy. Now George W. Bush has the chance to redeem his image and be a genuine environmental hero. As Ocean Conservancy president and Pew oceans commissioner Roger Rufe put it at the June 4 press conference: "We have an opportunity for the President of the United States to be the Teddy Roosevelt of the oceans."

STRIPER RECOVERY—NOT

--< >--

The Atlantic Ocean was full of striped bass in the early 1970s when I fished with master electrician-curmudgeon Jak Knowles. If they were over sixteen inches in length, you could kill as many as you wanted. We did. He would insist that we toast each big fish with S.S. Pierce Red Label, which was okay except in blitzes.

We didn't believe in selling our fish; but we sure believed in eating them. And after our spring trip Knowles would give one to each of his customers, then claim as income tax deductions the cost of tackle, gas and near-weekly repairs to his ancient green Willys. Once an IRS agent visited him, then backed out of his house, hands in the air and shouting: "Okay. Okay. Okay." That's how it was when you argued with Knowles.

Carrying our fish was impossible, so Knowles would order me to tow them through surf and estuaries. I didn't argue. I can still feel the rope cutting into my shoulder as I raced the ebbing tide under gaudy Nantucket dawns that seemed endless as youth and the great, silver fish strung out like stars across the continental shelf from the Carolinas to the Maritimes.

No one told us you could kill too many stripers. In fact the managers told us you couldn't. In 1973 when I complained to a high-ranking official of the Massachusetts Division of Marine Fisheries about the commercial harvest of striped bass, which peaked that year at 15 million pounds, he declared that there would always be "plenty of striped bass for both commercial *and* recreational fishermen."

With that, the Atlantic Coast striped bass population crashed. By 1980, instead of catching forty fish a trip, you might catch five a season. Basically, they were gone. The states had proven their inability to protect the resource, so in 1984 Congress approved the Atlantic Striped Bass Conservation Act which required the Secretary of Commerce to impose a moratorium on fishing for striped bass in any state not in compliance with a management plan hatched by the Atlantic States Marine Fisheries Commission (ASMFC).

The result, for the first time ever, was striper management. Suddenly there were highly restrictive commercial and recreational harvest regulations. For most states there was a recreational bag limit of one large fish a day. Over the next eleven years stripers proliferated. Knowles, who died on the dock with his boots on at 86, lived just long enough to see stripers start to come back. In the early 1990s, throwing long flies from boats, I began having forty-fish outings again; but with the size limit set at thirty-six inches, I was lucky to eat one fish a season.

All the gushing and oozing in the hook-and-bullet press about the managers' impressive "success story" made about as much sense to me as decorating a company commander for busting up drug traffic in his barracks. Then in 1995 ASMFC declared the stock "fully recovered" and approved Amendment V to the Atlantic Striped Bass Fishery Management Plan, thereby significantly increasing recreational and commercial harvest. When I told the managers that it was a reckless decision, they assured me that there would be plenty of fish for both commercial and recreational fishermen.

They didn't have it right this time either. Managing a healthy stock for abundance instead of maximum sustained yield—that is, maximum dead poundage on the dock—is utterly alien to the way fisheries managers think. Never have they attempted it; never has a constituency asked them to attempt it. The sensible, laudable and politically hopeless crusade by recreational anglers to win federal game-fish status for striped bass along the Atlantic Coast repulses managers. "It's wrong-headed," proclaimed one official of the Massachusetts Division of Marine Fisheries.

But what was wrong-headed was Amendment V. It might have worked had the number of recreational striper fishermen remained constant. (The commercial harvest has not increased as rapidly because it's mostly controlled by quotas.) In the 1970s, even before the crash, striper anglers were secretive and scarce—at least the serious ones who caught the fish. Few used boats. You saw them mostly on darkened beaches, hunched along the foam line like black-crowned night herons.

Even as stripers came surging back, populations of bluefish, tautog, winter flounder, scup, sea bass, sharks and tunas were bottoming out. Both commercial and recreational pressure shifted to stripers because they were available. In all other regions of the country recreational fishing pressure is falling off. But on the Atlantic Coast, thanks in large measure to the resurgence of stripers, it's increasing. In 1999, 13,218,936 pounds of striped bass were harvested by recreational fishermen—more than any other marine fish. Angler striped-bass-trip expenditures, adjusted for inflation, increased from $85 million in 1981 to $560 million in 1996—35 percent annual growth. During the same period the number of directed striped bass trips increased from roughly one million to seven million—an average annual increase of 38 percent. The Marine Recreational Fisheries Statistics Survey, administered by NMFS, estimated an increase in sportfishing trips for striped bass from 247,000 in 1990 to 691,000 in 1997.

Strict one- or two-fish bag limits are meaningless under that kind of pressure. So, for the last seven years, we've been killing about all the fish as soon as they hit legal size. Legal size varies from state to state and sometimes from month to month, but it's usually around twenty-eight inches except in Delaware, Maryland, Virginia and North Carolina where it's usually around eighteen inches.

"Since Amendment V we've seen the population trajectory flatten out," says John Carmichael a North Carolina state fisheries biologist who serves on ASMFC's Striped Bass Stock Assessment Subcommittee. "But there seems to be plenty of spawning stock out there to maintain the population. We're getting good year classes, a lot of recruits coming in. The question now comes down to what do we want to get out of the population. Is the goal to just get a lot of fish, which is what we're producing right now, or do you want to also get bigger, older fish? If it's the latter, then of course you have to fish them less."

Gary Shepherd, the National Marine Fisheries Commission's rep on ASMFC's Striped Bass Technical Committee, agrees with Carmichael. "In terms of total number of eggs, the spawning stock is now probably as large as it's ever been," he told me. "But the big fish are getting cropped off. Most of them are gone by the age of about 15, and stripers can live to 30. So we're limiting their life span to about half."

That raises a disturbing question: Can a population with a grossly skewed individual-size and age structure—in which virtually all individuals are removed before they have attained more than 50 percent of their age and growth potential—be said to be "recovered"? I submit that the answer is no. When a species evolves the capacity to spawn fifteen or twenty times in a lifetime, there are good reasons for it even if we don't understand them. One of those reasons might be a hedge against natural catastrophes and resultant spawning failures, always a danger with anadromous fish and particularly with stripers which are famous for largely missing year classes. But under present management they spawn once, and that's the end of them.

What's more, some biologists believe there's evidence of genetic selection for slow-growing and small fish. The larger fish also produce more eggs, so chances that the large-fish gene will be passed on to the population are nil under present management. Shepherd isn't sure if the biologists have it right about genetic selection. "Probably the only way to find out if they're right is not fish on striped bass for 20 years," he says. "And if hundred pounders start showing up again, they're wrong. But you're not going to do that experiment."

In 1999 commercial landings of striped bass totaled 1,103,812 fish, recreational landings 1,328,665 fish. But those stats are deceiving. For one thing, managers estimate that anglers caught an additional 12,514,721 fish which they released. For another, although commercial fishermen take just under half the fish, they are outnumbered by anglers by a factor of something like 500 to one. In my home state of Massachusetts, for example, there were 1,711 commercial striper fishermen on the water in 2000. In 1996, the most recent year for which data is available, the US Fish and Wildlife Service estimated that 886,000 anglers fished for stripers in Massachusetts.

Commercial striper fishermen take far fewer fish in the Northeast than they do in Virginia and Maryland. In 2000, commercials in Massachusetts harvested 40,256 fish weighing 779,736 pounds as compared with an estimated 175,533 fish weighing 2.5 million pounds by anglers.

Commercial striper fishing in Massachusetts is relatively clean because it's all hook-and-line. On the other hand, it takes out the most valuable brood stock—fish over thirty-four inches, of which 98.4 percent are females. Scarcely anyone depends on stripers for income, and a lot of the people involved are recreational anglers paying for their gasoline. You send in your $95, and you can start bashing. It's the same, or worse, in Rhode Island, New York and North Carolina. In Delaware, Maryland and Virginia—where a few people do depend on stripers—annual commercial quotas are, respectively: 193,447 pounds, 2,439,550 pounds, and 1,701,748 pounds. And commercial fishermen from Maryland and Virginia who operate on the Potomac get to kill an additional 883,850 pounds.

The reason so few commercial fishermen can take so many fish, the reason we have reckless management like Amendment V, and the reason game-fish status for striped bass gets shouted down everywhere outside New Jersey is that no one knows who the recreational fishermen are. They have a few effective organizations such as Coastal Conservation Associations and the Recreational Fishing Alliance but, basically, they are nonentities, political eunuchs. If they were required to purchase a saltwater fishing license—perhaps one for all fifteen ASMFC states—there would be a record of their names, phone numbers and addresses and they could be organized to influence managers and politicians. But they rail against the expense. To save the cost of one streamer fly or one surface popper they are willing to squander the health of the Atlantic Coast striper stock. It's hard to work up much sympathy for them or to get very angry at ASMFC for kowtowing to powerful, articulate, well-organized commercial fishermen.

Anglers have no right to vent their spleens about the commercial slaughter if they don't try to limit their own kill, which is even larger. The "harvest" is bad enough, but it gets lots worse when you figure in needless mortality of the "discards," as the managers call released fish.

North of Boston, where Ipswich Bay collects the Merrimack River, I never fail to encounter a procession of dead and dying striped bass floating in or out on the tide. Only a tiny fraction of the damaged discards ever show on the surface, reports Massachusetts Division of

Marine Fisheries director Paul Diodati, and he has counted as many as a hundred floaters on one tide.

Using artificial plugs and single hooks baited with sand eels and sea worms, Diodati and his colleagues conducted a striper-hooking-mortality study in a five-acre saltwater impoundment. They reported a 26 percent death rate for single baited hooks and an overall death rate of nine percent. Diodati's agency estimates that in 2000 Massachusetts anglers released seven million stripers, 571,000 of which died. Coastwide, recreational hooking mortality was estimated by ASMFC to be 1,031,454 fish.

A minimum size limit, at least where bait fishing is allowed, is stupid and wasteful. That's not to say that a *maximum* size limit—by which anglers have to release, say, fish bigger than twenty-five inches—is without dangers. It runs the risk of increasing harvest (because small fish are more vulnerable to angling) and thereby creating even more meat fishermen than already exist. But, with proper safeguards such as seasons, a maximum size limit could drastically limit hooking mortality because meat fishermen would get their fish and go home. Maine, Connecticut and New Jersey have figured this out, but they can't stand the idea of not killing the big female breeders. In Maine you can catch one fish between twenty and twenty-six inches or one over forty; in Connecticut it's one between twenty-four and thirty-two inches *and* one over forty-one; and in New Jersey it's one between twenty-four and twenty-eight inches *and* one over twenty-eight. "A slot limit is very appealing when there's a big group of fish moving through the fishery in that slot size," remarks the Striped Bass Technical Committee's Gary Shepherd. "But the trick is to keep it fixed. And if there's a poor group of fish, you have to stick with that too, take the good with the bad."

Rip Cunningham, editor of *Salt Water Sportsman* magazine, has crunched some numbers for his state of Massachusetts, but the general idea applies coastwide. "Assume a slot limit twenty-four–twenty-eight inches," he says. "In Massachusetts we are currently releasing 2,230,049 fish of this size each season. With [at least] eight percent mortality, 178,400 of them die. We're also taking 175,533 fish over twenty-eight inches. So, with that slot limit, you could take 354,000 fish without *any* additional impact to the stock. If you had twenty-three–twenty-eight-inch slot limit, it goes up to over 400,000 fish; with a twenty-two–twenty-eight-inch slot limit it goes up to 450,000. You'd be doing nothing you aren't doing today except allowing people to take home a fish."

Circle hooks could go a long way toward reducing hooking mortality. And if you can train yourself to let the fish hook itself rather then hauling back on the rod, they catch more fish. In virtually all cases they penetrate the lip only. There is ample evidence that circle hooks save fish of all species, but managers are reluctant to push them on the public because they're new and because no one has bothered to work up a definition of a circle hook, an easy-enough task. It's reminiscent of steel shot for waterfowl. It was new; the ammo companies wouldn't make it because it wasn't mandatory, and it wasn't mandatory because the ammo companies didn't make it. To its credit the Recreational Fishing Alliance is one fishing outfit loudly demanding mandatory circle hooks for bait fishing.

Finally, on charter and party boats both intentional and unintentional mortality need to be drastically trimmed. Clients are defined as "recreational" anglers but they are a different breed of cat than the folks you see bobbing around the saltchuck or trudging flats and beaches. "Charter and party boats need a one-fish limit and only six fish a day—not per trip, but per day," declares legendary Montauk flyfishing guide David Blinken. "Now they're allowed two fish per person per trip. They [the charters] have six guys on the boat plus the captain and mate, and they're taking twelve to twenty fish a day, all big breeders. They get the guys with the gold chains, beer bellies and slicked-back hair. I know lots of captains who want to release, but their clients want to kill, kill, kill. If the boats all switch at the same time, no one will lose business."

I worry about the future of striped bass because I know managers and their agencies. Rarely do they act for the resource. More often they *react* to the last and loudest special interest that shouted at them. Sometimes it's less their fault than the fault of our Pollyannaish public-comment process which wrongly assumes the public knows something about how to manage fish.

"With overall abundance high, you start getting into opinion," says Shepherd. "You ask a waterman in Chesapeake Bay what he wants to see. He wants to see as many eighteen- to twenty-five-inch fish as the system can produce. You talk to a surfcaster on Cape Cod about what he wants to see; and he says as many fifty-pound fish as the system can produce."

The trouble is that Shepherd and his colleagues are going to be hearing a great deal from watermen and relatively little from anglers.

In this prediction, I pray I am proved incorrect everywhere, but especially on the Hudson River. Now that this, the greatest striper source after Chesapeake Bay, is less contaminated with PCBs Governor George Pataki thinks it would be a dandy idea to open up commercial fishing: "Commercial fishing on the Hudson was a way of life for generations of New Yorkers. We owe it to today's New Yorkers to assess whether it's time to reestablish this tradition."

A state-assembled advisory committee has declared that Hudson River shad fishermen who accidentally kill about 23,000 pounds of stripers each season, should be allowed to sell them. "Being a bycatch in progress, it shouldn't have a major effect, since these fish are being caught now and discarded," proclaims a spokesman for the New York Department of Environmental Conservation. *But, of course it would have a major effect.* Only about 20 of the roughly 300 permitted shad fishing enterprises actually fish. With stripers, which bring far more than shad per pound, they'd get back on the water and launch a horrendous, targeted "bycatch" fishery.

"If you take more fish from the Hudson, you're going to have to give some up somewhere else," comments ASMFC's John Carmichael. "We're taking about what can be taken."

ASMFC will is about to finalize its draft of Amendment VI, a document that will serve as the source for public comments and hearings up and down the coast. If the final version turns out to be as bad as Amendment V, anglers will have no one to thank but themselves.

Why Should Anyone Listen to Striper Anglers?

—<( )>—

Striped bass have been declared game fish in Maine, New Hampshire, Connecticut, New Jersey, Pennsylvania, South Carolina and the District of Columbia. Unfortunately, that has not happened where they're most abundant—in Massachusetts, Rhode Island, New York, Delaware, Maryland, Virginia and North Carolina. And a federal bill that would give stripers game-fish status along the entire Atlantic coast—such as the one Rep. Frank Pallone (D-NJ) introduces every Congressional session—has as much chance of flying as a Perdue chicken.

One reason for this failure is that *recreational* anglers slaughter about 23 million pounds of stripers annually—more than three times the 7 million pounds taken by commercial fishermen. Therefore, recreational anglers have little credibility in the eyes of regulators and lawmakers when they demand an end to commercial fishing.

But recreational anglers squander their credibility in other ways, too. Consider the charade they put on in Massachusetts. This past summer I had a front-row seat. On Wednesday, July 12, 2006, I stumbled into the backyard at 3:00 a.m, looked approvingly at the overcast sky, dumped the sail bag of ice, birch beer and sandwiches into the cooler under *Assignment's* front seat, fired up the ancient Trooper, and struck out for Harwich, Massachusetts. Before sunup on your average summer weekday you might see one other trailer at the boat ramp. Now there were well over 100. I had to circle the lot twice to find a parking spot. "What the hell is going on here?" I asked the guy on the dock who caught my bow line.

"First day of commercial striper season," he replied.

That's what the state and the Atlantic States Marine Fisheries Commission (ASMFC) call it. But these are *recreational* anglers. They have fancy boats and tackle. They work nine-to-five jobs. No way do they need to be trafficking in cow stripers.

An hour and a half into the flood, the rips off Monomoy were starting
to cook, and standing waves piled over *Assignment's* transom. Dozens of
boats, alternatively appearing out the fog and vanishing into it, trolled
the seams or rode the fast current. I saw three near collisions, then fled
north to the cut. Here the fleet was pulling wire and umbrella rigs. From
all compass points I heard grinding reminiscent of Steve Martin's dentist
drill in *Little Shop of Horrors*. I couldn't figure what it was until I saw
an electric cable attached to a guy's reel. Enormous stripers, sometimes
three to a pull, flew over gunwales. Most of the fish were down forty
feet, but every now and then one would roll within fly-rod range. I killed
two three-footers. I never feel guilty about taking a legal limit, although
I often choose not to—especially if I'm about to travel and would
otherwise have to freeze the meat.

Had I bothered to send in $65 for a "commercial" license (the price
I'd get for one good fish), I could have killed twenty-eight more stripers
that day, provided they were thirty-four inches or over. These would be
almost exclusively breeding-age females; and, no matter what state you
live in, they are *your* fish. In summer the main body of the Atlantic striper
population hangs off Massachusetts, in winter off North Carolina and
Virginia. I could have killed 30 more fish each Tuesday, Wednesday and
Thursday and five on each Sunday until commercial anglers had *reported*
1,140,807 pounds.

But about three quarters of the roughly 5,000 Massachusetts anglers with
commercial licenses don't report *any* catch. It is not reasonable to assume
that they paid for a license and didn't fish or that they fished and caught
nothing in a season that may run two months. "The 'commercial fishery'
for stripers in Massachusetts is a farce," writes Brad Burns of Stripers
Forever. "Why would 74 percent of all commercial license holders have no
reported landings? These fishermen may simply have wanted a license just
in case they decided to sell a fish or two. But we believe that many of the
3,435 fishermen with zero reported landings are fish hogs who either want
to use their licenses fraudulently to circumvent the bag limits that apply to
everyone else, or make transportation of these fish legal until they can sell
them—unreported, of course—for cash under the table. Which is worse?
One is illegal; the other is simply reprehensible. ... As many as 98.98 percent

of Massachusetts commercial striped bass permit holders are simply paying for their fishing fun by selling their catch—legally or illegally—or filling their freezers under the guise of providing for the public."

The concept of managing a game fish for abundance, size and age-structure rather than maximum dead-on-the-dock poundage is utterly alien to Paul Diodati, director of the Massachusetts Division of Marine Fisheries. Diodati carries the torch for anglers who want to kill more than the two-fish daily limit, aggressively defending his make-believe commercial striper season against all who condemn it, and that includes the vast majority of the 550,000 unlicensed Massachusetts striper anglers. Diodati is also the chief architect of the ASMFC's rash petition to invite commercial and/or recreational fishermen from all Atlantic states into the stripers' last sanctuary—the Exclusive Economic Zone, extending 197 nautical miles beyond the 3-nautical-mile state limits.

Diodati makes no pretense that his "commercial" season provides anything more than gas-and-tackle money for recreational anglers or minor compensation for genuine commercial fishermen who, under his agency's watch, have wiped out other fish stocks. "The commercial fishery has also changed by attracting thousands of non-traditional participants who are lured by the thought of subsidizing an expensive hobby," he writes. "In addition, many full-time watermen who once paid little attention to this fish now focus their attention on the harvest and sale of stripers to help offset annual incomes that persistently diminish as regulations on other fisheries escalate."

The Massachusetts for-money, recreational striper season with its Orwellian moniker "commercial" represents everything that is wrong and ugly about how we treat this magnificent game fish. It teaches and encourages greed, and it is a prescription for poaching and black-market commerce.

For example, the season has spawned a common practice known in the law-enforcement community as "ice fishing." You buy commercial licenses for yourself, your wife, your daughter and your son. Then you go out on a non-commercial day, catch as many fish as you can, and ice them down. The next day you sell thirty fish, your wife sells thirty, and your kids unload the rest.

And commercially licensed anglers like to jumpstart the season before it opens because the first one to the fish market on opening day can get as much as $3.50 a pound. With the glut, the price may drop to $1.90 by the time you've legally filled your 30-fish limit, so stripers have a way of getting sold just a few minutes after the season opening at 12:01 a.m.

The very presence of a legal market elsewhere facilitates a black one in game-fish states. And in legal-commerce states poaching and illegal sale is even more out of hand. In New York City poachers are so brazen they no longer bother to be surreptitious about it, loading their boats with shorts in broad daylight. Report them, and they'll trash or sink your boat, as two of my guide friends can attest. Enforcement is nil.

Few states are more rapacious than Maryland. Because fish run small in Chesapeake Bay, Maryland wangled a special recreational size limit of eighteen inches, but then the charter fleet wanted a crack at the spawning cows that run up the Susquehanna in spring. So Maryland wangled a special regulation for them. Meanwhile the state's commercial fishermen are plundering the depressed, emaciated, and mycobacterium-blighted stock in the bay.

The greed feeds on itself. On August 23, 2006, with the Massachusetts commercial season winding down, agents from the state environmental police, the National Marine Fisheries Service, and the U.S. Coast Guard boarded five boats and seized 1,100 pounds of stripers illegally taken in federal waters. As one of the boats attempted to flee the enforcement team, the crew frantically threw fish overboard.

A month earlier Buddy Harrison, a well-known Chesapeake charter skipper who owns a fleet of a dozen boats, a restaurant, and a sea-food processing plant and had served as a member of Maryland's advisory board on striped bass, acquired his fourth citation for striped bass violations. This time for processing short fish.

In 2004 a two-year undercover sting by the Virginia Marine Police—aptly named "Operation Backdoor"—took down fourteen people at thirteen fish markets and restaurants for illegal trafficking in seafood, mostly striped bass provided by recreational anglers. An earlier operation had resulted in thirty arrests.

And in 2003 Tallman & Mack and Point Trap, both Rhode Island trap-net fishing companies, and Lotzzo's, a Massachusetts fish dealer, were busted by agents of the National Marine Fisheries Service and Rhode Island Department of Environmental Management for illegally selling and transporting at least 30,000 pounds of striped bass and providing false invoices. As part of their sentencing, which included major fines, the companies had to run public apologies in *The Providence Journal.*

No less ugly than legal and illegal commercial plunder are the wildly proliferating dead-on-the-dock striper tournaments conceived by and for recreational anglers. I know plenty of decent people who fish kill tournaments, but even they admit that these events attract, enrich and empower lowlifes and, at the same time, teach the public to kill the most and biggest. For example, a month before his most recent striper bust Buddy Harrison led a flotilla of boats filled with press and sundry dignitaries to the mouth of the Choptank River so that former Baltimore Orioles star Boog Powell could kick off the state's annual fishing tournament by releasing a tagged striped bass.

The same names have a way of popping up when you start checking who's who in Massachusetts "commercial" striper fishing, striper-poaching citations, and dead-on-the dock striper tournaments. For example, one of the tickets for over-the-limit—issued hours before the opening of the Massachusetts "commercial" striper season—was collected off the west end of Martha's Vineyard by one Bill Major, superstar of *On the Water* magazine's "Striper Cup." Sergeant Pat Grady of the Massachusetts Environmental Police won't release any details other than to confirm that he and another officer boarded Major's boat and issued the citation.

As of August 25, 2006 (pending the court outcome, avers *On the Water's* Bill Dean), Major was still listed on this year's "Striper Cup Leader Board" in the following categories for the following fish: twice for "Striper of the Year": 56.15 and 50.37 pounds; first place for "Angler of the Year (largest 5 fish cumulative pounds)": 231.86 pounds; twice in "Weekly Winners": 56.15 and 50 pounds; and three times in "Pounder Club Members": 39.16; 45.93; and 40.62 pounds. With recreational anglers killing all this brood stock for money and vanity why should legislators listen when they argue that commercial fishing should be shut down?

Is coastwide game-fish status politically feasible? "Probably not now," says Charles Witek, chair of New York's Coastal Conservation Association. "But I think it's a worthwhile goal in the sense that you're dealing with a fish that's pretty high up on the food chain and that doesn't respond well to overfishing. Game-fish status is something we'd all like to see, but we have to look at why we want it. If we want it to get the nets out of the water, to remove bycatch in some fisheries, to minimize discard mortality, to reduce mortality overall, it's probably worthwhile. If we want it because instead of them catching and killing the fish we're going to catch and kill the fish, then it's not a real big benefit."

Witek wouldn't mention names, but I will: the Jersey Coast Anglers Association and the Recreational Fishing Alliance. While they do a lot of good things, one of their main goals is more meat for themselves. Thanks to their influence, New Jersey didn't accomplish as much as it could have when it made the striped bass a game fish. The law took the stripers the ASMFC had allocated to commercials and let the recreationals kill them instead. So in New Jersey you can retain a third striper until the old commercial quota is filled. The net effect, of course, has been to further ventilate the already porous case that striped bass need coastwide game-fish status.

That's a shame because the argument isn't porous by nature; it has only been made that way by the behavior of the recreational community. On the other hand, the argument for commercial harvest is based entirely on untruths and distortions. It would be unfair, contend apologists, to deprive the poor and infirm who can't catch stripers for themselves of this glorious repast. But arguing that American shoppers should have access to wild striped bass makes as much sense as arguing that they should have access to wild turkeys. And Stripers Forever offers this: "There are four times as many people alive in America as there are [wild] striped bass. One bite each and the entire population would disappear in a meal!" Finally, nonfishers already have the chance to eat striper. All they have to do is buy farm-raised fish which are in far greater supply and virtually indistinguishable in taste.

Last year Stripers Forever released a study it had commissioned from the respected wildlife socio-economist Rob Southwick of Southwick Associates. Southwick found that 3,018,361 anglers from Maine to North Carolina annually generate 63,278 full-time jobs, $2.41 billion in direct retail sales, $289.4 million in federal income taxes, $18.2 million in state income taxes, and $105.1 million in state sales taxes. In all, they stimulate total new economic activity of $6.63 billion a year. This compares to $250 million for commercial fishermen. Moreover, if commercial fishing ceased, recreational anglers would stimulate $1.79 billion in additional annual economic activity.

The enormous economic value of stripers appears to be declining along with the population. While there are still lots of bass, it's time for managers to try a radical new approach—acting to *prevent* the collapse of a stock rather than reacting to it. In 2005 the ASMFC's population model indicated that stripers were being drastically overfished. But instead of managing the population it managed the model, changing it around so that stripers appeared to be in decent shape. Because the new model is being peer-reviewed there won't be an annual stock assessment in 2006; so, at the moment, anecdotal evidence is the only gauge we have to measure the health of the striped bass population.

While anecdotal evidence is notoriously unreliable, it can be frightening when it's independently provided by multiple sources. And people who know most about stripers are in near unanimous agreement that they're on the decline.

I know a great many striper guides, but not one who has a good feeling about the apparent population trend. Two of the most respected and successful of these are Capt. Terry Nugent (http://www.riptidecharters. com/info.html), who works both sides of Cape Cod, and Capt. Doug Jowett (http://home.gwi.net/~djowett/), a fly-rod-only guide based in Maine and the Cape.

"Nothing critical yet," declares Nugent. "But I have to say I'm seeing fewer and smaller fish. Four years ago at my big-fish spots every trip someone on the boat with light tackle would grab a forty-pounder. I haven't seen that in three years. I take a few, but not consistently. The spring run this year was particularly short."

Jowett's assessment: "I think stripers are in terrible shape. From where I sit the biomass has been going downhill for five or six years. We're missing year classes, and there's been an increase in harvest of very large striped bass which is exactly what happened in the last crash. This is the scary part—our daily fare [in Maine] is sixteen- to twenty-three-inch fish. Nothing smaller and nothing bigger in any numbers."

Supporting the observations of the guides, is the National Marine Fisheries Service's Marine Recreational Fishing Survey which shows a 40 percent decrease in striper-angler success since 1999.

Only recreational anglers can help arrest this trend. A smart first step, that would help repair damaged credibility, would be limiting the kill. I'm not talking about going to catch-and-release or even stopping at one fish, though I applaud anyone who does either. I'm talking about cooling it with the tournaments and reducing post-release mortality. As things stand now, at least half of all stripers killed by recreational anglers die after they go back in the water. That's an appalling statistic.

If you fish with bait, you need to use circle hooks. In fact, when the definition of a circle hook is nailed down (and we're not quite there yet), anglers should push for a law that makes it illegal for bait dunkers to use anything else.

Wasteful, destructive practices such as "yo-yoing"—i.e., stuffing a lead sinker or sparkplug down a porgy or pogie, sealing its mouth with a treble hook, then bouncing it on the bottom—need to be resisted and banned.

Even fly rodders can clean up their act. They have to quit nagging stripers to death with flimsy trout wands. Unless you're into a nest of small schoolies, you shouldn't use anything under a nine-weight. And even with the smallest flies there is almost never a need to go to tippet lighter than 20-pound fluorocarbon.

At the top of its website the Recreational Fishing Alliance issues this shrill warning: "Commercial fishermen and environmentalists are pushing their agenda on marine fisheries issues affecting you." That's true, though the rhetoric that follows makes it clear that the RFA perceives the agenda of environmentalists as somehow opposed to what it calls "our interests."

I don't mean to pick on the RFA; again it does a lot of good. But that kind of thinking has gotten all manner of fish stocks in the mess they're in. After all, is not every ethical angler an environmentalist? Can there be any among us who are not in favor of our surroundings, including—and, in this case, especially—a sea sustaining healthy ecosystems in which apex predators thrive? In the memorable words of Rich Landers, outdoor editor of *The Spokane Spokesman-Review*, "any sportsman who isn't an environmentalist is a fool."

Ethical recreational anglers and nonfishing environmentalists need to push their identical agendas on marine fisheries issues more aggressively. Currently they're being outshouted by commercial fishermen and *unethical* recreational anglers whose agendas are also identical—i.e., killing more fish for themselves.

SHARK ATTACK

―‹(·)›―

The first shark is a big blue of about 170 pounds. It vectors in on us as we ride the ground swells forty miles southeast of Bay Shore, Long Island, its glistening dorsal fin exiting the green sea like a knife tip through watermelon.

Soon it is ten feet off our stern, sucking in our menhaden baits. Captain Joe hauls back on one rod, then another, then a third; but each time there is only brief resistance. A second, smaller blue appears and is instantly hooked. We watch in disbelief as the first shark returns and mounts it, placing us in that tiny group of human beings who have witnessed shark copulation. As the animals thrash together on the surface, Leo, the first mate, slams the gaff into the unhooked male and hauls it bleeding up onto the deck. He points to the cartilage-supported, sperm-injecting appendages that extend from the pelvic fins and which scientists call "claspers" because Aristotle misidentified them as such. "Look," he tells me, "they got two penises—one for port and one for starboard." Then he gaffs the female.

Back on shore, at the field headquarters of what the National Marine Fisheries Service (NMFS) had called the best shark tournament in the East, I wade through a reeking stew of blood, bile and stomach contents. Then, in the quiet June evening when the crowd is gone, dozens of big sharks—blues, makos, duskies and sandbars—are hoisted by meat hooks into garbage trucks for the trip to the local landfill. The year is 1980; I am on my first assignment for *Audubon*.

My editors, Les Line and Gary Soucie, had sent me to the Bay Shore tournament because they had the aberrant notion that sharks were headed for trouble—especially off the East Coast where scores of species from two-foot-long bonnet sharks in warm shallows to thousand-pound makos in bluewater were being killed on purpose and by accident. Four years earlier—in the September 1976 issue—they had seen fit to inform the public about the vulnerability of sharks, warning that "contrary to belief in some quarters, there is reason to doubt whether the numbers of sharks in the sea could support a really extensive international fishery."

Cut to March 19, 1996. After ten years of a really extensive international fishery, America's shark resource is heading for disaster. Off our eastern seaboard large coastal species such as duskies and sandbars have declined more than 80 percent in one decade, a statistic that would qualify them as critically endangered under definitions set forth by the International Union for the Conservation of Nature. Recreational extinction (meaning you cannot go fishing with any reasonable hope of success) and commercial extinction (meaning sharking is so difficult it's no longer worth the effort) are already facts for many species, and biologists are even talking about biological extinction for some.

Scene: a conference room at the Day's Inn across from the Philadelphia airport at a meeting of the Mid-Atlantic Fishery Management Council—one of eight councils established by the Magnuson Act of 1976 to advise the NMFS and help it manage the nation's marine fishing regions. Suggested title for melodrama: *What Can We Do About Sharks Now That We Have Jeopardized the Resource?* Script: pure formula—as mindless and predictable as the plot of *Jaws*. I have heard it all dozens of times with nothing changed save the name of the plundered, critically-depleted fish—steelhead, salmon, haddock, cod, yellowtail flounder, striped bass, weakfish, swordfish, tuna, king mackerel, redfish …

But there's one big difference: the biological rules that apply to all these bony fishes do not apply to the primitive, cartilage-framed sharks. With protection, most bony fishes can recover from overfishing in a few years. Not sharks. They can take as long to reach sexual maturity as humans, and their gestation periods are comparable or longer. Young are usually born alive, and in dog-sized litters. The troubled sandbar shark, for instance, delivers eight or nine pups every other year. Duskies, also in bad shape, probably breed every third year. Embryos of the depleted sand tiger are not connected to the uterus by a placenta; they swim around in both uteri attacking and devouring their siblings so that by the time they are born there are only two forty-inch survivors. Hanging on the wall of the NMFS shark lab in Narragansett, Rhode Island, is the head of a fourteen-foot, 1,400-pound female great white. It was landed on light tackle after an epic, four-hour battle by Jack Casey, the scientist who headed agency shark research until he retired in 1995. It was one of the largest great whites ever taken by rod and reel in the Atlantic. And it wasn't even sexually mature.

The porbeagle—a swift, pelagic species allied to the mako and great white—became commercially extinct in the Northwest Atlantic in the 1960s, less than ten years after being targeted by the Norwegians and Japanese. Thirty years after fishing ceased, the population still hasn't recovered. "Historically, when shark species are fished, they are wiped out, often within five years," remarks shark biologist Samuel Gruber of the University of Miami who eight years ago had to move his lemon-shark research station from Florida to Bimini Island because there were no longer enough fish to study.

The shark disaster provides more support for my theory that there is no such thing as marine fisheries management, that it is an untested concept. Whenever I ask biologists for real-life examples, they cite recovery of striped bass or redfish or king mackerel, species we didn't pay attention to until we allowed their populations to crash. If that's management, Superfund remediation is landscape architecture.

What America has always done is react to crises caused by stupidity and timidity. In 1979 U.S. shark landings had been 300,000 pounds; by 1989 the figure had jumped to 16 million pounds. That was the year the NMFS—a tentacle of the U.S. Department of Commerce charged with regulating as well as promoting the fishing industry—started framing its shark-management plan, a process it dragged out until 1993.

The men and women who edited *Audubon* in the 1970s and 1980s and who had fretted about a shark crash five years before it started and seventeen years before our federal government saw fit to act, were not visionaries. They weren't even biologists. They were just question askers who paid attention to answers. But in 1996 the NMFS appears flabbergasted by the grim plight of sharks. The commercial fishing industry professes to have been blindsided and, as always, doesn't believe the data. Recreational anglers, many of whom responded to a bullish market for shark meat and shark-fin soup by selling instead of landfilling their catches, blame everyone but themselves.

Only a decade ago the NMFS was aggressively promoting sharks as "underutilized," as if nature makes a habit of festooning marine ecosystems with surplus parts. The agency gushed about the fine taste and nutritional value of shark meat and even handed out fax numbers of shark-fin dealers. "We are putting the bite on sharks rather than the other way around, and our revenge is sweet!" proclaimed one NMFS shark barker in 1985.

There is a young scientist standing beside me in the Day's Inn conference room in the City of Brotherly Love. His name is Carl Safina, director of the National Audubon Society's Living Oceans Program; and he has just started a war with the commercial fishing industry by recommending a zero quota on sharks. "No shark scientist believes [the resource] can recover to where it was in 1985 in under several decades," warns Safina. "In ten years, we have dug a hole that will take half a century to get out of *if we act now.* For each of us individually, this resource is changed forever. We can look forward to the benefits of recovery of striped bass, groundfish, even tuna. But we will never again see as many sharks as we had in the 1980s. This is a heartbreaking state of affairs."

Also standing beside me is another young scientist—Safina's policy analyst, Merry Camhi, an intense educator who never says die. She is having it out with a blond version of Captain Quint (the living cliche last seen sliding oyster-like into Jaws' ivory-gated gullet). The blond Quint is Willie Etheridge, 50, of Wanchese, North Carolina, who claims to process more sharks than anyone on the East Coast and who has just testified to the council that shark bites in Florida are up. He says he doesn't believe the biologists. "I look at the commercial fisherman's data as a hundred percent true," he says. "There's lies being used to cause the alarm that the fish stocks are in trouble."

"All the fisheries scientists who have been looking at these indices for fifteen years are saying that sharks are in trouble," answers Camhi.

"I don't believe it," says Etheridge.

The most convincing testimony and the best available scientific data is offered by Jack Musick, head of the Vertebrate Ecology and Systematics Programs at Virginia Institute of Marine Science. Musick, with the physique of a bear, the moustache of a walrus and the coolness of an air-traffic controller, has been monitoring shark populations off Virginia since 1973. He catches (and releases) them on "longlines" that trail one hundred baited hooks; and unlike data collected by commercial longliners, his has not been made suspect by financial interest. "The overwhelming trends in catch per unit of effort has been a massive decline that started somewhere in the early eighties," he says. "Right now the number of dusky sharks is probably ten percent of what it was in 1980. Sandbars are probably 15 to 20 percent. Tigers are 20 to 25 percent. Same is true of sand tigers ... I was a member of the action team that helped put together the 1994 stock assessment. We compared that data with other data bases—bycatch in shrimp fishery, observer information from the swordfish longline bycatch. All those other data sets showed the same trends."

Musick tells the committee that the assumed recovery rate on which the NMFS built its 1993 shark plan for the Atlantic, Caribbean and Gulf of Mexico is five to ten times higher than is biologically possible. He says scientists have been warning right along that something drastic must be done but that NMFS is "still treading water" and that "it's very frustrating for those of us in the scientific community who work with these animals to keep coming to these meetings, keep presenting the data, and have the NMFS blow us off."

When Nelson Beideman, director of the Blue Water Fisherman's Association, testifies that Musick's data needs to be peer reviewed by "NMFS shark experts" Musick correctly informs him that the data has not only been peer reviewed but *published* in a NMFS journal. "I've been told that it hasn't," says Beideman.

"Well, it has," says Musick. "In addition, I sent the publication to your consultants. I don't know what else you want me to do."

"My consultants say your data needs to be standardized," says Beideman."

"We standardized all that data in 1994."

The attack on the people working to save the shark resource by the people who make their living from the shark resource spills out of the room and onto the Internet where, the following day, Steve Branstetter, Program Director for the Gulf and South Atlantic Fisheries Development Foundation, charges that Musick is spreading "sensationalistic hype" and "working the sport magazines and newspaper sports/outdoors writers." Safina, he writes, has been "attempting to corrupt, sway, or otherwise influence [council] decisions."

Musick responds with ice instead of fire: "This was a *public* meeting … Neither Safina nor I attempted to 'corrupt' anybody on the council. At the request of committee chair Peter Jensen I presented the evidence … I have never 'worked the sport magazines' … I receive inquiries constantly from press of all kinds, and, working for a state agency, I must respond."

So goes the timeless clash. And above it all—seeking to keep a semblance of peace, avoid criticism and *always* to find "middle ground"— is the NMFS. The trouble with this approach is that there is no safe ground between what scientific data say should be done and what hearsay, fantasy and industry fiction say should be done; and if you travel as far as "*middle ground*," your renewable resource slides Quint-like into humanity's infinitely expandable gullet. "NMFS reacts to every bit of screaming, especially from the fishing industry and its full-time, paid lobbyists," says Ken Hinman, president of the National Coalition for Marine Conservation. "It is always looking for ways to avoid making waves, to manage without getting people mad, to have 'negotiated rule making,' 'interactive management' … They have a lot of phrases for it, but to me it's just trying to avoid making tough decisions."

Evolution of sharks has been slow because, until humans started slaughtering them en masse in the 1980s, they could cope with any limiting factor. The first sharks appeared before the dinosaurs, 350 million years ago. Today there are about 370 known species, with four or five new ones discovered each year. All are built on cartilage instead of bone and have slits for gill openings, but after that there's no generalizing. Earth's largest fish—the whale shark, which can measure sixty feet—eats the smallest animals in the sea, plankton, while the tiny cookie-cutter shark feeds on plugs it bites from the largest, the great whales. Whites commonly eat sea lions; tiger sharks are fond of sea turtles. Threshers herd fish with their long tails. Some sharks glow in the dark, some home in on sand-covered flatfish using bio-electric sensors. Mackerel sharks, including the porbeagle, mako and great white, are slightly warm-blooded and can chase down some of the fastest bony fish.

The slaughter of these ancient beasts is being driven by Asian lust for allegedly aphrodisiac shark-fin soup. Fins, which are mostly cartilage, are rendered into "noodles" by repeated soaking, drying and bleaching with peroxide. By 1990, Hong Kong was importing about 4 billion pounds of shark fins annually, China a billion. Today a pound of dried shark fins can fetch $200.

While shark meat is eaten everywhere, even in America, it is difficult and expensive to preserve. Therefore, much of it is wasted, especially when it comes up as bycatch in tuna and swordfish longlining operations. On our Pacific coast (except in California state waters) and in most of the world's oceans a practice called "finning" is still *modus operandi*. The animal is hauled on board, separated from its fins, then dumped back into the sea, usually alive. In 1987 two contestants in a Florida fishing tournament, reeled in finless tiger sharks which could only wriggle along the bottom and apparently had taken the cut bait only because they couldn't catch anything that swam. The NMFS shark plan has made finning illegal in the Atlantic, Caribbean and Gulf of Mexico where landings must now have a certain, reasonable meat-to-fin ratio. But some enterprising sharkers are getting around this by buying spoiled or unmarketable shark flesh, then dumping it after weigh in. And during periods when the season for large coastal sharks is closed the valuable, meaty fins of these species are reported to be mysteriously mixed with finless carcasses of pelagic species.

Even considering nothing but humanity, as we always seem to do, the mandate of "middle-ground" fisheries management—i.e., liquidating the resource faster than it can reproduce—seems insane. For one thing, a sea with an underabundance of sharks is unprofitable to *Homo sapiens*. We may be seeing some of the proof already along Florida's panhandle which is now beset by a plague of stingrays, apparently brought on by the removal of the hammerheads that used to prey on them. And in some areas off Australia a proliferation of lobster-eating octopuses, formerly controlled by sharks, may be the reason for the failure of the lobster industry.

Moreover, we'd probably be better off knowing why sharks are extremely resistant to disease, especially cancer, why serious wounds can heal in less than twenty-four hours, and why lacerations of shark corneas (which can be transplanted into humans) leave none of the clouding seen in other creatures. But we can't learn these things if there are no study subjects.

Sustainable commercial shark fishing, if there is such a thing, doesn't make much economic sense either. In 1986, when there were still a fair number of sharks around, anglers in New Jersey alone spent $2 million chasing them. Even in the free-for-all days of the 1980s the U.S. commercial shark industry never generated more than $8 million a year, but some sportfishing authorities estimate that a robust recreational shark fishery for the whole East Coast and Gulf of Mexico (with strict limits or perhaps a catch-and-release regulation) might be worth as much as $130 million. Ecotourism, based on shark watching, is big business all over the world. So popular is snorkeling among the whale sharks that congregate off western Australia's Ningaloo reef that spotter planes are now in use and regulations have had to be promulgated to control the number of vessels. Off the Maldive Islands in the Indian Ocean, underwater shark watchers spend $2.3 million a year. In the Bahamas, Walker's Cay Undersea Adventures puts 18,000 people a year in the water with sharks; and the NMFS has recruited guides to jab tags into the reef sharks, blacktips, lemons and hammerheads that come to frozen fish parts called "chumsicles." To a commercial fisherman these animals would be worth something like $50 each; but to Walker's Cay Undersea Adventures the figure is $10,000, according to Gary Adkison who started the shark dives five years ago.

"Isn't $10,000 per shark kind of stretching it?" I asked the University of Miami's Samuel Gruber.

"Not at all," he said. "There are at least three similar shark-watching operations on Nassau Island, but with only six to fifteen fish each. I did an estimate tourist revenue per shark and came up with a figure of $200,000 apiece for those sharks. Now a commercial fishing company has a proposal to take three metric tons of shark fillets a year from the Bahamas; that's probably 20 percent of the resident sharks."

Gruber agrees with Musick and Safina that unless the shark plan is drastically amended, sharks will not recover. But while NMFS shark coordinator Mike Bailey admits that the rebuilding schedule on which the plan is based was "overly optimistic," he argues that the plan "has gone a long, long way toward slowing down the shark fishery—certainly a lot more than other people think" and that "the commercial guys are really upset because we have cut back an anticipated 24 percent quota increase that they had planned their businesses around."

The shark plan covers only thirty-nine species. One of the species left to fend for itself is the dogfish (also called sandshark), one of the most vulnerable of all sharks in that a female can't bear young until she is fifteen or twenty years old, has the gestation period of an Indian elephant (about two years), then delivers a litter of only six to ten pups. While I was growing up on the North Atlantic the dogfish who were growing up with me (and taking longer to reach sexual maturity) were considered pests. I was taught that you always clubbed them at boatside, then deep-sixed their carcasses. Every angler, including me, carried a small baseball bat for this purpose. On most days you could catch several dozen cod or haddock until the dogs moved in and you started shark bashing.

Sonja Fordham of the Washington, D.C.-based Center for Marine Conservation groaned when I told her about how I used to treat these little sharks. Dogfish, she explained, are entrusted to the councils which aren't doing any better managing them than NMFS is doing with large coastals. "One of the lessons we're learning is that today's trash fish is tomorrow's delicacy," she declared. "It's very disturbing that managers don't differentiate between dogfish and groundfish. Dogfish are not cod; they don't start spewing millions of eggs at age two. That council meeting you went to in Philadelphia caused a big stir, but I think it was ironic that so much attention was paid to large coastals and *none* to dogfish."

At this writing a dogfish-management plan is at least two years away. To supply markets in Europe, where people have never been repulsed by the idea of eating dogfish, Americans are hammering the dogs, going after the big females which school together. Last summer, if you had ventured into a dogfish cutting house in Yankeeland or along the mid-Atlantic coast, you would have found yourself up to your ankles in embryos and ova. Now, with the big females pretty much killed off, fishermen are having to content themselves with intermediate-sized males.

The dogfish slaughter began only in the late 1980s. By 1993 annual landings had increased from about 9.9 million pounds to 44.5 million pounds. By 1995 the resource was drastically declining. "If you ever want to crash a population, just target the adult females," offers Tom Hoff, senior ecologist for the Mid-Atlantic Fishery Management Council. Hoff—a respected scientist doing the best he can with a tiny budget and staff—makes no excuses for the council's inaction. But biologists like Hoff only offer recommendations. Management decisions for species like dogfish are hatched by the eight regional councils which are dominated by fish mongers and their suppliers and whose membership is exempted by the Magnuson Act from standard federal conflict-of-interest regulations that apply to other managing bodies.

"You'd think someone would be saying, 'Let's not do this again,'" Fordham told me. No, I wouldn't think it, because I live in Massachusetts—home of the Yankee fleet where the main objective of marine fisheries management has always been to keep commercial fishermen from getting any angrier than they already are. The Massachusetts Governor's Seafood Task Force (a syndicate of fish-industry pooh-bahs and state bureaucrats) has just announced a program to promote "cape shark." I had thought I knew my native fish, but this one was new to me.

Seeking enlightenment, I consulted the newsletter of the Massachusetts Division of Marine Fisheries wherein I learned that cape shark is "a consumer-friendly name" for dogfish and that it is one of the "underutilized species" that the task force will be whooping it up for in the spring of 1996.

MARKETING MPAS

◅─◦ ◦─►

Marine Protected Areas (MPAs), traditional tools for conserving ocean resources, include national parks, national marine sanctuaries, national estuarine research reserves, national wildlife refuges, and sundry fish-management designations. In the North Atlantic, for example, Buzzard's Bay and Stellwagen Bank are MPAs because mobile-gear net fishing is banned in the former and oil drilling and mineral mining are banned in the latter. In the South Atlantic the MPA known as the Florida Keys National Marine Sanctuary has made it possible to zone jetskis out of bonefish flats and prohibit the destruction of coral reefs and their fauna by commercial collectors.

Flats guide and fishing writer Jeffrey Cardenas gets no argument from me when he calls for more instead of fewer restrictions in the Florida Keys National Marine Sanctuary. "I think the beautiful Marquesas atoll needs to have at least an idle-speed only regulation," he remarks. "And I'd like to see a [no-kill] zone, too." You could fish, but you'd have to release everything—not a problem for Florida fly rodders because they release everything anyway.

America has about 300 MPAs, and we're desperately in need of more, especially in light of the gross failure of fish managers to protect many of the stocks they've been entrusted with. That is why it grieves me to see MPAs given a bad name by certain environmental outfits who don't know fish or fishers but who claim to know what's best for both. For two years a nasty, absurd tiff between enviros and sportsmen has diverted both parties from real enemies they should be confronting together. It's as if Patton and Montgomery had called off the Italian campaign to engage each other in a duel with wet towels.

The trouble started on May 26, 2000, when President Clinton signed Executive Order 13158, thereby issuing a rallying cry for a coordinated, science-based network of MPAs, calling for public participation in

MPA consideration, and setting up a citizens' committee to advise the secretaries of Commerce and Interior on designations. The order came with no money and no new authorities. It was prudent, timely, precisely what marine fish needed. But environmental groups such as the Ocean Conservancy, Environmental Defense, the Natural Resources Defense Council (NRDC), and the Sierra Club took it as a call to arms. That might not have been such a bad thing had they proceeded intelligently, reaching out to sportsmen for advice and support. But they didn't.

"Marine protected areas, which restrict or prohibit fishing, offer one of the best tools for restoring depleted fishing stocks and damaged ocean ecosystems," proclaims NRDC. "Yet despite strong support from scientists and the general public, one group—sportfishermen—continues to try and block the creation of marine reserves ... Ironically, this group—sportfishermen—stands to benefit from this innovative tool." But MPAs don't necessarily, or even usually, "restrict or prohibit fishing." The rule establishing Stellwagen Bank National Marine Sanctuary even contains language prohibiting sportfishing restrictions. Sportfishermen read this baloney and believe it. No wonder they hate MPAs.

In late September 2000 NRDC invited fifteen marine scientists to its New York City headquarters to kibitz for a day-and-a-half about MPAs. A day and a half isn't much time to start thinking about MPAs and then decide where they need to go, especially MPAs as defined by NRDC which "restrict or prohibit fishing." After each scientist had scrawled out his wish list, NRDC used software to project the "polygons," as it called the hoped-for no-fishing zones, onto a map. As NRDC itself reports: "Overlaying the polygons revealed multiple nominations for five ocean areas comprising some 19.4 percent of the study area: the nine submarine canyons; the offshore waters near Cape Hatteras, North Carolina; tilefish habitat between Cape May, New Jersey, and Cape Cod, Massachusetts; a 35-kilometer (18.9-nautical mile) corridor of nearshore waters extending along the study area; and a band along the continental shelf break encompassing the upper slope." Basically, it consisted of everyone's favorite fishing holes.

With that, NRDC began distributing the maps to the public with no explanation that the polygons were just starting points for discussion.

Anglers were aghast. "If NRDC wanted to create opposition, they could hardly have done it any more effectively," says Dr. Carl Safina, head of the National Audubon Society's Living Oceans Campaign and one of the most well-spoken and outspoken advocates for MPAs. "It has been a public-relations blunder that is completely unmatched in the environmental community."

"The first instinct is let's get some proposals together, put them on the table and talk," comments Dr. Cheri Recchia, director of marine protected areas for the Ocean Conservancy (formerly Center for Marine Conservation). "But often it's not a good approach because people misunderstand. That can really antagonize." Recchia impresses with her directness and obvious commitment to ocean resources. When I asked her how sportsmen and enviros got into this spat she said: "The environmental community doesn't always do a good job of explaining. ... Sometimes there is a confusion about terminology, and that's been very damaging. When some of us use the term MPAs we mean closed to fishing; others mean something closer to the international usage which is a whole spectrum of areas including some closed to fishing." It was a perceptive and honest statement, especially given the fact that no group is more guilty of confusing terminology than her own.

Consider the conservancy's Ocean Wilderness Challenge launched in June 2001 "to promote a new ocean ethic and achieve wilderness protection for special sites in U.S. waters and in the Caribbean." The stated goal is to protect "at least five percent of U.S. waters as wilderness." That doesn't sound like very much until you reflect that anglers fish in about one percent, and no one's going to prohibit fishing where there aren't any fish.

But wilderness is a good thing, right? It has never limited fishing or hunting; in fact it has preserved and enhanced both by banning such habitat-wrecking activities as logging, roading, oil and gas exploration, mining, and tooling around in motorized off-road vehicles. For thirty-eight years conservation writers have preached to sportsmen that wilderness isn't a plot by the antis to "lock up" federal land, that hunters and anglers conceived the idea of wilderness, started the Wilderness Society, shepherded through the Wilderness Act. Some sportsmen are beginning to get the message. But motorheads and extractive industries fronting as wise-use groups keep hissing in their ears about "access" as if feet didn't work anymore. It's hard to educate people in a miasma of white noise. And now comes the Ocean Conservancy.

"Ocean wilderness will allow fishing, won't it?" I asked the conservancy's Greg Helms, who is heading an initiative to convert almost 25 percent of the Channel Islands National Marine Sanctuary off Los Angeles to ocean wilderness.

"Oh no," he said. "You won't be able to fish." I inquired about no-kill fishing for pelagics that don't stay in MPAs anyway. "Not that either," he said. "You can dive it; you can surf it; but there's no catch-and-release fishing. You can't do that with native fish in national parks or wilderness areas."

"You can't?" I intoned, scarcely believing my ears.

"No," he said. "Generally speaking, you can fish for fish that are placed there using user fees for the specific purpose of fishing them. But you can't harm an indigenous natural resource." That, of course, is incorrect. Non-indigenous fish are not stocked in national parks or wilderness areas, and catch-and-release fishing as well as catch-and-kill fishing is legal in both.

The Ocean Conservancy (by redefining wilderness) and NRDC (by redefining MPAs) have undone a generation of conservation education and propped up wobbling wise-use lies. Sportsmen, a naïve and paranoid lot even under the best of circumstances, freak out when they encounter real or imagined threats to access. They have not reacted well to the MPA initiative, but they have acted predictably. If the enviros had bothered to communicate with sportsmen, they could have avoided a war, gained allies, and learned what kinds of MPAs are genuinely beneficial to fish.

Anyone whose head wasn't in the sand or clouds could see the conflict coming. Mike Nussman, president of the American Sportfishing Association, told me this: "I went around for two years saying, 'Guys we're going to have a hell of a fight about this because there's nothing we value more than the public's ability to get on the water. And you're going to tell us we can't fish. Unless that's the only way to solve a fishery problem most anglers aren't going to be terribly receptive.' I preached and preached that, and basically everyone blew me off."

Nussman and his predecessor, Mike Hayden, have managed to convince the tackle industry that the best way to improve sales is to preserve and restore fish stocks; it was an idea that hadn't previously occurred to it. ASA is better and smarter than other trade associations, so I hate to see it coming out with press releases that have titles like: "Extreme Environmentalists Offer Misleading Statements on MPAs." "Extreme environmentalists" is the euphemism of polluters and habitat-destroyers for people who successfully disrupt their exploitation. The Earth Liberation Front is "extreme." The Ocean Conservancy and NRDC are just stupid.

Mostly, though, the ASA has maintained its cool. Not so the otherwise savvy, effective CCA (Coastal Conservation Association). For example, I and my fellow members received the following communication from President David Cummins. "Recreational fishing is under attack as never before ... attack by the feds and the radical environmentalists ... Environmental extremists are conspiring with federal bureaucrats to take away our freedom to fish ... These No Fishing Zones are a power grab; they're all about control of the citizens, not protection of anything ... Now picture this: the fish-no-more map proposed by these well-funded environmentalists. I've seen it, and I can tell you what it looks like. You'll be stunned. All along the Atlantic, from Maine on south, wherever there are aggregations of fish, they're proposing to ban fishing ... If you ever dreamed of fishing in the blue waters surrounding our 50th state, take your swimming gear but leave your fishing tackle home." With that Cummins launched into a come-on for the CCA Legal Defense Fund: "Will you help? Unless we are financially ready to defend against this insidious attack, we are not ready at all. P.S. These proposed No Fishing Zones are the most serious threat to sport fishing in my lifetime. The CCA Legal Defense Fund exists to beat back just these kinds of challenges."

CCA's reaction to the MPA initiative hurt it more than the MPAs would have. For example, Cummins' letter alienated the Norcross Wildlife Foundation which disburses major grants to groups working on behalf of fish and wildlife and on which I serve as a board member. Our president, Richard Reagan, responded as follows: "Dear Mr. Cummins: On reading your letter I find that Norcross apparently falls into the odious classification of being 'radical environmentalists' and 'environmental extremists,' simply because we support conservation of marine fisheries and fish habitat. ... Your letter is a poor imitation of the type of hysterical screed broadcast by the NRA and its president, Charleton Heston. In it, you have insulted the work of yeomen in fisheries conservation who focus on the environmental long view. ... For the foreseeable this suspends Norcross's support of CCA and its state and local chapters."

More unfortunate fallout of the ill-conceived, ill-executed MPA initiative comes in the form of the Freedom to Fish Act, written by ASA and now before the U.S. Senate. (Note: I used the word "unfortunate," not "unnecessary.") Basically, the bill would amend the Magnuson Act so that if a site is closed to recreational fishing, the managing agency would have to produce science showing that recreational fishing contributed to the problem. Once fish populations are restored the area would have to be reopened to recreational fishing. All that's fine, and ASA deserves credit for hatching the bill, if only to get the attention of the environmental community and force some kind of compromise.

But the danger of this kind of legislation is that it attracts the ugliest opportunists from the wise-use camp such as Sen. Kay Bailey Hutchinson (R-TX), one of the bill's two major sponsors and among the most vicious enemies of fish and wildlife in the Senate. Sportsmen prop up legislators like Hutchinson at their extreme peril. During the Clinton administration she pushed through a lengthy suspension of new listings under the Endangered Species Act. The voting criteria established by the non-partisan League of Conservation Voters shows her voting for the interests of fish and wildlife zero percent of the time for each of the last five years. Audubon's Carl Safina assesses the Freedom to Fish Act this way: "I think it's horrible, a real redneck reaction. Even the title. It slams the door on any dialogue on MPAs."

Environmentalists alienate sportsmen not just because they don't take the time to get to know them but because they don't take the time to get to know fish and fishing. Nowhere is an MPA more desperately needed than in the Channel Islands. This is because the indigenous and mostly sedentary groundfish live long and therefore reproduce slowly.

A cowcod, for instance, can make it to 100 years. The dark-blotched rockfish probably lives for 150 years. The groundfish resource around the islands has been essentially destroyed. Fishing should be banned for these species, and in a lot more than 25 percent of the sanctuary. Catch-and-release is not an option because when you haul up these fish their air bladders pop out of their mouths. Mortality is 100 percent.

But 200 feet above the groundfish there are thriving populations of highly migratory pelagics such as yellowtail, tunas and wahoo. They're in the MPA one minute, out the next. Why ban fishing for them? Or why not at least allow no-kill? Well, basically, it's "easier" to ban everything, say the enviros. But it isn't. Their refusal to bend on this issue is likely to derail not just the Channel Islands MPA by the entire network of MPAs proposed for the California coast.

In the needless alienation of anglers, fish managers frequently pick up where enviros leave off. Three years ago the Gulf of Mexico Fishery Management Council moved to set up a no-fishing MPA where reef fish such as groupers, snappers and amberjacks gathered to spawn. Such spawning aggregations are highly vulnerable to commercial and sport fishing, and that's why reef fish keep crashing. A no-fishing MPA for the reef-fish complex made lots of sense, and CCA, especially Florida CCA, endorsed it because the council promised to allow surface fishing for highly migratory pelagics. But at its last meeting, after all the public testimony had been heard, the council decided the enforcers' lives would be easier if it just prohibited all fishing. "We felt that they almost defrauded the public," says Florida CCA's director, Ted Forsgren. So CCA sued, eventually winning a settlement in which surface fishing for pelagics was reinstated, but not before lots of hard feelings and bad publicity for MPAs.

MPAs are valuable when they are used correctly, worthless or hurtful when they are not. One of the incorrect uses, standard with the MPAs now being pushed by the environmental community, is promulgating them independently of fisheries management plans. It does no good to save all the fish in part the ocean if we overharvest them in the rest of it.

"Fisheries are managed as a function of yield stream—based on adjusting some level of output from the stock, quotas, limits, etc.," comments

Louisiana State University's Dr. James Cowan, chairman of the Reef Fish Stock Assessment Panel for the Gulf Council. "But fishes within no-fishing reserves are no longer part of the yield stream. If you set aside 20 percent of the harvest potential, now 100 percent of the yield is going to come from that 80 percent. That's one of the tradeoffs, and we don't know enough about these tradeoffs to make informed decisions right now. When [no-fishing] MPAs are established you tend to see a relatively quick recovery of small fishes in the protected area. The forage base recovers, but a lot of the large fishes for which the reserve was set aside are relatively mobile, and if the fishing pressure isn't changed outside the boundaries, they don't recover."

Cowan believes that the enviros are being driven by the "crappy record" of fish managers, a record he claims is fast improving under the new language of the Sustainable Fisheries Management Act which mandates sustainability. At any rate, there is nothing mystic or unattainable about good fisheries management. It is entirely possible, as Florida and Texas have demonstrated with their spectacular successes with redfish. Although many managers have yet to try good fisheries management (thanks to the fact that the public, including enviros and sportsmen, have tolerated their dereliction), this doesn't mean we need to rush around decorating the ocean with no-fishing signs.

The sad thing is that enviros really could bring back fish stocks if they'd bother to learn what the limiting factors are. In the Northeast, for example, MPAs won't help as long as otter trawls are legal. Otter trawls remove fish stocks while simultaneously destroying their habitat. They "clearcut" the bottom, razing sea fans, coral and all structure that sustains juvenile fish and forage of adults.

"If environmentalists and anglers could get together and ban otter trawls, we could solve 90 percent of problem very quickly," declares Rip Cunningham, editor of *Salt Water Sportsman* magazine and chair of ASA's saltwater government affairs committee. "What does it matter if you go out and catch a codfish on a hook and line? I would like to see more benefits for commercial fishermen who make an effort to be cleaner— the hook-and-line commercial groundfish fishermen. That's the way we should be going. In Iceland, for example, it's virtually all hook-and-line for codfish. I went out just to see what it was like. Forty-foot, doubled-ended Norwegian high-sided trawlers with big rails and these automatic jigging machines spaced about three feet apart. When the line hits the bottom it goes slack and it brings back about two feet. Once it loads up with fish, gets certain amount of tension, it automatically hauls them up."

Sportsmen in Florida fought for years to ban inshore nets and get fish traps out of federal waters. During all that time not one of the major environmental groups now pushing MPAs assisted.

Two years ago the Florida Chapter of the Sierra Club made this pronouncement: "One type of gear may well be more 'destructive' than another, but ALL gear has negative environmental impacts. No-take needs to mean no-take and that means no fishing activity." If the Sierra Club would get out and fish a little, it would learn that catch-and-release fishing for, say, permit (with luck you'll exercise one per winter) has less "negative environmental impacts" than *any* activity permitted in no-fishing MPAs.

In spite of periodic lapses the Sierra Club is one environmental group that has made an effort to reach out to sportsmen. "Hunters and urban conservationists need each other," writes Sierra Club director Carl Pope—grandson of hook-and-bullet writer and conservation icon Ben East. "Never let that alliance break down."

But the "alliance" can't 'break down' because it doesn't exist. A sensible approach to marine fish management, including science-based MPAs that permit low- and no-impact sportfishing, might be a good way to start building one. Meanwhile, ASA's member firms ought to come out with metal sinker boxes that say: "Take an environmentalist fishing."

DO WE NEED SALTWATER LICENSES?

⥳ ⥄

The editor of *Fly Rod & Reel* magazine dropped by for dinner and to talk about an article he wanted on why coastal states need saltwater fishing licenses. Being an avid ocean angler, and having worked for a state fish and game agency, I was eager to get started and knew exactly who I would talk to.

My first source told me, "Anglers will almost certainly lose as the pieces of the marine fisheries pie are cut and distributed. They will come up short because, one, they are not counted with undeniable accuracy and precision and, two, their fishing effort and harvest cannot be established with statistical acceptability … Without [licensing] saltwater angling can pretty well expect to be crowded gradually out of the picture over the next decade or two." That source was Dick Stroud of the Sport Fishing Institute. The editor/dinner guest was John Merwin. The year was 1980.

A quarter-century later Stroud's prediction has come to pass, at least in the Northeast. The only coastal states (other than Hawaii) that don't have saltwater licenses are Maine, New Hampshire, Massachusetts, Connecticut, Rhode Island, New York, New Jersey and Delaware. For the sake of brevity, and because there are other peripheral issues in Hawaii, I'll focus only on the Northeast. Is it just that Yankee salts are tightwads? No, it's also because there are lots of facts about saltwater licensing they don't want to know.

Those facts are getting harder to ignore because in states that have implemented saltwater licensing management successes are increasingly spectacular. Mostly, this is because licensing provides contact information so that anglers looking after their own best interests—including groups of anglers such as the Coastal Conservation Association (CCA)—can organize, energize, educate and direct. And legislators pay far more attention to documented lists of resource users than someone's guesstimate of voiceless, nameless absentees.

In North Carolina (which didn't legislate a saltwater license until 2004) the Division of Marine Fisheries estimated that of twenty-nine species pursued by both anglers and commercials in 1999, anglers took 33 percent of the harvest. And yet there were an estimated 1.1 million to 1.5 million anglers compared to 9,232 licensed commercial fishermen. For the past decade the most popular recreational and commercial fish in the state, southern flounder, has been overfished to near collapse, mostly by commercials. A good recovery plan was shouted down by commercials. With the blessing of managers, commercial fishermen have nearly wiped out the state's blueback herring (important forage for all sorts of game fish). In the 1970s the annual herring harvest was about 20 million pounds; in 2003 (when the fishery should have been closed) the harvest was 100,000 pounds.

States that require saltwater recreational fishing licenses derive about 80 percent of their saltwater management revenue from this source. It's true that managers don't always use license revenue wisely (although they're getting better); it's also true that in most states they are fed and clothed by license revenue and that they cater to the interest groups providing it. This is why, on the inland scene, game and fish departments tend to ignore that 99.999 percent of fish and wildlife they call "nongame." This is why Northeast states let commercial fishermen call the tune; and this is why Alaska and coastal states in the contiguous U.S. from Maryland south around the Atlantic coast, west along the Gulf, and north to Washington have controlled or eliminated most commercial fishing. The phenomenon is called political reality.

As CCA chairman Walter Fondren puts it: "There is strength in numbers, but only if someone is counting. The owner of a seafood company that employs 100 people has historically wielded far more power in the fishery-management arena than a vast, silent, unknown population of recreational anglers. That seafood company's payroll, landings data and bottom line provide a tiny snapshot of the value associated with a particular fishery, but it may be the only snapshot. That monopoly on information translates into political power."

Because Texas has a saltwater license, it knows it has 900,000 anglers who fish in the ocean and who annually contribute $1.3 billion to the economy and provide 20,000 jobs. Armed with this information-and looking after the best interests of fish, anglers and themselves—managers have basically run commercial fishermen out of state waters (in this case, nine miles into the Gulf). Since 1980, when Texas banned gillnets, redfish and spotted sea trout have recovered from near extirpation to natural abundance. "Because of our saltwater license we have over thirty years of continuous monitoring data on all our recreational fisheries," declares Dr. Larry McKinney, coastal fisheries director for the Texas Parks and Wildlife Department. "This allows us to make very sound management decisions and identify problems before they become serious. I can't imagine why your [Northeastern] anglers aren't demanding a license. Until recreational anglers are willing to put money on the table to build programs, they're not going to be able to compete with commercial fishermen. It's just not going to happen."

"In providing saltwater fishermen with political standing, a license could revive Florida's decrepit sport fishery-even if all the revenue were blown on junkets and easy chairs," I reported in 1980. "But when the state hosted a series of public hearings on a saltwater license in 1978 and 1979 the response was loud and angry. Fisheries biologist Ed Joyce, who took a few unofficial polls, figures that 'More than 95 percent of the [recreational] fishermen were opposed.'" Thirty roller-rig gillnetters were basically running the show while 7 million recreational fishermen sat on the sidelines. Said one disenfranchised soul, as he scrawled a $100 check to the license-seeking Florida League of Anglers, "I was in a big school of kings and was getting good action. All at once an airplane started flying around, and shortly after that, four gill-net boats stormed into the area like PT boats. The captain of the boat nearest me ordered me to leave. I raised my hand and made a defiant gesture. He picked up a rifle. I decided to leave after all."

It took ten years; but, as commercial fishermen steadily wiped out mullet, redfish, ladyfish, snook, jacks, pompano, kingfish and other game fish, Floridians smartened up. In 1996, six years after implementing a saltwater license, the state banned all commercial netting. This would have been politically impossible had no one known how many saltwater anglers there were in Florida or who they were.

Mark Robson, the Florida Fish and Wildlife Conservation Commission's marine fisheries director, reports that saltwater licenses are now bringing in $15 million a year, of which, by law, 32.5 percent goes for research and management; 30 percent for fisheries enhancement; 30 percent for law enforcement, and 7.5 percent for administration, education and outreach. The state's artificial-reef program, which has had major problems, is fast improving under strict supervision of three fisheries biologists. The department now spends about $600,000 to partially fund 20 reef projects a year. There is less dependence on construction debris and more on scientifically designed "reef balls."

"In most states fees for saltwater licenses are very nominal," observes Jim Martin, former fisheries chief of the Oregon Department of Fish and Wildlife and now conservation director of Pure Fishing (a conglomerate of tackle manufacturers). "If fishermen believe they can't spare a little money to win these allocation battles with commercial fishermen and protect habitat, then they're just not paying attention. In Oregon the license protected a lot of our habitat and allowed us to track fisheries [with coded wire tags] so we could get the maximum quotas. If you're not tracking your fishery and you've got endangered salmon mixed in with abundant hatchery salmon, they just close the whole thing down. With saltwater-license revenue we were able to mark stocked smolts so that our ocean fisheries are now almost all on hatchery fish. [If you catch a fish with an adipose fin, you have to release it.] And we used license dollars for hooking-mortality studies so our fisheries could pass muster with [NOAA Fisheries'] endangered-species people."

In North Carolina, and every other state that has legislated a saltwater license, anglers made it happen. In every state without a license anglers are preventing it from happening. Basically, they see the license as another "tax." For example, Jim Donofrio, director of the Recreational Fishing Alliance, has this to say about New Jersey's proposed saltwater license: "Recreational fishermen should not bear the burden of increasing the state budget when we already contribute over $50 million in state sales taxes and over $2 billion to the state's economy overall."

According to the United Boatmen of New Jersey and New York, "a saltwater fishing license is another tax, pure and simple."

"This has shown the recreational fishing community that we really can make a difference," accurately proclaimed Doug MacPherson, legislative chairman of the Rhode Island Charter and Party Boat Association after his outfit led a vicious lobby campaign that defeated a saltwater license in 2003. Unfortunately, the difference wasn't a positive one.

"The Jersey Coast Anglers Association has always been opposed to a saltwater fishing license," writes its legislative chair, Tom Fote. "The recreational fishing community pays a considerable amount of taxes on tackle (regular sales tax plus 10 percent excise tax that goes into the Wallop-Breaux Fund). We also find ourselves taxed in other ways." Then, in the same breath, he complains that New Jersey isn't spending enough money on "marine resources."

Fote has it right when he notes that saltwater anglers already are taxed on tackle and other things (such as gasoline). What he and his allies apparently fail to comprehend is that by blocking saltwater licenses they are throwing away their own tax money and the tax money of all the saltwater anglers they purport to defend. What they're demanding and getting is taxation without representation. Under the Wallop-Breaux amendments to the Sport Fish Restoration Act, about a half-billion dollars are doled out to the states each year. Sixty percent of each state's share is based on the number of licensed anglers, 40 on land and water area. (No state can get more than five percent or less than one percent of available funds.) Under this program states can apply for up to 75 percent federal reimbursement on fisheries projects. So, by refusing to pay for a license, which would cost them roughly what they pay for three or four flies lost to bluefish in a morning, they are ensuring that all taxes they pay on fishing equipment and gasoline benefit everyone but themselves. They are getting nothing back in terms of enhanced enforcement, habitat protection or management; instead they are investing in such projects as Kansas catfish studies.

Northeast anglers fantasize that politicians will snatch their dedicated license revenue and spend it on things like welfare. First, most states have laws against this. Second, the Sport Fish Restoration Act provides powerful incentive against such behavior because it requires states that use license revenue for purposes other than fish and wildlife management or sportsman access to refund current and past federal aid (there's a similar program for hunters).

If you haven't logged onto Reel-Time, the Internet journal of saltwater fly-fishing (www.reel-time.com), do so because there is always fascinating and civil discourse and you can pick up lots of useful information (like where stripers, blues, tuna and albies are being caught on any particular day). But I get discouraged whenever the subject gets around to saltwater licenses. Citing Massachusetts Governor Mitt Romney's 2003 theft of the Inland Fish and Game Fund, one otherwise thoughtful and informed participant recently wrote: "Politics being politics, I agree with Capt. Ken. Believing license fees are going to be directed to the saltwater fishery is wishful, gullible thinking."

But there's nothing "wishful" or "gullible" about it. The point is this: When Romney attempted to steal inland hunting and fishing license dollars, the U.S. Fish and Wildlife Service informed him that the commonwealth would have to reimburse the feds to the tune of $4.7 million. Moreover, because Massachusetts' inland sportsmen have to buy licenses there's a list of who and where they are. Managers wasted no time telling them about the threat, and through their local clubs, sportsmen were in instant communication. Therefore they were able to lobby the bejesus out of the legislature. Romney never had a chance; he had to restore the Inland Fish and Game fund.

The studied ignorance of Northeast saltwater anglers regularly elicits laments from Reel-Time coordinator Capt. John McMurray who, for example, editorialized as follows in one of his weekly reports: "How come folks can get so worked up about a saltwater license that, more than likely, would have helped the fishery; start petitions; throw out conspiracy theories about how none of the money will go to the Dept of Fish and Game, etc.; but can't get a half dozen people at the Amendment 6 hearing to ask for lower mortality targets for striped bass? Unbelievable!"

I suppose Northeast anglers may be excused for fretting about the possibility of having to stuff their wallets with licenses from little states so close together that, in Long Island Sound, for instance, they commonly fish Massachusetts, Rhode Island, Connecticut and New York in the same day. "But New England could have regional reciprocity," comments Jim Martin. "We have it in the Columbia River—the border between Oregon and Washington. If you have either license, you can fish anywhere in the river." It's the same with freshwater boundaries most everywhere in the nation, including the Northeast. If states persevere in resisting saltwater licensing, warns Martin, the feds are likely to impose a license of their own. "There are increasing efforts to create one," he says, "and there's a good chance that money would not be dedicated."

There is virtually no marine enforcement in the Northeast because there's scarcely any license revenue for it. One guide friend of mine, whose name I can't mention because poachers will retaliate against him, writes as follows: "I invite you to watch the [New York City] poachers—every day dozens of different boats are going nuts in our area. There is no one to enforce against these guys ... I gave the Department of Environmental Conservation three hours of videotape of the poachers doing their thing, gaffing hundreds of shorts, faces and registration numbers in full view, and nothing happened ... I have personally had boats try to ram me and had one guy jump in my boat with a baseball bat. I have three children to support who need me more than the crabs on the bottom of the bay."

"Who are the 'sprots'?" fishing writer Jeffrey Cardenas once asked his Cajun redfish guide after encountering a message scrawled on a gillnetter's shack that read: "Fuck the sprots."

"We're the 'sprots,'" said the guide. Having licensed its saltwater anglers, Louisiana had banned gillnets, and the graffitist had been attempting to spell "sports." Even where they haven't been inconvenienced or put out of business, commercial fishermen don't like sport fishermen. So maybe the best case for recreational saltwater licensing is being made by lobbyists for the commercial fishing industry, who are fighting it like cats fight baths. If it is really an insidious plot designed to shake down sports, why are commercials suddenly so protective of anglers' fiscal well-being?

At the recent hearings in North Carolina, the only organized opposition to the recreational saltwater license came from commercial fishermen. "We don't like a license period," their chief lobbyist-Jerry Schill, president of the North Carolina Fisheries Association-told me this past November. But when I asked why he and his colleagues are so committed to conserving anglers' money, he said only that the license had a "bunch of holes in it."

"So you'd be in favor of a recreational license that didn't have holes?" I asked.

"No," he replied. "When you start making exceptions it sounds as though we favor a license, and we don't. We've opposed it for ten years. There are reasons to have a license, and the good reason is better data."

"So your association would favor a license that provided good data?" I asked.

"No," he said. "When you look at what the CCA has done in Florida and the Gulf states, it's pretty obvious what they want the power for. So it is my duty to do whatever I can to derail them from getting that power."

"Because you believe that, in fact, they will get power?"

"No. We were opposed to it because that was what they believed." When I told him I didn't understand anything he was trying to tell me he said, "Then you don't understand fish wars."

But if there's one thing I *do* understand it's fish wars, because I've been in the middle of them my entire adult life. Finally, I asked Schill if increased revenue for the management of southern flounder might not be salubrious for his industry, since that species is the number-one target of both commercials and anglers. "That's the old liberal notion—throw money at a problem, and we'll fix it," he replied. "And it's only been a recent revelation—like this year—that this state has been overfishing southern flounder."

It's "only been a recent revelation" because the state lacked data. It lacked data because it lacked funds. And it lacked funds because it lacked license revenue and the federal aid in sportfish restoration that goes with it.

Schill is not always this long-winded and unintelligible, especially when he is talking to his own people. So tight and terse was his diction in a 2003 statement to *The National Fisherman* that, in just fifty-five words, he was able to say everything I've been trying to say up to this point: "Look what happened in the other states," he declared. "Look what the CCA has done with that license when it's been put in place. In some states you've got fish that have been given 'game fish' status, taken off consumers' plates. In other states, gillnet bans. And in Florida, they got the ultimate: a commercial net ban."

Exactly!

THE HIGHLANDER HATCH

⤙ ⤚

The topping or crest, which moves so gracefully on the head of the lapwing, as he bobs about upon the fell, is often recommended for the body of a fly, but it is more praised for this purpose than it deserves, for the herl of an ostrich answers the purpose much better. No gentle angler will kill him for the sake of his crest nor the martin for the sake of his wing; and none but a downright barbarian—a scientific savage who would murder to dissect, or his purveyor, who would burke a young sweep for the price his teeth would bring at a dentist's—would think of shooting a wren, and she perchance a widow, with a small family of thirteen unfledged young ones dependent on her—her mate having fallen prey to a hawk or a weasel—for the pitiful reward of her tail.

—P. Fisher, The Angler's Souvenir, London, 1835

With all the other pressures on Atlantic salmon the relatively new demand for their smooth, pearl-like otoliths (ear bones) strikes me as abominable. Wealthy bird watchers, predominantly Latin Americans, have taken a fancy to camera and binocular straps studded and/or strung with as many as 400 otoliths from *Salmo salar* (each fish has but two). Otoliths from the coarse and ever-abundant freshwater drum, which are virtually indistinguishable, would serve equally well. But purists insist on "authentic" material. At this point most traffic appears legal, but a healthy little black market exists, and prices portend a larger one. For instance, some of the swankier shops, such as *Me Eche Español* in Buenos Aires, are getting up to $2,000 for a single strap.

I suppose I should now reveal that not a word of the preceding paragraph is true, but I bet it pushed your button. Hang onto the feeling; it will put you in a more receptive mood for what follows.

The term "traditional Victorian" salmon fly is an oxymoron. The gaudy concoctions with names such as Baron, Jock Scott and Green Highlander *replaced* traditionals that traced their origins to the fifteenth century. Bright flies first caught on in Ireland; and, as with many things Irish, including people, they were scorned when they showed up in England. Before bright patterns won acceptance in the last half of the nineteenth century, the Brits dismissed them as the "Irish Fly" and went so far as to ban them on the River Tweed because they were allegedly "a kind of bugbear to the fish, scaring them from their accustomed haunts and resting spots."

Anyway, depending on conditions, Victorian salmon flies work as well as any other sort of salmon fly. They are very beautiful. I have a few, and when I tire of looking at all the modern cigar-butt and deer-stool imitations, I tie one on just for the pleasure of fishing with it. Once, in the last half-hour of a disappointing trip to Newfoundland, I took a grilse on a Green Highlander for which I paid something like three dollars.

Victorian patterns (never that popular among New World anglers) have been collected here for wall decorations, though not obsessively until 1978 when Stackpole Books published Poul Jorgensen's *Salmon Flies, Their Character, Style and Dressing*. The fly-tying community acknowledges (and Jorgensen admits) that the volume created a monster in the form of lust for original materials. "I'm trying to remedy it because it wasn't really meant to be," he told me. "I researched and wrote up a lot of substitutes for these feathers—turkey, chicken, duck. That was the idea. But some of the guys just went wild, and started hunting down these rare feathers—tried to get them any way they could. They're corrupting these young tyers I'm trying to teach who tell me they want to tie flies but can't afford to."

Tyer and feather merchant Paul Schmookler of Millis, Massachusetts, gets as much as $550 for one of his Victorianesque flies that he models after neotropical butterflies. As of November 1991 Schmookler was offering 100-feather packages of blue chatterer (cotinga) and Indian crow (fruitcrow) for $700 and $500 respectively. He assures me that all his material is old and legally obtained and that he has never been hassled by the feds.

A section of the November 1991 price list of New York City feather merchant Sol Shamilzadeh reads as follows: "Indian Crow, pack of 20, $150; Florican [bustard]—The best pairs I've had in a long time. Per pair

$150." Among fly tyers the word "florican" often conjures images of the Great Indian bustard, banned for commercial trade by the U.S., which has designated it Endangered, and by the Convention on International Trade in Endangered Species (CITES) which lists it on its critical, no-export Appendix I. When I asked Shamilzadeh if this was what he was peddling he assured me that it was not, that his florican was the smaller, more abundant *Eupodotis bengalensis* or Bengal florican. All his material, he said, had been obtained legally at auctions.

In 1987 *Audubon* magazine, where I also write a conservation column, published a piece on Victorian salmon flies by Tom Rosenbauer of Orvis, who made a big effort not to glamorize "authentic" materials. It drew the following response from Kevin Schneider of Lakeside, California, with appropriate cc's to tyers and shop owners: "Illegal and immoral markets can only exist and prosper if there are buyers. As long as the demand for the traditional [authentic] Victorian Atlantic salmon fly continues, indigenous and exotic bird skins and feathers will be bought and sold … to the last bird." True enough, although the "last bird" part probably is an exaggeration. Yet Schneider makes a business of sating the buyers' lust for "authentic" material, supplying them with molted feathers from exotic pets and "birds that have died while in captivity." For instance, he offers a matched pair of tail feathers from the scarlet macaw (Appendix I) for $85 and a single feather from the speckled bustard for $275.

When I asked Schneider if his "Feather Way" mail order business didn't contribute to the commercialization of depleted birds and prop up the exploitative pet trade, particularly since the demand for feathers might tempt owners to assist their pets in "dying while in captivity," he said: "No. I'm against that myself. See, it's a very strange thing. I find feathers that would sell for a thousand dollars a pair. I sell them for five hundred, I work myself out of business, I go to another feather. I've done something for the planet."

When the subject gets around to the black market for Victorian salmon-fly material, tyers remind me of my old Sicilian friend who, with upturned palms and flailing arms, would intone: "Maaafia? Maaafia? What Mafia?" One feather merchant told me that "all the stuff was right here in this country," then urged me to abandon my writing project because publicity is "the worst thing in the world" for fly tying. "It's an unwritten kind of thing with our little hobby—don't show a large profile or the government is going to come down on you with a hammer. You have to hash that out with your own conscience." The hashing part was easy for me because I've learned that the surest indication that an environmental issue needs light is when the special interests involved start telling you it can't stand any.

"No one could afford to go down to South America," pronounced one tyer. "No one would dare," said another. Of course not. The stuff is procured by campesinos (the politically correct word for peasants) who make an average of $7 a day for machete work or canoe paddling. For the same fee, or less, they would gladly undertake the more relaxing task of sitting under a fruit tree, shotgunning Indian crows or any of the seven species of blue chatterers called for in the traditional fly recipes, including *Cotinga maculata* (Endangered and Appendix I).

Roxie Laybourne, a zoologist who examines feathers coming into the country for the U.S. Fish and Wildlife Service's Law Enforcement Division, has seen virtually all the old salmon-fly material (though never in big volume)—blue chatterer, cock of the rock (Appendix II, which requires an export permit from the country of origin), toucan, scarlet ibis (Appendix II and protected under the Migratory Bird Treaty Act), grey junglefowl (Appendix II but zero export quota from its native India), great Indian bustard (Endangered and Appendix I) and speckled bustard (kind of a bastard bustard that can be any of perhaps a dozen species).

"Mostly they try to mail it in," reports Chris Dowd, a special agent with the U.S. Fish and Wildlife Service. "We have good rapport with Customs. What they can they grab for us. We find stuff that was falsely invoiced under something like magazines, and it will end up being feathers. Unless you go undercover and prove criminal intent the courts won't touch it."

But I know two special agents who *have* gone undercover and *have* proved criminal intent on the part of some high-rolling feather merchants, shop owners and tyers. "[Illicit traffic] is hard to quantify," declares one of the agents. "But there are numerous, obvious violations of the Migratory Bird Treaty Act, the Endangered Species Act, the Marine Mammals Act and the Lacey Act. This interest in classic Atlantic salmon flies has generated a group of people for whom a fly is just another piece of artwork to hang on the wall, and how it's created doesn't matter as long as they get it. Those flies, done with the proper materials, are a who's who of endangered species and migratory birds. The British empire was trading all over the world when those flies were created.

"We found several shops and had leads on others that were talking about their sources of macaw and speckled bustard and junglecock and blue heron and on and on and on—all of which sounded illegal in context. We had an individual who was smuggling in large volumes of polar bear hair and bragging about how he could get all these junglefowl capes in from Canada, another individual who said he could get blue herons, another who was interested in waterfowl with spring plumage [waterfowl feathers may be used for commercial flies but only if birds are legally taken during fall hunting seasons]. In one shop we purchased a golden plover right off the wall. A guy even said he could get eagle feathers. ...."

Some junglefowl is now being raised in the United States, and is legally available at high prices. Some is being imported from England under special permit. And a whole lot is being smuggled in from India via Canada. "I've got all these guys going to Canada and asking me if I want them to bring me back junglecock," remarks New Hampshire fly-tackle dealer Al Bovyn. "Hell no, I don't. Someone's going to get in trouble, and I just don't want to get involved with it."

When word got out that I was asking questions about the black market, the feather merchants and tyers started contacting me. Schneider phoned to say that I had grievously offended at least three people, none of whom he would name. But several nationally-known tyers were pleased. One, who asked for anonymity, allowed that it was about time a magazine looked into the subject. "You go to any antique show or sportsmens' show, it's like a nightclub in the right part of town," he said. "You whisper and you can get the stuff, just like you can get cocaine. Chatterer, Indian crow, toucan, macaw ... There's lots of muffled talk, deals going down all the time ... We posture ourselves as righteous sportsmen and go into fits if we see a spin fishermen squeeze a six-inch brook trout. But we can put the kill order on birds in Venezuela."

No tyer that I contacted has even rudimentary comprehension of the laws. I talked to one who has just been busted for importing material from an outlet in Holland; it sounded like an innocent mistake.

Poul Jorgensen, the best-known tyer of them all, says the laws are a mystery to him and that *Fly Rod & Reel* should publish a synopsis.

Sol Shamilzadeh called back to say: "If you find that molted feathers from captive-bred populations are illegal, you must let me know because then what I'm doing needs to cease and desist. I've never completed the research. It is mind-boggling." Right he is. Here is what I found out for him: Depending on what permits one does or doesn't possess and what documentation one can or can't produce, most any exotic feather that one possesses and/or sells may be illegal or legal.

Schmookler says there are thirty fly shops he could walk into tomorrow with federal agents and close down. "Everybody is in violation," he proclaims. "One guy had florican bustard on his shelf. I asked him for a copy of his Endangered Species permit to sell these things so I could have a copy. He said he didn't have that. I think the laws are [complicated] purposefully. How dare the United States government tell us that we have to listen to the laws of a country that they don't even like, that they would go to war with?" But even Schmookler seems to have a poor grasp of the laws, referring to the "Endangered Species Convention" and repeating the ancient superstition that conservation officers can raid your house without a search warrant.

Fly Rod & Reel is holding back on the legal advice because it strikes us that distributing it to tyers of "authentic" salmon flies so that they can "play it absolutely safe" is like distributing condoms to teenagers for the same purpose. With recent fine-enhancement measures taken by the federal courts, penalties are draconian. You can be fined $5,000 and jailed six months for each count of illegally possessing parts of birds protected by the Migratory Bird Treaty Act. (Feathers from two birds equals two counts.) Then, if you sell or barter without the right paperwork, it's a Class E felony punishable by a fine of as much as $250,000 and a jail term of up to two years—*per count*. If a species happens also to be Endangered, you face an additional $100,000 in fines and another six months in the slammer. If the feathers have been obtained illegally in country of origin and/or transported over state lines, then the Lacey Act kicks in, carrying with it penalties that make the before-mentioned statutes appear lenient.

There is genuine safety only in abstinence. Jorgensen, for instance, saves money and sleep by avoiding all expensive "authentic" feathers from exotic birds. "You can imagine what would happen if the feds came over and raided this place and then I was written up in the paper," he says. He has another motive, too: "Shooting an Indian crow or blue chatterer is like shooting a Baltimore oriole. They're songbirds. They're rare." So Jorgensen, like most of the well-known salmon-fly tyers, is trying to popularize substitute feathers from common, often domestic species.

"The difference between a [cheap and legally available Eurasian] kingfisher feather and a blue chatterer feather lies basically in whether the little marking at the base is gray or black," comments Al Bovyn. "And I can't remember which is which. People will want to buy blue chatterer. Why pay fifteen dollars for a stupid little feather when you can buy a whole kingfisher skin for six or seven? I get calls at work. It's almost like they're having an orgasm—'I'm going to be a salmon-fly tyer and I want all the biggest and best feathers.'"

"Tying flies is nothing but deception," argues New Hampshire tyer Bill Hunter. "There are no rules, and when you start imposing rules, you start to limit what you can do."

Doubtless the most animated of the substitute-feather advocates is Massachusetts tyer Ron Alcott: "Joe Bates thought the sun rose and set on blue chatterer. It doesn't as far as I'm concerned. I use substitutes for Indian crow. I'm not going to pay these jokers ten or fifteen dollars a feather. It's ridiculous! That's what spoiled it ... You have this *mindless repetition* of the same recipes written over and over for the last hundred years." The very act of substituting feathers, he points out, was a tradition of the Victorian tyers—i.e., goose for swan, blue chatterer for kingfisher. And he, too, worries about impact on depleted birds: "Threatening the survival of a species for the sake of a few feathers is, and I emphasize, absolute lunacy."

Recently Alcott tied two Jock Scotts for the cover of *American Angler and Fly Tyer* in order to demonstrate that even the slick-talking experts can't distinguish "authentic" material from common, dyed substitutes. It worked.

Maybe Dick Stewart, Alcott's publisher at *American Angler and Fly Tyer*, says it best: "These feathers are being used for silly and superfluous purposes. There's no difference between putting them on womens' hats or in flies and hanging them on the wall. Nobody's fishing with these flies. Isn't it time that humanity takes another look at this sort of behavior?"

When I dropped in on Ron Alcott he gave me the grand tour of his fly-spangled living room. "Okay," he said, "when we pulled up alongside the two Jock Scotts. "Which is the 'authentic' fly?"

"Why, the one on top, of course," I replied without hesitating.

"Why?" he demanded.

"Because of the way the feathers lie."

"Are you positive?"

"Sure," I declared. "No doubt about it."

Long pause.

"Right," Alcott finally said, visibly impressed.

(Ron, I guessed.)

III
Salmon and Their Problems

EVERYTHING BUT SALMON

--- ⤙ ⤚ ---

The 407-mile-long Connecticut River dwarfed the continent's other Atlantic salmon streams. Each spring vast shoals of salmon moved from their rich feeding grounds off Greenland into Long Island Sound, then surged upstream. Through Connecticut, Massachusetts, Vermont and New Hampshire, they veered off into tributaries, climbing high into the Green Mountains and White Mountains, hurdling over falls, waiting out summer droughts, spawning under gaudy leaves, holding through winter, sweeping back to the sea on spring floods.

Then in 1798 the Upper Locks and Canal Company blocked this ancient migration with a sixteen-foot-high dam at Turners Falls, Massachusetts. Pollution and more dams followed, and within a few years Connecticut River salmon were extinct. Fish ladders and fry stocking in the 1870s and 1880s failed.

A second restoration attempt had just gotten underway in 1970, when I signed on as wildlife journalist with the Massachusetts Division of Fisheries and Wildlife. Quoting state and federal biologists, I assured the public that the Connecticut River system would sustain "thousands" of salmon within a decade. Today it sustains about seven million. Unfortunately, they're fry—stocked by the four states and the U.S. Fish and Wildlife Service. Annual returns of adults in 2001 and 2002 were forty and forty-four, respectively.

Something has gone dreadfully wrong with Atlantic salmon restoration, but not in the river. Juvenile salmon thrive in freshwater, then vanish at sea. It's happening not just to Connecticut River fish, but to the species throughout its range. Satellite imagery reveals drastic cooling of ocean habitat. One favored theory attributes it to runoff from the melting ice cap.

Among anglers, impatience has turned to pique. For example, the *The Lawrence* (Massachusetts) *Eagle-Tribune*'s respected outdoor columnist, Roger Aziz, charges that Atlantic salmon restoration "is perhaps second only to [Boston's] Big Dig in wasteful spending of other people's money." He suggests that funds go instead to more trout stocking, and he scolds managers for endangering upstream game fish by letting sea lampreys through fish-passage facilities. Meanwhile, restoration is being defunded by the Bush administration to the point that some hatcheries and holding facilities don't have money to feed fish or even pump water.

But while New England waited for salmon, a whole ecosystem came quietly alive. In 1970 managers argued about whether to call the program "anadromous fish restoration" or "Atlantic salmon restoration." Hoping to capitalize on the mystique of *Salmo salar*, they opted for the latter. They used the program to leverage clean-water standards as well as upstream and downstream fish-passage at six mainstem dams and seven tributary dams.

Steve Gephard, Connecticut's anadromous fish chief, keeps his boat moored on the river where he grew up, in Haddam, Connecticut. "The river reeked in the late 1970s," he recalls. "It would change color according to who was dumping what, and we'd have regular fish kills." Now there are no fish kills, and what he smells is the fragrance of salt marsh, tidal flat, and sun-baked driftwood. He can see his toes when he wades chest-deep to his boat.

With the 44 salmon in 2002 came 377,420 American shad, 3,054 gizzard shad, 77,430 sea lampreys, and 1,950 blueback herring. This was the smallest herring run since accurate records began in 1976, but apparently for a happy reason. In the reborn river below Holyoke herring are being swilled by an estimated 1.5 million striped bass. Other migratory fish such as white perch, alewives, sea-run brown trout, and American eels are thriving. Endangered shortnose sturgeon are on the rebound.

The alewife floater mussel—which had been excluded by dams because its larvae attach themselves to alewives and related species—are reappearing in old haunts. So are yellow lamp mussels and tidewater muckets which infect white perch and probably striped bass. Mussels—particularly the thin-shelled alewife floater—are relished by raccoons, muskrats, and otters.

In sterile, glaciated woodland ponds and streams, the huge influx of nutrients from the sea—in the form of fish carcasses, feces, eggs, milt, and young—has restored a host of native insect fauna which, in turn, has nourished fish. Sea lampreys, native Yankees which limit no marine fish, go blind on their spawning run and can't feed. They make nests with their sucker mouths, clearing pebbles and shaking out sediments; then they all die. The clean bottom attracts spawning salmon. Lamprey carcasses feed caddisfly larvae, which are then eaten by trout and young salmon. If the whole is beautiful, no part can be ugly.

Resident fish such as shiners, chubs, dace, darters, bullheads, suckers, sunfish, yellow perch, smallmouth bass, and largemouth bass are surging back into newly clean, newly fertile habitat. With the explosion of fish has come stunning increases in ospreys, eagles, mergansers, kingfishers, and herons.

The program has paid for itself many times over. So prolific are largemouth bass in the formerly foul and fishless Hartford area that it's a favored site for bass tournaments, including two national championships. Connecticut River shad fishing is now so spectacular that John McPhee has written a book about it (*The Founding Fish*, Farrar, Straus and Giroux, 2002).

The restoration program has alerted the public to the fact that fish are more than quarry for anglers. Coached and partially funded by the Connecticut River Salmon Association, Trout Unlimited, the Vermont Institute of Natural Science, and the Southern Vermont Natural History Museum, more than 100 watershed schools are hatching salmon eggs, rearing fry, and stocking tributaries. At least 18,000 people a year visit salmon fishways in Massachusetts; at least 70,000 visit state and federal salmon hatcheries. The public contributes 8,000 hours of volunteer work, mostly stocking fry and monitoring fishways.

About the only thing missing from the Connecticut River system are healthy runs of Atlantic salmon. As discouraging as this may be, the rebirth of the river's ecosystem has given salmon restoration a chance it never had, provided marine habitat improves. The few salmon that are returning are generally distinct from their principal ancestors—fish from Maine's Penobscot River that were stocked in the 1970s. The difference could be the result of crossbreeding with introduced stock from other rivers. Or it could mean that in barely more than thirty years, nature, with human help, has created something Earth had lost: a race of Atlantic salmon precisely suited to the Connecticut River. If this latter theory is correct, and studies support it, managers at last have the spark to rekindle a dead fire.

The Connecticut River's Atlantic salmon may not be doomed. If the black hole they're falling into at sea turns out to be a temporary phenomenon, and if there's really a new race of salmon honed and polished by perhaps the fiercest natural selection the species has ever known, there's a good chance that salmon restoration will finally succeed. Now is the worst possible time to let the spark flicker out.

SALMON STAKES

⤙(⟩⤚

In the fall of 2002 the Bush administration proved what everyone else already knew: Fish need water.

In an effort to appease irate irrigators, the U.S. Bureau of Reclamation (BuRec) had dewatered the Klamath River, which drains a 9,691-square-mile watershed of high desert, woods, and wetlands in southern Oregon and northern California. By July the agency had cut the flow from its Iron Gate Dam from 1,000 cubic feet per second—previously deemed by the administration as the bare minimum necessary to prevent extinction of the system's coho salmon—to about 650 cfs. From July 12 to August 31 more water went down the main diversion canal to irrigators than down the river to salmon.

Meanwhile, farmers were getting—and wasting—so much water that they were flooding highways and disrupting traffic. State fisheries biologists, commercial fishermen, sport fishermen, Klamath Basin Indian tribes, and environmental groups had repeatedly warned the Bush administration that such dewatering would devastate chinook salmon and steelhead trout populations and perhaps usher cohos into oblivion. After the National Marine Fisheries Service (NMFS) determined that BuRec's plan would indeed jeopardize the existence of coho salmon, the leader of the NMFS team writing the biological opinion (required by the Endangered Species Act when a federal action might affect a listed species) says he was ordered to change his finding and that, when he refused, his superiors made the changes themselves.

In mid-September, four months into BuRec's new ten-year water-distribution plan, chinooks, cohos, and steelheads from the icy Pacific hit the low, warm, deoxygenated river and turned belly up. The mortality estimate was 33,000 fish, mostly chinooks. From all reports, it was the largest die-off of adult salmon ever. Bright, robust fish, many over thirty pounds, covered gravel bars, blocking foot traffic, fouling the water, filling the air with a stench you could taste.

The Klamath system was once the nation's third biggest producer of Pacific salmon. All five species flourished there, as did steelhead, green sturgeon, the Lost River sucker, and the shortnose sucker. Now chinooks and steelheads are down from their presettlement abundance by something like 90 percent. Sockeye, pink, and chum salmon are extinct in the basin. Cohos are listed as threatened. Until the 1970s the Klamath tribe caught thousands of pounds of suckers; now it takes one fish a year for ceremonial purposes. Both sucker species are endangered, and the green sturgeon is being considered for listing. These fish have been flickering out because BuRec's ninety-five-year-old Klamath Project has replumbed the Klamath system with a network of six dams, 185 miles of canals, 516 miles of lateral ditches, and forty-five pumping stations. Now water flows everywhere it never belonged.

About 280,000 of the basin's original 350,000 acres of wetlands and shallow lakes have been drained or filled. Still, the Klamath Basin—a.k.a. "Everglades West"—provides refuge for 80 percent of all waterfowl that negotiate the Pacific Flyway. In winter these birds help sustain the largest population of bald eagles in the contiguous states. The U.S. Fish and Wildlife Service operates six national wildlife refuges in the basin. But, like BuRec, the service is part of the Department of the Interior; and, under the Bush administration, it has become part of the problem.

Klamath Basin farms get about twelve inches of rain and 100 growing days a year. Before there were crop surpluses, water shortages, and endangered species, it seemed a dandy idea to make this high desert bloom. These days it's an insane waste of money and resources—like transporting iron ore by air. Until October 31, 2002, when *The Wall Street Journal* ferreted it out, the Bush administration had been suppressing a peer-reviewed U.S. Geological Survey (USGS) study that found that agriculture in the Klamath Basin generates $100 million a year compared with the $800 million generated by recreation, such as camping, boating, rafting, swimming, and fishing, and that restoring water to the river would boost this last figure to $3 billion. The study also determined that buying out the farms and protecting the land would create $36 billion in benefits at a cost of $5 billion. In an internal USGS memo obtained by the *Journal,* an agency scientist revealed that the regional director "wants to slow [the release of the study] down because of high sensitivity in the Department right now resulting from the recent fish kill in the Klamath. Suffice it to say that this is not a good time to be handing out this document."

In the Klamath Basin the government gets farmed a lot more than the land. There is scant demand for most of the crops grown; sometimes they're even plowed back into the ground. Originally it cost farmers nothing to get a permanent irrigation hookup to BuRec's public-financed Klamath Project. Now, on top of this, they get electricity to operate irrigation pumps at one-sixteenth of fair market value, a lower rate than their ancestors paid in 1917. During the dry summer and fall of 2001, basin farmers-some irrigating normally with emergency wells drilled at public expense-harvested $48.6 million in state and federal relief. Many reported their most profitable year ever.

Those who did best didn't own land; they leased it from the Fish and Wildlife Service at $1 per acre while reaping a minimum of $129 per acre in farm subsidies. They farmed the Lower Klamath and Tule Lake refuges, supposedly devoted to waterfowl and (in the case of the latter) bald eagles, which depend on waterfowl. These two refuges, once the flagships of the refuge system, are now national embarrassments. Of America's 540 national wildlife refuges, they are the only two that permit commercial agriculture. The farming program, administered on 25,600 acres, requires about 60,000 acre-feet of Klamath River water per year; pollutes river and wetlands with phosphates and nitrates; and loads land and water with pesticides, including two neurotoxins, fourteen endocrine disrupters, and eleven carcinogens. When water is scarce, as it usually is in the basin, marshes go dry so farmers can get water. Waterfowl have plummeted from 6 million or 7 million in the 1960s to about 1 million today.

On both refuges the Fish and Wildlife Service is in gross violation of the National Wildlife Refuge Improvement Act of 1997, which stipulates that permitted activities be "compatible with the major purposes for which such areas were established." The service attempts to justify its farming-first policy with the Kuchel Act of 1964, which permits agriculture in national wildlife refuges. But the statute requires that such agriculture be consistent with fish and wildlife management. After dewatering, polluting, and poisoning marshes and river, farmers produce potatoes and onions and grain—far less nutritious to waterfowl than wetland plants.

For anyone still in doubt, the summer of 2001 proved that there isn't enough water in the Klamath River for fish, waterfowl, and agriculture. Something had to give; that was agriculture and refuges. The river's endangered suckers and threatened coho salmon had first dibs on water. Then came tribal-trust resources—mainly chinook salmon. If there was any water to spare, it could go to agriculture and refuges. That's what state water law and the Endangered Species Act said.

But politics said otherwise. Incited and assisted by property-rights groups, irrigators organized a "bucket brigade." (This was modeled after the Jarbidge Shovel Brigade of Elko County, Nevada, which fantasized that it had "sovereignty" over federal lands and, on July 4, 2000, hacked an illegal road through the Humboldt-Toiyabe National Forest and habitat of the threatened bull trout.) On May 7, 2001, some 15,000 farmers, politicians, and property-rights activists (many bused in by the Farm Bureau) scooped buckets of water from a lake that feeds the Klamath River and passed them hand to hand through downtown Klamath Falls and into an irrigation ditch. The media circus attracted politicians, who puffed and blew about the evils of the Endangered Species Act. Senator Gordon Smith (R-OR) vowed to introduce a bill that would "reform" the act. "We must never feel it's okay to say that sucker fish are more valuable than the farm family," he proclaimed. Representative Wally Herger (R-CA) called the situation a "poster child" for Endangered Species Act reform. And Representative Greg Walden (R-OR) lamented that surgery on the act had to start with another "dust bowl." Later, an organizer of the Jarbidge Shovel Brigade arrived with a ten-foot-tall bucket. The Pioneer Press, a local weekly, started a "virtual bucket brigade" by e-mail, in which 70,000 people expressed support for the irrigators.

On June 29 an irrigation-canal headgate was illegally opened and water released from Upper Klamath Lake. BuRec shut it. Twice more an angry mob, now encamped, opened the gate, and twice more BuRec shut it. On July 4 about 150 demonstrators formed a human chain, shielding vandals who cut off the headgate's new lock with a diamond-bladed chainsaw and a cutting torch. The sheriff announced that he wouldn't bust anyone, because they were only "trying to save their lives." A deputy drove up in his cruiser, lights flashing, removed his hat, and replaced it with a farmer's. With that, he opined that Oregon environmentalists were likely to elicit such violence as "homicides." He even suggested two potential victims: Andy Kerr and Wendell Wood of the Oregon Natural Resources Council. Finally, BuRec called in U.S. marshals.

Two weeks later Senator Smith's amendment to the Interior appropriations bill—it would have required federal agencies operating in the Klamath Basin to ignore the Endangered Species Act, legal obligations to Indian tribes, and the Clean Water Act—failed by a vote of 52 to 48.

On July 24 Interior Secretary Gale Norton divined that there was water to spare in Upper Klamath Lake and ordered 75,000 acre-feet released to farmers. "Unfortunately," she declared, "none of this water will reach the national wildlife refuges because there simply is not enough water to do more than provide a little relief to some desperate farm families during the remainder of this season." She went on to suggest that wintering bald eagles could be artificially fed.

The drought was much less severe in 2002. Still, with great fanfare, the Bush administration cut off minimum flows to fish, tribes, and refuges in order to provide irrigators with full deliveries. On March 29 the headgate at Klamath Falls was again opened—this time by Agriculture Secretary Ann Veneman and Interior Secretary Gale Norton, who were on hand to emcee the ceremony. Veneman spoke of the administration's "commitment to help farmers and ranchers recover from losses suffered last year." Norton gushed about how nice it was to be "providing water to farmers."

Diverting so much of the Klamath for irrigation required brand-new science. Under the mandate of the Endangered Species Act (ESA), the NMFS had issued a biological opinion that such dewatering would jeopardize coho salmon, and the U.S. Fish and Wildlife Service had issued a biological opinion that it would jeopardize the suckers. So Norton asked the National Research Council (an offshoot of the National Academy of Sciences) to review the two documents. In February 2002, after just three months, the NRC panel hatched an interim draft report, alleging that the biological opinions weren't supported by enough science. Armed with this opinion, the president's Klamath advisory team (consisting of the secretaries of Interior, Commerce, and Agriculture, and the chairman of the President's Council on Environmental Quality) ordered new findings from the NMFS and the Fish and Wildlife Service.

On October 28, 2002, Michael Kelly, the NMFS biologist assigned to write the biological opinion, filed a federal whistle-blower disclosure with the U.S. Office of Special Counsel, charging that the team's recommendations for minimum flows were twice rejected under "political pressure." His main complaint was that the required analysis for the Reasonable and Prudent Alternative—the part of a biological opinion that tells an agency (in this case, BuRec) what it should do to avoid jeopardizing a listed species and which, in this case, had been suggested by BuRec—was intentionally not carried out, and that a specific risk to coho salmon that he and his colleagues had identified had been intentionally ignored.

A month after his disclosure, in his first interview with the media, Kelly told me this: "We were ordered to interpret the NRC report as recommending that the Bureau of Reclamation could avoid jeopardy by operating as it had for the previous ten years. But simple logic and a basic understanding of the Endangered Species Act regulations can demonstrate that any 'recommendation' in the NRC report does not make sense in an ESA context. One of the problems we have with the NRC report is that the panel never defined what kind of confidence they wanted. We biologists felt like they were a bunch of Ph.D.'s accustomed to reviewing peer-reviewed scientific-journal articles that require a very high level of confidence. A biological opinion is not that kind of document. The regulations say you use the best information available. You have to make a conclusion. And when you're unsure, you give the benefit of the doubt to the species."

Most whistle-blowers put up with lawbreaking until late in their careers, when they haven't got much to lose. But Kelly is only 37 and has a young family to support. When the Public Employees for Environmental Responsibility came to his defense, it warned him that if he blew the whistle, he might get lucky and hang on to his job, but that he should pretty much expect to lose it. I asked Kelly if blowing the whistle had been worth the risk. "They [his team's superiors] did a masterful job of forcing us to the point where I just couldn't participate any longer," he said. "The only way for me to continue would have been to violate the Endangered Species Act. I just couldn't do that. I wouldn't want to be continually participating in such egregious rule breaking and mismanagement of resources. In the past there was always subtle political pressure. I'd hear a supervisor say, 'Well, we can't recommend that under this administration.' It was de facto pressure. But this was finally something that was so blatant I had to say something."

Since Kelly's disclosure, two Oregon State University researchers who had been investigating the NRC document—fisheries professor Douglas Markle and graduate student Michael Cooperman—have reported that it is riddled with errors, such as incorrect water-quality data, faulty fish-population models, selective use of data to support "a conclusion they had already reached," and even reference to nonexistent species.

Enemies of the ESA and the press framed the controversy as a choice between fish and farmers. "The Bush administration knew exactly what side they wanted to be on—the side of the farmers," says Mike Daulton, Audubon's assistant director of government relations. "So, dismissing the opinion of the NMFS and others and disregarding the downstream tribal fishermen, they decided to put on paper this ten-year plan to basically guarantee flows to irrigators."

There is only one solution to the Klamath water crisis: End lease farming on the refuges and buy farms and water rights from willing sellers. Before the summer of 2002 the federal government was committed to just this. But it gave up when it ran into fierce resistance from business interests that profit from farming, such as pesticide and fertilizer distributors, and from farmers who lease land cheaply on the refuges and therefore profit from subsidies. In an October 23, 2001, letter to Representative Wally Herger, the Tulelake Growers Association tried to get Phil Norton, who was then manager of the Klamath refuges, disciplined for alleged violations of the Hatch Act, which proscribes lobbying by federal employees. As evidence the association cited comments attributed by the media to Phil Norton, such as: "We are trying to fix the system so that it works again, but there's a lot of land that, frankly, never should have been put into agriculture production."

Last June the Fish and Wildlife Service, which is controlled by the Secretary of the Interior, completely reversed itself, issuing a Finding of No Significant Impact from farming in the Tule Lake National Wildlife Refuge. And despite a 94 percent favorable response in the public-comment period, the service rescinded its 1999 ruling that irrigation on the refuges would be permitted only in years when there was enough water to sustain wetlands. It abandoned its buyout effort. No longer did refuge spokespeople say that lease farming on the refuges "had to go." Instead, they proclaimed that farming was "compatible" with their mission.

The Klamath Water Users Association prevailed on Representative Greg Walden to kill an amendment to the 2002 Farm Bill that would have provided $175 million to buy farmland from willing sellers in the Klamath Basin. This so infuriated farmers who own land and have long favored a buyout that fifty of them wrote the association as follows: "To prevent this unfortunate situation from reoccurring and to prevent any future legal action, we request that all future association activities purporting to represent Klamath Basin Water Users on any major issues, such as retirement of land, be submitted to a vote of the landowners prior to any public announcement or official position statement."

Among the signers was John Anderson, 50, who runs beef cattle and grows a few crops on 3,500 acres in Tulelake, California. The drought of 2001 hurt him badly, wiping out 100 of 150 acres of peppermint and making him even more determined to get into a business more practical and profitable than trying to make the desert bloom. "The buyout has become an emotional issue that has built on itself," he says. "Logic has been lost. People go around saying, 'By God, we're not going to let the government take it,' and 'These environmentalists are full of bull.' I'd say more than 50 percent of the farmland is available for federal buyout right now." A lot of landowners aren't talking because they've been intimidated by property-rights barkers. Anderson, who is not among them, says he has received death threats by phone in the middle of the night.

On October 2, 2002, after salmon had been dying in the lower river for two weeks, the Pacific Coast Federation of Fishermen's Associations, the Earthjustice Legal Defense Fund, the Wilderness Society, Trout Unlimited, the Yurok tribe, and Representative Mike Thompson (D-CA) held a press conference outside the Department of the Interior building in Washington, D.C., to announce their lawsuit against BuRec and the NMFS for violating the Endangered Species Act. Thompson had the Yuroks ship out 500 pounds of dead salmon with which he and his fellow plaintiffs festooned the park across from the Interior building. So rancid was the shipment that Federal Express at first refused to deliver it. "It was amazing how quickly the flies found those fish," recalls the Wilderness Society's Pete Rafle. "I now understand why the theory of spontaneous generation held sway. I've got a pair of shoes that I'm going to have to resole or burn. I wasn't expecting puddles."

"I think there's been a real lack of understanding that the salmon are connected with the farming practices," Representative Thompson told me. "Unless you know the area, you don't necessarily know that the two are connected, and that's been a big problem. So it has come down to God-fearing farmers versus hippies and fish. That's not what it's about at all. It's about livelihoods in the lower basin."

The only people to express surprise at the fish kill worked for the Department of the Interior. Steve Williams, director of the Fish and Wildlife Service, showed up at the press conference to lament the plaintiffs' "premature rush to judgment" and proclaim that it was "too soon to draw conclusions" about what might have killed the salmon— roughly the equivalent of a parachute manufacturer suggesting that sky divers scraped from asphalt might have died on the way down from food poisoning.

Sue Ellen Wooldridge, Gale Norton's deputy chief of staff, asserted that the government can't release much water from Upper Klamath Lake because of the endangered suckers, failing to mention that if it hadn't diverted the river for full deliveries to irrigators in violation of the Endangered Species Act, there would have been more than enough water for suckers, salmon, and refuges.

Finally, James Connaughton, chairman of the President's Council on Environmental Quality, offered this explanation: "There will always be setbacks because we don't have an ultimate authority on how natural systems work. The trick is to manage risk in a way that minimizes and localizes and creates limited opportunities of time for those setbacks to occur."

In other words, the president's top environmental adviser expects the public to dismiss what's apparently the biggest salmon kill in history as just another bum hand in a game of five-card draw, played with the public's fish and wildlife as the ante. The Klamath tragedy isn't an isolated event. On September 30, when the salmon die-off was at its peak, the administration was giving away federal water a thousand miles east, on the Gunnison River in Colorado, thereby desiccating the Black Canyon of the Gunnison National Park and jeopardizing four endangered fish and a world-famous trout fishery. Earlier in the month Interior declined to appeal a bizarre court ruling that canceled the water right of Deer Flat National Wildlife Refuge in Idaho, a refuge dedicated to waterfowl. Since 1973, when the Endangered Species Act outlawed these kinds of risks, no other administration has been willing to take them. Now they're a habit with the Bush team, and it isn't winning any pots.

Have Salmon Endangered Maine?

—‹‹ ›› —

In 2000, when the last populations of Atlantic salmon in the U.S. were protected under the Endangered Species Act, politicians and industry lobbies warned that the ESA listing would ruin Maine's aquaculture and forest-products industries. But the sky has yet to fall. The Endangered Species Act is currently under attack by the Bush administration, which is seeking to neutralize it by fiat, and by conservative politicians who are trying to gut it legislatively. Leading the charge in Congress is House resources chairman Richard Pombo (R-CA) who proclaims that the law is "broken," has been a "failure," and is used by "radical environmental organizations [to] prohibit legal land uses of nearly every kind."

Such talk infuriates Steve Moyer, Trout Unlimited's federal advocacy coordinator, who helped procure the last reauthorization of the ESA in 1988 when he was a lobbyist for the National Wildlife Federation. "We don't enforce the Clean Water Act aggressively enough," he declares. "We weaken some federal lands laws to cut more forests. We don't bother to update a federal mining law from the 1800s. We don't make the Magnuson Act conserve marine fish. We don't provide adequate funding for federal and state wildlife programs. On and on and on. We put a huge burden on the ESA (thirty species of trout and salmon from coast to coast, for example), and then some have the nerve to blame it for being 'broken.'"

But what of the human misery allegedly caused by the ESA? Consider the nation's wild Atlantic salmon—which exist only in Maine. There has been plenty of time for onerous federal regulations to trash a state's economy. Has this happened?

The aquaculture industry, the forest-products industry, the blueberry industry, the property-rights community, and just about every state and federal politician in Maine said it would. Consider some of the pronouncements of then governor Angus King: "It will kill the [aquaculture] industry dead.

D-E-A-D, dead." The feds have "betrayed" Maine with "a partial takeover." "They're trifling with people's lives and I resent the hell out of it."

State Rep. Robert Daigle (R-York) likened the ESA listing to a "nuclear bomb." U.S. Sen. Olympia Snowe (R-ME) fretted about "disastrous consequences" including "an end of aquaculture." U.S. Sen. Susan Collins (R-ME) warned of "serious implications for the aquaculture, blueberry, cranberry, and forest products industries," and lamented the "cruel irony" of federal intervention after the state had already embarked on its own recovery plan. Jonathan Reisman, president of the Maine Conservation Rights Institute (a wise-use outfit) and associate professor of economics and public policy at the University of Maine-Machias, circulated the following statement over the Internet: "What they're saying to Washington County is, we don't really care about the violent sodomization you're enduring—just turn the other cheek, cooperate with your tormentor, and you'll learn to enjoy it. Personally, I've always thought violent rapists should be executed to protect the community from repetition."

Less than a month after the November 13, 2000, ESA listing, the State of Maine filed suit (unsuccessfully) against the federal government. It was joined by the state Chamber of Commerce, Atlantic Salmon of Maine (an aquaculture venture), Stolt Sea Farm Inc., the Maine Aquaculture Association, the Maine Pulp & Paper Association, the Wild Blueberry Commission, and blueberry growers Jasper Wyman and Sons and Cherryfield Foods.

When the U.S. Fish and Wildlife Service (USFWS) and the National Marine Fisheries Service (NMFS) first made noises about listing in 1996, then-Sen. William Cohen (R-ME) informed then-Interior Secretary Bruce Babbitt that "the disposition of this [Atlantic salmon] petition will greatly affect my views regarding changes to the Endangered Species Act that might be warranted." Babbitt, who took the threat very seriously, backed a state restoration plan that supposedly would make listing unnecessary. It was a nice try by Babbitt who, during his tenure, single-handedly saved the act, but he underestimated Maine's recalcitrance and torpor.

On December 18, 1997, Interior's USFWS, along with the Department of Commerce's NMFS, approved the state plan, simultaneously withdrawing the proposal to list the salmon of seven Down East Maine rivers. Salmon advocates were less sanguine about the state plan than the sundry bureaucrats and politicians who oozed and gushed about it that day in Augusta. For one thing, it had no funding mechanism. For another, measures were largely voluntary. "It was a plan to avert impacts to business and industry; it wasn't about salmon restoration," says Ed Baum, who retired as the state's salmon restoration coordinator in 2000 after thirty-two years with the Salmon Commission. Even when Baum worked for the state he dared to tell me this, on the record: "There has never been a serious attempt to restore salmon runs in Maine."

One indication the state plan would fail was in 1999, when Cherryfield Foods asked to dewater the dangerously low Pleasant River. The state ignored its own plan and its own salmon biologists and told the company to go ahead. Another indication was that, right up to listing in November 2000, the state stridently maintained that there were no wild salmon to protect. "It's hard for me to understand how an animal that numbers in the millions can possibly be in danger of extinction," commented then-governor King. "If you carry it too far, everything's an endangered species: I guarantee that a mouse in Waterville, Maine, is different in some ways than a mouse in Watertown, New York."

Even as the governor was venting this kind of gas and wind, his senior salmon biologist, Baum, was confronting him with the truth, calling America's remnant wild salmon a "treasure of national significance." One of the nation's most respected geneticists—Tim King, of the U.S. Geological Survey—had demonstrated for the feds that America's wild Atlantic salmon were indeed unique. As the USFWS and NMFS put it, "The loss of these populations [endemic to the Dennys, East Machias, Machias, Pleasant, Narraguagus, Ducktrap, and Sheepscot rivers and Cove Brook] would restrict the natural range of Atlantic salmon to the region above the 45th parallel and beyond the borders of the United States. ... The genetic resources of these most southerly stocks are considered vitally important to the species' future survival." It was the best science available, all peer-reviewed.

But the governor's office dismissed it as "junk science," and hired two obliging researchers, one from the state university, to confirm the allegation. Then, armed with their own junk science, the governor and his industry cronies went after the USGS's Tim King. "This was just outrageous, completely politically motivated," says Leon Szeptycki, Trout Unlimited's eastern conservation director. "It was incredibly wasteful and damaging. This poor guy Tim King got dragged through the mud. It got really personal. Tim didn't have a dog in this fight; all he cared about was doing the work. He provided really elegant genetic and statistical evidence of a native population structure." Maine's congressional delegation bought into the governor's bogus accusation, diverting $500,000 from salmon restoration to order up a redundant genetic study by the National Academy of Sciences. Lo, more than two years later, NAS reported that Tim King had gotten everything right.

So what happened to Maine's aquaculture industry? Is it, as former-governor Angus King predicted, "dead, D-E-A-D, dead"? Well, salmon farming looks like it might be heading in that direction, which is some of the best news for wild salmon that's come out of the state since listing. Production is a third of what it was in 1999, and far fewer escapees are showing up in the rivers. But what, if anything, has the ESA to do with the industry's current woes?

"As far as we can tell the only industry more regulated than we are is nuclear power," says Sebastian Belle, executive director of the Maine Aquaculture Association. "We had one major operation, Fjord Seafood, a Norwegian company, pull up stakes entirely. We have other companies that have scaled way back, and the last independent salmon farmer in the state [Erick Swanson of Trumpet Island Salmon Farm in Blue Hill Bay] is quitting."

Long before Belle mentioned the listing he went through a long litany of other grievances, particularly foreign competition and the February 2002 court order to get rid of European fish, which supposedly grow faster than North American strains but threatened to genetically swamp them. Interestingly enough, this order resulted not from the ESA but from the Clean Water Act. Fish farms are major sources of pollution, fouling water with feces, decaying feed, pathogens, antibiotics, pesticides and exotic genes—all of which are regulated under the statute. Forced depopulation of European stock did in Atlantic Salmon of Maine and crippled other operations. They'll even admit they are victims of the Clean Water Act.

But in fact, they are victims of themselves. Before listing they used every possible legal and political maneuver to retain their European fish. Despite the fact that this violated state and federal law, the governor's office and the congressional delegation backed them, talking the feds into looking the other way. The stubborn commitment to European fish caused major loss of production because the court not only required salmon farmers to get rid of their alien fish but to do so immediately. They had to depopulate their pens and, for the rest of the season, were left with nothing. Heritage Salmon, Inc. and Stolt Sea Farm, Inc.—based in Canada, where European stocks have long been outlawed—had North American fish on hand and therefore were able to convert their Maine operations.

In addition to fining salmon farmers for violating the Clean Water Act, the court required them to "fallow" production sites. "As a result we have about 400 people out of work in Washington County," complains Belle. "When you're mandated to go [temporarily] out of business by a court order I would say that's a pretty imposing event." True. On the other hand, fallowing—vacating a site for at least one growing season—is nothing more than good sense and standard procedure in many types of agriculture. Because the industry had declined to take this precaution, sea lice proliferated. Lice themselves are a major scourge of penned salmon, but they transmit a far more deadly scourge—infectious salmon anemia, a rapidly spreading virus that replicates in gills, kidney, liver, intestine, spleen, muscles and heart, causing hemorrhaging and killing victims in under a month. In 2002 an outbreak required Maine salmon farmers to destroy most of their stock—every fish in Cobscook Bay, about 1.5 million adults. Heritage Salmon Inc., in whose pens the outbreak apparently started, was fined $15,000 for failing to report positive test results. Another outbreak in 2003 required more destruction. Yet another outbreak is underway as I write. And now, to the alarm but not surprise of wild salmon advocates, the virus is showing up in Penobscot and Merrimack salmon.

Maine's last independent salmon farmer, Swanson of Trumpet Island Salmon Farm, isn't going out of business. He's just switching to mussels. It's a growing trend, and great news for everyone, especially wild salmon. Around the time of listing, salmon (by value) accounted for about 95 percent of Maine's aquaculture industry; now they're down to half. Oysters and mussels are taking up most of the slack, but a state-of-the-art aquaculture center at the University of Maine is figuring out how to raise cod and halibut. "There's a real effort to prop up the industry and go to alternative species," says Andy Goode, director of U.S. programs for the Atlantic Salmon Federation. "I think there's recognition that, with salmon, the industry just can't compete." The fortunes of any undertaking are enhanced by diversity; so, to the extent that the ESA has provided incentive for conversion from salmon to shellfish, it has helped Maine aquaculture.

Maine's blueberry industry, which produces half the continent's wild blueberries, is having its share of problems, too—none of which is related to the ESA. For one thing, the brutal, largely snowless winter of 2003–2004 freeze-dried the buds, wiping out half the crop. For another, in 2003 a jury ruled that three Maine blueberry processors had illegally conspired to fix prices. With triple damages and attorneys' fees the processors would have had to cough up about $60 million. The growers, who had brought the suit and who couldn't survive without processors, agreed with the defendants that this would put everyone out of business and eventually settled for $5 million.

Still, Dave Bell, director of Maine's Wild Blueberry Commission reports that the industry's general health is "very good." One reason is that, unlike salmon farmers, blueberry growers devised contingency plans when it became clear they could no longer irrigate their crop by dewatering salmon rivers. Even without the listing, state and federal clean water laws would have forced growers to develop alternative water sources. Now they irrigate mostly from distant wells and artificial ponds. So, as a motivator for wise business practices, the ESA listing has benefited the blueberry industry, too. "There are some cost-share programs to help growers develop alternative water sources," says Bell. "As long as everyone works together proactively to address issues and solve problems we can co-exist. I've always believed that if we can have salmon in Down East

Maine again, it's good for everyone." That sure sounds more positive than some of the industry's pronouncements when the commission was suing the feds for listing salmon.

Foreign competition, not the ESA, has hurt Maine's forest-products industry. But, according to Michael Barden, director of Environmental Affairs for the Maine Pulp & Paper Association, there have been encouraging recent developments such as the booming economy in China, where there isn't much pulp capacity, and the decline of the dollar, which is making it more profitable for U.S. firms to export their product. Barden's association was also a partner to the state's unsuccessful suit opposing the listing of salmon, but since then all association members have sold their forestland and therefore aren't suffering even imaginary inconvenience. The only measurable effect of the listing on the forest-products industry has been to provide it with a windfall in the form of state, federal and private funds used to buy its development rights. International Paper, for example, has sold a conservation easement that protects a 1,000-foot corridor on both sides of 210 miles of the Machias River and six major tributaries. The public still gets to hunt and fish, and IP still gets to cut its timber, albeit on a sustainable basis. The second phase of the project will protect the river's headwater lakes. "This kind of habitat protection was called for under the state plan," says Tom Rumpf of The Nature Conservancy, the deal's lead negotiator. "But no way could the state have afforded it without ESA money."

"After listing, all the fighting became moot," says Baum. "There's much more cooperation among the state fisheries agencies [Inland Fish and Wildlife, Marine Resources, and the Salmon Commission]. During most of my career the commission would have to get a permit from IFW to stock salmon; and there were often rivers that were off limits. Also, IFW was stocking browns, rainbows and splake and other species in the salmon rivers and never consulting with us."

The Atlantic Salmon Federation's Goode agrees. "A year after listing you started to see a lot of collaborative projects between industry and the NGO community," he says. "For example, three big aquaculture companies got together with ASF and TU, and we designed an effective new containment management system at every site."

With help from Senators Snowe and Collins, now ardent salmon advocates, federal money is pouring into the state, and, as a result, more state and private funds are becoming available. Some of this money is funding the work of local watershed councils, now heavily invested in salmon recovery; they're controlling non-point pollution and siltation, reporting violations, buying land, and otherwise protecting habitat. According to Salmon Commission director, Pat Keliher, there are now about twenty-eight biologists working on Atlantic salmon; before listing there were about seven. The newly moneyed commission is gearing up for a massive liming project on the Dennys River, which has been blighted by acid rain. About three quarters of the riparian habitat on that river had been unprotected; now the state has locked up about 60 percent of that. "We have every major stakeholder, including the entire state Congressional delegation, in the harness working together," says TU's Steve Moyer.

For political, not scientific, reasons there was no listing for the genetically unique salmon of Maine's Penobscot River—America's biggest Atlantic salmon river and one that sustains more fish than all Down East streams combined. Nor was there a listing for the salmon of the Kennebec and Androscoggin rivers. Yet the ESA will benefit all these runs. The second part of the National Academy of Sciences study—an inadvertent result of the ESA in that it was ordered up by Maine politicians panicked by the alleged threat of listing-was released in December 2003. It recommended dam removal, a no-brainer for anyone who knows salmon; but most politicians don't know salmon. "To have the NAS say this has been hugely beneficial," says the Natural Resources Council of Maine's Laura Rose Day, who directs an environmental coalition called Penobscot Partners.

Beneficial indeed. Last June representatives of Pennsylvania Power and Light Corporation (owner of the most hurtful dams on the Penobscot), the Penobscot Indian Nation, the State of Maine, Interior's Bureau of Indian Affairs, the National Park Service, the USFWS, American Rivers, the Atlantic Salmon Federation, Maine Audubon, the Natural Resources Council of Maine and TU signed an agreement that will open 500 miles of river habitat to easy access for salmon and ten other species of migratory fish. Under the agreement PPL will get to increase generation at six dams once it sells three dams on the lower river—Veazie, Great Works and Howland dams-to the Penobscot River Restoration Trust. Veazie and Great Works will be removed; Howland will be by-passed by a large channel; and improved fish-passage will be installed at four other dams.

Even the Bush administration likes the idea. At the final agreement in June 2004 there wasn't going to be a press conference. But when U.S. Secretary of the Interior Gale Norton heard this she demanded one, then joined Maine governor John Baldacci and other state and federal dignitaries on the banks of the Penobscot. "Today," she declared, offering an eloquent (albeit inadvertent) defense of the ESA, "it seems perfectly plausible that executives of a power company that owns dams on the river, environmentalists and sportsmen who have tried to get the dams torn down, the governor of Maine, representatives of state and federal agencies responsible for the fish in the river, and members of a Native American tribe that has fished the river for 10,000 years are all working together."

SALMON OF THE ST. LAWRENCE LAKES

◄-(-)-►

"Landlocks" weren't always those slender, dainty fish that snatch Gray Ghosts from prop wash or bend alder reflections as they sip dry flies. The extinct races of Atlantic salmon that inhabited Lakes Ontario, Cayuga, Onondaga, Seneca, Champlain, Memphremagog, and other sprawling waters that feed the St. Lawrence River were huge, some approaching fifty pounds. Technically, they were not landlocked because they had access to the sea, though it's doubtful that many took advantage of it. A few probably migrated in reverse, running downstream and then up the big tributaries of the St. Lawrence where they spawned alongside and maybe with sea-runs.

The Salmon River, collected by Lake Ontario at Pulaski, New York, was named for Atlantic salmon—not, as is commonly supposed, the chinooks and cohos that darken it each fall. In 1884 the bulletin of the U.S. Commission of Fish and Fisheries noted the following catch from the river: "In October, 1836, two men took two hundred and thirty salmon between 8 p.m. and 12, with spears and fire-jacks, and after 12 til morning two other men in the same skiff took two hundred odd, the average weight of the entire lot [was] fourteen and three-quarters pounds." In 1892 the same publication filed this report: "It was nothing uncommon for teams fording the rivers and creeks at night to kill salmon with their hoofs. An older settler living in the town of Hannibal told Mr. Ingersoll that one night while driving across Three-Mile Creek the salmon ran against his horses' feet in such large numbers that the horses took fright and plunged through the water, killing one large salmon outright and injuring two others so that they were captured. The farmers living near the smaller creeks easily supplied their families with salmon caught by means of pitchforks."

Restoration with a mixture of races from Maine is underway. Whether or not it succeeds in any significant way depends on the ability of Atlantic salmon advocates to do three things: 1. Get over their saltwater fixation; 2. Dispel the popular superstition—advanced by the charter industry—that Atlantic salmon in Lake Ontario are part of an international plot to do away with the mass hatchery production of Pacific salmonids; and 3. Convince the environmental community that Atlantic salmon are not just "sportfish" but a cog in an imperiled native ecosystem, part of earth's biodiversity they keep saying we need to save.

Today the lakes are radically different environments than when they were prowled by wild, native salmon. At least sixteen alien fish species are established in Lake Ontario alone. The nutrient-sucking zebra mussels that showed up in 1980 are short-circuiting energy flow. Here and in the upstream lakes the biggest threat to Atlantics isn't sea lampreys but alewives. Alewives, which arrived in Lake Ontario via the Erie Canal or perhaps were introduced in the mistaken belief that they were shad, contain thiaminase, an enzyme that degrades vitamin B1 (thiamine) in predator fish that eat them, thereby killing fry in the swim-up stage. In the late nineteenth century the few Lake Ontario salmon that made it past dams probably were already critically deficient in thiamine. The last wild fish was seen in 1898.

It's tempting to speculate what would have happened if, in the 1960s, Great Lakes fish managers had stocked Atlantic rather than Pacific salmon. But eggs weren't available, and Atlantics are much harder to hatch and rear. This was an important consideration because the mission was not to create a sport fishery but to control the alewives which had taken over the lake and, in regular, massive die-offs that never overtook recruitment, were fouling beaches and clogging water intakes. Today the alewife population is about 20 percent of what it was then.

In addition to lampreys and alewives, Atlantic salmon must now contend with competition from hordes of cohos, chinooks, steelheads, browns and rainbows. The Salmon River system, for example, may be disgorging as many as a million chinook smolts a year, and when the adults surge back up in the fall they tend to run everything else out of the main channel. None of this means that Atlantic salmon habitat is anywhere near gone. It's a big lake; and the tributaries keep getting cleaner.

But neither the Province of Ontario nor the State of New York is making much of an effort at restoration. The Ontario Ministry of Natural Resources stocks about 200,000 fry a year strictly for research purposes. It's collecting data on competition with other salmonids and on how stream habitat such as substrates affect survivability. In the late 1980s and early 1990s the province stocked yearlings in the Wilmot River on the east side of Toronto and the Credit on the west, ceasing when returns proved consistently low compared to returns of Pacifics. But returns of Atlantics are always low compared to returns of Pacifics. According to Sandra Orsatti, manager of the ministry's Lake Ontario Fishery Unit, an element of sportsmen feel threatened even by the tiny research program, "fearing a decrease in hatchery production of Pacific salmon."

There has been more activity and better results on the New York side. Thirteen years ago, in a courageous move for which it took considerable heat, the Department of Environmental Conservation quit stocking Pacific salmon in the Black River system (in the eastern basin) and switched to Atlantics. Managers were fed up with all the illegal snagging, and the Canadians were complaining about the chinooks that kept straying down the nearby St. Lawrence River and showing up in sea-run Atlantic salmon streams. But Atlantic returns were low compared to returns of Pacifics. There was pressure from anglers to stock Pacifics, and the program was cancelled in 2001. Now chinooks are being stocked again, albeit in smaller numbers.

Twenty years ago New York started stocking Atlantic smolts in three high-quality streams—Little Sandy and Lindsey creeks (in Lake Ontario's southeast corner), and Irondequoit Creek east of Rochester. "In June 1986 I caught fifty-seven adult Atlantics in the Little Sandy," says Fran Verdoliva, the department's Salmon River Coordinator. "The biggest was thirty-nine inches. There was natural reproduction—twenty-nine young of the year per surface acre. Not much compared with 1,500 to 7,000 steelhead, but the steelhead had been in the system for twenty years." After only four years the state abandoned the program. The idea that one native Atlantic salmon might be worth a whole bunch of alien Pacifics just didn't compute with the managers or the public. "Frankly," says Verdoliva,

"I think that for the average angler 'a salmon is a salmon.' Today we live in a world where fast and easy is the way to do it. Then there's the conspiracy theory that we're stocking these fish so we can phase out Pacifics. People really believe that. I had one guide tell me that he'd kill every Atlantic that came into the Salmon River because he wanted the program to fail."

Currently, the department stocks close to 100,000 smolts a year, mostly in the Salmon River system. While the fish face horrendous competition from Pacific salmonids, they have more going for them than you'd think or than some hatchery bureaucrats acknowledge. For one thing, Atlantics can tolerate warmer water than the other salmonids (although chinook smolts are out of the river their first spring before temperature is a factor). In summer, when parts of the mainstem are in the high 70s, only juvenile Atlantics are present there. That's a real niche. In 1996 the federal government relicensed the river's hydro plants, requiring minimum flows that induced the state to stock Atlantics. The good water conditions allowed the chinook population to explode but also gave the Atlantics—with their big fins—a home-court advantage in the new riffles and fast water. "There has been a lot of talk that Atlantics can't compete with steelhead and Pacific salmon," Verdoliva says. "Well, we've been doing studies in the tribs, and that's just not true."

When the first adult Atlantics showed up in the summer of 1998 Verdoliva caught seven eight-to ten-pounders in one evening on a traditional Atlantic salmon fly called an Ackroyd. Since then fish up to twenty-five pounds have been caught. In 2001 Verdoliva saw twelve Atlantics up to eighteen pounds at fish-cleaning stations being sliced up with cohos and chinooks by anglers who didn't know what they had.

Oak Orchard Creek, midway between Rochester and the Niagara River, is also being stocked. There are scant data on returns, but a local flyshop owner claims he saw 35 adults brought in last fall and estimates that about 200 were caught—a dubious statistic because they're mixed in with big browns.

Upstream from Lake Ontario good numbers of stocked salmon are present in Cayuga and Seneca Lakes (along with lampreys and alewives), but there's no reproduction. Onondaga is too polluted for salmonids. During the winter of 2002–2003 at least six Atlantics were caught through the ice in Oneida Lake thanks to past stockings by the Atlantic Salmon Fish Creek Club, whose mission is restoring the species to Fish Creek and the Oswego River system. The strategy is first to show that it's possible, then stoke state, federal and public enthusiasm. In March 2003 the club obtained 15,000 eyed eggs that, at this writing, are being incubated at Carpenters Brook Fish Hatchery in Elbridge, NY.

The fact that not a single Atlantic was ever seen in the Niagara River above the falls or in the upper Great Lakes confounded early settlers, which also explains why they were shocked when the fish stopped coming up Lake Ontario tributaries they'd dammed. But, while salmon weren't native in the upper Great Lakes, establishing them there is no different than extending ocean runs by providing fish passage around waterfalls. Atlantics have been stocked in all the upper lakes but never with any sustained effort and never, until now, with any noticeable result. In 1987, however, Lake Superior State University, in cooperation with the Michigan Department of Natural Resources, began releasing smolts in the St. Marys River at Sault Ste. Marie. The fish travel sixty miles downstream into Lake Huron where they gain weight quickly. Now twenty-pounders are returning; and, while the run isn't big, the fishing in riffles and powerhouse outfalls is better than on lots of Canadian streams. Last year anglers voluntarily turned in 180 fish to the lab. Apparently, there's some reproduction because smolts are fin-clipped, and now and then an adult shows up with all fins intact.

The spectacular success story was (and soon will be again) Lake Champlain. The first serious fish survey—by New York in 1929—revealed that salmon had been extirpated. Dams had the most to do with it, but sea lampreys probably helped. Sea lampreys, it now turns out, are native to Lakes Ontario and Champlain, but not one of the historical accounts of salmon or lake trout catches mentions a fish bearing a circular wound. So the native races of salmonids (now extinct) apparently had adapted to the presence of sea lampreys.

Sporadic efforts were made to rehabilitate—with hatchery strains— salmon runs in the Champlain Basin, but it wasn't until 1973 that New York, Vermont and the Fish and Wildlife Service engaged in serious, coordinated stocking. Very quickly it became apparent that something was limiting the fish. They'd grow fast and then, at a certain size, disappear. All evidence pointed to sea lampreys, so in 1985 a chemical control program was proposed. It wasn't rocket science. After all, the main poison of choice—TFM, the stuff that allowed lake trout restoration in Lake Superior and Pacific salmonid management in all the Great Lakes—was 1950s technology. TFM, applied to spawning streams, is pretty benign and pretty selective, though hard on aquatic salamanders like mudpuppies. Still, federal law required a full-blown Environmental Impact Statement (EIS), a process the participants managed to drag out for five years. When the EIS was finally hatched, in 1990, it was only good for eight years.

However, from 1990 to 1997 New York and Vermont knocked Champlain's lampreys from hell to breakfast, and the salmon population took off. "Some of the guys were fishing the Ausable, Boquet and Saranac instead of going up to the Gaspe," says New York's regional fisheries manager Larry Nashett. "Up there they might spend a lot of time and money and catch one fish. Here, on good days, they were taking three-fish limits." The better salmon were seven or eight pounds. There was even some natural reproduction.

But when the EIS expired in 1997, the dawdling and red tape started all over again with a "supplemental EIS." Coordinated control by New York and Vermont didn't resume until 2002. But now there's another danger—alewives. They've shown up on the Vermont side in Lake St. Catherine, which drains into Champlain. Biologists suspect that they were unleashed by bass fishermen who had been watching too many ESPN shows about how alewives fatten largemouths in southern impoundments. The Vermont Department of Fish and Wildlife is looking at ways of containing the alewives and has even talked about trying to eliminate them from the system. So far they haven't been seen in Lake Champlain.

Sportsmen are solidly behind Champlain salmon restoration. "Anglers favored salmon so strongly that lake trout took most of the hit when we had to trim stocking by 40 percent to protect the smelt forage base," reports Vermont's district fisheries biologist Brian Chipman. But the environmental community seems clueless that the salmon program is not just about fish for anglers or that tradeoffs, such as limited mudpuppy mortality, are part of the cost of restoring native ecosystems. On October 30, 2001, for example, the Vermont Public Interest Research Group, Audubon Vermont, and Sylvia Knight (a private citizen) challenged the supplemental EIS in federal district court, claiming that it inadequately protected mudpuppies and rare mussels. Mudpuppies, however, bounce back and mussels are little affected. On September 6, 2002, the judge upheld the supplemental EIS. The plaintiffs are being unfairly and stupidly mocked by local anglers for their concern about mudpuppies and mussels. Still, that commendable concern appears not to extend to other parts of Champlain's native ecosystem such as Atlantic salmon. In announcing its lawsuit Vermont PIRG went so far as to quote an alleged authority from academia who proclaimed that Atlantics were being stocked "strictly for sport fishing."

Currently both states release 270,000 smolts a year. A portion of these are the result of fry stocking (biologists do the arithmetic based on the assumption that five percent of the fry make it to smolthood). As with sea-run restoration, fry stocking has great potential and produces adults indistinguishable from wild ones. Recently Vermont managers obtained stock from Maine's Sebago Lake. They'd been relying on fish from Maine's West Grand Lake, which evolved to migrate downstream. "We think we've been losing a lot of our salmon down the Richelieu River," says Chipman. "We have good returns of salmon that have gone through one lake year, but then they kind of disappear."

East of Champlain, the sea-run-size salmon of the Clyde River, which feeds Lake Memphremagog, had attracted anglers from all over the world until construction of Newport No. 11 dam in 1957 obliterated the run. But the dam breached in 1994 and was removed two years later. Now the salmon in the lamprey-free, alewife-free river and lake are doing splendidly.

Even if managers do all the right things in the big lakes that feed the St. Lawrence, Atlantic salmon aren't going to be spooking horses in your lifetime. And even in Champlain and Memphremagog natural reproduction by itself isn't going to sustain populations. It's true, as environmental groups have pointed out, that the salmon being stocked are not original strains. Those strains are extinct. But it's important to have the next closest thing

(Maine strains) swimming, and to some extent breeding, in these lakes—just as it's important to have introduced tundra and Canadian anatum peregrine falcons flying and nesting in the old range of America's extinct strain of eastern peregrine.

To have the chance to catch an Atlantic salmon in these lakes and their tributaries, to see one, or just to know they're out there should matter to Americans and Canadians—whether they fish or not. These fish can never be what they were, but they can at least be there, a little piece of something beautiful, part of our history and of earth's.

As Maine Goes, So Go the Salmon

---- ⤜ ⤛ ----

Trusting America's last wild Atlantic salmon to the State of Maine is like trusting the original *Whistler's Mother* to Mr. Bean. In case you missed the movie, he accidentally transfers the contents of his fountain pen to the painting via his handkerchief, proceeds to wipe off the ink (as well as Mom's face) with paint remover, then "restores" everything with Magic Marker. A few lonely salmon activists have been saying this in politer diction for the past twenty years. Finally they have the attention of the feds.

In 1993, with runs flickering out, a Massachusetts group called "RESTORE: The North Woods" petitioned the National Marine Fisheries Service and the U.S. Fish and Wildlife Service to protect Atlantic salmon under the Endangered Species Act. Industry moguls, state bureaucrats and veteran salmon anglers gasped and spluttered. The Atlantic Salmon Federation called RESTORE "an upstart environmental group" whose sole mission was "to further its own agenda" and declared, "We don't mind taking on the forestry, hydro or agriculture interests one at a time, but we weren't prepared to take them on all at once, and that's what this petition is forcing us to do."

So horrified were industry and the state at the thought of a spotted fish playing spotted owl in Yankeeland that they hatched a radical new idea—resource stewardship. They called it "Project SHARE" (Salmon Habitat And River Enhancement). They'd band together with the public to protect the things that Atlantic salmon depend on, like woods and water. They'd set up citizen "watershed councils" and actually give them money.

Governor Angus King—ardently committed to the preservation of Maine from the Endangered Species Act (though not of America's Atlantic salmon from extinction)—had an even grander idea. He convened a task force to develop a "plan" by which the state would promise to get serious about restoration and conservation of America's wild Atlantic salmon and whose purpose would be to so impress the feds that they'd go away.

The impending "train wreck" of an ESA listing would be alchemized into a "win-win" scenario by which everyone, even the salmon, would prosper. And, as with those fourteen-day miracle diets, there'd be no pain. The plan would be essentially a volunteer effort, demonstrating once again the selflessness of industry and the innate goodness of human nature.

Eighteen months later—in March 1997—the King administration delivered a one-inch-thick document loftily entitled "Atlantic Salmon Conservation Plan for Seven Maine Rivers" defined as "a five-year, comprehensive directive of conservation actions designed to give wild Atlantic salmon every advantage to successfully propagate and thrive."

The feds—in form of the National Marine Fisheries Service and the U.S. Fish and Wildlife Service—really did go away. On December 15, 1997, Secretary of the Interior Bruce Babbitt and Assistant Secretary of Commerce Terry Garcia appeared on the steps of the Maine State House, effused over the salmon plan, and formally withdrew their proposal for listing, as threatened, the "Downeast stocks" of the Sheepscot, Ducktrap, Narraguagus, Pleasant, Machias, East Machias and Dennys. As Roberta Scruggs of the *Maine Sunday Telegram* aptly noted, there hadn't been so many smiling faces seen in one place since the Up with People concert. With that, the State of Maine got busy doing what it always had done for Atlantic salmon: basically nothing.

That's not to say that some real good hasn't come out of both the fear of the plan and the plan itself. "The petition to list was great," Maine salmon biologist Ed Baum told me four years ago. "It has been a club held over everyone's head ... All of a sudden, during the past two years, we have people with whom we never dealt almost falling over themselves to see what they can do to help." And, while the councils are woefully underfunded and have yet to understand that their role is protecting habitat rather than managing salmon, it's nice to see the people of Maine thinking about natural resources. The Ducktrap Council, which existed before the plan, and the Sheepscot Council have led the way and set the example. And, while the five Down East councils are further removed from the populated state capitol of Augusta and therefore have been less effective, they are clearly on the right track. In fact, the watershed councils were the only aspect of the salmon plan to get good marks in the March 1999 review by the feds: "The creation of the watershed councils and their actions to date are a tremendous accomplishment. We believe the watershed councils have the potential to have great benefits not just for Atlantic salmon but for the entire ecosystems."

In the first year of the salmon plan politics rather than science determined how much water agriculture could suck from salmon streams. But in April 1998 the Land and Water Resources Council (the state entity that administers the plan) recommended that Cherryfield Foods, Inc., which irrigates its blueberries with water from the Pleasant River, leave at least 36 cubic feet per second in July and 30 cfs in August and September. Cherryfield Foods had wanted 24 cfs across the board. Ed Baum had wanted 60. Still, having seen how things went before the plan, Baum isn't upset. "I can live with that," he says. So can the salmon, provided everything else works out for them.

But everything else isn't working out. In 1997 and 1998 the runs of all seven Down East rivers reached all time lows. The 1998 estimated rod catch was 15 from the Narraguagus, five from the Machias, zero from the other five. On the Dennys, a river in which biologists counted *565 redds* in 1978, only one wild fish was seen (after two kids had stabbed it to death with sticks). Most biologists agree that at least fifty individual adult salmon of each sex are needed to maintain a stock's genetic integrity, so maybe it's already too late.

The salmon plan is limited to stocks of the seven Down East rivers. But since the feds dropped their listing proposal, Dr. Tim King of the National Biological Service has analyzed the genetic make-up of naturally reproducing salmon populations from Cove Brook and Kenduskeag Stream (tributaries of the lower Penobscot) and Bond Brook and Togus Stream (tributaries of the lower Kennebec). These strains, distinct from each other, turn out to be the most unique on the continent. The wild salmon that occur in Eaton Brook, Felts Brook, the South Branch of the Marsh River (all tributaries of the lower Penobscot), the Passagassawaukeag River (which flows into Penobscot Bay) and its tributary Wescott Stream may be unique, too, although Dr. King didn't have enough samples to make that determination. "These are only the places we've looked," remarks Maine Trout Unlimited Council chair Jeff

Reardon. "Every place there have been rumors of remnant populations of wild Atlantic salmon we've found them. I think if we look closely at tributaries and small streams that are still in decent shape, we're going to encounter these fish."

When the National Marine Fisheries Service and the Fish and Wildlife Service decided not to list Atlantic salmon as threatened they redefined the "distinct population segment" (an Endangered Species Act designation more relevant and meaningful than "species") from the Down East stocks to stocks from all rivers collected by the Gulf of Maine. But in its 1998 annual progress report the state says that it "is not convinced the conservation plan is the appropriate vehicle for addressing other river runs of Atlantic salmon under the circumstances." And, while the report notes that the state's Atlantic Salmon Authority has the statutory charge to develop a statewide conservation plan, the authority doesn't even have the funds to tend the fish it's already committed to.

As I write, water withdrawal for property owners by the Cobbessee Watershed District is killing hundreds of alevins in Cobbossee Stream, a lower Kennebec tributary where adult Atlantic salmon were seen over redds last fall. These alevins might be pure-blooded Atlantic salmon. Or, as the state correctly notes, they might be brown trout or brown salmon hybrids. The point, however, is that because our distinct population segment of Atlantic salmon is every bit as important to America as, say, our distinct population of grizzlies, its guardian needs to err on the side of caution. Because Maine has never understood this, it is unwilling to fund sufficient salmon staff even to investigate these kinds of potential disasters.

There's no element of doubt about the disasters happening on the Sheepscot and Kenduskeag. The state lets cows walk, wallow, urinate and defecate *in* salmon habitat because, like their crooning, federally subsidized western counterparts, Maine cattlemen "can't stand fences." Last summer there was so much cow dung in the Sheepscot that a state salmon biologist couldn't see his boots while electro-fishing. Bob Wengrzynek of the U.S. Natural Resources Conservation Service has walked, often beside the cows, down the Kenduskeag's 128-mile length from source to tidewater. "At one location over 100 cows were using an access point twenty-five feet wide," he told me. "The stream was dead for a quarter to a half mile because of the nutrient loading. The bottom of that stretch was bombed with cow pies. For a couple thousand yards wherever the sunlight would hit the stream there'd be blobs of algae."

In September 1998 Doug Watts of Augusta, founder of Friends of the Kennebec Salmon, inspected what, according to Wengrzynek, is an "even worse" section of the Kenduskeag. Watts's report: "Attached to each rock and stone in the streambed were five- to ten-foot plumes of olive-green, filamentous algae 'gook.' In many places the algae blooms were so thick they completely covered the stream bottom. A mile upstream I saw the probable source: a feed yard for more than 100 Holstein cattle a few yards from the banks. ... The feed yard was so pounded and mashed by hooves that it resembled a black soup of mud, cow urine and cow manure, all oozing into the stream."

According to Watts, Bond Brook's salmon were allowed to receive the following TLC by the state and the City of Augusta as recently as last December: "Every single tree and shrub was removed along more than 400 feet between Burbank Brook, a Bond Brook tributary which has been turned into a drainage ditch for much of its length by commercial development. ... The brook was clearcut to enhance the visibility of a new stainless steel Denny's Diner."

Watts describes a logging operation on the Marsh River in November 1998: "The loggers had built (gouged is a better word) a makeshift logging road through the stream channel and on top of a coldwater feeder brook to gain access to timber on the other side of the stream. The skidder tires left waist-deep ruts in the soft soil for hundreds of feet up the steep slope, creating a perfect conduit for silt and mud-filled runoff into the stream. The logging operation was located a quarter mile upstream of some of the best salmon and native brook trout spawning habitat in the stream."

Probably the greatest threat to America's last wild salmon is the aquaculture industry. Salmon stocks that evolved in Europe are radically different from those that evolved in North America, a fact that has led to a protocol by the North Atlantic Salmon Conservation Organization (NASCO) to ban their use in the United States and Canada. Canada complies; the U.S. defies. Governor King says there's no problem because the industry will start "containing" its fish. But since the industry obviously has never wanted its fish to escape and since most of the fish returning to the Down East rivers are now escapees, that pronouncement hardly inspires confidence.

In May 1999 I filed a Freedom of Information Act request for all correspondence between Maine Department of Marine Fisheries commissioner George Lapointe and Atlantic Salmon Authority chairman Henry Nichols regarding the proposed Long Island and Bartlett Island aquaculture lease sites. Nichols had urged that European fish not be used "due to the close proximity to the Ducktrap River and Cove Brook and Kenduskeag Stream." The paranoid, ill-informed response by Lapointe cuts through all the purring and posturing of the King administration to expose its real priorities. He accused Nichols of presenting "a position which does not represent the views of all members of the authority" and charged that "since the ASA plans to develop a position statement on aquaculture, we believe your comment letters are premature and should not have been presented as the position of the ASA at this time. The comments in your letters have broad policy implications for salmon aquaculture on a statewide basis and go far beyond specific concerns about the Blue Hill Bay sites."

So poor Ed Baum—Maine's ever-patient, ever-lonely salmon professional who for thirty-one years has presented Maine bureaucrats with facts they don't want to know, had to draft the following response: "The Salmon Board members in attendance authorized the chairman to express all of these concerns to the Maine Department of Marine Resources in the letters which were subsequently drafted. ... I am unaware of any plans by the ASA Board 'to develop a position statement on aquaculture.' ... Considering the large number of board members that there are and the infrequent attendance by some of them, in my opinion it would be impractical to have the board review contents of comment letters that are signed by the chairman."

Now that the Defenders of Wildlife and other environmental groups have filed a lawsuit challenging the legality of the salmon plan, Governor King has averred that the state is doing "everything humanly possible" to save Atlantic salmon and that he will fight the plaintiffs to the bitter end. According to sources in his own administration, his defense will be that the feds and Tim King have it all wrong and that America doesn't really have any unique Atlantic salmon.

Meanwhile, the National Marine Fisheries Service and the Fish and Wildlife Service have about run out of patience. "The Atlantic Salmon Authority," they told the state in a recent review of its progress report, "has several staff experts on Atlantic salmon biology, yet numerous examples are provided where they have not been involved in major decisions that affect the future of this fish. ... This response [on why the state hasn't acted to save wild salmon outside the seven rivers] lacks the needed commitment and delays attention to these rivers and tributaries to an uncertain future date. ... We do not believe that the ASA currently has adequate resources to conduct the necessary Atlantic salmon management activities on the seven rivers."

Trout Unlimited is at the end of its pick pole and kicking logs. "Case law that has subsequently interpreted the [Endangered Species] act has consistently held that voluntary, executory conservation measures such as those in the plan cannot be a substitute for listing," writes Charles Gauvin, TU's attorney president. "Given the state's failure to provide funding to implement the plan during the last 15 months, and its failure to respond to numerous calls for improvements in the plan, it's hard to imagine the State of Maine even coming close to restoring wild Atlantic salmon. Maine has no enforceable fish-health protocol, and even the regulations contained in the restoration plan are completely voluntary and rely on aquaculture operators to report their own violations. Where salmon farming is concerned, the state's approach is 'see no evil, hear no evil.'"

Even the Atlantic Salmon Federation has promised to recommend listing if the state fails to take just one of the following six corrective measures: 1. Assign salmon management to one agency; 2. Manage all wild salmon, not just Down East stocks; 3. Adequately fund the watershed councils; 4. Control all water withdrawals; 5. Ban use of European aquaculture stock; and 6. Site aquaculture cages no closer than twenty miles from salmon rivers. At the end of April, Governor King informed the federation that Maine would not be banning European stocks. So, unless there's a change of heart on either side, the Atlantic

Salmon Federation will recommend listing under the Endangered Species Act. It scarcely seems that five years has elapsed since the federation was scolding RESTORE: The North Woods for doing the same thing.

I guess what it all means is this: There is an excellent reason to have a strong Endangered Species Act. The people who framed the law twenty-six years ago knew what they were doing, and they knew human nature. America's self-induced Atlantic salmon debacle teaches a lesson that no one who's been paying attention needed to learn—that volunteer regulations are effective only in making everyone feel warm and fuzzy. That's why all the toothless endangered species legislation enacted before 1973 failed; and that's why the current statute has been and is a beacon for the nation and the world.

SALMON SHELL GAME

-‹‹· ·››-

I have a Brittany; my son has a German shorthair; my cousin has a Newfoundland. What's more, there are hundreds of thousands of these domestic canids in households all across the United States. Genetically, they are "no more than moderately divergent" from gray wolves, as the policy wonks at National Oceanic and Atmospheric Administration (NOAA) Fisheries—formerly the National Marine Fisheries Service—like to say, whatever that means. In any case, dogs can hybridize with gray wolves and produce fertile offspring. Ergo: gray wolves are no longer endangered.

This is precisely the logic behind a Bush administration policy, released May 28, 2004, proclaiming that Pacific salmon and steelhead trout of hatchery origin can count as wild fish when determining if an ESU (evolutionarily significant unit) needs protection. NOAA Fisheries gets to decide whether the genetics of a hatchery stock are less than or more than moderately divergent from the whole ESU. With no tool for making such a determination and no definition of "moderately" or "divergent," the agency then decrees whether a hatchery stock should be excluded or included. Under the new policy, hatchery fish included in an ESU are counted in assessing population status.

The policy is a return to the thought processes of the early twentieth century when huge federal hatcheries were going to provide all the "mitigation" needed for mega-dams built without adequate fish-passage. As a cure for dwindling salmon runs, hatcheries were as effective as leeches for anemia. Hatchery fish, selected for everything wild fish are not, survived badly. Those that returned suppressed wild fish and spread diseases and defective genes. To make sure hatcheries were full, crews harvested eggs and milt from the first fish that returned, thereby eliminating later runs. Even non-fishermen know that in the Pacific Northwest, hatcheries are the second biggest factor—after the dams that spawned them—in suppressing salmon and steelhead. Can it be that the Bush administration hasn't heard this?

No. The policy was lobbied for by logging, power, livestock and agribusiness interests who, for years, have tried every possible way to get threatened and endangered salmon and steelhead stocks delisted so they can destroy and pollute habitat with impunity. Nothing, until now, has worked. But this brilliant ruse renders habitat obsolete—just keep mass-producing hatchery fish, and there's no need for unobstructed rivers shaded by forests in which water flows all year.

"Hatchery salmon are just as good as so-called 'wild' salmon," explains the Pacific Legal Foundation—the Seattle-based property-rights outfit representing special interests in lawsuits and petitions for delisting. "Millions of fish from each of the five Pacific salmon species are flourishing from Alaska to California. The fact that you can buy salmon for $3.99 a pound in your local supermarket should make that pretty clear."

In 2001 U.S. District Court judge Michael Hogan ruled that NOAA's exclusion of hatchery fish from the listed Oregon coastal coho ESU was arbitrary and capricious. Since then, the administration has repeatedly stated that this decision forced the new policy. But the decision did no such thing. All Hogan said was that if you include hatchery fish in a threatened or endangered ESU, you must list the whole ESU. He didn't say anything about having to include hatchery fish. Hogan ruled that, if the Bush administration so chose, it could separate wild and hatchery fish and list only the former. Another option the administration had would have been to appeal. After all, the Endangered Species Act plainly states that threatened and endangered species must be protected in their "natural habitat."

The Hogan decision precipitated a blizzard of petitions from industry to delist the Oregon coastal coho and fourteen other stocks. A coalition consisting of sixteen organizations, including Trout Unlimited and American Rivers, countered with petitions to list just the wild fish in these fifteen stocks, since Hogan had ruled that this was perfectly permissible. The upshot was a lengthy review by NOAA Fisheries. In 2002 the agency did the right thing, what it had always done: It agreed to count only wild fish. But, after intense pressure from special interests, it flip-flopped.

In March 2004, almost a month before the new policy was made public, six of the nation's foremost fisheries scientists exposed the Bush administration's manipulation and suppression of data. These scientists had been hand-picked by NOAA to serve on its independent Recovery Science Review Panel. In the spring of 2003 NOAA asked them to determine research needs on hatchery issues and advise it concerning how those issues affected recovery for twenty-seven threatened and endangered salmon and steelhead stocks. NOAA liked their advice on research needs. However, when the scientists informed it that hatcheries were not a solution but part of the problem, NOAA told them that this part of the answer wasn't acceptable for a government publication.

So, publicly complaining about being censored, the scientists published their findings in the respected, peer-reviewed journal *Science*. "Hatchery fish usually have poor survival in the wild and altered morphology, migration, and feeding behavior," they wrote. "On release, hatchery fish, which are typically larger, compete with wild fish. Their high local abundance may mask habitat degradation, enhance predator populations, and allow fishery exploitation to increase, with concomitant mortality of wild fish. The absence of imprinting to the natal stream leads to greater straying rates, and that spreads genes not adapted locally."

Less than a month later, with impeccable timing, someone leaked a one-page summary of the new policy to *The Washington Post*, which published it on April 28. Industry and agribusiness moguls were ecstatic. Washington Association of Wheat Growers lobbyist Gretchen Borck, for example, opined to Reuters that salmonid extinction had its good points: "I applaud the people that are trying to save species that are endangered. But it might be good that we don't have dinosaurs now. We've gotten oil from the dinosaurs. If we had preserved the dinosaur, we wouldn't have that oil. Hopefully this will get us a breather from environmental lawsuits."

Also celebrating were Indian tribes, among the most rapacious exploiters of salmon and steelhead, regardless of origin. In an interview with the Associated Press, Charles Hudson, spokesman for the Columbia Intertribal Fish Commission, was quoted as saying: "If you talk about other endangered stock—antelope, condor, for example—they've long used trapping, transporting and artificial reproduction to restore them. For some strange reason salmon have not been allowed that flexibility."

But anglers, fisheries biologists (including many at NOAA), environmentalists and commercial fishermen were aghast. Scientists from NOAA's Recovery Science Review Panel vented in a May 24th telephone press conference sponsored by Trout Unlimited. "They [NOAA scientists] had no idea what the policy announcements were going to be," said Dr. Russell Lande, of the University of California at San Diego. "It came as a complete surprise to them and they actually had to send a list of questions to the policy branch."

Dr. Ransom Myers, of Dalhousie University in Halifax, also a panel member, said that if the policy is not withdrawn, "it's only a matter of time before salmon stocks presently listed are delisted and habitat critical for their long-term survival is eliminated."

Conservation groups like American Rivers quickly weighed in. "Hatcheries aren't habitat," said Rob Masonis, the organization's northwest regional director. "When you remove protections for endangered salmon, you also remove key protections for the rivers they inhabit. This could lead to lower water quality and further degradation of streamside forests, and it could hurt communities and businesses that rely on healthy rivers. Hatchery-reared replacements will never substitute for wild salmon runs since the need for hatcheries indicates a broken river ecosystem."

Bill Bakke of the Native Fish Society summed it all up with: "Politics trumps science."

Remarked Kaitlin Lovell of Trout Unlimited: "This policy circumvents the most basic tenets of the Endangered Species Act and effectively lets the federal government off the hook for any responsibility to recover salmon and healthy rivers and streams."

The National Wildlife Federation's Jan Hasselman accused the Bush administration of "deliberately blurring the important distinctions between wild and hatchery-raised salmon [and] trying to loosen safeguards designed to protect salmon habitat and clean water in the Northwest." Glen Spain of Pacific Coast Federation of [commercial] Fishermen's Associations charged NOAA with "trying to redefine reality" and "turning conservation biology on its head."

Newspapers around the country also pummeled the White House. "The Bush administration has now found a novel way around these [Endangered Species Act] inconveniences," editorialized *The New York Times.* "A new policy on counting fish, its practical effect would be to eliminate the distinction between wild salmon and hatchery salmon, which can be churned out by the millions. This sleight of hand would instantly make wild salmon populations look healthier than they actually are, giving the government a green light to lift legal protections for more than two dozen endangered salmon species as well as the restrictions on commerce that developers and other members of President Bush's constituency find so annoying."

Oregon Governor Ted Kulongoski, condemned the "bleeding in" of hatchery fish to ESUs and explained that his state was committed not just to more fish but to "water quality," "stream banks" and "the general quality of the watershed."

Sen. Maria Cantwell (D-WA) voiced concern that the administration was abandoning science and law in favor of "political expediency" and that the new policy would plunge the region "into uncertainty and conflict through protracted litigation." Rep. Mike Thompson (D-CA) accused the White House of concocting a "recipe for disaster." And he helped draft a letter of protest, signed by seventy-six members of Congress, which rebuked the President and his staff for reneging on "repeated statements that they want to use the best science and resources in all natural resource policy decisions."

If, as has been suggested, the White House leaked the policy on purpose to "test the water," it got some compelling results. The public firestorm elicited a NOAA announcement that it would not, as it had promised just two weeks earlier, "propose relisting at least twenty-five species [sic]." At least not right away.

Crocodile tears gushed from the policy's ghost writers, most notably the Pacific Legal Foundation, which vowed to sue the administration. "We'll let them justify to a judge how they think hundreds of thousands of fish are threatened with extinction," Russell Brooks told the press. Timothy Harris, general counsel of the Building Industry Association of Washington, which is suing NOAA in hope of getting delistings, called the failure to immediately delist "a step backwards" and recycled the old industry and administration untruth that the Endangered Species Act requires hatchery and wild fish to be considered as the "same species."

Still, the strategy of the special interests and the administration was successful and clear. Suddenly it's possible to use hatchery fish to write off habitat, to replace wild water and wild watersheds with concrete raceways. The administration can announce delistings anytime it feels like doing so—which, obviously, won't be before the election. But if there's a second Bush term, the heat will be off, and the administration and its allies will be free to start picking apart trout and salmon habitat.

The likely scenario is that the White House will secretly encourage lawsuits from the Pacific Legal Foundation, then settle in favor of industry or mount token defenses, lose on purpose, and refuse to appeal. That's been its consistent game plan for unraveling other environmental laws— the Clean Water Act, for example. Dr. Robert Paine, of the University of Washington, another member of the Recovery Science Review Panel, explains: "I think that NOAA Fisheries will do as they've said; they're not going to delist some big fraction of these stocks. The implication of that, is it will set into action an increased series of lawsuits by the people who initially pushed the Hogan decision through. ... Then [the administration] is off the hook in terms of responsibility."

American Rivers' Masonis and Trout Unlimited's Lovell are especially worried about a part of the administration's proposal that the angling community hasn't picked up on—counting resident rainbow trout as steelhead. Already NOAA Fisheries has proposed downlisting the endangered Upper Columbia steelhead whose population, it alleges, "includes resident rainbow trout."

"Our fears turned out to have been well founded," says Masonis about the administration's latest fiction that, just because the DNA happens to look the same to bureaucrats who lack the technology to read it anyway, a rainbow is a rainbow is a steelhead.

"If there are lots of resident rainbows, the administration assumes they'll just turn into steelhead and replenish the population," says Masonis. "There's potential here, too, to use hatchery fish to escape listings."

Lovell worries about the "enormous implications" for anglers—who may be prevented from fishing for resident rainbows, which no sober scientist would claim require listing—and for all manner of truly imperiled fish and wildlife that may be denied protection simply because, in segments of their range, they sometimes hybridize with close relatives. At risk of being written off, for example, are any number of cutthroat races, which interbreed with rainbows or other cutts.

"NOAA Fisheries doesn't have the genetics for almost 99 percent of these wild fish," Lovell says. "So when it applies [the new ESU criteria] it uses a whole bunch of 'proxies'—what kind of brood stock did you use, have you been using the same hatchery population, what are your release strategies; are your fish coming back at different times than wild fish?"

In February 2003 more than sixty scientists, including twenty Nobel laureates and nineteen recipients of the National Medal of Science (awarded by the President), provided irrefutable evidence that this salmon shell game is merely business as usual for the Bush administration. The scientists' report, entitled "Scientific Integrity in Policy Making: An Investigation into the Bush Administration's Misuse of Science," charges the administration with "distorting scientific data and suppressing scientific analysis in numerous policy areas, including environmental protection" and "repeatedly censoring and suppressing reports by its own scientists, stacking advisory committees with unqualified political appointees, disbanding government panels that provide unwanted advice, and refusing to seek any independent scientific expertise." One of many examples offered by the scientists was the suppression of an EPA study revealing the dangers of eating mercury-contaminated fish, this at a time when the administration was pushing a major revision of the Clean Air Act that would permit certain coal-fired power plants and refineries to increase pollution.

The Orwellian transformation of hatchery salmonids into "wild" ones is odd policy if, as Mr. Bush and his people profess, they are committed to fish and fishing. While the president isn't into trout or salmon, he has rhapsodized about the joys of going bassing with Ray Scott and bluefishing in his father's cigarette boat. The vice president gushes about fly-fishing for trout in Wyoming. And Bush's interior secretary, Gale Norton—James Watts's old protégé at the Mountain States Legal Foundation—offers the following: "Fly-fishing conjures images of grace, to be sure, but its mastery requires patience and commitment. Less well known, however, and deserving of far greater recognition, is the vital role fly fishers have played and continue to play in conservation in the United States."

Norton, an accomplished abuser of science herself, at least has it right about fly fishers. But she might have added this, perhaps in a note to Trout Unlimited and its allies: "The most vital part of that vital role has been to expose and hold accountable elected officials who sacrifice, for short-term profit, wild salmonids and the water and land that sustains them."

IV
MANAGING/MISMANAGING

SOMETHING'S FISHY

⤜( )⤛

Americans adore fish hatcheries. At their home waters, anglers greet stocking trucks the way kids greet ice cream trucks. At the hatchery itself there's the zoo experience, but beyond that there's the warm feeling of encountering all that rippling energy soon to recharge fresh and salt water, the perception of humankind making nature right again with artificial milk and honey. The Bonneville Hatchery, part of the Bonneville Dam complex in Cascade Locks, Oregon, is even on the National Register of Historic Places. Its fifty-eight concrete raceways (consisting of descending rectangular pools) annually produce about 10 million fall chinook salmon, 400,000 coho salmon, and 250,000 steelhead trout.

On the damp, cold morning of October 30, 2004, the facility is crowded with people as well as fish. Mothers tow snack-munching kids; lovers stroll hand in hand; foreign students photograph one another in front of display tanks. Everywhere there's a low murmur of appreciation. There's a line at the pellet dispenser. Insert a quarter and you get a handful of processed fish chow to throw at adult rainbow trout, kept here for display. They surge upward, making the raceway boil, and when their dark backs cleave the surface, I can see their deformed fins—pectorals and caudals, scarred and rounded by cement, each dorsal nipped to a fleshy stump by the ravenous horde. When I walk along the raceways, the fish follow me like city pigeons. The salmon and steelhead are smaller because they'll be dumped into the Columbia River system as smolts—the juvenile stage that acclimates to salt water, sweeping tail first to the sea. When they go through generating turbines like the ones at Bonneville Dam, they get disoriented and become easy targets for predator fish. In the impoundments there is little current to guide survivors downstream, so they mill around, feeding more predator fish. Trucking and barging them around dams has proven a dismal failure.

Despite its enormous popularity, there's a problem with the Bonneville Hatchery: It doesn't work. Hatcheries, like drugs, can be healing, or hurtful and addictive. They can and do serve as genetic reservoirs, saving species from extinction until habitat is repaired, and they can and do provide fishing in waters where there was never a chance of natural reproduction. But when their mission is to replace habitat degraded by industrial and municipal pollution; siltation from watershed disturbances; loss of streamside shade; and, especially, the construction of dams, they fail.

The Bonneville Hatchery and hundreds of others built to "mitigate" the loss of salmon and steelhead caused by habitat destruction are of the latter sort. Despite their prodigious output—and, to some extent, because of it (although dams are the major culprit)—runs have been declining for more than a century. In the late 1800s Washington State hatcheries produced roughly 4.5 million juvenile chinooks a year; by 1950 they were producing 30 million; by 1968, 93 million. By the 1980s and early 1990s the Columbia alone was being doused with 100 million to 120 million hatchery smolts a year. At that point, wild and hatchery runs in the system had dwindled from perhaps as many as 16 million returning adults to about 2 million. Throughout the Northwest, 159 wild stocks (races adapted to specific rivers) faced extinction. Despite fluctuations caused by varying ocean conditions, runs continue to decline. Even today some hatcheries still measure success not by numbers of adult fish that come back from the sea but by numbers of smolts they stock. As Yogi Berra might say, the bottomless pit just keeps getting deeper.

"A colossal failure of adaptive management" is how Kurt Beardslee, director of the native-fish advocacy group Washington Trout, describes the saturation bombing of Northwest rivers with hatchery fish. "The [state, federal, and tribal] hatchery bureaucracy continues to make the same mistakes over and over and over again, each time expecting a different result," he says. "That's one definition of insanity."

Trout and salmon are not turnips, and if they are to survive in the wild, they cannot be produced like turnips. They are sentient beings with learned survival skills and physical adaptations molded by their environment. For example, to migrate from their natal streams to the Gulf of Alaska or, on the Atlantic side, to Greenland, salmon depend on the sharp, full fins they lose in hatcheries. Wild juvenile salmonids are largely subsurface feeders. Reared on pellets, they become surface feeders, vulnerable to predatory fish and birds. When salmonids detect a moving shadow, they need to flee, not rush forward in hope of getting fed.

In order to fill space and maximize growth, traditional hatcheries take eggs and milt from the first fish that show up in the river, thereby selecting for early returning fish, so that runs naturally staggered throughout most of the year are compressed into weeks. When eggs and milt are taken from hatchery brood stock, progeny can be warped by inbreeding. Wild fish compete for mates and spawning sites, so the fittest are favored. Traditional hatcheries mix eggs and milt randomly. Wild fish have evolved to fit conditions in their rivers of origin; if, for example, a river is fast and steep, the native stock may be lean, with noticeably large fins. But traditional hatcheries play musical chairs with stocks, taking them from one watershed and dumping them in another.

Salmonids reared in traditional hatcheries are selected for domesticity. They adapt to crowded conditions because there is no alternative; they learn not to seek cover because there isn't any. In short, they are molded to be everything wild fish are not.

In a 1970 experiment Montana fish managers stopped stocking a section of the Madison River with hatchery trout. Four years later large trout (three years and older) were up 942 percent. How could this be? After all, the more turnip seeds you stick in the ground, the more turnips you harvest. But again, salmonids aren't turnips. Those produced by hatcheries are relatively short-lived, but because they are reared in conditions that make them fight viciously for food, they survive long enough to eat wild juveniles, outcompete wild adults, and often spread diseases in the process. As a result of the Madison River experiment, Montana no longer stocks its rivers.

All this is not exactly breaking news. John Cobb of the old U.S. Bureau of Fisheries complained about "an almost idolatrous faith in the efficacy of artificial culture of fish for replenishing the ravages of man and animals," and noted that "nothing has done more harm than the prevalence of such an idea." That was in 1917. Have we learned anything since? Well, some of us have, and some of us haven't.

Squarely in the latter group are people making the major decisions. On June 3, 2004, the Bush administration appalled the scientific community—including its own fisheries biologists—by proclaiming that hatchery salmon and steelhead can count as wild fish when determining if a stock needs protection under the Endangered Species Act. To be so counted, said the administration, a domestic hatchery stock must be no more than "moderately divergent" from the wild stock. The domestic chicken is only "moderately divergent" from its progenitor—the endangered jungle fowl. Thanks to Frank Perdue and other factory chicken farmers, there are now millions of chickens on the planet; so by Bush logic, the jungle fowl is fully recovered. The salmon policy is intended to circumvent the Endangered Species Act—the law most loathed by the special interests that brought the Bush administration to power and, to a large extent, comprise it.

The idea to pass off hatchery fish for wild ones was promoted by Mark Rutzick, Bush's former salmon czar at the fish branch of the National Oceanic and Atmospheric Administration (NOAA Fisheries). Rutzick had caught the administration's eye when, as a lawyer in Portland, Oregon, he led the timber industry's effort to avoid regulatory inconvenience with the same shell game. The Pacific Legal Foundation, which provides counsel to plaintiffs seeking delisting of salmonids, has also been pushing for this shell game. "Millions of fish from each of the five Pacific salmon species are flourishing from Alaska to California," the foundation proclaims. "The fact that you can buy salmon for $3.99 a pound in your local supermarket should make that pretty clear."

Foundation attorney Russell Brooks, who met with Rutzick a month before the plan was announced, represented the timber industry in a 2001 case in which U.S. District Court Judge Michael Hogan ruled that the government's exclusion of hatchery cohos from the threatened Oregon coastal coho stock was arbitrary and capricious. The official line from the administration is that its new salmon policy was forced on it by Judge Hogan. But all Hogan said was that once NOAA decided "that hatchery spawned coho and naturally spawned coho were part of the same [evolutionarily significant unit], the listing decision should have been made without further distinctions." He never said that NOAA had to make the decision to lump hatchery and wild cohos together.

A year earlier the agency had asked six of the nation's top fisheries scientists to review salmonid policy, including the use of hatcheries, and to advise it on how best to recover twenty-seven listed stocks. But their report, released five weeks before the Bush plan was made public, contained facts the administration didn't want to know—basically, that hatcheries were counterproductive in salmonid recovery. The scientists were told their findings were inappropriate for a government publication; so, expressing outrage at the censorship, they published their report in the respected, peer-reviewed journal Science. One of the team members—Ransom Myers, of Dalhousie University in Halifax, Nova Scotia—offers this statement: "Unless [the policy is] changed, it's only a matter of time before salmon stocks that are presently listed will be delisted, and habitat that is critical for their long-term survival is eliminated."

Most of this critical habitat has already been lost to dams. Not only have hatcheries failed to mitigate for this loss, but some function as dams themselves. The idea was to block a river so returning fish could be easily captured and stripped of eggs and milt, and so the hatchery would be insulated from disease. This extinguished wild runs and deprived upstream ecosystems of vital nutrients provided by decaying carcasses of spawned-out salmon. Consider the U.S. Fish and Wildlife Service's Leavenworth Hatchery on Washington State's Icicle Creek. It blocks endangered Upper Columbia River steelhead from twenty-one miles of prime spawning and nursery habitat, while dewatering habitat of the threatened bull trout. "This is just outrageous," exclaims Washington Trout's Beardslee. "The agency charged with recovering bull trout is harming them more than any landowner in the entire Wenatchee Basin. Farmers are reprimanded and required to take restorative action if they dewater rivers to raise crops. It's the height of hypocrisy when the agency is doing things every day that the farmers are not allowed to do once." Washington Trout is preparing a lawsuit.

For years the feds refused to remove a series of three deteriorating, useless dam-weir complexes that blocked Icicle Creek, arguing they were "historically significant." Under fierce pressure from the public, they finally relented, appraising removal costs at $4.8 million. Then they announced there was no money. So the Icicle Creek Watershed Council, a local citizens group funded largely by philanthropist Harriet Bullitt, decided to take on the job. In August 2003 the council retained a Spokane contractor, who did the work for $249,000. All that remains is for the feds to open one upstream gate. "The Fish and Wildlife Service was okay with our removing the dams," Bullitt told me. "We followed all their specs and rules; they monitored the job. We finished in five weeks. We revegetated the banks, recycled the rebar and cement. Then we told the hatchery staff to open the gate. We waited and waited, and nothing happened. Now they're telling us that opening the gate is 'against policy.'"

Bullitt and her group are up against something more impregnable than any dam—the hatchery bureaucracy. It has its own political base and social structure; in states like Washington—which churns out salmon and steelhead from nearly 100 hatcheries—it dominates fisheries policy and squashes dissension. "If you cross a sacred cow with a military base in Washington State, you get a fish hatchery," says Bernard Shanks, former director of the Washington Department of Fish and Wildlife, who in 1998 was hounded out of office for merely suggesting that hatchery production be deemphasized.

Collectively, Northwest hatcheries are still a threat to wild salmonids; but they are undergoing major reform—all of it driven by the Endangered Species Act, which holds them accountable for damaging listed stocks. Eggs and milt are increasingly taken from wild fish, and juveniles are often stocked in rivers of origin. Some hatcheries now release smolts at only one location so they won't imprint to other parts of the river where, as returning adults, they'd have more opportunity to spread defective genes. Two years ago Oregon cut the flow of hatchery cohos to its coastal rivers by 90 percent. A few hatcheries, particularly tribal facilities on the Columbia, are experimenting with shade, cover, predator-avoidance conditioning, and curved raceways with sediment on the bottom that produces natural food in the form of macroinvertebrates.

Modern hatcheries, and even most traditional ones, now clip the fleshy, vestigial adipose fin from young salmon and steelhead so adults can be distinguished from wild fish. When commercial or recreational fishermen catch a fish with an adipose fin, they have to let it go. In fact, the adipose fin has become a status symbol, eagerly sought by anglers who didn't want to kill the fish anyway. Rob Masonis, an avid steelheader and northwest regional director for American Rivers, says this: "One of the most encouraging things I've seen in the last five years has been a much greater understanding among anglers of the importance of wild fish and the desire to catch wild fish. They get it; and it's those voices that need to rise up in the policy debate."

Does the hatchery-reform effort hold promise for restoring self-sustaining salmonid runs? Probably not. For one thing, even after one generation, hatchery stock starts losing its reproductive capacity. "My best expectation would be that hatcheries will be reformed to the point they're no longer harmful," declares Jim Lichatowich, former assistant chief of fisheries for the Oregon Department of Fish and Wildlife, and author of the acclaimed book *Salmon Without Rivers*.

So, with hard work and luck, hatcheries may one day cease providing substitutes for the wild salmonids they eliminate and only provide partial mitigation for people prevented by habitat loss from taking wild fish. In other words, they'll become efficient producers of meat and sport. Environmentalists need to understand there's nothing wrong with that. One of the most eloquent advocates of native fish restoration is Jim Martin, Oregon's former fisheries chief and now director of the Berkley Conservation Institute. "Hatchery management has changed tremendously over the last ten or fifteen years," he told me. "But there's just as much hatchery bashing by environmental groups as ever. A lot of fisheries managers in this country are disgusted with the environmental community because no matter how much they do to improve hatcheries, it's not enough. We're not wiping out any cities or reclaiming any farms for wetlands, so we're stuck with a hell of a lot of habitat loss. Hatcheries currently support 70 percent of the anadromous salmonid fisheries in the West. Without them, there'd be very little fishing."

The problem with hatchery bashing is not that there's too much of it but that it's too unfocused, and one reason hatcheries provide so much fishing is that they impede natural reproduction. However, the fact that some hatcheries are grossly abused doesn't mean that others aren't desperately needed. Without hatcheries to hold rare stock all but lost in the wild, there would be no self-sustaining lake trout in Lake Superior.

Greenback cutthroat trout—once believed extinct—would not be almost fully recovered. Utah would not have its Bonneville cutthroats back. There'd be scant hope of saving Snake River sockeye salmon, coaster brook trout, westslope cutthroats, Rio Grande cutthroats, Apache trout, Atlantic salmon, Gila trout, Gila topminnows, and pallid sturgeon. In tailwaters and reservoirs all across the continent, hatcheries provide fishing where none would otherwise exist. In these waters, at least, game fish like trout, landlocked salmon, walleye, and striped bass are stocked as juveniles, growing fast, regaining muscle tone and color. It may not be natural fishing, but at least nature is involved. It gets the public outdoors, invested in clean air and water. Martin is right in everything he says.

But there's more to be said. I object to the hatchery bureaucracy not just for what it does to wild fish but for what it does to people. It creates the illusion—perpetuated by the Bush administration—that habitat is expendable. (Why protect clean, free-flowing rivers and watersheds from dams, pollution, and watershed abuses when you can mass-produce salmonids in concrete fish factories?) And it impedes development of what George Bird Grinnell, nineteenth century sportsman and outdoor writer, and founder of the first Audubon Society, called "a refined taste in natural objects." Anglers conditioned by hatcheries chase stocking trucks like herring gulls, then fish with pellet imitations. It would be cheaper and more efficient to replace the fish tanks in trucks with seats and haul the anglers to the hatcheries.

One bright June morning, amid a blizzard of mayflies called pale morning duns, I worked my way up Utah's Logan River, catching and releasing brown trout. I'd been hoping to add to my life list a Bonneville cutthroat—a descendant of the massive predators, bigger than most salmon, that prowled ancient Lake Bonneville and had been considered extinct until the late 1950s, when they were rediscovered by Colorado State University fisheries professor Robert Behnke. But no Bonneville showed, and I was happy enough exercising the browns—strong, stream-bred fish with perfect fins, ocher spots, and buttercup-yellow bellies. I was reaching down to shake another brown from my barbless fly when I saw what looked like a large goldfish, but which, on closer examination, turned out to be an albino rainbow trout. Despite their extreme vulnerability to predators, the state breeds them and tosses them in with normal, less visible rainbows so the public spots them easily and doesn't complain that the stocking truck hasn't been around.

More recently I found myself in the mountains of West Virginia, inspecting acid-mine damage to brook trout habitat. I came away encouraged, not only by the remarkable progress being made in bringing dead water back to life with innovative lime treatments, but by the many pristine streams that still teem with these gaudy little natives. West Virginia's brook trout are a national treasure that should be promoted. But the official patch of the state's Department of Natural Resources features a white-tailed deer, a cardinal, and a rainbow trout—native to the Pacific Northwest. This fish—called a West Virginia Centennial Golden Trout— is a pigment-impoverished mutant that turned up in a hatchery in 1954 and has been cultured ever since. It's so popular that Pennsylvania borrowed the warped genes to concoct what it calls its "palomino trout."

All sorts of other Frankenstein fish are patched together in hatcheries; and because they're hybrids of species unlikely to meet in the wild and because they're frequently sterile, they help perpetuate the hatchery bureaucracy. These include "tiger muskie" (a cross between a muskellunge and a northern pike), "tiger trout" (brown trout crossed with brook trout), "wiper" (white bass crossed with striper), "saugeye" (sauger crossed with walleye), "splake" (speckled trout crossed with lake trout), and "cuttbow" (cutthroat crossed with rainbow). The more Frankenstein fish that hatcheries pump out, the more demand they create. Conditioned by such values and policy, anglers rebel when enlightened managers attempt to restore imperiled native fish by poisoning out introduced aliens and mongrels.

Just before I left the Bonneville Hatchery, I hiked along its water source, Tanner Creek, starting in the mist beside 350-foot-high Wahclella Falls and moving downstream. I'd almost reached Interstate 84 when I saw a flash of red. A pair of wild coho salmon were spawning. Having never witnessed this, I watched transfixed as the two fish shivered and turned on their sides over the depression the hen had cut in the gravel with her tail. The scene reminded me of what we'd lost but also of the tenacity of the life force, the ability of wild creatures to rebound when given half a chance.

Getting Past Hatcheries

If traditional hatcheries worked, America wouldn't have a salmon crisis on both coasts. Saturating rivers with mass-produced domestic smolts or fry wipes out wild fish through competition and introgression. Traditional hatcheries strip fish of genetic diversity, and—because managers select for early-run fish by taking the first eggs they can get hold of, the better to fill available space—runs are homogenized and compressed so that in rivers where salmon and steelhead migrated throughout most of the year they now blast through in a few weeks. Because domestic stocks do poorly in the real world, adult Pacific salmon of hatchery origin can cost $300 apiece. But there's an additional insult that doesn't get talked about much. Hatcheries physically block migrating fish.

Consider Washington, the nation's most hatchery-dependent state, where ninety-six hatcheries (more than any other state or even the federal government) pump out 300 million fish a year and where the hatchery bureaucracy accounts for fully 25 percent of all Department of Fish and Wildlife employees. "If you cross a sacred cow with a military base in Washington State, you get a fish hatchery," says Dr. Bernard Shanks, the department's former director, who in 1998 was hounded out of office because he dared to gently crusade against traditional hatcheries and aggressively defend wild salmon against overharvest. "Our hatchery system is an entrenched culture complicated by Native American tribes that have treaty rights on runs often dependent on hatchery fish."

For the most part, hatcheries in the Pacific Northwest were built as "mitigation" for wild runs destroyed by dams. Because the managers didn't want pathogens flowing into the hatchery with the water supply, they erected dams and weirs to prevent those nasty wild fish—"feral fish," they call them—from contaminating the water upstream. "You build a hatchery to supplement the runs and then you truncate the runs to protect the hatchery; so you end up paying for something you were getting free, and then the hatchery doesn't work," comments Jim Lichatowich, former assistant chief of fisheries for the Oregon Department of Fish and Wildlife. "A lot of these diseases are secondary problems that result from poor rearing conditions. Everyone has cold germs on them, but they don't get sick unless they're stressed. If the fish in a river can cause disease problems in a hatchery, it would strongly suggest to me that conditions in the hatchery are creating stress. The fish are being crowded or the water isn't right."

In 1991 Washington Trout wrote the first in a series of requests to the Washington Department of Fish and Wildlife, the tribes and the US Fish and Wildlife Service (USFWS) to inventory fish-passage barriers at their respective hatcheries. The tribes and USFWS ignored the requests, but the state complied (though not until 1997), reporting fish-passage problems at thirty-eight hatcheries. "Removal of these things should be a no-brainer, but it almost seems like we can get more cooperation out of real-estate developers than from the fish farmers of the agencies supposedly in charge of salmonid recovery," declares the biologist who first alerted me to the problem. "The real test is whether the state, tribes and Fish and Wildlife Service have the courage to change the hatcheries so that they are relevant and can actually assist in wild fish recovery. ... If we aren't going to change the way we do business, maybe we're better off just folding our tent and starting a dot.com. It doesn't seem to be getting any better. The hatcheries are some of the largest blockages of fish passage in the state. There's very little self-initiative to resolve these problems. The only places we're doing anything is where we're getting pressured by wild-salmon groups."

Such a place is the hatchery on Tokul Creek, a Snoqualmie River tributary that has the highest density of Puget Sound fall chinook redds in the Snoqualmie-Snohomish basin. Since 1990, when a fish ladder at the water-intake dam blew out in a storm, chinooks, cohos, steelhead and resident cutthroat and rainbow trout have been illegally blocked from .7 miles of habitat. According to a report by Washington Trout, "an additional 53 miles of habitat may have historically been accessed by summer steelhead." The facility raises primarily steelhead but also brook trout and introgressed cutthroats and rainbows for stocking high mountain lakes. "But often these lakes have streams that flow into native trout water," says Kurt Beardslee, director of Washington Trout. "We have examples of coastal cutthroat systems that have been devastated by non-native cutthroats. They'll swear that those lakes don't have outlets, but they do. If you can find something that's beneficial about the Tokul Creek hatchery, let me know, will you?"

While the wheels of bureaucracy seem finally to be turning at Tokul because of pressure from Washington Trout, genuine resolution of its fish-blockage might lose a race with a glacier. "We've just concluded a review on capital projects as they relate to hatcheries," explains Doug Hatfield, complex manager for Tokul and four other hatcheries in the Snohomish and Lake Washington drainage. "Because of public interest Tokul has risen from about a third of the way down to number two on the capitals list. We'll be looking for money from the legislature this next session [January 2001]." According to Kevin Amos, the state's chief pathologist, this means that "two or three years" will elapse before any work begins. So exactly ten years after the Tokul Creek hatchery began blocking wild salmonids, the fish-passage project assigned the second highest priority on a list of thirty-eight is still in the talking stages.

Most of the Tokul Creek watershed is owned by Weyerhaeuser, which, under a binding agreement with the state, was required to survey and remove all its blockages. It found thirty-one hanging culverts, promptly fixed thirty; and, if the last one hasn't been fixed by the time you read this, it will be before year's end. If Weyerhaeuser had failed to remove these blockages in a timely fashion, the state—which for a decade has procrastinated on installing fish passage at its Tokul Creek hatchery and still doesn't have a timeline for the project—would have issued the company a citation. The state also requires Weyerhaeuser to leave buffers along Tokul Creek, the largest buffers ever required in the State of Washington. If large, woody debris—vital to the survival of juvenile salmonids—falls into Tokul Creek, Weyerhaeuser can't legally salvage it. Were it to do so, the state would cite it. But when that same debris fetches up on the state hatchery dam, instead of tossing it back into the river on the downstream side, the workers haul it out, cut it up and burn it to heat the hatchery building.

Public outrage seems also to have budged the bureaucracy into some kind of motion at the USFWS's hatchery on Icicle Creek, at Leavenworth,

Washington. But the federal government is moving even slower than the state. The facility was constructed in the late 1930s as mitigation for the 1,400 miles of spawning and nursery habitat cut off by the Grand Coulee Dam on the Columbia River. Two of the hatchery's dams illegally block twenty-one miles of stream, mostly in the Alpine Lakes Wilderness Area of the Wenatchee National Forest. Bull trout (federally threatened) and wild Upper Columbia River steelhead (endangered) are denied access to this stretch. Wild spring chinook (endangered) are denied access to about two miles of it.

Four "diffusion" dams (in which water is released from the bottom) were built above the hatchery along a one-mile stretch to create pools, and each pool was sealed by a weir. This way fish could be held until they were ripe, then netted and stripped. The flow in the holding pools needed to be about 200 cubic feet per second; but in a normal spring Icicle Creek can run at 6,000 cfs, and after one spring storm it hit 14,000 cfs. To keep the fish from getting blown out, a 4,000-foot-long canal was dug with a spillway dam at the bottom so that flood water could be shunted past the holding pools and dumped back into Icicle Creek on the downstream side. In 1979 the USFWS abandoned the diffusion dams and weirs and, below the canal's spillway dam, constructed two holding ponds and a fish ladder running directly into the hatchery. Since then the one-mile stretch has silted in and the dams and weirs have deteriorated to the point where fish could get past them if they weren't blocked by the first diffusion dam they encountered. That dam is equipped with fish ladders, but they're closed. If they were opened, the fish would then be blocked at the top of the one-mile stretch by an iron-gate water-control dam.

A lot of people, including the Yakama Indians and local sportsmen, are more than content with this arrangement because the first diffusion dam concentrates large numbers of fish downstream, and as long as the hatchery gets the 1,800 fish it needs for eggs and milt, it lets Indians and sportsmen help themselves to the surplus, which this year is expected to be about 10,000.

The Yakama Nation has been a leader in the crusade for wild salmon; in fact, it is trying to restore cohos to Icicle Creek. But it wants Leavenworth maintained as a traditional dump-and-strip operation complete with introgressed fish and migration barriers because, as it explains, dams have destroyed most of the other good dip-netting places and it needs salmon for "ceremonial" purposes (although it also does a brisk business selling them on the commercial market). As the tribe recently explained to the USFWS: "The existing barrier dam is an important factor in the success of the fishery. The holding behavior of chinook in the deep pool at the base of the dam allows tribal fishers to use traditional dipnets, as well as hook-and-line, to capture the fish. This is a consistent feature of successful tribal dipnet fisheries, which depend on natural or human-caused obstacles to slow or concentrate the salmon migration. The opening of an efficient passage route around the dam to the upper Icicle may reduce the tendency of salmon to hold, as they do now, at the base of the dam. Experience in the Yakima River basin showed that improving adult fish passage efficiency at irrigation diversion dams reduced the fishing success of tribal members."

Sportsmen also like the big concentration of surplus hatchery fish. And they worry that if endangered chinooks show up in upper Icicle Creek, the feds will shut down all angling. It's possible, I suppose, but elsewhere the National Marine Fisheries Service requires only that wild fish (distinguished from hatchery stock because their adipose fins haven't been chopped off) be released. "It is well known that whitefish fishermen hook steelhead," comments Dick Rieman, of the Icicle Creek Watershed Council, a wild-salmon activist who has tried mightily to get the Fish and Wildlife Service off its butt. "Yet neither the National Marine Fisheries Service nor state has closed the whitefish season on the Wenatchee River." And, if the feds do get spooked about incidental take, Rieman explains, they can always order that Leavenworth hatchery smolts be separated from their adipose fins.

Pushing the USFWS to go slow in removing its illegal fish blockages is none other than the Icicle Valley Chapter of Trout Unlimited. "This [surplus hatchery stock] is all there is left," argues president Doug Allan, "and we should be very stubborn about messing with the one successful gold piece we have left. If I seem a little radical about my one last gold piece, I mean it when I say I will not give it up. Who will stand with me?"

Going slow is one thing hatchery bureaucrats do well. Those who look after the Leavenworth facility have decided that opening the fish ladders on the first of four useless diffusion dams and removing (or maybe just opening) the equally useless water-control dam so that salmonids can gain access to twenty-one miles of traditional spawning and nursery habitat might somehow compromise the natural environment and therefore requires a full-blown Environmental Impact Statement. So they've called in the fluvial geomorphologists, the hydrologists, the hydraulic engineers, the wetlands specialists and all manner of other lofty literati who—by the time they've finished studying the river, canal, dams, weirs, water velocities, seasonal flows, seasonal runoffs, benthic communities, sediments, soils and God knows what else, and then removing the illegal blockages (if that's what they decide to do)—may blow through $4.8 million, according to the USFWS's own estimates. The EIS team will even have to consider impacts on the weirs and dams because two years ago the hatchery got them added to the National Register of Historic Places.

In 1997, when wild salmon activists began nagging the USFWS for action, it recited a litany of defenses for blockage and excuses for torpor. First—until its own disease expert dismissed the argument as nonsense— it claimed it had to protect its introgressed stock from pathogens. Then there was all this hydrogen sulfide that might sweep down and stink up property along the lower river. When this also proved to be nonsense hatchery pooh-bahs fretted about toxic metals, even though the watershed is mostly wilderness and underlain by granite bedrock. Finally, they averred that the Yakamas needed the blocked flood-control canal to imprint cohos. But now USFWS biologists say the sediment holding pond will work just as well.

Most of the dams and weirs deemed by the federal government to be "historically significant" are on property now owned by Harriet Bullitt, a member of the Icicle Creek Watershed Council. When the feds built the hatchery they forced Bullitt's mother to sell them an easement along the one-mile stretch where the holding pools were to be built. "Those structures are on my property," declares Harriet Bullitt. "I own both sides of the river there, and they didn't ask me about this historical stuff. The rules for listing structures on the National Register of Historic Places are very clear. Negotiations have to be with the landowner, not the easement holder. Easements have nothing to do with it. The hatchery has a nature trail. They teach kids about riparian habitats. They let the local ski club run ski trails around the land. They have a salmon festival every year where they celebrate fish. But the wild fish in the river are dying. We would like to see the Fish and Wildlife Service pay more attention to those wild fish."

Bullitt would also like to see the service commit itself as decisively to the defense of natural objects as it has to the defense of unnatural ones. Dams are historically significant only as monuments to human folly. Any fool can make one, and many fools have; but only God can make wild salmonids. What about their historical significance? Wild salmon, steelhead and bull trout don't have time to hang around, abrading their snouts on cement, while hatchery bureaucrats contemplate their navels and hire consultants to count pebbles.

As U.S. Secretary of the Interior Bruce Babbitt likes to say, "In America we do not build dams for religious purposes." Yet to watch how some of his employees worship useless ones, you'd think we did.

WANT ANOTHER CARP?

—‹‹ ·›› —

Under President Clinton the U.S. Fish and Wildlife Service did well compared to its performances under past administrations. There were, of course, high points and low points. This column is about one of the latter. My devout hope is that the Bush administration can use the information to avoid similar disasters, reverse a gross injustice to one of the agency's most talented and dedicated professionals and, in the process, save the Mississippi River system from yet another Asian carp.

In 1990 the Fish and Wildlife Service assigned fisheries biologist Jerry Rasmussen, a fifteen-year agency vet with superb performance reports and eight major awards, to coordinate a new twenty-eight-state organization for cooperative fish management called the Mississippi Interstate Cooperative Resource Association (MICRA). Rasmussen was directed in writing via a memorandum of understanding (MOU) signed by the Fish and Wildlife Service and the MICRA states to "promote MICRA's interests," *not* the interests of the Fish and Wildlife Service as they are sometimes imagined by certain of its senior bureaucrats.

Without even a secretary, Rasmussen built MICRA into a powerful, effective force for fish conservation and restoration. He did everything, even produced MICRA's nationally acclaimed bimonthly publication, *River Crossings*. To the man, the state fisheries chiefs, who represent their agencies at MICRA meetings, adored him. In 1994 he received personal letters of commendation from Secretary of the Interior Bruce Babbitt and Vice President Al Gore. In 1995 he became one of the few federal employees ever to get the American Fisheries Society's coveted President's Conservation Award. With one of the twelve agency awards for his work at MICRA came a letter signed by regional director Sam Marler and Assistant Regional Director John Christian which read in part: "We are stretched very thin, and some dedicated federal employees respond to this challenge by working smarter and for longer hours than can be reasonably expected. They commit more of themselves for the resource than their job requires."

But in helping the twenty-eight states in their effort to stop the aquaculture industry from infecting the Mississippi drainage with a *fourth* Asian carp Rasmussen committed a bit more of himself than some people in the Fish and Wildlife Service's Washington office had counted on. By doing his job—that is, telling the truth about the black carp, largest and most ecologically dangerous of the imported Asian carps and helping the MICRA states defend themselves against it—he so irritated the industry that it complained to U.S. Senator Blanche Lincoln (D-Arkansas) who had worked for Clinton when he was governor. On July 24, 2000, Sen. Lincoln hauled Fish and Wildlife Service Director Jamie Clark into her office and sat her down in front of the two industry spokesman who had set up the meeting and who also had worked for Clinton while he was governor.

The spokesmen were black carp producer Mike Freeze of England, Arkansas, and Ted McNulty, vice president for agriculture and aquaculture at the Arkansas Development Finance Authority. Neither man had been shy about letting Clark know how he felt. "I want to voice my objection to USFWS subsidizing a radical and uninformed organization such as MICRA," McNulty had written in response to a notice she had posted in *The Federal Register* soliciting comments on a proposal to list the black carp as an injurious species under the Lacey Act. "Taxpayer money is being spent to post lobbying positions on a government web page and to accuse people trying to make a living of being selfish. At best this is a waste of money and might be considered illegal. I ask that the USFWS immediately sever all connections with MICRA and end its memorandum of understanding with the MICRA states immediately."

Freeze told me this: "The meeting began when she [Clark] turned to Senator Lincoln and said she'd discovered that one of her employees had been involved in some activity she didn't approve of and that she intended to make sure that type of activity didn't occur again." The day after the meeting Clark ordered that Rasmussen be removed from MICRA. Simultaneously, the service withdrew MICRA's funding and voided the MOU with the states. At this writing MICRA has no federal coordinator and is more or less in limbo.

The charge against Rasmussen (conflict of interest) was first raised by USFWS fisheries chief Cathleen Short, a delegate to MICRA who never bothered to attend a single meeting, even when she was in the same building on the same day. Short claimed that Rasmussen had helped the twenty-eight states prepare a petition to his own agency (the Fish and Wildlife Service) to list the black carp as injurious. It was true. But it was also true that Rasmussen's written orders in the MOU required him to do precisely this—i.e., "promote MICRA's interests." Before Clark got leaned on by the "Arkansas Mafia" (as some Fish and Wildlife Service personnel now refer to Sen. Lincoln and her Clinton-connected aquaculture constituents) and while the MICRA states were still preparing their petition, Rasmussen met with or spoke with his supervisors dozens of times and never once was the issue of conflict of interest mentioned.

Getting twenty-eight states to agree on anything, much less a strongly worded petition on the dangers of an alien fish, should have been grounds for yet another award. Instead Washington demanded Rasmussen's head on a platter. At this point the regional office stepped in, asking that it be allowed to at least reassign him to an invisible position at the Rock Island, Illinois office of the La Crosse, Wisconsin Fishery Resource Office. In agency doublespeak, he was being shielded from "a situation that could be perceived as conflict of interest." So when I asked Short about Rasmussen's treatment she was able to accurately state: "That really was a regional decision and a regional action." Then she said, not so accurately, that her "whole involvement has been relative to the petition to list black carp under the injurious wildlife provision of the Lacey Act."

According to the Public Employees for Environmental Responsibility (PEER), which came to Rasmussen's defense, he has been ordered not to talk to anyone, especially the press. However, I had no trouble getting information from his many friends and colleagues inside and outside federal government, among them Dennis Riecke, a fisheries biologist with Mississippi Department of Wildlife, Fisheries and Parks.

"We were told [via the feds] you don't talk to him," says Riecke. "That's bullshit. Someone who's not my employer is gonna tell me *I can't talk to someone in the United States?*"

It was Riecke who blew the whistle to MICRA about what was going down in Mississippi where, as in so many other southern states, resource agencies run and jump for aquaculture as if they were circus poodles. To understand the black carp crisis in Mississippi you have to go back ten years to when Donald Robohm, president of SeaChick fish farm in the south coastal town of Escatawpa, wanted to raise tilapia—a sunfish analogue from Africa which was already wreaking ecological havoc in Florida. When Robohm, a prolific and passionate letter writer, was informed that state law prevented this, he took his case to the legislature which promptly changed the law. The best the state could do was require him to install screens and filters to guard against escapement, which is about like guarding against an amphibious landing by planting poison ivy. In short order the tilapia were loose and reproducing in the Thompson's Branch of the Pascagoula River, where they remain to this day. It was the fault of ospreys, says Robohm. When the mouth-brooding male tilapia get taloned they spew fry over any water that happens to be underneath.

Wildlife, Fisheries and Parks sent down a crew which made an unsuccessful attempt to eliminate the naturalized tilapia with rotenone, removing six truckloads of the aliens along with just one bucket of native fish. When the department revoked Robohm's tilapia permit temporarily (today he's probably the biggest producer in the state) he claimed he was being abused and took his case to the legislature, which promptly transferred regulatory authority for fish farms to the Department of Agriculture. So when Mississippi catfish farmers started playing with black carp there wasn't a thing Wildlife, Fisheries and Parks could do except give advice to the Deparatment of Agriculture, an outfit that doesn't care much or understand much about aquatic ecosystems.

Pack any species together in tight quarters and parasites are going to flourish. Three years ago a trematode which moves from pelicans to ram's horn snails to fish started killing a few commercially raised channel cats. Black carp, which can grow to six feet and 154 pounds, eat snails and mussels; so they can break the cycle by cleaning out the ram's horn snails in a fish pond. Chemical alternatives such as copper sulfate and lime are available, but they're more expensive and perhaps less effective. Native molluscavores such as redear sunfish, blue catfish, and freshwater drum might also work, but they've not been evaluated. After black carp wipe out the snails and mussels (except for zebra mussels, which they can't pick off structure), they eat crustaceans (such as crawfish) and God knows what else. The threat to native fish, many of which depend on mollusks and crustaceans, is significant; the threat to freshwater mussels—the most endangered group of animals in North America—is enormous. Waterfowl such as canvasback ducks feed heavily on the fingernail clams of the Mississippi system. If black carp get established there, these already stressed ducks will take a hit from which they may not recover.

An "injurious" listing for the black carp isn't going to mean a whole lot because the species is already in the country being propagated in research and production facilities in Arkansas, Florida, Louisiana, Mississippi, Missouri, North Carolina, Oklahoma, Texas and maybe elsewhere. Although black carp haven't yet turned up in the wild, they may already have escaped into the Mississippi system from a catfish farm in Missouri. At least injurious-species status would proscribe future importation from Asia and impede (but not stop) interstate transport.

Farmers of channel catfish contribute about $500 million a year to the U.S. economy or about half the volume of the entire aquaculture industry. What catfish farmers want, catfish farmers get; and what they want is black carp. The Mississippi Department of Wildlife, Fisheries and Parks pled with the state Department of Agriculture to at least make the catfish industry use sterile ("triploid") black carp, not that this is much protection because in order to make triploids you have to have fertile "diploids," and virtually every hatchery in existence has had fish escape from it. Also, fish may be mistakenly certified as triploid when they're actually diploid. But diploids, explained the Department of Agriculture, are cheaper and more readily available, and the industry just *had* to have them. So Mississippi catfish farmers are flinging black carp around the state and even importing them from Arkansas.

"If we could remove Arkansas from the Mississippi drainage, we'd be a long way to improving conditions for some of our native fish," declares MICRA member and past chairman Marion Conover, chief of fisheries for the Iowa Department of Natural Resources. It was Arkansas and its fish farmers that gave us the other three Asian carps—grass (now extant in forty-five states), silvers, and bigheads. The grass carp were going to eat aquatic weeds. The silvers and bigheads were going to clean up pollution by eating phytoplankton and zooplankton respectively. The industry assured all hands that it wouldn't let them escape, and if by some act of God or osprey they did escape, it assured all hands that reproduction in North America would be impossible.

Today in parts of the Mississippi River commercial fishermen can't lift their nets because they're so full of bighead carp. In October 1999 a Fish and Wildlife Service biologist investigating a fish kill on a Mississippi backwater in southern Illinois counted 157 silver carp, 18 bighead carp, nine grass carp, 30 common carp, and one individual each of five native species. On a recent visit to find what swims in the waters of Mark Twain's mighty Mississippi a Japanese film crew encountered acres of carp rolling and leaping, occasionally landing in their boats. One cameraman got hit on the head.

"We prohibit black carp in Iowa," says Conover. "But we can't keep them from swimming up the Mississippi River. We prohibited bigheads, too, and we have millions of pounds of them. Ted McNulty and the whole industry have it exactly backward. They say that unless you prove black carp are harmful they should be allowed to use them. They stuffed that down our throat in St. Louis at a MICRA meeting we hosted with the catfish farmers. They're in tight with [Sen.] Trent Lott [R-MS] and other politicians, and they're just going to walk right over the natural resource agencies."

Such walking was recently accomplished by another prolific and passionate letter writer, one Pete Kahrs of Osage Catfisheries, Inc., Osage Beach, Missouri. By persuading the state Department of Conservation's policy-setting commission (comprised of lay people) to "reign in," as he puts it, the professional fish managers, he got the department to raise black carp for him. This despite the fact that his fish farm was the one from which black carp may have escaped into the Mississippi system (via the Osage and Missouri rivers) after flood waters swept over the ponds in 1994. "Three fish were unaccounted for," Kahrs told me. "But maybe they died." Anyway, he says, black carp are now being widely and inadvertently distributed throughout the Midwest with baitfish from

Arkansas. The fact that black carp haven't been seen in the wild doesn't prove anything because they look so much like grass carp that they may have gone unnoticed. At least the state will be providing him with triploids, and it vows to wean him (and the other fish farmers who will get the fish) within five years so that the state can be "black-carp free."

Kahrs, McNulty and Freeze have attacked Rasmussen for using "inflammatory" language and publishing "misinformation" in *River Crossings*. Wrote Kahrs in one of his letters, this to Anita Gorman of the Missouri Department of Conservation Commission: "MICRA posts lobbying positions on government web pages using state and federal electronic mail, to accuse people, i.e., private taxpayers trying to make a living in the aquaculture industry, as 'selfish' and 'whose only interest is the financial gain of the few' as it relates to the use of black carp."

Rasmussen's exact words in *River Crossings* were as follows: "All of the Asian carps will thus likely be thought of by our grandchildren as 'natives'; and even worse, our grandchildren may never see or know that species such as the paddlefish, buffalo, and others ever existed—all because of selfish, self-serving decisions made for the benefit of a few people in the late 1900s!" If that statement is inflammatory, it's because it's the exact truth. Moreover, I'd say it's about time federal resource managers started talking that way! If more of them did, they'd get more respect and our fish and wildlife wouldn't be going down the tubes so fast.

"Jerry did the right thing," comments MICRA chairman Bill Reeves, chief of fisheries, for the Tennessee Wildlife Resources Agency. "He stood up for the resource, and he got punished for it. I didn't know that people in federal service got treated like that. All us fish chiefs have talked to each other about it, and we agree that Jerry did what any good employee for the Fish and Wildlife Service would do. He's a go-getter. He's always been a credit to the service. He's dedicated; he's passionate about big rivers and riverine resources. And that passion and desire to do good is what got him in trouble. When this black carp issue came up in Mississippi, allowing fish farmers to utilize diploid black carp, MICRA took it up as an issue. I told everyone that, since I'm the chair and not from a catfish-producing state, I could be used to take the heat. And that worked well until that delegation from Arkansas went to visit Senator Lincoln."

Marion Conover agrees. "I think I can speak for hundreds of professionals that Jerry was a casualty of fish politics," he says. "It wasn't handled correctly at all, and certainly he had done nothing wrong. It's sad when one contact with a senator can do that. But it wasn't just Jerry. As far as I'm concerned the twenty-eight state partners got dumped on big-time by the Fish and Wildlife Service. There was no consulting with MICRA, no follow up, no questions. The decision was made with no input from states."

I find it astonishing that, after trashing our aquatic ecosystems with hundreds of alien species, including three Asian carps and a European carp, we are now arguing about reintroducing a *fifth* carp. Over the past century we've unleashed at least 135 alien species on the Mississippi system alone. Measured just by dollars, this has been a national disaster. But we've learned nothing. We still talk about miracle fish from abroad which are going to eat all the bad stuff and leave all the good stuff. We wander down expressways like sleepwalkers; and when smart, tough resource professionals such as Jerry Rasmussen yell at us to wake up we still round them up and ship them to Siberia.

As Marion Conover observes, we've got to forget about proving a species is "injurious" and banning it and, instead, ban everything that we *haven't* proved harmless. The regulatory framework for preventing infestations of alien species is hopelessly inadequate. We need new federal legislation. And, more than that, we need the courage and decency to stand behind the good people who try to show us the way.

FISH-POISON POLITICS

⤙( )⤚

The most beautiful creature in Massachusetts, if you ask me, abides in Hyla Brook, an icy rill bright with cowslips and watercress, undefiled by hatchery trucks and, because Boston drinks it, embraced by big, roadless woods. And I'll go on to opine that the ugliest creature in Alberta abides in Moraine Lake—the fifty-acre slab of polished turquoise you used to see on Canadian $20 bills. In both cases I'm talking about fish—the same fish, the brook trout. Before managers started flinging them around the continent like wedding rice, they used to call them "eastern brook trout."

Native ecosystems, like great works of art, can be rendered repulsive when smashed and smeared. Treasuring them is hardly a new or radical idea. More than fifty years ago Aldo Leopold advocated it when he called for an "ecological conscience." More than a century ago George Bird Grinnell, editor of the sporting weekly *Forest and Stream*, advocated it when he called for "a refined taste in natural objects." Today America and the rest of the world value fish and wildlife more than ever, but anything will do; there is scant concern for the conservation of genes or the sanctity of species.

One would expect that sportsmen, because they interact more directly with nature, would lead the effort to repair native ecosystems. Certainly this would be in their best interests. For one thing, fish and wildlife generally do better in their native habitats than do aliens that evolved elsewhere; witness, for example, Colorado's robust greenback cutthroat trout in the streams formerly polluted with scrawny, stunted browns, rainbows, hybrid cutts and brookies. But "better" means much more than increased size and condition of quarry. In healthy, native ecosystems the acts of hunting and fishing take on new meaning and significance; the sportsman becomes a true participant in nature instead of just another interloper in a ruined system.

Some sportsmen are indeed leading the way, but the majority can't educate the ecologically illiterate because they qualify as such themselves. With only a few exceptions, the sporting press doesn't provide them with useful information but instead plays to their fears and superstitions, the better to hawk ad space. Meanwhile, the chemophobic general public—no better served by its media—imagines that the short-lived and utterly benign chemical piscicides rotenone and antimycin are somehow going to pollute their surface and even ground water.

Where fisheries professionals have not been hamstrung, their work with chemical piscicides has produced spectacular results. In California alone, Little Kern and Volcano Creek golden trout, as well as Lahontan and Paiute cutthroats, owe their continued existence to the use of rotenone by state and federal agencies. In 1992 Utah spent $3.7 million applying 878,000 pounds of powdered rotenone and 4,000 gallons of five-percent liquid rotenone to Strawberry Reservoir in order to provide a sanctuary for Bonneville cutthroat-presumed extinct until they were rediscovered in a few desert streams that still run into the dry basin of ancient Lake Bonneville. Today the wild Bonnevilles—which grow much larger than the introgressed and ill-adapted alien trout that had formerly populated the reservoir—provide a sport fishery worth $6 million a year.

The bull trout—a big, square-jawed char of western North America—is listed as threatened in the United States and as a "species of special concern" in Canada. One of its major problems (virtually its only problem in Canada's Banff National Park) is genetic swamping by brook trout. Brook trout—stocked in the days when managers, too, were ecologically illiterate—have taken over most of the park's streams and lakes. To its credit Canadian Heritage, the federal agency that oversees national parks in Canada, has decided that Banff's Moraine Lake should be as beautiful on the inside as it is on the outside. In 1997 it announced that the park should restore bull trout, Alberta's provincial fish. In order for this to happen brook trout and introgressed cutthroats and rainbows will have to be removed. Physically, the task won't be difficult. For one thing, it's a headwater lake and its three feeder streams are too cold to support the alien trout with which it has been defiled. For another, it's small and easily accessible by truck and snowmobile. Politically, however, the task may be impossible.

If you would like to learn about proposed bull trout restoration in Moraine Lake, don't read *Real Fishing Magazine*. "Trout genocide" and "ethnic cleansing" is what editor Craig Ritchie calls it. "No one," he wrote in the April 2000 issue, "knows how long it will take insects, amphibians, plants, aquatic invertebrates, birds and other creatures that will be killed off in the process to repopulate-or even if they will."

But people who read the literature do know. Amphibians, few of which are killed by rotenone and fewer still by antimycin, bounce right back, as do the few insects and other invertebrates that are killed. Piscicides don't affect birds or plants, though I suppose it's conceivable that a plant or two or a bird or two might be killed if explosives are used in conjunction with chemicals. The real motive of Parks Canada, Ritchie averred, is that it "wants to outlaw fishing, and this is a way of pushing it through." But fishing—including catch-and-release for bull trout—is part of Banff National Park's plan, a plan approved by Parliament. The park couldn't change that plan even if it wanted to; and it doesn't want to, says Charlie Pacas, the biologist who will head bull trout restoration if it ever happens. Ritchie says he never contacted Pacas or any other Banff official (the only thing Pacas agrees with him on). However, Ritchie did tell me he erred in reporting that TU Canada (which he also failed to contact) is an enthusiastic accomplice in the proposed trout genocide. He says he's since learned that "TU is very much opposed." But even this turns out to be untrue. While TU Canada heartily endorses "recovery efforts for native species at risk such as bull trout," it has no official position on what's been proposed for Lake Moraine, because there is as yet no written plan.

Ritchie has succeeded in whipping up Citizens for Private Property Rights, based in Santa Ysabel, California. "Brook trout," the group sardonically proclaims, "are bad, evil trout and must be eliminated and … bull trout are ever so much more precious in God's eye." And the Canadian Taxpayers Federation echoes Ritchie in calling bull trout restoration "ethnic cleansing." The Canadian Alliance Party calls the proposal "obscure" and worries that it could offend "the animal-rights people," not explaining why anyone should care. If the Canadian Alliance Party cares, then it has reason for concern: People for the Ethical Treatment of Animals—whose members don't give a damn what kind of animals inhabit the planet so long as none of them die—calls the proposal "cruel" and declares that it is "unconscionable" to kill one species so that another may live.

When I interviewed Brad Bischoff, the media point man at Banff, he seemed jumpy as a dusted grouse. "Any decision we make will be posted for public comment, and no final decisions are going to be made until those public comments are reviewed," he told me. About the third time he said the park hadn't made any final decision, I began to wonder if it ever would.

Neither an ecological conscience nor a refined taste in natural objects is more apparent south of the Canadian border. American sportsmen, flimflammed by special interests and deceived by their own media, are in a hissy fit about Montana's proposal to create a seventy-seven-mile sanctuary for westslope cutthroat trout on upper Cherry Creek—a Madison River tributary currently infested with brook trout and introgressed rainbows and Yellowstone cutts. Herewith, some brief background: Westslope cutts, petitioned for threatened status under the Endangered Species Act, have been eliminated from all but two percent of their historic range in the upper Missouri River system. The Montana Department of Fish, Wildlife and Parks—among the nation's more enlightened state resource agencies—has committed itself to a recovery plan whereby ten healthy westslope populations will be established in five distinct drainages, each at least fifty miles long. "We'll keep monitoring for surviving fish, and if necessary, we'll do more treatments," says project leader Pat Clancey. "Right now we plan on doing treatments two years in a row." While the department hopes to avoid the expense and red tape of federal listing, its commitment to the project is based on the belief that saving this lovely and unique subspecies is simply the right thing to do.

Because of a twenty-five-foot waterfall on its downstream end, the project area had been fishless until about eighty years ago, when it was first stocked with trout. So critics are correct when they say westslopes were never part of upper Cherry Creek's native fauna. On the other hand, westslopes belong in the Missouri watershed; rainbows, brookies and Yellowstone cutts do not; and there aren't many good barrier-equipped westslope sanctuaries available. The naturalized aliens now caught in the system evolved in lower, warmer, wetter conditions; a fish of twelve inches is a trophy. I've fished smaller streams where westslopes average twelve inches.

If you seek balanced perspective and accurate information on the project, don't read *Outdoor Life*, which in June 1999 ran an article with the inflammatory and misleading title "Playing God on Cherry Creek." The text, also inflammatory, relies heavily on sources who lack scientific credentials (but not opinions) and recycles their rumors, often with no attribution. For example, it states that if a bear eats the poisoned fish, "it could become sick." Decades of scientific literature demonstrate that this is nonsense. "Both antimycin and rotenone will also exterminate the stream's aquatic insect populations," it asserts. But these chemicals kill very few insects, and populations that are reduced recover in a few months. It wrongly reports that "a lawsuit has been filed to halt the project on the grounds that it violates the federal Clean Water Act." Then in a grotesque mime of objective journalism, the editors invite readers to vote for or against the project. Surprise: 98 percent were opposed.

Readers of *Range* Magazine were served as badly. In the Winter 2000 issue the Forest Service, a partner in the project, is accused of "contradicting" the Wilderness Act; but the act provides for exactly this sort of management. The article asserts that if even one of the grayling that were once stocked in Cherry Creek (and never again seen alive) turns up dead, the project "would be illegal on its face, directly afoul of the Endangered Species Act." But grayling aren't even listed. Range reports that Fish, Wildlife and Parks failed to procure "a discharge permit that the Clean Water Act requires before any foreign 'pollutant' can be put into waters." But such permits aren't needed for chemical piscicides. Range reports that Cherry Creek "could be used as a natural hatchery, providing highly adapted eggs to help restore Yellowstone cutts to other, similarly demanding high-country environments." But the resident cutts are mongrels and don't belong in this part of the state anyway. When I asked Clancey why he hadn't explained all this to *Range* Magazine he said that no one from the publication had ever contacted him or anyone else in the department.

Instead, *Range* relied on rumors and fatansy provided by the two maestros of opposition—William Fairhurst, president of the Public Lands Access Association, and attorney Alan Joscelyn, who represents Montana's cyanide, heap-leach mines. By filing an appeal with the state Board of Environmental Review, Fairhurst and Joscelyn managed to keep the project from proceeding on schedule in 2000; and, although the appeal was dismissed last September, the board has put a stay on restoration work so Fairhurst and Joscelyn can take their case to district court. If they do this, and apparently they intend to, they may delay restoration yet another year. Fairhurst is in a snit because something like 70 percent of the project area is on the ranch of media mogul and fish-and-wildlife restoration hero Ted Turner who, like many Montanans, doesn't invite the general public onto his land and who is picking up $343,350 of the project's $475,000 tab. Joscelyn has fleas in his shorts because Turner funds the environmental groups that keep suing the polluters he represents. Ted Turner, Fairhurst tells the press, is "playing God in Montana." He submits that westslope restoration on Cherry Creek is actually a plot keep the public out of the entire watershed.

Fairhurst recently joined the Montana Mining Association, which has come out against westslope restoration on grounds that the project supposedly will "poison a public water supply"—even though the association has successfully lobbied for weaker water-quality standards and even though its members have done plenty of water poisoning themselves. "The enemy of my enemy is my friend," Fairhurst told *The Bozeman Chronicle*. In July 1999, when Jill Andrews was the Mining Association's director, she revealed her outfit's real motive in a statement to *The Montana Standard*: "He [Turner] funds 350 of those [environmental] organizations. They oppose almost everything we try to do."

The entire quantity of chemicals from which Fairhurst, Joscelyn and the Montana Mining Association say they want to protect the public is twenty gallons of antimycin and ten gallons of rotenone, to be delivered to the main stem and all feeder streams of the seventy-seven-mile-long drainage over the course of two years. The stuff breaks down in hours and isn't toxic to people. Chemical control of unwanted fish by professional managers has been happening in North America since 1934 without a single documented human injury.

Today most managers most managers perceive the importance of native ecosystems, but when they try to restore them they often get lynched by the mob. In 1994, pike, unleashed by some bucket biologist, turned up in 4,000-acre Lake Davis, which supplies water to about 2,500 people in north-central California. The lake—extremely fertile and, in its shallow sections, full of aquatic plants—is the quintessential pike factory; and it connects to the San Joaquin and Sacramento River systems, where endangered races of chinook salmon and steelhead still cling to existence. Accordingly, the California Department of Fish and Game launched an expensive but practical plan to rotenone Lake Davis, after which it would stock rainbows that grow as fast in the lake as they do in the hatchery. This time sportsmen were on board, but from the way the general public reacted you'd have thought the state had proposed atmospheric nuclear testing.

As Fish and Game prepared to deliver the rotenone in October 1997, locals held protest marches and all-night candlelight vigils along the lake shore. "Burn in Hell, Fish & Game!" shrieked one placard. Some protesters wept; others cursed; still others donned wetsuits and swam out into the 52-degree water, where they chained themselves to a buoy. When Fish and Game agents unchained the swimmers, shore-based protesters shouted, "Shame, shame." For crowd control the state deployed 270 uniformed officers consisting of Highway Patrolmen, game wardens, Fish and Game biologists and technicians, and deputies from the Plumas County Sheriff's office. A two-man SWAT team took up positions on a water tank.

As frequently happens with big fish reclamations, not all the rotenone was neutralized as it flowed down the outlet, and some hatchery rainbows and browns expired along several miles of Big Grizzly Creek, which hadn't been fit for even stocked trout before the dam went in. It wasn't a big deal, basically a cost of doing business. But the Plumas County District Attorney filed criminal charges (promptly dismissed) against Fish and Game and three of its employees. The City of Portola filed a $2 million claim in preparation for a civil lawsuit alleging that the state deprived citizens of their right to safe drinking water. The Central Valley Regional Water Quality Control Board hit Fish and Game with a $250,000 administrative fine, which it was allowed to pay by stocking extra trout (many more than it had accidentally killed) and doing habitat restoration along Big Grizzly Creek. A sign over a Portola restaurant proclaimed: "We don't serve Fish and Game." Angry, grossly ill-informed locals pushed through a law stipulating that henceforth the Department of Health Services, not Fish and Game, would be in charge of any chemical treatment of drinking water.

The hassle, horrendous though it was, seemed to have been worth it. The endangered Sacramento and San Joaquin salmonids appeared to be safe from the saber-tooth aliens. But then in May 1999 pike—stocked by angry residents or missed by the rotenone—again turned up in Lake Davis. After a five-year pummeling by the public and the press, Fish and Game had no more belly for confrontation, and who can blame it? The ignorati had won. Now the department proposes a "multi-faceted" plan—devised by a team dominated by city, county and state bureaucrats who wouldn't know a trout from a pout—whereby pike are to be removed by barriers, drawdowns, explosives, electro-fishing and nets. Fish and Game admits that the plan won't eliminate pike, just knock them way down. But removing most of an alien population is like amputating most of a gangrenous appendage; it doesn't accomplish a whole lot.

Here, from a letter to the California Fish and Game Department, is what the California–Nevada chapter of the American Fisheries Society thinks of this approach: "We believe any action less than eradication is in violation of state law and biologically and ecologically irresponsible. … It is clear to us that little or no sound fishery science has been used to develop this plan. It appears the Department has adopted objectives, control techniques, and monitoring programs based on consensus of non-biologists. In doing so, the Department has abdicated its legal and professional responsibilities."

Too bad that fisheries professionals are getting beaten down as they labor to repair the remnants of humanity's only real wealth. Strange that the public should pay for the education of fisheries professionals, pay for their salaries and benefits, pay for their buildings and equipment, then push them aside and undertake fisheries management itself. But not at all strange that native fish should then flicker out.

BIG WATER BLUES

⤙ ⤚

On the last morning of winter 2001 I stood four miles out in Lake Okeechobee—the shallow, rich 470,000-acre heart and lungs of the Everglades and second largest freshwater body wholly in the United States. Behind me, to the north, flushing Florida's prairie country, were the Kissimmee River and other arteries straightened and cut off from their spongy floodplains. In front of me, on the distant southern shore and beyond—all blocked from view by water draped over the curving Earth—lay the sparse, working-class communities of Clewiston and Belle Glade, sprawling sugar cane plantations, the Everglades, and Florida Bay.

I saw none of the high grass that had ringed the lake before it was re-plumbed by humans. And I could only imagine the custard apple and moonvine jungle that had dominated the southern rim and the dense forest of cypress, water oak, popash, maple, and palmetto to the north where beef cattle now cycle alien Bahia grass, dairy cows convert silage to milk and phosphorus, and chemical-addicted orange trees goosestep along chalk-lined rows. The vegetation around the lake had been so impenetrable, and the land so wet, that the basin wasn't even circumnavigated until 1883. This was America's last frontier—through the nineteenth century wilder and less known than Alaska. Okeechobee, which means "Big Water" in Seminole, had been semi-mythical to whites until Christmas Day 1837, when Colonel Zachary Taylor proved its existence by chasing the tribe into a trap they'd set for him on its northern shore.

Flanking me in the lake were two of its most tireless and effective advocates—fisheries biologist Don Fox of the Florida Fish and Wildlife Conservation Commission and Paul Gray, manager of Audubon's Lake Okeechobee Sanctuaries. Hosed by near-horizontal rain—the first significant precipitation in six months—we slogged toward the surviving portion of Audubon's Indian Prairie Marsh over acres of white mussel shells, through wet muck, up onto cracked muck, and finally onto a high, brushy berm that now seals the marsh from the life-giving lake.

We had swerved and skidded our way here from a mudflat called Little Grassy ten miles to the north and two miles offshore. In 1988 the lake wind over Little Grassy had tussled the tops of bulrushes, sending green waves sweeping across their 250-acre expanse. But about that time the U.S. Army Corps of Engineers decided to raise the lake one foot—to 15.5 feet above sea level—because, well, the water might be needed by thirsty sugar cane, citrus, and Gold Coast lawns. More than a decade of high water had drowned the bulrushes, reducing them lakewide from 10,000 acres to about 700. At Little Grassy, where there had been about 18 million stems, there were just 188 by April 2000. The victims' remains, along with other emergent plants living and dead, had been ripped up by waves and pushed into the shallows to form the berm.

The mud the plants had once held in place—and the algae proliferating on the nutrients they used to eat—blocked sunlight, so that 50,000 acres of submerged plants died too. Food for wading birds disappeared or, in the deepening water, became unavailable; nesting pairs declined from about 6,000 to zero. The apple snails, on which endangered snail kites depend, had laid their eggs on the bulrush stems. In 1996 there had been thirty-five active snail-kite nests on the lake; for the last two years there have been none.

The decision to drown Lake Okeechobee's marshes and kill off their ecosystems had not resulted from any dearth of scientific data. It was a calculated transaction that expended the public's fish and wildlife so that agribusiness and cities could be spared an increase in water "demands not met" of three percent, which might have cost them $20 million but which also could easily have been cancelled by old-fashioned conservation.

No one had bothered to tally what the lost fish and wildlife would cost South Florida's economy. Recently, though, the Florida Fish and Wildlife Conservation Commission has calculated that the value of black crappie, largemouth bass and various other sunfishes dependent on an acre of bulrushes is $24,000. So the lake's 9,300 acres of lost bulrushes had been worth $223.2 million, not counting other values, such as the dabbling ducks that used to attract hunters from all over the nation. In Fisheating Bay, twenty miles southwest of Little Grassy, the commission had counted an average of 11,886 dabbling ducks during the winters of 1981 and 1982. Between 1991 and 2000 it counted an average of 338 *for the entire lake.*

The absurdity of this and other transactions became even more apparent to me when I stepped back—or up—and perused the whole watershed from a Cessna 172. The still air was hazy from wildfires whose convection columns bloomed like thunderheads to the northwest and southwest. Directly below us the gutterized corpse of the Kissimmee River marched straight as a drill column to the lake. Six miles east we cut the course of Taylor Creek, named for Zach, now bilious with algae after collecting seepage from dairy-farm manure lagoons (state-of-the-art treatment even in the twenty-first century). Scattered over the prairie were potholes where otters, waterfowl, shorebirds, and wading birds breed and raise their young. The metastasizing citrus groves had cut many off from the prairie and its cycles of flood, drought and fire. Clogged with brush and polluted with nutrients, they no longer function as wetlands. All this happened when the lake was supposedly being restored under the state's Surface Water Improvement Management Plan, implemented in 1989. "After twelve years of 'restoration' the lake is in the worst shape it's ever been in," remarked Gray.

Another tireless lake advocate—Nat Reed of Hobe Sound, Florida who served presidents Nixon and Ford as assistant secretary of Interior—said this: "I consider the near death of Lake Okeechobee the single greatest environmental defeat I have suffered on my watch. The defeat is painful and nags at me. I am determined with 'time left' to turn the situation around. … The saga of Lake Okeechobee is one of the great pollution stories in the sense that since 1971 (in my case) the key decision makers knew that the problem existed and was growing more serious. It is a story of studies and more studies because action seemed either impossible politically or pragmatically. Having stated the obvious, who will save the lake?"

Maybe it will be Reed, Gray, Fox and other activists who have been piling up some impressive victories. In June 2000—six months before President Clinton signed the Comprehensive Everglades Restoration Plan—the Florida legislature enacted the Lake Okeechobee Protection Plan which allocated $38.5 million for restoration of the northern part of the watershed, including landowner assistance programs and stormwater treatment areas. The treatment areas, full of nutrient-loving cattails, will function as artificial kidneys, doing some of what the natural river systems used to do for free

Thirty miles from the lake the straight gutter we'd been following came to an abrupt end; and suddenly the old Kissimmee River reappeared, braiding and coiling through its ancient floodplain. In an enormously significant reversal that advertises the folly of gutterization to the world, the Corps and the water management district are returning twenty-two of fifty-six miles to original condition. Seven miles had been restored just in the last year, and already it looked wild and natural. Part of the plan—set in motion by the Florida legislature in 1976, just five years after the Corps' dragline took its last bite—calls for buying all the land in the five-year floodplain.

Not all the dead trees we flew over were the victims of high water. Many had been injected with herbicide by the district. These were melaleuca from Australia, the bane of native ecosystems and planted by the Corps to stabilize the flood-control dike. In the Everglades, melaleuca are still out of control; but on Lake Okeechobee the district is winning. And last year it, the Florida Department of Environmental Protection, and the Corps replanted the dike with 10,000 native trees—custard apple, red maple and bald cypress.

Out over the lake the picture brightened even more. Blowing east across the newly exposed flats like shreds of black silk were small, tight formations of pintail, blue-winged teal, green-winged teal, and Florida mottled duck—the first push of pioneers. Far to the southwest the marshes of Audubon's Lake Okeechobee Sanctuaries merged with haze and horizon, regreening in the sunlight and newly dried soil or blackened by desperately needed prescribed burns. Further out, where the lake turned silver, we could make out the chartreuse brush strokes of surviving bulrushes and bulrushes planted by Fox and his volunteers. Now, for the first time in more than a decade, they were producing seeds. "To go back and restore all the 18 million plants we lost on Little Grassy would cost $6.3 million," Fox had told me. "Now nature's doing most of it for us."

Last January, at its conference in Stuart, Florida, the Everglades Coalition (an alliance of forty-one environmental groups, including Audubon)

predicted that if restoration is allowed to proceed, within ten years roughly 50,000 acres of submergent plants and 100,000 acres of emergent plants will have returned to the lake's littoral zones and with them most of the missing fish and wildlife, including at least thirty nesting pairs of snail kites.

Despite the explosion of life caused by the first low water in a dozen years, enormous problems remain: Lake Okeechobee gets 500 tons of phosphorus annually from dairy, citrus, and ranching operations in the north and, in the south, polluted flood and irrigation water "backpumped" from by the sugar industry—i.e., pumped back into the lake so the sugarcane won't drown. Natural inflow is roughly 100 tons. In 1987, about the time the lake began to blanch with massive, malodorous blooms of blue-green algae, Florida's legislature established a phosphorus goal of no more than 400 tons a year—300 tons *over* what the lake and the Everglades can handle. With luck the treatment areas currently planned on the north shore will remove 90 tons of phosphorus per year, but an additional 310 tons must be removed if lake and Everglades are to live. "If we don't restore the lake, nothing else will work," said Gray. "We're spending $7.8 billion on the Comprehensive Everglades Restoration Plan but only half a billion of that for the watershed north of the lake where most of the pollution comes from [mainly for additional stormwater treatment areas and dredging muck from streams]. That's not going to get the Everglades fixed."

Before humans messed with it, Lake Okeechobee had expanded and contracted like any other healthy heart and lungs. During the summer rainy season the shore would move six miles inland and the surface rise to twenty feet above sea level, spilling over the southern rim into a 40-mile-wide, 100-mile-long swath of sawgrass. The Everglades, as English surveyors started calling this marsh 150 years ago, was like no ecosystem on the planet—a river of grass nourished by the lake. It filtered out solids, sucked up nutrients and delivered sweet, soft water to aquifers and Florida Bay.

The contractions of Lake Okeechobee were as vital as her expansions. When the water receded, the organic muck that had built up on the bottom dried, decomposed, burned, and blew away. Dabbling ducks wobbled down onto shallows rife with seeds and young, succulent vegetation.

Shorebirds scampered over wet flats, gorging on the aquatic larvae of dragonflies, damselflies, midges, mayflies, and caddisflies. Then these insects would grow wings, shuck their larval skins and billow up in great clouds of beige and black that wafted like woodsmoke across lake and marsh, nourishing the whole food chain from fish and frogs to the birds, turtles and alligators that ate the fish and frogs.

In autumn insect blooms would fuel the continent's largest migration of swallow-tailed kites and coincide with the arrival of insectivorous neotropical birds—warblers, tanagers, vireos, nightjars and the like, all funneling down from half a continent through the tip of Florida, exhausted and desperate for energy to carry them across the gulf. In the spring they migrated the other way, again refueling on the lake's insects after the arduous gulf crossing. Then, during the 1990s, the flying insects crashed. Taking their place were sludge worms—useless to birds and virtually all the other life that had depended on the insect blooms.

The first major assault on Lake Okeechobee began in 1887 when humans connected it to the Gulf of Mexico via the Caloosahatchee River. Then, in 1926, they connected it to the Atlantic via the St. Lucie River. This way the lake could be flushed whenever bureaucrats supposed that it was "too high." In 1967 the Army Corps of Engineers finished girdling the lake in a thirty-eight-foot-high dike. All these manipulations shrank Okeechobee, desiccated the Everglades, sickened Florida Bay by depriving its flora and fauna of the brackish water in which they had evolved, and in the St. Lucie and Caloosahatchee estuaries, killed sea grasses, oysters, crabs and other organisms intolerant of freshwater.

Yet the tweaking continued. In 1971 the Corps finished what it called its "improvement" of the Kissimmee River, ripping it from the embrace of its wildlife-rich wetlands, yanking out its lazy curves, forcing it into a dragline-excavated ditch, dredging out its life and magic, even the magic of its name which now became "C-38."

The old river system had been the lake's kidneys—or one of them— cleansing roughly half the inflow as the Everglades used to cleanse the outflow. Now, along with the other gutterized tributaries, it express delivers nutrients and solids straight into the lake, where they settle, choking benthic life and plants, and toppling the ecosystems built upon them.

When the devastation gets bad enough even the bureaucrats take note. It was, in fact, the extirpation of snail kites that helped set real restoration in motion in 1997. That year, the Fish and Wildlife Service declared Lake Okeechobee critical snail-kite habitat which meant that, by continuing to flood the marshes, the Corps violated the Endangered Species Act. If Audubon, the lead group in the fight for Okeechobee, had sued—and it would have—the lake's water management would likely have been taken over by a federal judge. So, on April 25, 2000, the Corps let the district declare an environmental emergency, authorizing releases calculated to bring the lake down to Thirteen feet above sea level by May 23.

Then came an additional reprieve for the flora and fauna of Lake Okeechobee—a drought which by April 20, 2001, had dropped the surface to 9.77 feet above sea level, the lowest ever recorded. Now a new water-level management plan has been implemented that is better than the last, though still inadequate. It will allow levels as low as 13.5 feet, at which point 19 percent of the marshes would be exposed. "A quarter of the lake is marshes," said Gray. "So we can restore 25 percent of Okeechobee just with a good water regime, which means occasionally allowing the level to go down to twelve feet [at which point 75 percent of the marshes would be exposed.]"

Even with the great promise of restoration that I saw on the lake and on the upper Kissimmee, public resistance is daunting. The popular and respected James Bass—who rode with his father in the old cattle drives to the East Coast before there were real roads and who still runs 2,000 head of cattle on the dry floodplain of C-38—speaks for many of his neighbors when he calls freeing the river from the big ditch a faddish "reversal" instigated by "newcomers." "You can't go backwards," he told me. "Everyone wants to preserve. How would you like to own land here and be preserved?"

Bass says he spreads as much phosphorus on his rangeland as he can afford. But recently the ag-school literati, who had been telling him and other ranchers to do just that, have taken to saying it's a waste of money because grass had always known something they've just learned—that the hardpan below the dirt, into which it sends its roots, is rich with natural phosphorus.

The lake's single biggest problem is the inflow of phosphorus and pesticides from the sugar industry's flood and irrigation water. The growers, who are accustomed to getting their way, appear intransigent. While the water management district has always allowed them to backpump to get rid of flood and irrigation water, it has just given them permission to backpump merely to keep the lake full for future irrigation. "It's difficult to talk to environmentalists sometimes because they don't want to look at the facts," declares George Wedgworth, president of the Sugar Cane Growers Cooperative of Florida.

But here's a fact that environmentalists *have* looked at: Soon there will be no excuse for backpumping because treatment areas on the south shore will serve as receptacles for excess water from the sugarcane fields and because water needed for future irrigation will be available from all treatment areas. About half the wetlands in Florida have been drained, so now there is water to spare. In an average year the lake gets about 7.7 surface feet, five of which evaporate. About one foot goes to irrigation, about six inches to the big cities on the lower East Coast, and about a foot needs to be vented. It is this excess foot with which managers have been killing the salt-dependent St. Lucie and Caloosahatchee estuaries by dumping it on them and killing the freshwater-dependent Everglades and Florida Bay by not dumping it on them.

"Water backpumped from sugar cane is the cleanest entering the lake," proclaimed Wedgworth. "Somewhere in the high 90s [ppb phosphorus]," chimed in his VP for communications, Barbara Miedema. (According to the South Florida Water Management District, the *average* phosphorus concentration from the biggest backpumping station in 1999 was 300 ppb.) And Wedgworth blames environmentalists for demanding the emergency release and thereby making backpumping "necessary." "Lowering the lake has caused the worst drought that South Florida has seen in over twenty years," he continued. (According to the district, 450,000 acre feet of water was released during last year's emergency, the same amount taken by the sugar industry; and from October 2, 2000, to April 2, 2001, the industry took an additional 287,612 acre feet.) But then, speaking of the storm that had drenched Don Fox, Paul Gray and me, Wedgworth said something eminently true and with which all interests agree: "We had about two inches of rain last Monday, and instead of putting that back into Lake

Okeechobee they dumped it to sea. I don't think that's very prudent for the natural system, for wildlife, for agriculture or for people who drink scotch and water on Miami Beach." It is this agreement that has allowed Lake Okeechobee and the Everglades to suddenly acquire a future.

If resistance to restoration seems unstoppable, so does support. The increased backpumping has outraged and mobilized the year-old, 200-member Friends of Lake Okeechobee. "At the same time the district authorized more backpumping it decided not to restrict water usage," says Larry Harris, editor of the group's newsletter. "The district made a conscious decision to pollute the lake on the south end which is extremely sensitive and which was showing the best recovery. Now they're dumping all this stuff in there; I hate to call it water. You have to look at it to understand."

"The lake's health is more important than having just-in-case water for the sugar industry," adds Friends' president, Carroll Head. Along with Audubon and the Florida Wildlife Federation, Friends is petitioning the district to reverse its decision.

When I tried to contact the loud, angry property-rights group Realists Opposing Alleged Restoration (ROAR) I learned that it was no longer active. Apparently, its voice has been drowned out. Louder and angrier than ROAR ever thought of being is Fishermen Against Destruction of the Environment. "It's a new day dawning, and I'm glad to see it," comments the group's take-no-prisoners president, Wayne Nelson. "For 15 years I've been trying to tell the bureaucrats that if you don't clean up Okeechobee, you can forget about the Everglades. Finally they're listening. Now what this lake needs is a governor who will be its champion. [Governor] Jeb Bush told me he's fished it. But when I asked him to come see it with me he hemmed and hawed."

On my last day in Florida, driving east toward the Gold Coast, I looked for a sign from the lake. Finally, I thought I saw it—a snail kite hanging over the St. Lucie Canal and wobbling on the west wind like its namesake. Later, I learned that snail kites don't have forked tails, and that this was "only" a swallow-tailed kite. Still, it was hawking insects, perhaps dragonflies emerging from the lake's reborn shallows. As an omen, it would have to do.

DAMN THE TAXPAYERS, FULL SPEED AHEAD

‹‹‹ ›››

In 1999 the U.S. Army Corps of Engineers adopted an official prayer, in which it thanks the "engineer of all eternity" for "holding the plumb line of the cosmos" and beseeches him to guide it in "making rough places smooth, crooked ways straight and ... our calculations accurate." At least in the last of these requests, the agency's prayers had already been answered. In April 1998, Donald Sweeney, the Corps' own Ph.D. economist, presented preliminary figures on a proposed plan to double the length of seven 600-foot locks on the Upper Mississippi River System. The expansion would allow 1,100-foot tows of fifteen barges to go through the locks without uncoupling, saving about an hour per lock. The cost of the project would be about $1 billion, the benefits about $750 million. Sweeney, a twenty-two-year veteran of the agency who had been recognized as a superstar in every performance report ever issued by his superiors, hadn't just punched buttons on his pocket calculator. For five years he had headed a team of fourteen economists and five contractors who monitored barge traffic, studied congestion, analyzed grain exports, and accurately calculated benefits.

But what the Corps prays for and what it really wants are entirely different things. According to a sworn affidavit Sweeney filed in February 2000 with the Office of Special Counsel (OSC), he was ordered to "ignore" and "alter" data and "arbitrarily reduce" expenses in order "to produce a seemingly favorable benefit-to-cost ratio for immediately extending the length of existing locks." The OSC has determined that Sweeney's charges have merit, and an investigation by the Army Inspector General is under way.

In his affidavit, Sweeney reports that on September 18, 1998, Gerald Barnes, deputy for project management of the Corps' St. Louis District, "told me to find a way to justify large-scale measures in the near term for the [study], or the Mississippi Valley District office would find an

economist who would, and I would be out of my job as technical manager."
Sweeney replied that he was constrained by professional integrity. A week
later he was removed as leader of the economic study team. (Barnes says
he cannot comment because the investigation is ongoing.) The new team
leader, economist Richard Manguno, also found that the lock expansion
was not economically justified. According to sworn written testimony he
gave to Senate investigators in April, Manguno says that he, too, was told
to alter his figures, and eventually he complied. Now the Corps is saying
that the costs don't outweigh the benefits after all, and that actually the
reverse is true.

After Sweeney was taken off the study, he had nothing to do, so the
Corps did what it does best: make work. Despite the fact that he is an
economist, it ordered him to oversee construction of a harbor on the
Mississippi in southeastern Missouri. "Fine," he said. "Teach me how." His
superiors allowed that training would indeed be prudent, but somehow
they didn't get around to providing any. He was told to do the project
anyway, and when he said he wouldn't because he couldn't, he was given
a three-day suspension for "insubordination." That's when he wrote his
whistleblower affidavit.

Attached to the affidavit are internal memos from the Corps' military
brass that reveal a secret plan to further engorge the annual civil-works
appropriation of the Mississippi Valley Division by $100 million per year
for the next five years. "If that goal is met, we are all going to be very
busy," effused the Division's Lenard Ross in a summary of a meeting
with the Corps' military commanders. "To grow the civil works program,
[headquarters] and the Division have agreed to get creative. They will be
looking for ways to get [studies] to 'yes' as fast as possible. We have been
encouraged to have our study managers not take 'no' for an answer."

On September 25, 1998, team member Dudley Hanson summarized
orders from Major General Russell Fuhrman, then the Corps' director of
civil works, in this memo to the team: "If [data] do not capture the need
for navigation improvements, then we have to figure out some other way
to do it. ... He [Fuhrman] directs that we develop evidence or data to
support a defensible set of capacity enhancement projects. We need to
know what the mechanism is that drives the benefits up."

The Corps even has an internal computer slide presentation on how to bloat itself by $2.2 billion over the next five years. In one slide it cites its own "Principles & Guidelines" as first on a list of "Impediments to Growth."

The Corps' definition of the "Upper Mississippi River System" is the 858 miles of main stem from Minneapolis to Cairo, Illinois, the Illinois River, and the navigable portions of the Minnesota, St. Croix, Black, and Kaskaskia rivers. The system accommodates about 125 million tons of barged goods a year. If the locks are expanded, that figure could double in fifty years, and it is this rise in traffic that would have the most serious effect on the river's ecosystem.

Up until the late 1800s, before the Corps began systematically "improving" the Upper Mississippi, the entire floodplain was a rich mosaic of wooded islands, wetlands, sloughs, ponds, lakes, prairies, and bottomland forests. In spring the unimproved river would creep over its floodplain, laying down a gentle snow of nutrients that fueled the whole ecosystem, scattering fish that had evolved to broadcast their eggs over flooded bottomland and whose young fattened on the rich plankton blooms that poured from the saturated earth. Now most of the islands are underwater, 50 percent of the floodplain is sealed off by levees, and much of the main channel is locked into place by wing dams, revetments, and riprap. In order to provide a nine-foot-deep channel for barge traffic, thirty-six dams have converted a rising, falling, life-giving river system to a chain of deadwaters.

"There are some sacred cows for the Corps," observes Scott Faber of American Rivers, the Washington, D.C.-based advocacy group, "and one is the Upper Mississippi. It's their personal turf. For years they've run it like a military junta runs a third world country."

Consider the case of Major Charles Hall, a district engineer at Rock Island, Illinois. In 1927 he was ordered to study the economic feasibility of dam construction for navigation. Like Sweeney, he presented accurate calculations that showed costs to outweigh benefits, and like Sweeney he was overruled by his superiors when special interests complained. Two years later Hall was ordered to study the impacts the dams and locks would have on fish and wildlife. He found that making a nine-foot-deep barge canal out of the Upper Mississippi would "radically change" the ecosystem by creating a "succession of stagnant or sluggish pools." Businessmen in Minneapolis complained to Hall's superiors, asserting that commerce was being stifled by an individual "not in sympathy with the project." The Minneapolis Journal called Hall's findings "gratuitous opinions" and described his duties as "neither floral nor faunal, but engineering." Hall was taken off this study, too. On June 3, 1930, Congress authorized the dams, even though the Corps' final report wasn't out. It has been ever thus.

These days the special interests pressuring the Corps to disregard its own economic data are the barge owners. Their lobby, the Midwest Area River Coalition 2000, is claiming that the Corps didn't cook the books at all but is being victimized by the "pernicious attacks" and "hyperbole" of environmental extremists whose "orchestrated effort apparently aims at reversing the vision our forefathers had in harnessing the power of rivers."

But the vision of our forefathers wasn't always 20/20. For instance, Minneapolis has never had any real need to be connected to the barge channel of the Mississippi. Yet when Hubert Humphrey was elected mayor of the city in 1945, he began crusading for two monstrous, horrendously expensive locks to circumvent a steep waterfall. And he kept at it when he moved to the U.S. Senate three years later. Construction began in 1950. That's how Corps navigation projects have always been conceived—not by necessity but by politician. Today Minneapolis is working on a riverfront plan that would re-move all industry and close the city port.

There has been no increase in barge traffic on the river since 1992. Still, taxpayers are paying 90 to 95 percent of the cost of maintaining the Upper Mississippi's navigation system (about $158 million a year, and that's not counting the $1 billion for lock expansion). You'd think the tax hawks would be as mad as flipped-over snapping turtles, and they are. Ralph DeGennaro, executive director of Taxpayers for Common Sense, declares that the Corps is "out of control" and that its credo is: "Damn the taxpayers, full speed ahead."

On the morning of April 5, 2000, in the Upper Mississippi River National Wildlife and Fish Refuge near Wabasha, Minnesota, I caught a glimpse of the river the way it used to be, before Congress turned the Corps loose on it. What, I wondered, is the dollar value of the two dozen bald eagles I saw from the U.S. Fish and Wildlife Service's outboard-powered skiff? Along the banks and in the backwaters they dipped out of silver maples, orbited nests in ancient cottonwoods, and rose from the river into the brightening sky, shaking water and flashing sunlight. And how much for the pileated woodpecker swooping up onto the snag; or the muskrat sneaking under the bank with his mouth stuffed with greens; or the great blue herons and tree swallows sailing overhead; or the hooded mergansers and wood ducks bursting out of the sloughs; or the turtles that left their eggshells all over the sandy islands; or the pike, bluegills, catfish, paddlefish, sturgeon, and smallmouth bass that cruised beneath us? All these creatures provide real economic benefits that, to some extent, will be sacrificed by the increase in barge traffic that lock expansion will promote. If the Corps tallied these costs, its proposal would flunk even the bogus, post-Sweeney analysis. A 1999 study for the Fish and Wildlife Service by Industrial Economics, of Cambridge, Massachusetts, sets the economic contribution of fishing, hunting, wildlife viewing, and sightseeing along the Upper Mississippi at $6.6 billion per year.

With me on the river were Bob Drieslein and Cindy Samples of the Fish and Wildlife Service's Winona, Minnesota, office; MaryBeth Garrigan, director of the National Eagle Center in Wabasha; and Dan McGuiness, director of the National Audubon Society's Upper Mississippi River Campaign. The refuge's 200,000 acres extend 261 miles southward from Wabasha to just upstream of Rock Island, Illinois, providing habitat for at least 292 species of birds, 57 species of mammals, 37 species of amphibians and reptiles, and 118 species of fish. It's the most popular of all national wildlife refuges, attracting about 3.5 million visitors a year—more than Yellowstone National Park.

To celebrate the refuge's seventy-fifth birthday, McGuiness, accompanied by staff and volunteers, spent most of August 1999 traversing 751 river miles in a houseboat called the Audubon Ark, discussing the real costs of lock expansion with about 1,200 visitors and 50 reporters. "Are we just accountants bartering fish and wildlife for barges?" he asked them.

So far, that's exactly what we are. For example, according to the Corps' own data, pressure or direct impact from the huge propellers of a single tow boat can be expected to kill or maim fourteen adult gizzard shad, shovelnose sturgeon, and smallmouth buffalo fish per kilometer. This means that on the 858-mile trip from Cairo, Illinois, to Minneapolis, each tow boat could kill 19,730 of these fish, and there are 124 other species in this section.

Another cost is habitat loss caused by more barge wakes. The waves erode shoreline vegetation, muddying the water, which, in turn, kills aquatic vegetation by cutting off sunlight. In 1986, when the Corps got final permission from Congress to build the planet's biggest civil engineering project—Locks and Dam 26 in Alton, Illinois—it promised that this was all the navigation expansion needed, that it wouldn't be back for more. As part of the deal the Corps agreed in writing to do sixteen studies on the impact of the increased barge wakes on fish and wildlife. But most of these studies were never done, and most of the questions still haven't been answered, even though the Corps has spent $40 million on the study Sweeney worked on.

Now 10 percent of the species that occur along the Upper Mississippi are classified as rare, threatened, or endangered in one or more of the basin states (Illinois, Iowa, Minnesota, Missouri, and Wisconsin), and seven are listed under the Endangered Species Act. The river had one of the world's richest mussel faunas, but pollution, dredging, dams, barges, and commercial harvest have reduced documented species from fifty to thirty. Two of the survivors are federally endangered, and fifteen others are state listed. One of the disappearing species—the ebony shell, whose larvae attach themselves to the gills of skipjack herring in order to move upstream—used to be the dominant mussel in the Upper Mississippi. But when the dams went up, skipjacks couldn't migrate, and the population of ebony shells crashed.

At least fifteen species of Mississippi fish now face extirpation. Most of them require gravel bottoms or quiet backwaters without excessive sedimentation. The ancient giants of the Mississippi—the endangered pallid sturgeon and the plankton-grazing paddlefish (a candidate for listing)—must move great distances to find a rock-rubble bottom for spawning. But dams block them and slow the flows so that silt settles and covers up the rubble. Even where the bottom remains unburied, the females will reabsorb their eggs if they don't sense rising water.

This nation has a large and powerful adversary," the Corps explained in one of its old films on remaking rivers. "We are fighting Mother Nature. … It's a battle we have to fight day by day, year by year; the health of our economy depends on victory." The war is going badly.

Since World War II the Corps has spent nearly $100 billion (in 1999 dollars) trying to stop U.S. rivers from flooding, yet average annual flood damage has steadily climbed, to nearly $8 billion. "We harnessed it, straightened it, regulated it, shackled it," bragged the Corps as it fitted the Mississippi River system with an alleged flood barrier—a phalanx of levees longer, higher, and thicker than the Great Wall of China. Assured by these kinds of pronouncements, the public confidently moved into the floodplain. Then in 1993 the river yawned, as it does every few decades, inundating the dams, blowing apart the levees, killing 47 people, displacing 74,000 others, and destroying $15 billion worth of property. It was an act of engineer, but America called it "an act of God."

A full year later, as I surveyed flood damage along the Upper Mississippi in Illinois and Missouri, I saw fish and new vegetation in floodplain ponds that had been dry since the levees went up in the mid-1920s. Before then, fingers of the unimproved river would reach into these ponds every spring, collecting young fish and spreading spawners. Now, seventy years later, water and fish had arrived once more, and aquatic plants had sprouted from seeds that had been waiting in the earth all that time for the river to do its thing. On the inundated floodplain, behind the busted levees, smallmouth and bigmouth buffalo fish—native suckers that once sustained local economies—outproduced alien carp for the first time in the six years that records had been kept.

This is how the river had worked for 10,000 years before the dams and levees started going in. Spring floods would clear out some of the old hardwoods, spreading their seeds over rich earth newly washed with sunlight. Summer droughts would follow, leaving exposed mudflats where the seeds of cottonwoods could germinate and where shorebirds could feast on invertebrates.

Now both shorebirds and cottonwoods are disappearing, because we've bartered mudflats for barges. And the mast-producing oaks and hickories, so valuable to wildlife, are being replaced with a monoculture of willow and silver maple, species tolerant of the perpetual high water caused by dams.

Last April I saw a carpet of reed canary grass everywhere I looked in the backwaters of the refuge. River ecologists believe that the loss of the natural flood cycle has somehow caused this native ground cover to become invasive. And Bob Drieslein blames the invasion, along with the unnatural profusion of water-tolerant trees, for degrading the habitat of the eastern massasauga—a diminutive, swamp-dependent rattlesnake being considered for listing under the Endangered Species Act.

In Big Lake, one of the numerous backwater impoundments created by the dams, we ran aground on loose silt and had to turn back after traveling only 100 yards. In its early years, before it started filling in, Big Lake provided rich habitat for waterfowl and other wildlife. Low flows expose sediments to the air, allowing them to compact and harden into mudflats where emergent plants take root. But Big Lake has never had a chance to dry out and grow new plants that can serve as windbreaks. And the existing windbreaks—cattails, phragmites, and bullrushes—are being battered by wind-generated waves. Their loss, in turn, permits even larger waves that further erode the shoreline, creating and stirring up even more light-blocking sediments. The silt is also killing the wild celery relished by ducks. Ten miles downstream, at a similar backwater lake called Weaver Bottoms, waves and sedimentation are killing the arrowhead. Tundra swans used to stop here by the thousands on their spring and fall migrations, glutting themselves for weeks on arrowhead tubers; now a few hundred stop for only a day or two. Thus do the ecosystems of "improved" rivers unravel.

The Corps is preparing a draft environmental-impact statement on the lock expansion, which the public needs to scrutinize and challenge, Sweeney says. As for Sweeney, he is putting in his time with the Corps, but he says his relationship with management is "coldly professional" and that he is no longer allowed to do anything important. "We can't have the Corps doing its own feasibility studies," he told me. "It's like having my 11-year-old son do a study about how much ice cream he should have after dinner. I know what the answer's going to be. Your readers should view with skepticism anything the Corps proposes to do. The current system is structured to give a biased answer."

Just how lawless has the Corps become? I asked Sweeney if civilians still control it, as federal statute requires. "Absolutely not," he replied. "I would say more than ever it's a military-run organization." The Corps' military pooh-bahs have traditionally used trick arithmetic to justify environmentally hurtful, make-work projects, but Sweeney says they're getting more brazen: "There has always been this subtle, unstated pressure. But when I first started 22 years ago, if it really wasn't a feasible project, it was okay to say so. And if the politician wanted to go ahead and build it anyway, that was his call, and he'd have to pay the price without our support. In those days you would give a project as many breaks as you reasonably could, but nobody would ask you to go past the line where you just said professionally, 'I can't do this anymore.' Now it's not okay to say no."

When I asked if he was going to keep working for the Corps, he said, "I don't see how I can." That's a shame, because there aren't many Corps employees with his kind of sand. For every Don Sweeney who won't break the law, even to keep a job, there are 100 who flout it just because that's the way the outfit does business.

Perhaps Sweeney has not sacrificed his career in vain. "If there is any good that can come of my disclosure," he says, "it would be a truly independent evaluation of Corps proposals. Maybe the creation of some sort of really independent study authority. Maybe make the Corps of Engineers just engineers." For all on earth who advocate the conservation of fish, wildlife, and tax dollars, that's a consummation devoutly to be wished. And for the great engineer in the sky, it may be the best of all prescriptions for making "crooked ways straight."

DAM REMOVAL

─── ⤙ ⤚ ───

"Dams are not America's answer to the pyramids of Egypt. We do not build them for religious purposes." So declared America's tireless dam-busting cheerleader Bruce Babbitt when, with joyful swipes of his ceremonial sledgehammer, the former U.S. Secretary of the Interior regularly presided over the dismantling of useless, decrepit, dangerous dams. In 1993 this behavior was considered so bizarre that President Clinton dressed him down for it.

Today the notion that dams are not sacred monuments to be preserved for all time is universally accepted by state and federal agencies. As yet, however, there is no such acceptance by the general public, a fact that should alarm all thinking Americans regardless of how they feel about fish and wildlife. A dam's average life expectancy is fifty years, and a quarter of America's 76,000 dams defined by the Corps of Engineers as "large" or "high-hazard" (in which failure is apt to kill people) are more than fifty years old. By 2020 the figure will be 80 percent.

Impoundments behind large dams, most of which are unlikely to be removed in the foreseeable future, can stratify and take on the ecological features of genuine lakes. But most impoundments are mongrels, possessing neither riverine nor lacustrine characteristics; and while they may support organisms that evolved in both environments, they support neither well. For example, in Wisconsin—which leads the nation in dam removal—anglers caught smallmouth and largemouth bass in the impoundments above the four dams on the Baraboo River, but the fishing was pretty lousy.

When the last of these dams was removed in February 2001 (making the Baraboo the longest river freed by dam busting in the nation), both bass species, as well as catfish, walleye and sauger, surged back in numbers that astonished even state biologists. Crews from the Wisconsin Department of Natural Resources had shocked eleven fish species above the Waterworks and LaValle dams, the dominant one being carp. Eighteen months after the dams were taken out the crews shocked twenty-four species above the remains of the Waterworks dam and twenty-six species above the remains of LaValle, and in both cases the dominant species was smallmouth bass. Before the demise of the Waterworks dam the crews had shocked three smallmouths; eighteen months after removal they shocked eighty-seven. Recovery has barely gotten underway and already the unshackled Baraboo's smallmouths are drawing national attention. Although smallmouths may thrive in lakes and large reservoirs, they do best in rivers because that's where they evolved. Largemouths evolved in still water; but they're doing far better in the free Baraboo than they were in the impoundments because they're no longer suppressed by carp.

Of course, there would be no recovery of Baraboo game fish without recovery of the complex ecosystem of which they are part. In the tepid, eutrophic impoundments midges, sludge worms and bloodworms had dominated benthic fauna. Now caddisflies and mayflies dominate cool, oxygenated riffles newly cleansed of sediment. With the species sought by anglers have come lake sturgeon, paddlefish, darters and the giant native sucker called bigmouth buffalo—all moving freely, breeding in restored habitat, feeding game fish with their eggs and fry. And with all the fish have come mussels which, as larvae, migrate through the system by temporarily attaching to fins and gills.

Today the energy flow of the freed Baraboo is increasing geometrically from Hillsboro to the Wisconsin River, through 120 miles of mainstem and up into hundreds of tributaries veining the slopes of the 650-square-mile basin, out and up into meadow, muskeg, forest and sky—to the muskrats that eat the mussels, the owls, weasels, bobcats and wild canids that eat the muskrats, to the otters, eagles, ospreys, herons, kingfishers, turtles and snakes that eat the fish, to the salamanders, frogs, bats and woods warblers that eat the clouds of aquatic insects. Dam removal is about life, not death, rebirth not destruction.

The Prairie River, which in 1944 produced Wisconsin's record inland brook trout of nine pounds, fifteen ounces, was arguably the best trout stream in the state. Now, released from its four dams, it's fast regaining its former status. The Prairie Dells dam, nine miles from the river's confluence with the upper Wisconsin, had been rebuilt for hydro power in 1904 when it was already twenty-four years old. But power generation never happened because the engineer had stuck a decimal point in the wrong place. Once the dam was finished there was no reason to waste perfectly good turbines on it, so for eighty-seven years it did nothing except collect sediment, block fish and otherwise unravel the rich, river-based food chain.

In 1991, when the dam was taken out, the 2.6-mile-long impoundment regurgitated 20,000 cubic yards of muck, discoloring the river for miles. Dam defenders shrieked; environmentalists cringed. But three seasons of snowmelt flushed the system clean. Brook trout reproduction jumped thirty fold, and the state quit stocking hatchery fish.

Pennsylvania has done nearly as well as Wisconsin. When the state Fish and Boat Commission removed a dam on Lititz Run, water temperature dropped twelve degrees in twenty-four hours. Lititz Run is a tributary of the Conestoga River which had been a limestone trout stream before dams turned it into a series of stagnant, methane-belching sumps. Now, with the removal of twenty dams in the system, water quality has improved to the point that the state can stock hatchery trout, and the goal of re-establishing self-sustaining populations is no longer a pipe dream. Already American shad, moving up from the Susquehanna for the first time in a century, have reproduced.

The benefits of dam removal had been no secret before all the good work in Wisconsin and Pennsylvania, but the lessons went unheeded by a large segment of the public. Restoration of the Baraboo was plenty contentious. Pennsylvania had an easier time on the Conestoga, although the Fish and Boat Commission's Scott Carney wishes the state had more angler support. "The biggest challenge we face is trying to restore stocks like shad that haven't been fished in anyone's memory," he told me. "Getting anglers excited about fishing for something they have no experience with and trying to justify taking out an impoundment they've fished their whole lives can be challenging."

Local resistance was downright nasty during restoration of the Prairie River. The last dam to go was the 21-foot-high, 675-foot-long Ward Dam at Merrill, built in 1905. It had been producing $34,000 worth of electricity per year and costing the owner, International Paper, $50,000 a year to operate. Moreover, it was riddled with cracks, and test borings into the concrete produced pure powder for the first sixteen inches. DNR proclaimed it a safety hazard and ordered International Paper to either rebuild it or tear it down.

From May 1998, when International Paper applied for a removal permit, until drawdown in September 1999, locals mounted nine legal challenges. Then, after drawdown got underway, they temporarily halted work with more legal challenges. There were bomb threats, including one from a fellow who vowed to blow up International Paper's buildings, by which act he would have done away with the impoundment he was trying to save because the buildings were part of the dam complex. DNR crews who supervised the project were harassed and threatened. Dam defenders festooned the town with black crepe paper and "Save the Lake" signs. They proclaimed that the exposed mud flats would release volcano-like plumes of blastomycosis (an often fatal fungal lung disease endemic to wetlands of northern Wisconsin). When a local doctor publicly testified that this was nonsense and that the bottom of the impoundment was probably the only blasto-free habitat in the watershed, his practice was boycotted. For standing alone among his neighbors in defense of his home water, the River Alliance of Wisconsin proposed to honor him with an award; but he declined it because he didn't want any more bad publicity.

The state council of Trout Unlimited fought hard for removal of the Ward Dam, but such was the local intimidation factor that TU's Merrill chapter refused to take a position. Even the Friends of the Prairie River, which exists for no other reason than to restore the river's health, stayed out of the controversy. The homeowners around the impoundment were eager to have anyone and everyone (except themselves) spend $2 million to rebuild the dam, and this in a town that had just defeated a referendum to rebuild the library. The day the dam came out International Paper got seventeen phone calls from townspeople who confided that the company had performed a grand public service but that they'd been afraid to voice their support for fear of reprisals.

I don't mean to be a scold or to imply that there isn't lots of dam removal that's going easily and well. But with the exception of Trout

Unlimited and a few other enlightened angling groups, America's sportsmen have been sitting on the bench. More disheartening is the fact that when sportsmen do get involved, they're often on the wrong side. Seeking information on the removal of the Condit dam on Washington State's White Salmon River, I contacted officers of the seventy-member White Salmon River Steelheaders. To my astonishment I learned that what the group is working to preserve is, of all things, the dam. The 125-foot-high Condit dam, built in 1913, is thought to be the tallest dam slated for demolition in the nation. Six years ago the Federal Energy Regulatory Commission imposed $30 million in license conditions, including fish passage, on the owner—PacifiCorp. Since the dam produces a mere nine megawatts of electricity and its removal would cost only $17.5 million, Moe Howard could have made that business decision. Removal of this, the only dam on the White Salmon River, will open up sixty-five miles of mainstem and tributary habitat for desperately depleted Columbia River salmonids. The Washington Department of Fish and Wildlife estimates that removal will reestablish runs of about 700 adult steelhead, 4,000 spring chinooks, 1,100 fall chinooks, and 2,000 cohos. Babbitt called the project "the Northwest's epicenter of hope." How could any sane, sober steelheader possibly be opposed?

In separate interviews the president of the White Salmon River Steelheaders (Jim Anderson) and a board member who used to be president (Gary Lawson) went on and on about the importance of protecting, not wild steelhead, but the stocked, introgressed trout dumped into the impoundment by PacifiCorp as mitigation for its impassable dam. They called it a "family" fishery but offered no cogent explanation as to why families can't fish for wild salmonids, migratory or otherwise, or crappies or bluegills elsewhere, or, for that matter, stocked, introgressed trout in all the thousands of other places where they unfortunately are available.

I encountered the same disconnect in Oregon, where Portland General Electric wants to disappear its Marmot Dam on the Sandy River. The state stocks the river below the dam with hatchery steelhead and chinook salmon, then sorts returning adults, passing only wild ones. By reopening 100 miles of spawning and rearing habitat from the Pacific to the headwaters on Mt. Hood, Marmot's removal would ultimately produce more fish and fish of quality; but because no sorting would be possible, the present gravy train of fin-clipped, genetically impoverished hatchery stock would have to cease.

This makes perfect sense to sportsmen with what Aldo Leopold called an "ecological conscience," but not to the 250 businesses, organized guides and organized anglers in Oregon, Washington, Idaho and Alaska who call themselves the Northwest Sportfishing Industry Association. "We were blindsided by Trout Unlimited, American Rivers, Oregon Trout and the Native Fish Society," complains Director Liz Hamilton. "You can't convince someone that they need to put money away for college, which is the long-term stuff, when you're taking dinner off the table. I think Portland is trying to make a deal with the National Marine Fisheries Service so the feds can get a quick [endangered species] victory and the city can protect its water supply somewhere else. The deal was done behind closed doors; there was no public process."

Ignorance among sportsmen is no less rampant on the other side of the continent. In the last session of the Maine legislature, Down East bass guides got a bill introduced to halt all dam removal. It failed, but sponsor Rep. Albion Goodwin (D-Pembroke) predicts future success. He has it straight from the guides that native alewives would wipe out alien smallmouths if they re-colonized the St. Croix drainage (this despite the fact that the two species happily coexist everywhere else they share habitat). In the 2000 session Goodwin succeeded with a bill to prohibit the state from allowing passage of alewives (along with everything else that negotiates the St. Croix) without a vote of the legislature. Most of Maine's lawmakers swallowed it all hook, line, boat and motor.

Goodwin in full cry is something to behold. "We have dams all over the state, and people are trying to tear them all out," he laments. "It's dangerous because you're gonna form up about 1,500 terrorists. You know what a terrorist cell is? It's a person who lives on a pond that pays taxes and has a little dock and a canoe, and he wakes up one morning and he lives on a brook that's a half a mile away. The director of Inland Fish and Wildlife cannot introduce alewives without a vote of the legislature. That's what I did with my bill. That includes the Marine Resources idiot, too. They're two commissioners from away—one from Arizona and one from Virginia. I told the governor to hire a Maine person who knows the lakes and rivers, but he's from Virginia. What does he care? Fred Kircheis [director of the Maine Atlantic Salmon Commission] is running for cover because I told him I was all done funding him. I'll shut him off, and he'll start running back to Minnesota. The goddamned Canadians wanted to raise alewives for fertilizer and bait. I told those sons of bitches to build a fishway on their side of the river. I sent 'em all packing: 'Get the hell out of Calais before I have you run out as terrorists.' And away they went a-running."

Such attitudes discourage, especially in a state that tore down the Edwards Dam on the Kennebec River, thereby providing the nation with one of its most spectacular river-restoration success stories. Now, twenty-seven miles upstream, residents of Waterville are bringing lawn chairs to the Kennebec's banks to watch the aerial acrobatics of sturgeon and salmon. Now, seventeen miles upstream, all ten anadromous fish native to Maine are headbutting the ninety-four-year-old Ft. Halifax Dam at the mouth of the Sebasticook River. Under conditions of the Ft. Halifax Dam's operating license the appearance of these fish requires the owner, Florida Power and Light, either to install fish passage or excise the dam. But bass fishermen are crusading to save the impoundment. Writes Maine guide James Gorman of Winslow (incorrectly): "All the meadows and farms you see in the Sebasticook Valley exist because the beavers kept the river dammed, which created natural impoundments allowing silt to settle, thus establishing top soil." Ken Fletcher of Save Our Sebasticook calls those who want to free the river that his outfit is pretending to save "an elite group of artificial-lure fishermen."

Last summer members of Save Our Sebasticook and other dam defenders went canoeing on the impoundment with staffers of the Natural Resources Council of Maine. "It was just clogged with algae," recalls the council's Laura Rose Day. "Yet these folks stretched their hands out wide in the sunshine and said: 'How could you ever want to change a river like this?'" Then one of them accused her of plotting to return all Maine's rivers to their "primitive state."

Forty miles east of Ft. Halifax, the proposed removal of the West Winterport Dam on Marsh Stream is eliciting similar reaction. The four-mile-long impoundment is depriving brook trout and Penobscot River salmon of important spawning and rearing habitat. Such a liability is this dam that the owner gave it to Facilitators Improving Salmonid Habitat (FISH)—a river-restoring group hatched by the Maine Council of the Atlantic Salmon Federation. Now Winterport is threatening to take it by eminent domain, a move that residents may find unappetizing because it would require the town to pay fair market value of $50,000 and assume the far greater expenses of repair, maintenance of the thoroughly inadequate fishway and liability. Public hearings have been ugly. Herewith, the most representative expressions of dam logic mailed to FISH in defense of the dam: "Mother Nature needs to be left alone."

"The earth is all we have, and sometimes it's honestly much better to leave things as they are."

"You might as well personally take a bag of explosives and literally destroy every bass, pickerel, catfish, eel and the many turtles and accompanying fowl that use the waterway ... bald eagles ... Canadian geese, hawks and falcons, and the multitude of ducks and herons."

"A family of ducks have been back every year to lay and raise their young just above the dam."

Rodman Dam, a vestigial organ of the Cross Florida Barge Canal aborted by President Nixon in 1971, is the only dam in the nation that doesn't have even an alleged purpose. It just sits there, plugging up sixteen miles of Florida's Ocklawaha River and blocking travel routes of bears, turkeys, bobcats, Florida panthers and countless other species that need to move between the St. Johns River Valley and the Green Swamp. To maintain Rodman Reservoir—a vile, six-foot-deep, 9,000-acre stew of herbicides and decaying and sprouting alien pond weeds—taxpayers must spend more than $1 million a year. In "return" their shrimp, crabs and marine fish get deprived of vital nutrients, and their striped bass, shad, channel cats, eels, mullet and manatees get cut off from the sea.

Forty-six environmental groups organized as the Alliance to Restore Ocklawaha River want the dam out. Every Floridian with even rudimentary appreciation for natural ecosystems—even Governor Jeb Bush—wants the dam out. But in 1998 Sen. Jim King (R-Jacksonville)—the majority leader who tools around the impoundment on a jetski—derailed the project. In this mischief his enabler was none other than a 1,700-member largemouth-bass-fishing organization called Save Rodman Reservoir, Inc., which sponsors the annual "Save Rodman Bass Tournament" and gets free office space from the City of Palatka. President Ed Taylor—who organizes for-profit bass tournaments when he's not working to "SAVE Rodman from Evil Destruction," as his card puts it—has told me and other reporters that Save Rodman Reservoir has the blessings and support of Operation Bass, Bass Anglers Sportsman Society, Ducks Unlimited of Florida and the Florida Bass Federation. But this is a half-truth; Operation Bass wants the dam out, and DU has no position.

In 1999 the Save Rodman Bass Tournament weighed in its all-time record poundage. That was the year one of the 174 competing bass boats, violating no rule, left the reservoir via the Buckman Lock and traveled down the river that Sidney Lanier, who negotiated it by steamer soon after the Civil War, called: "the sweetest water-lane in the world, a lane which runs for more than a hundred and fifty miles of pure delight betwixt hedgerows of oaks and cypresses and palms and bays and magnolias and mosses and manifold vine-growths." Twenty-seven miles down the Ocklawaha the two-man team caught 23.27 pounds of bass, swung their boat around and raced twenty-seven miles back to the reservoir, arriving in time to win the tournament. Somehow that part of the story never made it into Save Rodman Reservoir's newsletter.

WHERE BAITFISH DON'T BELONG

—<( )>—

Wild trout water more beautiful than northern Maine's Big Reed Pond doesn't exist. It is embraced by one of the few remaining old-growth forests in the East. It is one of about 307 lakes in the nation (305 in Maine) that still sustain native brook trout undefiled by hatchery genes and one of only 14 waters in the nation (all in Maine) known to sustain native populations of blueback trout, a grievously imperiled race of arctic charr.

In the early 1990s guide Gary Corson found smelts in Big Reed. Smelts are native to Maine, but not to Big Reed. They're legal bait in Maine, but not in Big Reed. Someone—apparently in an effort to grow bigger brookies and bluebacks—had illegally introduced them.

It worked spectacularly. In fact, the bluebacks, which had averaged about ten inches (big for landlocked charr) were suddenly attaining lengths of over twenty inches. There was a problem, however. Recruitment all but ceased. The smelts were chowing down on blueback and brookie fry, then competing with surviving bluebacks for zooplankton. Corson, who used to fly his clients into Big Reed at least three times a week says he wouldn't fish there today. "In the deeper water we'd get the occasional two- or three-pound brookie; and the shoreline was full of smaller fish. Everything disappeared." So it goes when baitfish are unleashed where they don't belong.

Thousands of other native fish populations across America have been undone by baitfish introductions. Anglers have dumped bait pails on purpose and by mistake, and bait dealers have introduced non-native baitfish in order to have additional waters to seine. One thing is certain: If baitfish are used in water where they do not occur, they will become naturalized.

While the literature is rife with warnings about dangers to salmonids of non-native spiny-finned fish like perch and bass, it scarcely mentions baitfish. But the former blight is a function of the latter. Few bait dealers know what they're selling, fewer anglers know what they're buying, and no one knows what they're seining. Often juvenile spiny-fins (perch, bass, sticklebacks and the like) are mixed in with the soft-fins (shiners, suckers and the like.); and while the target soft-fins may be legal, non-target soft-fins in the haul frequently aren't.

An informal survey of bait dealers in Wyoming turned up juvenile trout infected with whirling disease mixed in with legal baitfish. And baitfish shipments, especially in the West, are often contaminated with sticklebacks which promptly take over new habitat, carpeting the bottom and blowing off primary production. What's more, sticklebacks provide scant forage to game fish (largemouth bass actually lose weight when they eat them). The loudest complainers are the bait dealers themselves because the sticklebacks they inadvertently spread around wipe out the baitfish they target.

Greg Gerlich, senior aquatic biologist for the Colorado Division of Wildlife, dispatched crews to purchase sixty baitfish from each of a dozen bait shops. "Only two of those shops had mono-specific cultures, like all fathead minnows," he says. "The rest contained everything from goldfish to small carp to suckers to yellow perch to sticklebacks. Minnows are expanding beyond their range. We're seeing new populations of sticklebacks, yellow perch, carp and goldfish."

"I think we're making some headway with baitfish introductions," says Maine's chief fish biologist, John Boland. "Ice fishermen [the primary baitfish users in the East] are much more cognizant about not dumping bait down the hole." Still, the level of ignorance is appalling. Most ice anglers receive their education, not from managers like Boland, but from internet, newspaper and barroom commentary, much of it provided by baitfish dealers. For example, in the February 18, 2007, *Kennebec Journal* the head of the Maine Bait Dealers Association, Stephen Staples, offers the following about alleged dangers of baitfish becoming naturalized in salmonid habitat: "If that happens, so what? Shiners are much needed forage for our fisheries and not harmful to the watersheds."

Try that out on the people who used to fish Oregon's sprawling Diamond Lake, so high in the headwaters of the Umpqua River that it was fishless until rainbow trout were stocked circa 1912. The rainbows grew an inch a month, commonly reaching ten pounds. But sometime in the 1940s tui chubs were introduced by bait anglers or perhaps by bucket biologists as "much needed forage" for rainbows. The rainbows ate the chubs, but not enough to make a difference. Instead of rainbow flesh, the lake produced tui flesh. The chubs cleaned out the zooplankton, slicing off the rainbows' food chain at the base and enabling the proliferation of toxic blue-green algae on which the zooplankton had grazed.

In 1954 the state successfully reclaimed the lake with rotenone, and the trophy fishery recovered, eventually attracting 100,000 anglers a year. But around 1990 someone introduced tui chubs again. Again the chubs took over, dominating the biomass and facilitating poisonous algae blooms that made it unsafe to swim or even fish (for the few who still bothered). Once the lake became turbid and toxic the chemophobes, who had held up rotenone treatment, backed off. Finally—in September 2006 at a cost of $6 million in federal, state, county and private money—the state again reclaimed Diamond Lake, killing an estimated 90 million tui chubs. "In two or three years we hope the nutrients tied up in the chubs that were killed will recycle back into invertebrates and zooplankton," says Rhine Messmer, of the Oregon Department of Fish and Wildlife. "We'll then ramp up our stocking, and hopefully we'll have the trophy fishery we had before."

But such happy endings, if this turns out to be one, are rare. Most bait-infected salmonid water is too big or has too many inlets, springs or marshes to be reclaimed. We lose it forever. Consider the fate of native brook trout in New York State's Adirondack Park as reflected in the microcosm of the Saranac Lake Wild Forest management unit. An estimated 94 percent of the unit's 19,010 acres of ponded surface water historically supported brook trout. Today three percent support brook trout; and the figure would be only .5 percent had the state not done reclamations. Only one of the 156 ponds and lakes in this unit is thought to have been affected by acid precipitation. The rest have been rendered troutless by alien fish.

Golden shiners, white suckers and yellow perch are among the worst invasives; and all appear to have been moved around in bait buckets. Of the thousands of Adirondack ponds that have been lost to soft-fins and spiny-fins, only a few are suitable for rotenone treatment. But there's another problem—key people within the Adirondack Park Agency choose not to learn about rotenone and therefore fear it. And, largely because an ecologically illiterate NGO called the Adirondack Council keeps hissing in the agency's ear, it forbids helicopters in state-designated wilderness during summer (the only practical way of transporting equipment and the only time surveys and reclamations are possible). "We have people in the Park Agency telling us our data is too old to justify management," says Bill Schoch, the Department of Environmental Conservation's regional fish manager. "And, at the same time, the agency tells us we can't fly into these ponds to get new data. It's incredibly frustrating."

The ongoing game of musical chairs we play with baitfish endangers more species than those that titillate us by bending our rods. For instance, non-native baitfish—especially red shiners—are impeding restoration of federally threatened spikedace and loach minnows (which occur only in the Gila basin of Arizona and New Mexico) and threatened pike minnows and endangered razorback chubs in the Colorado River system.

Although golden shiners can be a major threat to wild salmonids when humans fling them around the waterscape, they're every bit as important to their native ecosystems as brook trout are to theirs. The European rudd—with which bait dealers and bait anglers have polluted the Great Lakes, the St. Lawrence River system and now Maine—threatens to hybridize our native golden shiners out of existence.

Not all tui chubs are prolific. Two races—the Mohave tui chub of California's Mojave River (the fish's name has been anglicized) and the Owens tui chub of California's Owens Valley—are now federally endangered largely because non-native chubs, unleashed in their habitat by bait anglers or bait dealers or both, are crossbreeding with them. The Owens tui is a victim of the common tui, while the Mohave tui is being undone by the arroyo chub which has managed to hybridize with it across the genus line, producing sterile offspring. The California Department of Fish and Game would like to keep these endangered fish on the planet by reclaiming a little of their lost habitat, but antimycin is illegal in California, and the department's senior fish biologist, Steve Parmenter, correctly notes that use of rotenone isn't "politically feasible." In other words, public ignorance, which got these fish into trouble in the first place, is now preventing their recovery.

Damage to native fish habitat in the West, grievous as it is, palls beside damage in the East. One reason is that many western states have decent regulations (if not enforcement), while regulations in the East are hopelessly inadequate. Montana and Wyoming have banned live baitfish west of the continental divide—their best trout water. Colorado has banned live baitfish in water above 7,000 feet—its best trout water. Washington and Oregon prohibit all live baitfish in freshwater. California has a virtual ban. West of the divide New Mexico permits only fathead minnows.

New York, on the other hand, hopes to narrow down legal baitfish species to fifteen including the golden shiner and white sucker with which it has had so much trouble. But at this writing, just about any soft-fin goes (though all baitfish have been banned and will continue to be banned in important native brook trout water). In Pennsylvania it is actually legal to seine baitfish from water where they are native or naturalized and release them in water where they are neither. Maine, which has lost about 90 percent of its wild brook trout habitat but nonetheless retains an estimated 97 percent of all ponded native brook trout water in the nation, has also banned live baitfish in much of its remote trout water. But major brook trout strongholds—including the ninety-two-mile-long ribbon of lakes, ponds, rivers, and streams know as the Allagash Wilderness Waterway—are still open.

Among the twenty-three species of baitfish Maine still permits are the golden shiner, lake chub, fathead minnow, and common shiner (which it has determined pose a "moderate" threat to brook trout), smelt, longnose sucker, creek chub (a "high" threat), and white sucker (a "severe" threat—more severe even than yellow perch, brown bullheads, and largemouth bass, which it bans).

Only in Maine has the threat of baitfish attracted major media attention. The flap started with two proposed pieces of long overdue and desperately needed legislation almost pathetically modest in their goals—about like Oliver Twist asking for seconds on gruel.

One was introduced on behalf of the Sportsman's Alliance of Maine (SAM). The bill would ban live baitfish from a few of the "B List" ponds—where brookies are self-sustaining and haven't been stocked in at least twenty-five years. "This is nothing but a continuation of the bill passed in 2005 that protects 'heritage trout' in 305 unstocked ponds—the 'A List,'" declares Gary Corson, the Maine guide who discovered smelt in Big Reed Pond and who serves on SAM's Fishing Initiative Committee. "The state recognizes 284 B List ponds, but at least 36 of these have been stocked with species other than brook trout. SAM wants them off the list; it's unreasonable to ask the department to stop stocking landlocked salmon, for instance. And some of the waters don't qualify as principal brook trout waters; we want those off the list, too. We're not looking for big numbers." As Corson notes, ice fishing isn't allowed on most of B List ponds anyway. After all the subtraction, ice anglers would be prevented from using live bait on only 14 ponds out of over 1,100 available to them. And even on these fourteen they would be able to use jigs, worms and dead baitfish (very effective for brook trout and lake trout when fished on the bottom).

The other bill, introduced on behalf of the Dud Dean Angling Society (DDAS), would ban just four of the twenty-three legal species of baitfish—the ones the scientific literature lists as alien to the state. These are the spottail, blackchin and emerald shiners, and the eastern silvery minnow. Emerald shiners are of special concern because they are primary vectors of Viral Hemorrhagic Septicemia (VHS), a devastating fish disease now established in the Great Lakes and the St. Lawrence River System.

"Ice fishers and bait dealers have been stirring the pot on the internet, getting everyone all charged up," says Corson. "These guys don't know what the hell they're talking about, and no one on our side is willing to get into that kind of a fight with them. We haven't heard a peep from open-water bait fishers."

The noise from Maine carried all the way to New York City, and on March 13, 2007, *The Wall Street Journal*, in typical fashion, spun the baitfish controversy into what it called a "class war" between native, blue-collar ice fishermen and rich, yuppy flyrodders "mostly 'from away.'"

Whipping ice anglers to a froth of fear, loathing and paranoia has been Maine's property-rights community which has seized on the proposed legislation as a means of vilifying those who value native ecosystems—

i.e., the ubiquitous, liberal "greenies." SAM, it alleges, has been infiltrated by "environmental extremists," "eco-fundamentalists," and "fly fishing elitists"; SAM, TU and the "Duds" (DDAS) have conspired to push traditional anglers out of the way "so they can have the resource all to themselves"; sponsors and supporters of the bills who once lived or were educated in other states are "invasisve species themselves," the legislation is "incrementalism," "a government jackboot in the door," "the first salvo" in a meticulously planned offensive to ban all ice fishing.

Among the more prolific of Maine's conspiracy theorists is one Alfred Moore of Milbridge who spends his days crusading on internet newspaper comment boxes, blogs, forums and chat rooms against what he calls "the Environmental Industry" (always capped). According to one of his daily warnings, the "anti-live bait legislation could ban use of live bait forever." He defines brook trout as "the 'new' Atlantic salmon" and proclaims that "Environmental Industry groups are already buying up land to 'protect the natives'" which he expects will soon be listed under the Endangered Species Act, first in the long list of federal statutes he detests.

Similar rhetoric issues from bait dealers, particularly their chief spokesman—John Whalen, a former state game warden and Maine's only propagator of alien emerald shiners. "Ethically, the fly fishermen don't like ice fishing," he told *The Wall Street Journal.* "They view it as consumptive, removing 'resource' from the environment." Whalen defines advocates of the baitfish legislation as "ring-tailed barstards [sic]" out to "eliminate ice fishing and general law fishing opportunities and to just screw with traditional Maine fishers."

A mantra from Moore, Whalen and the rest of the Maine anti-bait-reg lobby is that there's no proof that spottail, blackchin and emerald shiners, and the eastern silvery minnow are non-natives. That's true (although the only Maine biologist to have studied them says they are). It's also irrelevant because a baitfish doesn't have to be alien to a state to ruin a fishery in that state; it only has to be alien to the body of water in which it is unleashed. Witness, for example, the fate of the brookies and bluebacks that used to abound in Big Reed Pond. Moreover, the burden of proof that these baitfish are alien should not be on those who seek to protect wild trout. The burden of proof that these baitfish are native (and none exists) should be on those who want to risk seeding them throughout the state.

In the last decade or so the Maine Department of Inland Fisheries and Wildlife has done a much better job of managing the national treasure it has been entrusted with. Its brook trout specialist, Forrest Bonney, reports a significant increase in the percentages of older and bigger fish. Draconian bag limits—down to one fish on some ponds—have done wonders.

Thanks to scientists like Bonney and fisheries chief Boland, Maine also has some excellent management policies in place. It's just that, with so much political heat from special-interest groups like bait dealers, those policies don't always get implemented. Considering all the department's talk about the dangers of alien fish, you'd think it would want to prohibit use of at least the four baitfish alien to the state. But it testified against the DDAS bill, and, on the department's advice, a legislative committee has recommended that only the blackchin shiner be banned. "Why?" I asked Boland.

Boland is a very good biologist, but his answer made no sense to me. He explained that the twenty-three species of legal baitfish are "extremely difficult to identify," that "we don't have reliable records for their distribution," and that "it wouldn't make a lot of sense to saddle the wardens with this kind of enforcement." I can't think of three better reasons to restrict the use of all live baitfish in and near wild trout water until biologists figure out what lives where.

At this writing the department doesn't have an official position on SAM's bill, but Boland doesn't like it. Two years ago, at the legislature's direction, the department convened a working group to determine what additional wild trout ponds needed protection from baitfish. "Right in the middle of this comes this bill from SAM," says Boland. "In a way I look at it as undermining the group's efforts." But the department waited ten months to call a meeting, and SAM got impatient.

Natural Resources Committee chair Rep. Theodore Koffman (D-Bar Harbor), who introduced SAM's legislation, offers this: "Mr. Boland probably won't come in with a better bill; that's troubling. The folks I've been working with—former department staff, anglers and guides—feel that the department has fallen way short and is hobbled by pressures. I can't confront it head on; so this is the way I'm trying to do it."

There's a small minority of ice anglers and bait dealers vindictive and/or selfish enough to intentionally disperse baitfish as well as alien game fish they happen to favor, especially pike. Draw maps of Maine's major baitfish dealerships, its major ice angling activity, its major rudd infestation, its major emerald shiner infestation, its major pike infestation, and you pretty much have one map.

On February 20, 2007, a hearing was held on the DDAS bill at the Statehouse in Augusta. One of the participants, TU and DDAS member Jeff Levesque (who until recently served on both the state's brook trout working group and SAM's Fishing Initiative Committee) told me this: "As we were all leaving, one of the leaders of this whole [anti-bait-reg] crew came up to me and said: 'If you fly fishermen keep pushing to ban these invasives, they're just going to get spread around.' That's the mentality of these guys. It doesn't surprise me that they're applauding the pike introductions."

Meanwhile, in Maine and across the nation, bait anglers and bait dealers continue to purposefully and accidentally festoon aquatic habitat with alien baitfish and whatever other aliens are mixed in with them. And, as in Maine, education, enforcement, and legislative reform move at the pace of continental drift.

Native fish, especially wild salmonids, don't have that kind of time.

Management by Politician

◄─(- -)-►

You can never take the politics out of fish and wildlife management. But you can and must take the politicians out. Politicians, by their nature, will try to seize control of fish and game agencies, and they succeed wherever sportsmen and environmentalists remain apathetic and unengaged. Usually, the first step is stacking the agency's policy-setting commission, the members of which are generally appointed by the governor and sometimes confirmed by the legislature. When politicians control commissions (and, thereby, fish-and-wildlife decision making) they cater to the big money that underwrites their campaigns—large, extractive industries inconvenienced by the needs of fish and wildlife.

"One of the big things that has led to politicization of fish and game agencies in the Northwest is the [ESA] listings of salmon and steelhead," says Bert Bowler, who retired as Idaho's salmon biologist last September and continues to defend the resources as native fisheries director for Idaho Rivers United. "The governors said, 'This is bigger than you fish and wildlife agencies. We need to get involved here because our constituents are at risk from the feds.' The sad part of all this is that the states aren't standing tall representing the needs of the fish. Oregon, Washington and Idaho have been neutered. I've never seen it this bad. The fish need strong agencies, and they don't exist."

Rod Sando, former director of the Idaho Department of Fish and Game agrees. "It's a generic problem particularly here in the West," he says. "I think it comes down to the transition that's going on from the extractive economy to the new economy of tourism and recreation. In the Idaho Fish and Game Commission and others—Wyoming, Colorado, Utah, to some extent Montana—you see commissioners who are not fish and wildlife advocates so much as advocates for ranching or timber or mining. In Washington the commission isn't bad on resources, but the department is in trouble with the legislature." Indeed it is. In February 2001 a bill was introduced in the state House of Representatives that would remove budgetary authority from the Fish and Wildlife Commission and let the governor appoint the Fish and Wildlife director.

No case study more graphically illustrates what Sando is talking about than his own forced resignation on January 23, 2002. If there's one thing the threatened and endangered salmonids of the Columbia system needed, it was a strong, principled Fish and Game director in Idaho, a leader willing to stand up to the powerful commercial interests preventing recovery. Sando, who had distinguished himself as head of the Minnesota DNR for eight years, was just such a leader. When he arrived in Idaho on April 1, 2000, he found the department in shambles. The agency was hemorrhaging money; morale was at an all time low.

The mess had been created and left by Stephen Mealey, a director who displayed no commitment to anything save telling sportsmen, environmentalists, politicians, and resource extractors what they wanted to hear. He promised the moon and the stars and the planets, then delivered glow-in-the-dark ceiling decals. Eventually this modus operandi angered the resource extractors, and they had him fired. One of the things he promised was that he wouldn't let the commission come out with a statement of simple biological truth—that the best way to recover Columbia Basin salmon and steelhead was to remove the four lower dams on the Snake River. But at a hearing in May 1998 overwhelming testimony in favor of dam removal forced the commission to do just that.

The legislature was apoplectic. In retaliation it held hostage a desperately needed license-fee hike, offering to pass it only if the commission reversed itself and proclaimed that salmon and dams could coexist just fine. It tried to strip the department of salmon-management authority and tried to fire the head of the salmonid program and the chief of fisheries. The governor prevailed on the Fish and Game Commission to remove from state hatcheries all displays suggesting that a free-flowing river might be salubrious for salmonids.

"I was at the hearing when our commission made its stand on salmon in 1998," says Bowler "They didn't say go out and breach the dams. They just reported our science—that if you want to recover the fish, a free-flowing river is the way to do it. The governor's office had brought in all these tobacco scientists to try to counter it. That's how it always was. When we would put out the science, the governor's people would come out with tobacco science in an effort to convince the public that you couldn't trust us or our data: 'Well, gee, we just really don't know if salmon need water.' It got almost that ludicrous. They would counter with: 'No, the dams aren't a problem. They're actually better for the fish.' Idaho took the lead on this in the Northwest because the governor's office seemed so threatened by what these fish might do to the status quo. The status quo in Idaho is water and dams on the lower river for navigation to Lewiston."

To show how much he really loved salmon, Kempthorne set up a September 1999 photo-op at Redfish Lake in which he flounced around releasing hatchery-bred sockeye adults while uttering such banalities as: "There's something spiritual about this. This is exactly what nature intended." Really? Nature intended more sockeyes to reach their historical spawning habitat via governor than by swimming themselves? Nature intended that the entire natural run of sockeyes that year—the second highest return of the decade—would be seven fish? Nature intended that the lower river be transmogrified to a series of warm, predator-infested, silt-choked deadwaters where humans collect smolts in nets, tote them seaward in barges, and then pretend that it works? When nature was running the show, the Snake River rose and fell with the seasons, chilled out in tall forests and shaded canyons, rushed and tumbled and breathed in oxygen, picked up and spread gravel and dead wood. In those days the river produced almost half the chinooks spawned in the entire Columbia system. Combined runs of all salmonids are thought to have approached eight million.

Leaned on by Kempthorne and the legislature, Mealey issued a gag order to department personnel, forbidding them from talking publicly about Snake River salmon recovery. (Immediately thereafter wads of toilet paper appeared in the mouths of all the mounted fish on display at the Boise headquarters.) When reporters asked questions about salmon and were told that it was verboten to speak of such things, First Amendment removal became a bigger story than dam removal.

Mealey had been brought in by Kempthorne's predecessor, Phil Batt, to restrain what Batt perceived to be a rogue agency. Kempthorne found

Mealey useful for that purpose, also. But after Mealey's dismissal by the commission, the legislature gave Kempthorne a more reliable device— a new bureaucracy called the Office of Species Conservation that stripped the department of management authority for all threatened and endangered species and placed it with the governor. Kempthorne—who, as a U.S. Senator, led western Republicans in a failed jihad against the Endangered Species Act—is using the Office of Species Conservation not to recover Snake River salmonids, bull trout, wolves and the like, but to filter professional science coming out of the Fish and Game Department so that special interests won't be inconvenienced by the Endangered Species Act. Not only does the office bleed $500,000 a year from the state budget—a huge amount in Idaho—it shortstops federal dollars and decides how Fish and Game will spend them. Running the office is Jim Caswell who, as supervisor of the Clearwater National Forest, presided over the destruction of its fragile soils, forests and trout streams while fighting the roadless initiative offered by his enlightened boss, Mike Dombeck.

Sando was just the prescription fish and wildlife needed—a smart, tough pro who said what he meant, never showed his back in a fight, and stood up for the resource and his fellow biologists. Staff and sportsmen adored him. He rebuilt morale and got the department out of the red and well into the black. It wasn't long, however, before he got crosswise with the legislature and governor. Kempthorne had instructed state employees that, when discussing salmon management, they were to speak with "one voice"—his voice, the voice of ignorance. But, unlike Mealey, Sando couldn't do that. His written mandate was to follow fish and game policy, and the commission, not the governor's office, sets it. Until he heard otherwise from the commission, the department's policy was going to be that a free-flowing Snake River is what salmon needed. Two months before the governor forced him out the commission gave him a raise.

Under Sando the department moved aggressively to protect and restore fisheries resources, both resident and anadromous. His main priority was instream flows. But, although water rights were purchased from willing sellers, this displeased irrigators, particularly the Idaho Farm Bureau Federation. There's a lot of trout habitat in Idaho that has been dried up by irrigators—on the Big Wood River, the Lemhi, the Little Lost, the Pahsimeroi, to mention just a few. Sando wanted to restore dewatered trout habitat, and he would have if he'd had the chance.

While the department doesn't own or manage much land, it tells federal agencies such as the Forest Service and BLM what they need to do to protect and restore fish and wildlife. For example, cows shouldn't be allowed to wallow in trout streams and rip up their banks as they currently do throughout Owyhee County and on such waters as the East Fork of the Salmon River, the Pahsimeroi, Bear Valley Creek, and Marsh Creek, one of the most important spring chinook producers on the Columbia system. The Idaho Cattle Association deeply resented this advice, even when it was ignored.

What also incensed the Idaho Cattle Association, its allies in the legislature, and a small but shrill group of elk hunters in the Clearwater country was Sando's alleged softness on predators. On the Clearwater National Forest elk are way down because the winter range can no longer support them. Huge fires in the early 1900s created massive brush fields and, in turn, an explosion of elk. But as trees matured, the elk faded away. "A lot of the winter range there is probably on a 500-year [growth-burn] cycle," says Lonn Kuck, Fish and Game's former big-game manager who retired last July after thirty-two years with the department. "There is an element out there that is convinced that predators are the limiting factor. That element simply can't comprehend that habitat isn't always constant; it thinks that if you kill the predators, we'll have elk coming out of our ears."

Helping me understand what Kuck meant was one Ed Lindahl, board member and past president of the Concerned Sportsmen of Idaho— as far as I can determine, the only hunting-and-fishing outfit that was glad to see Sando go. "Sando was an embracer of wolves," he declared. "That put him at odds with us. We're dead set against wolves. What our forefathers did to them should have remained so. Reintroducing wolves was the most extreme of environmentalism. I'm a retired Army officer, and I take the same view of militant Marxism throughout the world." According to Lindahl, the elk that get away from the wolves are eaten by bears and cougars. Almost as bad as predators are trout fishermen, with their preservationist mindset against clearcutting and roading: "I bump up against the Orvis men of the world who don't want to see the forest opened up," he declared. "You know, the purists who want only wild fish—groups like Trout Unlimited that file knee-jerk appeals and law suits on any timber sale that may help elk." And, of course, there's the "extreme environmentalism" pushed by the Rocky Mountain Elk Foundation which "embraces the roadless initiative that the Clinton administration rammed down the West's throat." Such talk makes eminent good sense to a lot of Idahoans.

Last October a golden ax, in the form of gross "predator coddling" by Sando, fell into the laps of the Concerned Sportsmen of Idaho, the governor, the Idaho Cattle Association, the Idaho Farm Bureau Federation, and the legislature. According to the report filed by conservation officer Bob Sellers, this is how the incident went down: The wife of a caretaker at a ranch near Mountain Home, an area where cougars have co-existed with people and livestock for decades, saw a small lioness and her two cubs at one end of a pasture. They seemed to be looking at some horses at the other end—hungrily, she thought. Neither she nor anyone else saw the cats chasing the horses. But guessing what they had in mind, she phoned a local hunter, Bob Corbus. When Corbus arrived the cougars were nowhere to be seen, so he drove around in his truck until he found them, then shot all three. The mother and one cub died quickly. The other cub, unable to move, lived for another day until Corbus got around to shooting it again. In Idaho you can only kill cougars if they're attacking your livestock. So—after getting clearance from his supervisor and the local prosecutor—Sellers cited Corbus for game-law violations. Although Corbus wasn't a member of the Idaho Cattle Association, president-elect Ted Hoffman wrote a letter to Sando, demanding that he fix the ticket.

Sando's response—that he wasn't into fixing tickets, and that it was illegal anyway—was described by the association as "a political move." With that, the association passed a resolution authorizing Hoffman to "cause the Idaho Fish and Game Department to follow the existing law." Scenting blood, the Idaho Farm Bureau Federation proclaimed that Sellers had been "overzealous" and demanded that he "be removed from duty and thoroughly investigated." Sen. Robbi King-Barrutia (R-Glenns

Ferry) and Rep. Mike Moyle (R-Star) announced that they would file legislation to enable livestock owners to more easily kill predators. The prosecutor dropped the charges, but that wasn't enough. Corbus filled a six-page complaint with the state, and now Sellers is being investigated by the Attorney General.

A heavy predator-control element in the commission left Sando with only a one-vote margin, and one of his supporters—Nancy Hadley, who had cast the tie-breaking vote for his raise—was coming up for reappointment. Clearly, Sando was toast.

When Sando left the department Kempthorne expressed astonishment. But Don Clower, one of the governor's own appointees to the commission, set the record straight. "I watched on TV as the governor said that neither he nor his staff had anything to do with Rod's forced termination," he told me. "That just wasn't true. They took us into little groups of twos and threes so they didn't violate the open meeting law. They spent forty-five minutes telling us all the bad things Rod had done and to go fix the problem." Clower reports that the governor himself showed up for one of the meetings.

Kempthorne sees Clower, whose term is up June 30, as a major mistake. But Clower has built an enormous following among sportsmen, and it's not clear that they'll let the governor replace him. I asked Clower what sportsmen in other states needed to do to keep the politicians out of wildlife decision making. "Get involved," he said. "As a group, we're an apathetic bunch. The only time we rise to anything is when we're directly threatened."

While Idaho hunters, anglers, and environmentalists were contemplating their navels the state legislature was eroding the Fish and Game Commission system, doing away with staggered terms and shortening term length from six years to four so that new governors could bring in more new members. Kempthorne, for example, brought in four.

But now that Idaho's sportsmen have lost the director they so badly needed, they've joined with environmentalists in a twenty-two-group coalition and are fighting back. As former Interior Secretary and former Idaho governor Cecil Andrus aptly puts it, Kempthorne and the legislature "have jabbed an old hibernating bear in the fanny with a stick." The coalition is circulating a petition for a ballot initiative next November that would reduce the number of commissioners from seven to five, strip the Senate of confirmation power, and require the governor to appoint members from candidates elected in caucuses around the state.

A good measure of the initiative's worth is the reaction it is eliciting from the governor and Farm Bureau Federation. In March the coalition summarily dismissed a "compromise" offered by Kempthorne in the form of a five-man commission in which sportsmen supplied two members, the Farm Bureau supplied two, and the governor appointed the fifth. Andrus accurately defined it as "three to two against wildlife." Showing its first-ever concern for sportsmen, the Farm Bureau refers to the "unholy alliance" between sportsmen and environmentalists and warns that "if true sportsmen go for this ruse, the hunter, fisherman and outfitters will be out of business."

"The current situation is forcing the public to take this kind of action," says Lonn Kuck. He speaks of "this subtle pressure" that made it impossible for him and his fellow professionals to do the work they were hired for. "It was very difficult to make hard decisions," he says. "No one said I couldn't do something, but lots of times my recommendations weren't carried out. If you don't agree with the direction, you're slowly and insidiously ostracized from the decision-making process to where you become ineffective. That happened to me. It reached a point where I didn't even participate in the last round of big-game season-setting."

Maybe the coalition can pull the State of Idaho up by its bootstraps. I doubt that it realizes its own power. "Whenever sportsmen combine with environmentalists, you have 60 to 70 percent of the population, an absolutely irresistible coalition," remarks Chris Potholm, founder of the Potholm Group, a polling and strategic advice company that has engineered sixty environmental referenda victories in thirty states. I'd hate to think that men like Sando are too good for states like Idaho. Maybe there's a state that deserves Sando now, but he's 60 and tired of directing (or trying to direct) resource agencies. He's flat-out not going to do it anymore.

So what *is* he going to do? Well, at this writing he's off to a place about as far as you can get from Idaho politicians and Idaho resource extractors—New Zealand. For a full month he's going to fish for non-threatened steelhead.

Robbed by RATs

It sounded okay when Congress authorized it in 1996. The few sportsmen and environmentalists who even noticed vacillated between disinterest and mild approval. Starved for funds, as always, the Forest Service, Bureau of Land Management, National Park Service and Fish and Wildlife Service would charge the public new or increased fees for accessing its land to fish, hunt, boat, drive, park, camp, walk. ... It was going to be an "experiment"—a three-year pilot program. That's why it was called the "Fee Demonstration."

Americans were used to paying entrance fees at national parks and wildlife refuges. But after Fee Demo was extended through 2001 they expressed outrage about what they came to call the Recreation Access Tax (RAT) on national forests and BLM land. Late in 2004 RAT was extended yet again—this time for ten years—when Fee Demo was replaced with the Recreation Enhancement Act, a law that empowers the four agencies to charge even more access fees.

Scott Silver, director of the Bend, Oregon-based Wild Wilderness—one of the very few environmental groups that has sounded the alarm—lives two blocks from the Deschutes River, world famous for its steelhead. "At the end of town the Deschutes National Forest begins," he says. "Upriver for maybe five miles is what the Forest Service now calls a High Impact Recreation Area, and I cannot go anywhere there in a car without having paid. An access road runs parallel to the river, and there are about three perpendicular roads to it. You may be a mile away, but as soon as you enter one of those perpendicular roads you're confronted by a sign that says 'Entering Fee Area.' I use a kayak. You're not going to carry a kayak a mile."

"These fees have been very controversial to say the least," comments Rick Swanson, the Forest Service's respected river and wetlands point person. "Look at the reaction you get when you talk about saltwater licenses. The whole gauntlet of, 'Hell-no I won't pay,' to 'Yeah we really need to kick in more.' It's the same thing with fees. Some people realize what's out there and what's at stake and how we're having trouble trying to provide recreation for the American public. The money is getting to the ground.'"

Swanson's saltwater-license analogy is especially apt, but not in the way he imagines. The real benefit of saltwater licenses has not been revenue for management but representation in management decisions for recreational interests (in this case anglers). The same is true of RAT. But what recreational interests are we talking about?

Fee Demonstration and the Recreation Enhancement Act were the work of the motorized-recreation industry. There was no Congressional debate or public involvement. Both RAT laws were slipped through as midnight riders tacked to appropriation bills because the industry knew they couldn't survive democracy.

Facilitating Fee Demo via cost-share partnership with the Forest Service was the powerful American Recreation Coalition (ARC) whose membership is comprised mainly of manufacturers of ATVs, motorized trailbikes, jetskis and RVs. And joining ARC in lobbying aggressively for both RAT laws have been the National Off Highway Vehicle Coalition, the National Snowmobile Manufacturers Association and such odious "wise-use" fronts for the motorized recreational industry as the Blue Ribbon Coalition.

As a result, anglers now have few places to find quietude and wildness or listen to birdsong or the music of rushing water or wind through forest canopies. Hike into any remote stream or pond in nonwilderness and you're likely to be assaulted by the screech and whine of internal-combustion engines. Pretty discouraging when you've invested two or three hours, and the guys on the machines have invested ten minutes.

Largely as a result of RAT legislation, 10,000 new ATVs (including trailbikes) get registered each year in Idaho, the contiguous state with the most national forestland. Now the total is 100,000. Colorado had about 11,000 registered ATVs twelve years ago. Now it has 90,000. Today ATVs account for five percent of all visits to national forests and grasslands. Ninety percent of BLM lands are now open to motorized recreation; the agency even sponsors races. And the machines themselves have grown from little farmyard putt-putts to monsters with double seats, megashocks, and 700-cubic-centimeter engines.

Recreational vehicles need to be regulated, not banned. "You're not going to get rid of them," says Scott Silver. "But you can't let these agencies look at motorized recreational industries and call them 'partners' and 'stakeholders.' That's nonsense. The environmental community is under the delusion that motorized recreation is somehow going to be managed with these user fees. No. It's going to be used and abused to give the industries the best advantage they can negotiate. Because we don't understand reality, they're negotiating better then we are."

But the recreational-vehicle issue is just sidebar. While Rick Swanson has it right about RAT funds getting to the ground (at least in most cases), appropriations from Congress keep disappearing into bureaucratic black holes. So RAT money—virtually none of which goes to fisheries research or enhancement—has become both a replacement for squandered wealth and an incentive for continued profligacy.

Instead of shaking down visitors for a few extra bucks on top of what the IRS has taxed them to buy and maintain the property, on top of what state game and fish departments and the Park Service have charged them for fishing licenses, on top of what the Fish and Wildlife Service has charged them to buy and maintain refuges, and on top of what campgrounds charge them to spend the night, the agencies might try not wasting the money they already have. For instance, the BLM and Forest Service could save $2 billion a year and dramatically improve fishing and hunting by desisting from below-cost timber sales and unnecessary road building. The maintenance backlog for Forest Service roads (which could circle the globe 19 times) is $10 billion. It can't even take care of the roads it has, and yet it's building new ones.

What's more, the non-motorized people paying RAT fees are the very ones most invested in public lands and who, in many instances, have volunteered to staff visitor centers, maintain trails, pick up litter, find lost hikers, remove invasive exotic plants, restore stream habitat, and backpack trout fry to high-country lakes. The best analogy I've seen is the Park Service sending France a bill for refurbishment and maintenance of the Statue of Liberty.

"I fish," wrote John Voelker in probably the most quoted statement on angling since Walton, "because I love to, because I love the environs where trout are found, which are invariably beautiful, and hate the environs where crowds of people are found, which are invariably ugly." But RAT puts federal resource agencies in the business of attracting crowds of people, thereby disfiguring the environs of trout. It motivates managers to ignore sportsmen and promote instead activities that damage fish and wildlife and conflict with fishing and hunting. Recreation becomes a business. Our rivers, lakes, grasslands and forests become Disneyfied amusement parks.

Noted outdoor writer and *Field & Stream*'s erstwhile conservation editor Michael Frome offers this: "Stewardship of public lands—especially wilderness—often requires limitation of use, but [RAT] provides a powerful incentive for managers to avoid anything that will limit use—the more use they can generate, the greater their budgets. Money is not the simple answer, but Congress must provide the funding to do the necessary administration to maintain these national treasures for future generations. It should not order administrators to merchandise the resource in order to pay their salaries."

We're seeing the results of this incentive in a new Forest Service program under way (sans public participation or Congressional oversight) called "Recreation Site Facility Master Planning." The agency evaluates recreation facilities on each forest, then assess them for profitability. In some forests this means closing almost half the recreational sites— the ones that generate the least revenue. The remote campgrounds and trailheads—places to which an angler seeking a quality fishing experience would naturally gravitate—are first to get disappeared. Bulldozers are knocking down campgrounds, dismantling latrines, even removing fire pits. You won't be able to even park.

For instance, the new master plan for the Mark Twain National Forest in Missouri calls for reducing "Recreation Areas" (containing one or more campgrounds, picnic areas, boat accesses or trailheads) from fifty-three to thirty, campgrounds from thirty-six to twenty-two, picnic areas from forty-one to twenty-five, and trailheads from fifty-one to thirty-eight. In Colorado about half the 140 campgrounds and other recreational facilities on the Grand Mesa, Uncompahgre and Gunnison national forests face closure. The BLM has just announced a similar plan.

RAT fees provide an excuse for Congress and the administration to chip away at critically needed programs such as the Land and Water Conservation Fund (derived from oil and gas exploration leases). The four agencies use the fund to purchase fish and wildlife habitat, an activity the President frowns on because the privatizers inside and outside the White House who have his ear contend that the feds shouldn't be "tying up land." The Land and Water Conservation Fund is supposed to provide $900 million a year for public-lands projects to offset damage caused by offshore drilling. For 2007 the President has asked for $84 million.

The Western Slope No-Fee Coalition estimates that the Forest Service will decommission about 3,000 campsites, day-use facilities, picnic areas, trailheads, and parking places. "Very little budget money from Congress is getting to the ground, says the group's president, Robert Funkhouser. "About 80 percent is used for administration." As for anglers getting any return on their RAT investments, Funkhouser says this: "I stay pretty close to this subject, and I have never heard about fee revenue going toward fish or fish habitat. I would feel pretty comfortable saying it doesn't."

The same grim scenario is unfolding on our national wildlife refuges which the Bush administration—again, at the behest of privatizers—has placed on a starvation diet. RAT fees aren't helping. Last December I visited the Pahranagat Valley National Wildlife Refuge in southern Nevada—a ten-mile ribbon of green in the Mojave Desert and one of the few places in this, our driest state, where the public can fish. The Upper Lake has a good population of largemouth bass, but it's infested with carp. The carp muddy the water, degrading bass habitat and preventing photosynthesis in plants that sustain waterfowl.

To keep the carp out the refuge installed weirs on the pathetic, irrigation-depleted remains of its water source, the White River. But it has no money to maintain the weirs (which are rotting where they stand) and no money to control the carp. This is a land of imperiled desert fishes—relics from extinct glacial lakes that have miraculously adapted to desert life. The refuge contains many springs that probably sustain federally listed species such as threatened White River Springfish and possibly endangered roundtail chubs (clinging to existence in a nearby artificial pond and thought to be extinct in the wild). But the refuge can't even afford a biologist to inventory the springs. "I need that data to make good decisions," declares refuge manager, Merry Maxwell.

In January the Fish and Wildlife Service's eight-state, fifty-four-refuge Midwest Region announced a plan to reduce the workforce by about 20 percent. "Our sense is that about a third of the refuges in that region are going to be in 'preservation status,' which means they'll be unstaffed," says Jeff Ruch, director of Public Employees for Environmental Ethics.

Summing up the whole sorry mess for all federal resource agencies is district ranger Cid Morgan of the Angeles National Forest in California: "We're going to have to do more with less until we do everything with nothing."

As abusive as RAT fees are in their own right, the Forest Service is abusing them further by playing fast and loose with the law. The Recreation Enhancement Act of 2004 was supposed to fix all the problems with Fee Demo. No longer would the public be charged just to, say, go fishing, but only if a site had "significant investment," which the act defined as six amenities: security services (staffers who check to see if you've paid), parking, toilets, picnic tables, permanent trash receptacles, and permanent interpretation (signs with such messages as "Don't feed the animals").

What happened on the Deschutes National Forest is typical. "One day," says Scott Silver, "and I mean one day, the Forest Service goes out and buys a bunch of thirty-gallon, galvanized trashcans and some chains and padlocks and drops them off at places they'd been charging without being in compliance."

A site has to have all six amenities. But the Forest Service has dreamed up a way of getting around the law by designating sections of forest as "High Impact Recreation Areas" (HIRAs). One corner of a HIRA has a sign; another corner, perhaps two miles away, might have a trash can. Three miles from both might be a parking lot. The Recreation Enhancement Act makes no reference, oblique or otherwise, to anything like an HIRA. The concept is simply Forest Service slight of hand. And HIRAs are being set up all across the national forest system.

The Forest Service has been flouting even its own bizarre interpretation of the law. Last year it admitted to the Senate Subcommittee on Public

Lands and Forests that 739 HIRAs didn't have the six amenities. Moreover, it had not bothered to report 627 of these HIRAs to Congress, a violation of the Recreation Enhancement Act which forbids designation of new fee sites without public participation. And there are at least 3,000 former Fee Demo sites outside HIRAs that are still charging fees, many of them illegally.

When Scott Silver got a ticket for refusing to pay a RAT fee in a Deschutes HIRA he informed the U.S. attorney that he would be representing himself in court. The feds immediately dropped the charge. But they prosecuted Christine Wallace, a Tucson legal secretary, who wouldn't pay two tickets for what amounted to hiking without a license on a Coronado National Forest HIRA in Arizona. While the Recreation Enhancement Act allows RAT fees, it specifically prohibits the Forest Service and BLM from charging entrance fees. Accordingly, the court found that by charging a fee for entering the HIRA and for parking, the Forest Service had illegally implemented the law.

But the agency appealed and on January 16, 2007, won a reversal. If the ruling stands, it establishes case law that makes it a crime to fish or even get out of your vehicle on your own land without finding a ranger station (if one is open) and coughing up money that even the motorized-recreation axis that hatched RAT fees never intended for you to pay.

When federal agencies come to depend on funding from special interests the special interests wind up running the show. On the fish-rich Sawtooth National Recreation Area in Idaho, as on so much public land entrusted to the Forest Service, the campgrounds have been taken over by concessionaires. After a public-relations disaster in this land of fed haters managers here have recently backed away from RAT fees. But the damage has been done.

"Services at the concessionaire-run campgrounds are minimal and charges are high," says former Idaho conservation officer Gary Gadwa, who now directs the Sawtooth Interpretive and Historical Association and volunteers for the Forest Service. "You might as well be paying to stay in an RV park. That's how expensive the campgrounds have become. We get 1.5 million visitors a year. This area is very popular for fishing—high-mountain lakes, streams, rivers, and steelhead in the Salmon River.

But very little of the [RAT] money went to fisheries or fisheries research and with all the fishing opportunities the need is great."

There's also a pressing need on the Sawtooth and elsewhere for monitoring species listed under the Endangered Species Act such as Chinook salmon, sockeye salmon, steelhead, and bull trout. But the Recreational Enhancement Act explicitly prohibits the agencies from spending RAT fees for this purpose. The law was written by Rep. Richard Pombo (R-CA) whose career-long crusade against the Endangered Species Act got him defeated in the last election.

Empowered by RAT fees, concessionaires are taking over our national parks as well as our national forests. So bad has the Disneyfication process become that in 2005 the Park Service nearly succeeded with a "draft directive" in which it would have raised additional funds through corporate sponsorship. Gale Norton, then secretary of Interior and the Bush administration's queen privatizer, called the proposal "exciting." Most any corporate enterprise, even alcohol, tobacco and gambling companies, would have been eligible for sponsorship. Had not the public recoiled in disgust, the promo might have read: "Fish Grand Teton National Park, brought to you by Wonder Bra."

Still, the Park Service has what it calls "Proud Partners" (American Airlines, Discovery Communications, Inc., Ford Motor Company and Unilever) whose monetary contributions allow them to cash in on the Park Service logo. And another overt effort like the draft directive of 2005 would be anything but a surprise.

Pombo and the motorized recreational industries who brought us RAT fees never intended them to benefit fish, wildlife or any of the other natural attributes that make our public lands so special. A veteran Park Service biologist told me this: "Back in 2000 the Bush campaign talked about the maintenance backlog in the parks. The strategy, as I perceive it, was to redirect fee dollars away from all the important projects that parks were spending them on—planning, resource work, management. The Recreation Enhancement Act has basically taken away the ability to fund those programs. And now the administration can say, 'Oh look we're spending millions on maintenance.'"

RAT fees are just part of a decades-old campaign to privatize government and the land it manages. Perhaps that agenda is best articulated by Republican spinmeister Grover Norquist, who runs the anti-tax lobbying outfit Americans for Tax Reform and hosts weekly meetings in Washington, D.C., for just about every conservative lawmaker and libertarian think-tank wonk in town: "I don't want to abolish government. I simply want to reduce it to the size where I can drag it into the bathroom and drown it in the bathtub."

As long as Bush/Reagan-era privatizers wield power in the legislative and executive branches of government the future looks bleak. On Feb. 2, 2007, the Forest Service's northern regional forester, Abigail Kimbell, took over for retiring chief Dale Bosworth, a decent, competent man who tried and often was not allowed to do the right thing and who pursued the administration's privatization agenda but without much enthusiasm.

Kimbell, on the other hand, has compiled a long record of brutal timber extraction and punishing her employees for doing their jobs, especially when it comes to defending fish and wildlife.

She says she wants to increase access fees.

V
HEAVY DUTY ECO ISSUES

SAVING THE NORTH WOODS

—‹‹ ›› —

At least the fish were still there. It takes more than oily marinas, motorboaters, partyboaters, waterskiers, jetskiers, parasailers, windsurfers and second-home developers to deplete smallmouth bass, the resilient bread-and-butter fish of Down East Maine. And, insulated as they are by forty feet of epilimnion, lake trout—"togue" in Mainespeak—were nearly as prolific as they'd ever been. With the increase in angling pressure more landlocked salmon were being stocked, so, if anything, they were more abundant than in the days when this watershed was wild.

The twenty-foot, square-end Grand Laker canoes used by the guides had been replaced by low-slung, glittery bass boats powered by enormous, time-conserving outboards. There used to be almost fifty guides in the thirteen towns between Grand Lake Stream and Forest City—more guides per surface acre than anywhere else in Maine, or New England, for that matter. Now there were none. There had been more fishing and hunting lodges here than anywhere else in the Northeast. Now they were out of business. But who needs guides when you can propel yourself with a foot-operated trolling motor and find fish with a sonar unit that beeps like a tipped-over telephone? And why travel almost to Canada for lodge-based, guided suburban bass fishing when you can do it yourself an hour by air out of New York, Boston, Chicago, Philly, Detroit or Atlanta?

Although some species of wildlife were on the way out, white-tailed deer had undergone spectacular recovery now that all the "no trespassing" signs had reduced hunting pressure. And while the economy had crashed after the guides, lodge owners, loggers and forest-products workers moved away or went on welfare, and after the Baileyville pulp and paper mill went belly up, the dollars were now pouring in (or, more accurately, out) as multinational corporations developed the former Georgia Pacific holdings, starting with the valuable shore-front property.

As I gazed up along the Farm Cove Peninsula from Leen's Lodge, I saw a phalanx of trophy houses. Twelve miles down the lake they faded into the summer haze, betrayed only by their docks, diving rafts and moored boats. I encountered all this last July—but only in a "daymare" as I studied the North Woods and contemplated its future from a float plane en route from Bangor to West Grand Lake. After a thirty-year hiatus, I was returning to this sacred land of lakes, streams and woods as the guest of the Downeast Lakes Land Trust and the New England Forestry Foundation (NEFF). There was still time to save it all, but the window of opportunity was closing fast.

Out on West Grand Lake once more, in the Grand Laker steered by guide and folk singer Randy Spencer, I scanned the shoreline for signs of change, and failed to find any. Doubtless there were new cottages, especially on the lake's south end, but I hadn't noticed the cottages in the 1970s, and I didn't notice them now. Nothing looked new, obtrusive or out of place. Most of the 14,000-acre lake still appeared untouched by humanity. It was silent save for the yodeling of loons and the lapping of waves. It was still embraced by a healthy mixed northern forest that stretched to the horizon or rose to meet purple ridgetops—not wilderness in the technical sense perhaps, but a damn fine facsimile. Collected by West Grand are the waters of thirty-two lakes, ponds and streams, all as wild or wilder. As nearly as I could discern, there hadn't been any change, but change was bearing down from all compass points.

Throughout the North Woods—that 26-million-acre swath of green from Machias, Maine, to Syracuse, New York—timber companies, beset by changing world markets and hounded by ravenous stockholders, are hawking their holdings. These days they tend to manage their forestland not on time scales dictated by natural regeneration but by the average corporate life expectancy of their CEOs (less than ten years). So, from the industry perspective, growing cellulose on shore-front property has become fiscally imprudent. It's more profitable to slick off the timber and sell the land. The primary threat to fish, wildlife and the local economy is liquidation cutting, subdivision and loss of public access. "It's happening all around us," declared Downeast Lakes Land Trust director Steve Keith as we strolled along the remote beach at the narrows below Pocumcus Lake, where American

Indians had speared sea-run salmon. "Even in Washington County you can go fifty miles from these lakes and find everything we're trying to avoid."

In 1999 the locals got a major scare when Georgia Pacific sold 446,000 acres—nearly all its property in Maine—to timber investors who consigned it to the care of Wagner Forest Management, Ltd. The initial concern of the guides was not suburban sprawl; woods and waters were so immense that they couldn't imagine such a thing. They worried instead about loss of access. Would the new owners festoon the forest with posted signs, cutting sportsmen off from favorite streams, ponds, grouse coverts, trap lines and deer stands? It wasn't long, however, before they realized that their livelihoods depended not just on access but on wildness. It's true that these lakes provide some of the best smallmouth fishing in the world, that the landlocked fishing is unexcelled south of Canada, and that lake trout are so prolific the state discourages their release, fretting that they'll get ahead of the forage base. But anglers don't come here from all over the world just for the fish. They come here for the North Woods experience—to be poled on still waters in Grand Laker canoes, to listen to the loons and warblers and the summer wind through birch, maple, spruce and balsam, to breathe sweet air undefiled by gasoline fumes. There are far more deer per acre in my central Massachusetts woods than in Down East Maine, but there is not one hunting lodge.

So in 2001, the guides allied themselves with sportsmen, lodge owners and local environmentalists to form the Downeast Lakes Land Trust. Their mission: purchase and permanently protect the entire 27,000-acre Farm Cove Peninsula. Skeptics, including professional biologists, foresters and land conservators, smiled condescendingly. Only rich folk from, say, East Hampton, New York, attempt to do this sort of thing; and even when they succeed they're lucky to save 100 acres. When approached by the land trust the Wagner company suggested that it find an experienced outfit to work with. So the land trust turned to the New England Forestry Foundation. By anyone's standards the land trust had been thinking big with its dream of saving the entire Farm Cove Peninsula. But NEFF had just wrapped up the largest conservation easement America has ever seen. In two years it had raised $32 million, mostly from private sources, and, for $37.10 per acre, protected 762,000 acres of forestland in northern and western Maine owned by the Pingree family.

NEFF suggested that the Downeast Lakes Land Trust collaborate with it in an undertaking called the Downeast Lakes Forestry Partnership. Farm Cove Peninsula would be purchased outright, then conservation easements would be obtained on additional forestland, bringing the total area protected to 342,000 acres. The project would include 78,000 surface acres on sixty lakes, 54,000 acres of wildlife-rich wetlands, 445 miles of lake shoreline, 1,500 miles of river and stream shoreline. Last March the partnership (with its other member, the Woodie Wheaton Land Trust) completed the St. Croix phase, raising $3.2 million and purchasing a 500-foot wildlife corridor/buffer along 13 miles of Spednic Lake (another world-famous smallmouth fishery) and 36 miles along the St. Croix River (the international boundary with Canada). Purchase of the Farm Cove Peninsula will cost $12.5 million, the easement on the remaining land $13 million. The partnership has committed to close on the deal by December 31, 2004. It's a tough time to be raising money, and help is needed. Still, at this writing, everything's on schedule.

Moreover, the timing has been perfect. As the partnership was signing options to purchase the land and easements, New Brunswick had just bought and protected 390,000 acres from Georgia Pacific's Canadian holdings, 72,000 acres of which, mostly on Spednic's north shore, has been designated as wilderness reserve. Throw in state federal reserve lands, Passamaquoddy and Penobscot lands, and other protected parcels, and you get a nearly contiguous block of one million acres of fish and wildlife habitat saved from development.

Aspects of the Downeast Lakes Forestry Partnership offer important lessons. First, nothing like this has ever been attempted anywhere. Other protection projects—even NEFF's monumental Pingree coup – have targeted unpeopled woods. No other project has been community based, community spawned and designed to preserve the local economy and traditional lifestyles. People live and work in these woods. The Baileyville mill, now owned by Domtar, is the biggest employer in the region. Without it the economy, along with the forest products industry, would collapse and Wagner would be forced to sell outright to developers. The partnership guarantees continued logging under responsible, though not oppressive, guidelines. Guaranteed also is public access and all traditional uses including hunting, fishing, trapping, snowmobiling and even ATV riding. The project is a model and a mold-breaker, the only practical way to avoid the Californication of Maine. As NEFF's director and Maine resident, Amos Eno, comments, "We should strive to lead, consistent with our motto 'Dirigo,' [I lead] and not follow California's example. ... A half century ago California was self-sufficient in wood. Today the state imports 80 percent of what it uses. ... Maine is a state on its knees financially, and Washington County in downeastern Maine is on the economic floor." The Downeast Lakes Forestry Partnership offers salvation of the environment and the economy which, here and everywhere, are one and the same.

Washington County is the epicenter of the wise-use movement in Maine, but there's been little noise. In all my research I was able to turn up only one published harangue—a June 19, 2003, op-ed in The Portland Press Herald by wise-use guru Jon Reisman of Cooper. "I expect more than half a million acres between Routes 1 and 6 will be 'protected' in one manner or another, creating the Down East National Salmon Wilderness Reserve, or DENSWR," lamented Reisman. "Wilderness is winning over jobs, and for most of Washington County it means less opportunity. Unless you're in the business of protecting salmon habitat or publishing beautiful multi-colored Green propaganda."

The partnership's project manager, Frank Reed, met with Reisman to try to reason with him. "He couldn't call this a bad idea," recalls Reed, "because then he'd be saying the landowners shouldn't do what they want with their land. I kept saying: 'Jonathan, are you saying you want to tell the landowner what to do with his land?' 'Oh, no, no, no,' he'd say. 'Then what are you trying to tell me here?' He finally said, 'Well, landowners ought to be able to do what they want, but uh, uh, uh. ... '"

If you follow FR&R's Conservation column, you may recall my report about the nasty and embarrassing tiff over the Champion lands acquisition in Vermont in which a tiny group of opportunists whipped up paranoia and property-rights fervor among economically disadvantaged residents by claiming (falsely) that the deal had been put together in secret by government bureaucrats and the Green mafia from out of state. But because the Downeast Lakes Forestry Partnership involves neither government nor environmental groups and because it was hatched and is being steered by locals, especially guides and sportsmen, wiseusers have no one to co-opt. The big peg for the wise-users in Vermont had been the ecological reserve in which the prescribed management was no management. "Come and watch healthy trees grow old, fall over and die," puffed James Ehlers, editor of (Vermont) *Outdoors Magazine*. But last January the board of the Downeast Lakes Land Trust unanimously voted to a establish a 3,500-acre ecological reserve in the upper Machias River watershed—habitat of Maine's endangered anadromous Atlantic salmon—that will abut a 3,800-acre ecological reserve established by the state and a 3,700-acre parcel to be managed by the land trust on 100- to 150-year cutting rotations. "Ecological reserves are important," says Bill Cherry, who worked twenty-nine years as an industrial forester for St. Regis, Champion and International Paper and is now coordinator of the Machias and East Machias River Watershed Council. "They provide valuable controls, baseline data. If we're doing something wrong elsewhere in the forest, ecological reserves can tell us what it is." And ecologist Janet McMahon, a consultant for the project, told me this: "These woods are all pretty young. The oldest stands are along the water, and they're only about ninety-year-old hemlocks, about a third of their natural age. What's missing is older, closed-canopy stands. Most of the beech has been cut; that has hurt bears. The oaks have been cut off the ridges, and that has hurt both deer and bear. We know old growth is good for deer yards, and in most cases reserves in Maine are surrounded by land with lots of browse. Reserves provide big trees and snags for species like marten, woodpeckers, wood ducks, hooded mergansers and owls. That's the part of the North Woods that's missing."

In Down East Maine at least, sportsmen are starting to understand this.

I did not argue with the land trust's Steve Keith and NEFF's Tim Storrow when they proclaimed that if you just walked around in these woods (or "puckerbrush," as Downeasters call it) you wouldn't see much of anything, that the only way to get a feeling for this country is by water, and that since I was going to be on the water anyway, I might as well tote a fly rod. First stop was Tomah Stream, a bit of an anomaly in the area known for its smallmouths, landlocks and lake trout, because in spring it provides spectacular wild brook trout fishing. One of the reasons is that Tomah sustains the highest diversity of caddis species ever found in the United States. It also sustains the state-threatened Tomah Mayfly, one of the very few predatory mayflies. But in high summer Tomah is low and warm, and I'd have to content myself with smallmouths.

For half a day we paddled and pulled canoes through the heart of the project area via as wild and lovely a stream as I have ever encountered. Raptors (barred owls and red-shouldered hawks I think, but couldn't get positive IDs) flushed ahead of us and sailed toward Grand Lake Flowage, only to flush again. A ruffed grouse and her brood buzzed out of the alders. Ebony jewelwing damselflies in fantastic numbers fluttered over dry sandbars and perched in iridescent, green-black clusters on brush, sedges and the drooping seedheads of grass. We drifted over fallfish nests—piles of gravel three feet across and a foot high. Smallmouths, some a foot and a half long, ghosted out of the shallows. Jeff McEvoy, my stern man and new owner of the storied Weatherby's Lodge at Grand Lake Stream, regaled me with local lore, while his Springer bitch, Madison (named for the river), pranced along the bank. McEvoy, formerly with the Natural Resources Council of Maine and, before that, a U.S. Fish and Wildlife Service refuge manger, has been a source of biological enlightenment and political savvy for all committed to the protection of woods, waters and traditional livelihoods. We caught smallmouths—clean, ruby-eyed fish with caudal fins you could shave with—and fat, grunting fallfish on Clousers and beadhead Woolly Buggers. I enjoyed the plucky fallfish nearly as much as the bass. "Cousin trout," Thoreau called them.

I had the first landlock—a sleek 17-incher that snatched a fast-moving Elkhair Caddis and, though she never showed herself, fought like a fish twice her size. Soon I was into another that came unbuttoned as I slid it into an eddy. Whittemore landed a decent smallmouth. But Storrow had the fish of the morning—a stream-bred, golden-hued salmon of at least 18 inches that ascended three times to absurd altitudes. Its enormous pectoral and ventral fins reminded me why, in fast water, Atlantics have the advantage over all other fish, native and alien.

A misty rain was blowing across the valley when the guides pulled up in their trucks, Grand Lakers in tow. "You look like you want to go fishing," declared Chris Wheaton as I bit off my 6X tippet and tied on a yellow balsawood popper. I told him he'd figured me right, so off we drove to the landing at Big Lake in Princeton. Big Lake is shallower than West Grand, with more structure along the shore. There isn't finer smallmouth water on the planet. It's not a big deal to catch 50 bass a day. And the slot limit, which spares bass between 12 and 16 inches, has created a trophy fishery.

Big Lake, too, was just as wild as I remembered it, and its south and southwestern shore are in the project area. As I eased my first bass toward Chris's outstretched net something big and black and checkered with white spots shot under the canoe, missing the mesh by inches. It was the "obnoxious loon." He surfaced four feet away, watching the bass. Pin feathers protruding from the back of his neck gave the manic air of Woody Woodpecker. To my delight and Wheaton's pique, he followed us for two miles, eyeballing my rod and surging to the boat each time it bent. An immature eagle sculled over spruce spires. Kingfishers dipped and rattled. There is nothing like fly-fishing out of a cedar-and-ash canoe for North Woods smallmouths, especially when you're being poled within an easy cast of sunken boulders. That's the way bass fishing used to be. Chris Wheaton, one of two people who still build Grand Lakers, has strong opinions about what has befallen bass fishing. If he's guiding you and you want to liven up the conversation (not that you're likely to encounter the need), just ask him what he thinks of all the fancy bass boats they have on the TV shows. Or better still, ask him if he is planning to get one. And as you're fishing keep looking around you. That's the way it can be in Maine and everywhere in the North Woods.

SLUDGE SLINGING

—‹‹ ›› —

Coal mining is a nasty business, especially in water-rich West Virginia, Virginia, Kentucky, Tennessee, and Pennsylvania. Precipitation, running off the stumps of mountains hacked down by coal companies or up from deep mines, picks up sulfuric acid, coal dust, and heavy metals that magnify through the food chain. But that's just what flows unimpeded into streams. Because Appalachian coal is associated with all manner of impurities, it must be washed with chemical flocculants before it can be burned. The rinse water is even worse than the runoff—blacker, more viscous, more toxic. "Sludge" it's called.

Like "overburden," the industry's word for everything that isn't coal, sludge is dumped on streams—except usually not on purpose and never legally. Coal companies attempt to contain it by damming up valleys. Sometimes the dams fail; more often the impounded sludge blows out through old mine shafts. Almost all of the 653 active sludge reservoirs in the United States are in Appalachia, and 230 of them are built over underground mines.

The danger to fish, wildlife, and people is enormous, but lessons aren't being learned, precautions aren't being taken, and federal culpability is being denied. Meanwhile, the Bush administration is trying to do away with the few rules that control sludge production and "mountaintop mining," as the administration and industry like to call it, or "mountaintop removal," as everyone else calls it. But thanks to a smart, tough mining engineer named Jack Spadaro, the White House appears to be learning one important lesson about the dangers of uncontrolled coal extraction: Few political messes are harder to cover up than sludge spills.

But first some history. On February 26, 1972, a dam owned by Pittston Coal Company failed, sending a tidal wave of sludge through seventeen communities along Buffalo Creek in Logan County, West Virginia. One survivor—Patty Adkins, now of Barboursville—told me this: "The water kept getting higher. And we saw all this debris—heaters and furniture and car parts. Then we heard this loud noise, and all this water came rushing around the bend, breaking loose houses and carrying them off. We saw an old couple in their truck get washed away. The McCoys' house had washed down and lodged at the train trestle, and these two men pulled out a woman's body. They put her beside the tracks, and one of the men took his raincoat off and covered her up. My sixth-grade teacher, Mrs. Ramey, and her husband died." In all, 125 people were killed and 4,000 left homeless. Pittston blamed God, claiming it was His "act." Although the company settled with the victims for $25 million, it settled with the state for just $1 million in a deal accepted by then-governor Arch Moore, later convicted for taking a bribe from another coal company.

Spadaro, at this writing employed by the U.S. Department of Labor's Mine Safety and Health Administration (MSHA, pronounced "EM-sha"), is among the leading experts on sludge spills. At the time of the Buffalo Creek tragedy, he was a twenty-three-year-old instructor at West Virginia University's School of Mines, one of the world's top institutions for training mining engineers. "Right then," he says, "I made a pledge to dedicate my life to doing whatever I could to prevent this type of thing from happening again." There had been all sorts of warnings, such as failures at this and every other sludge dam along the creek. For at least four years valley residents had been warning officials the dam was unsafe. As staff engineer for the commission assigned by the governor to investigate the disaster, Spadaro wrote the report. But during the process he got crosswise with the commission chair, Jay Kelley, who, according to Spadaro, wanted to take it easy on Pittston and who, as dean of the School of Mines, was also Spadaro's boss. So in order to protect his voice on the commission, Spadaro resigned from the university. No one except the governor could fire him from the commission, and he stayed on, not equivocating, not excusing, not retreating. Eventually eight commissioners agreed with Spadaro that the fault lay with Pittston, not God. Kelley wrote the one-man minority report.

Spadaro never bought into the notion that environmental regulators shouldn't also be environmental advocates. Two years later, on his own time, he helped found Save Our Mountains, one of the first groups to oppose mountaintop removal.

In 1981 he offended another bureaucrat—J. Steven Griles, then in charge of the Department of the Interior's Office of Surface Mining (who went on to become George W. Bush's Deputy Secretary of the Interior, after working as a mining lobbyist). Spadaro, who had transferred to the OSM, signed off on a decision to close a coal-preparation plant. "There were serious environmental problems there," says Spadaro. "But I was told by the regional director to vacate the closure order. I refused." Spadaro and his lawyer, Hope Babcock (who went on to become Audubon's general counsel), met with Griles. "He was so angry he was almost spitting," Spadaro recalls, "but he couldn't fire me." Instead Spadaro was suspended for thirty days sans pay. But he made agency brass even madder by winning an appeal through the Merit Systems Protection Board and making the OSM cough up his back pay.

Although Spadaro continued to anger certain of his superiors by doing his job and by exercising his First Amendment rights, he managed to get performance evaluations that basically alternated between "outstanding" and "exceeding standards." In 1992 he won Interior's highest honor, the Merit Service Award. In 1993 Interior named him Engineer of the Year. In 1997, his first year as superintendent of MSHA's National Mine Health and Safety Academy, in Beckley, West Virginia, he won the prestigious Bravo Award. The person who hired Spadaro—Davitt McAteer, MSHA's former director (officially known as "Assistant Secretary of Mine Safety and Health")—calls him "a good man." Celeste Monforton, who served as special assistant to the director, calls Spadaro "a great guy [who] did a tremendous job." She told me that "he really brought the academy into the twenty-first century."

When I met Spadaro, at the West Virginia capitol building on February 17, 2004, he was receiving yet another award—for "public service" from the West Virginia Environmental Council. Over the phone he'd spoken as softly as Mister Rogers, so I was surprised to encounter a big, square-shouldered, former football star with a Paul Bunyan beard. That evening, at a reception for award winners, Spadaro complained about the lack of regulations for sludge impoundments. And he condemned mountaintop removal. "There's no need for it," he said. "It's just cheaper for the companies."

Patty Sebok of Coal River Mountain Watch, who had just received the Environmental Council's award for "environmental courage," who lives beside a sludge-polluted stream, and who is married to an underground miner put out of work by mountaintop removal, presented Spadaro with a whistle, saying: "We want you to keep blowing this long, hard, and loud." Then the crowd broke into a chant of "Bring back Jack. Bring back Jack." But from what?

Well, on June 4, 2003, Spadaro was placed on "administrative leave"—a prelude to termination. Then, on October 1, he was informed that he would presently be fired for "abusing his authority," taking "unauthorized" cash advances, and generally failing to follow "instructions" and "procedures." He gave me his two-inch-thick response to the charges so I could read his side of the story.

Meanwhile, he would show me some sludge reservoirs, but no one can see them from the ground. Like the people who permit and encourage them, they're all in high places, and the companies gate access roads. So I turned to SouthWings, a group of volunteer pilots who show journalists and others the tracks of industry as they exist on the landscape instead of glossy promos. Our pilot, Sue Lapis, had flown me over these same coalfields in 2001. With us in the Cessna 182 was the Ohio Valley Environmental Coalition's Janet Keating—perceived as Freddy Krueger by mountaintop removers everywhere—who had stepped to the podium after Spadaro to receive the Environmental Council's Mother Jones Award. Keating and her outfit are only just beginning to realize how many allies they have across America. Recently a woman from Ohio called the council's office to complain about flooding caused by the removal of overburden from coal seams. She'd been referred by the Department of the Interior.

Five minutes out of Yeager Airport I was again reminded that mountaintop removal is itself a euphemism for mountain-range removal. "Almost level, West Virginia," proclaim the bumper stickers. I noticed major progress toward that end just in the past three years. As far as we could see and in all directions, the mountains of the Cumberland Plateau were being clear-cut, along with the most diverse and productive temperate forest on earth, home to 1.5 million life-forms per acre, not counting microbes. Four thousand feet below us, draglines, bulldozers, trucks, drills, and detonation crews chipped away at mountains like Mr. Tooth Decay and his henchmen in the old Colgate Dental Cream ads. "We're wiping out whole ecosystems," said Spadaro. "Everything from I-64 south to Kentucky will be gone."

Spadaro pointed out failing valley fills sloughing off the sides of Kayford Mountain, where I'd righted Patricia Fraker's gravestone, knocked off its base by shrapnel from what is thought to be mankind's single biggest nonnuclear explosion—just one of many by which this mountain is being converted to a seventy-square-mile stump. "These fills start failing as soon as they're created," said Spadaro. "The companies riprap water channels, but the rocks are always too small and they wash out." During the Carter administration, valley fills had to be compacted every four vertical feet as they filled up, and they were limited to 250,000 cubic yards. Spadaro wrote those rules; but when Ronald Reagan came in, Griles and his colleagues virtually did away with them. Today some valley fills contain 500 *million* cubic yards of mountain rubble, and there's no compacting. Two thousand miles of streams have been obliterated. And rule reduction continues under George W. Bush, whose OSM, again under Griles, proposes to do away with the last major impediment to mountaintop removal: the regulation that prevents valley fills and other mining activity within 100 feet of perennial streams.

"This is just outrageous," declares Ben Stout of Wheeling Jesuit University in Wheeling, West Virginia, who studies sludge reservoirs and mine runoff. "The administration is pulling the rug out from under the Clean Water Act. I really think in twenty years eastern Kentucky and southern West Virginia are going to be humanly uninhabitable. That's even without considering the ecosystem component. Humans are not going to be able to live in this region where there's no potable water. ... Insects are indicators of stream health. With valley fills, which obliterate streams, insect mortality is 100 percent. And in watersheds with longwall mining, we've found a 50 percent reduction in both numbers and species. You kill rivers by cutting off their fingers. Headwater streams provide linkage with the forest. Insects convert leaves and sticks to fats and proteins—very scarce commodities in the woods. These fats and proteins are available to almost everything—salamanders, frogs, birds— and at a time in the spring when these neotropical migrants are coming back. It's a mass emergence. Lose the insects and you lose the linkage."

Impressing Keating and me as much as the valley fills were the sludge reservoirs, enormous deltas of coal dust spreading from intake pipes into black stews of grime, grit, toxic flocculants, and heavy metals. All perched directly over communities, one over an elementary school. At 143 mph, it took us ten minutes to fly around Massey Energy Company's Brushy Fork sludge reservoir above Whitesville. The dam, made by blowing up a mountain for fill, is 950 feet high. The only evacuation route is the road toward the dam.

Brushy Fork is a Buffalo Creek blowout waiting to happen. The rock formations under the dam have not been checked for fractures. And Massey has been cited by the state at least thirty-seven times for permit violations, such as failure to monitor the reservoir, failure to control erosion, failure to control sediment, and failure to control pollution.

Sludge spills can be prevented with monitoring, maintenance, and enforcement, yet they continue on a regular basis. In the Ohio River watershed there have been 13 spills on the Little Coal River since 1997; six on the Big Coal River since 1987; thirteen on the Big Sandy River since 1994; four on the Levisa Fork since 1972; nine on the Tug Fork since 1972; and three on the Gauley River since 1970.

The worst occurred on October 11, 2000, when Massey's Big Branch sludge reservoir in eastern Kentucky (designed by the same engineers who designed Brushy Fork) collapsed into the underground mine it straddled, blowing 310 million gallons of sludge out the side of the mountain and down 110 miles of the Big Sandy River system, obliterating riparian habitat; killing millions of turtles, snakes, frogs, salamanders, mussels, and fish, including imperiled paddlefish; polluting public water supplies; clogging water-treatment plants; flooding houses; and shutting down schools, restaurants, and laundries. The sludge spread over valleys like lava. Twigs stuck in it remained upright, moving along with the flow. It was the worst environmental disaster in the history of the eastern United States. The governor of Kentucky declared ten counties a disaster area. Massey blamed God, claiming it was His "act."

As a member of the team assigned to investigate the disaster, Spadaro accumulated compelling evidence that clears God and implicates both MSHA and Massey (a major GOP contributor). Moreover, an internal report vindicates his findings. At first the team made good progress. It interviewed almost fifty witnesses and plowed through boxes of documents. But things changed under George W. Bush. The new Secretary of Labor, Elaine Chao—wife of Senator Mitch McConnell (R-KY), among the Senate's top five recipients of coal-industry largesse—appointed former mining executive David Lauriski as MSHA's new director. Both his deputy directors are former mining executives. On the first day of the Bush administration, the leader of the investigation team was replaced by MSHA's Morgantown district manager, Tim Thompson. According to Spadaro, among the first words out of Thompson's mouth were: "We're gonna wind down this investigation." And: "We're not going to allow any arrows to be pointed in the direction of MSHA." Thompson, however, denies this, saying he "only wanted to move the investigation along."

The team wanted to interview or reinterview at least twenty-five more people. "Thompson allowed us six more interviews," says Spadaro. The team had already met with an MSHA engineer who in 1994 had inspected the Big Branch sludge reservoir and written a memo about its deplorable condition, including major fractures and major leaks. To avoid a "very possible" disaster, he made nine recommendations for remedial action, such as installing devices to monitor the quality and quantity of leaking water and reevaluating concrete seals separating abandoned and active sections of the underlying mine. After MSHA's chief of technical support, Mark Skiles, had read all agency documents related to the sludge reservoir, he wrote the following to Davitt McAteer, then MSHA's director, who had ordered the review: "I would conclude from this investigation that after the 1994 failure that [MSHA] did not follow [the 1994] recommendations." Skiles's memo—undated but written on October 31, 2000, according to the Department of Labor's Inspector General—was a draft, intended only for internal use, but it got leaked to the press. Spadaro says his investigation team never saw the response—dated October 31, 2000—until May 2001, when it seemed to appear out of the ether.

"There wouldn't have been a spill if MSHA had followed those recommendations," Spadaro told me. "Not only did they ignore them, they fabricated a response and backdated it to cover themselves." He said he had recently turned over the proof to the proper authorities. When I asked who those authorities were, he said he'd been instructed not to say, but the previous day he'd canceled an appointment with me in order to help the U.S. attorney with the criminal grand jury investigation into the spill. When I phoned Lauriski's office to get the agency's side of the story about this and all other charges by Spadaro, I was referred to MSHA's assistant secretary for public affairs, Bob Zachariasiewicz, who declined to comment, although he went on and on about Spadaro's alleged transgressions.

Zachariasiewicz also refused to answer my questions about the Skiles memo. But if MSHA's response wasn't a backdated fake, all personnel involved in drafting it should get Bravo Awards for snapping out of their bureaucratic torpor and moving at a speed never before seen in federal government. In the space of a single workday MSHA supposedly faxed or otherwise delivered Skiles's three-page document with twenty pages of attachments from Arlington, Virginia, to the agency's Pikeville, Kentucky, district office; analyzed the contents; and hatched a five-page response, which painstakingly rebuts each point. Pikeville district manager Carl Boone, who was in the office in October but was transferred two months later, can't recall whether or not he wrote the response without "going through [his] files." McAteer, who quit after Bush was elected but was on the job in October 2000, doesn't recall seeing it. The Inspector General reports that Celeste Monforton, then special assistant to the director, first saw an unsigned version of the response in April or May 2001 and questioned Bob Elam (the acting director after McAteer) about it, and that "later that same day, Elam provided Monforton with a signed copy." Monforton informed me there had been pressure on Skiles to retract his memo.

The investigating team wanted to charge Massey with ten federal violations. But MSHA issued two. Now, because the two were relatively weak, an administrative law judge has dropped one, and the federal fine has been reduced from $55,000 to $5,600—this for a spill of toxic waste about six times the volume of oil lost from the Exxon Valdez. "From January 2001 through October of 2001 there was constant intervention by top management in formulating the violations and the conclusions of the report," says Spadaro, who sat in on meetings after he'd resigned from the team. "In determining responsibility and whether there was or was not negligence, the report failed." So he refused to sign it and, on April 11, 2001, quit the team, stating in his letter of resignation that the investigation had found Massey to have "submitted incomplete and inaccurate information to [MSHA] over a number of years, but Mr. Thompson does not want to issue any violations to the company or to thoroughly discuss this shortcoming," and expressing concern about a concerted effort "to leave unreported unexamined serious defects." This kind of language did not go over well with MSHA brass.

Nor did the five complaints Spadaro filed with the Labor Department's Inspector General, nor the two whistleblower complaints he filed with the Office of Special Counsel. He charged that MSHA director David Lauriski and deputy director John Caylor had been passing out illegal sole-source, no-bid contracts to their friends. One contract, alleges Spadaro, went to one of Lauriski's pals for an academy course. "All district managers and other supervisors have been encouraged by Mr. Dave Lauriski ... to attend these [$1,025 per person] classes," Spadaro wrote. He told me that the government sometimes had to pay more than $40,000 per week. "The information was nowhere near as useful to mine inspectors as the accredited twenty-five-week-long entry-level training courses we already offered." In a memo to the Inspector General's office alleging other violations, Spadaro wrote: "Mr. Caylor threatened me and said that he would have me 'taken out of here' if I interfered with the contracts."

When I asked Monforton if she'd heard any talk from Bob Elam and others about punishing Spadaro for quitting the Big Branch investigation and for publicly criticizing MSHA, she said: "I can't recall their exact words, but there was definitely word in the air that they were going to get Jack for doing this."

Monforton's comment rang true when I read the charges against Spadaro. Some I had to read twice to convince myself there hadn't been typos. Without exception, they call to mind the charges filed against Alice by the Queen of Hearts. First, MSHA accused Spadaro of misusing his government credit card by not getting $22.60 in bank charges for cash advances approved before he took visiting mine officials to dinner. This despite the fact that, even though the $22.60 had been a legitimate business expense, Spadaro had paid it back long before MSHA knew about it. Another charge was that Spadaro "abused his authority" by granting waivers for food and lodging to visiting mine-rescue teams and to an academy instructor stricken with multiple sclerosis. In fact, he had been ordered to do so and was fully authorized by an MSHA policy directive. According to MSHA, Spadaro "created the perception, if not the reality, of antiunion animus" by *suggesting* that a union leader employed as an industrial hygienist move her office downstairs so she could work with another hygienist on a mine-safety project. She objected, so Spadaro didn't move her.

The whistleblowers who survive—the smart, effective, legitimate ones like Jack Spadaro—don't go just a little public. Spadaro is blowing his whistle as if his bird dogs were running deer. His relationship with his superiors is chillier than ever. And they are less than enthusiastic about the kinds of projects he is working on these days—such as guiding *Audubon* writers around the sludge reservoirs and mountain stumps of Appalachia. On the other hand, they won't let him back into his office. They've even changed the locks, denying him access to files he needs for his defense.

There is a scene in *Star Wars* where Obi-Wan Kenobi says to Darth Vader (accurately, it turns out): "If you strike me down, I will become more powerful than you can possibly imagine." So it has been with Jack Spadaro, who gets more powerful with each passing day; who speaks daily with reporters, legislators, and environmental leaders across the nation; and who isn't getting fired after all. A five-month delay following a notice of termination is unheard of, but now MSHA is playing a different, safer game. On February 24, 2004, Spadaro was informed that he was being transferred to Pittsburgh and demoted one full pay grade. He's staying in West Virginia while he appeals, and advancing his radical notion that regulatory agencies should serve the public rather than themselves and industry.

SAGGING STREAMS

<-( )->

Over the past decade the coal industry has generated copious ink by ripping the tops off American mountain ranges, in the process burying and polluting streams and converting some of the planet's most diverse temperate forests to desert. Meanwhile, beneath the surface, the industry is also ripping apart the earth and destroying streams with a less visible technique called longwall mining" or "total extraction." Welsh coal miners introduced the practice to the U.S. in 1875, but it didn't really catch on here until about 1980.

Traditional deep miners leave "pillars" of coal along the seam so that they and their equipment don't get buried. As a side benefit, the earth doesn't collapse under streams and manmade structures, at least not right away. With longwalling the whole coal seam, which runs for miles and may be seven feet high and 1,000 feet wide, is removed the way a dentist excavates a root canal. These days a "shearer" moves back and forth on a track set across the face of the coal seam as if the whole deposit were a stick of salami being abbreviated by a whirling meat slicer. Hydraulic roof supports are inserted and removed as the shearer progresses along the seam. As this happens the earth collapses into the cavity, and fish, wildlife and humans above are treated to what the industry chastely calls "planned subsidence." Buildings crack or fall apart. Wetlands, springs, ponds and streams vanish into the bowels of the earth. Even as they are dewatered, streams lose their riffles, transmogrifying into a series of stagnant pools sealed by dams that mark the edge of the collapsed mine. Sometimes the industry converts traditional deep mines to longwalls by going back in and removing the pillars. Leaving coal in the earth for any purpose is anathema.

Longwalling happens everywhere there are major coal deposits—in Pennsylvania, for instance, in West Virginia, Kentucky, Wyoming, Utah, Ohio, Illinois, Alabama, and New Mexico—and it's increasing because it's the cheapest method of getting coal out of the ground. Currently there are fifty-three longwall mines operating in the U.S. "Longwall mining, which revolutionized underground mining operations in the United States over the past twenty years, is one of the main reasons why coal is used today to generate 52 percent of the nation's electricity," reports the industry publication *Longwall USA*.

In Pennsylvania, fourth largest coal producing state after Wyoming, West Virginia and Kentucky, longwalling now accounts for 75 percent of underground soft coal production. There's no reason to suppose that the practice is more hurtful here than in other states; the difference is that it has not gone unobserved. So Pennsylvania's experience offers the only clear vignette of the national scene.

Watching and collecting data have been personnel from the U.S. Fish and Wildlife Service's Pennsylvania field office and the Raymond Proffitt Foundation, a Philadelphia-based NGO specializing in environmental protection. By state and federal law damaging perennial streams by longwalling (or any other means) is illegal, but when the industry controls the economy, staffs the legislatures and appoints its own regulators often from its own ranks, enforcement tends not to happen. As the Raymond Proffitt Foundation observes in a lengthy report on longwalling, "Pennsylvania wetlands [including streams] are being destroyed by the high-extraction (longwall) mining of bituminous coal underground. Quietly. Inexorably. Without regulation. Pennsylvania protects wetlands from other types of construction activities. Its laws do not exempt longwall mining from wetland regulation. But wetland law enforcement is absent when mining permits are approved." Because of the "inadequate and unlawful implementation of the regulatory process for permitting new longwall mines," charges the foundation, "streams are dried up or altered to the extent that fish and invertebrate populations are devastated. Entire aquatic ecosystems are permanently changed." According to the foundation, the laws are apparently being broken with the tacit approval of the state Department of Environmental Protection's Bureau of Mining and Reclamation (BMR): "Examination of the BMR files ... leads to the inescapable conclusion that BMR seeks deliberately to ignore the requirements protective of wetlands, the same requirements that the

Department of Environmental Protection imposes upon other types of industrial and construction activities statewide."

Typical of the examples offered by the foundation is permit 30841316 for the expansion of Consol Energy's Bailey Mine. DEP approved it on Feb. 24, 2000, thereby adding 11,120 acres to Consol's underground mine permit area and 4,126 acres to its subsidence control plan area. The land overlying the expansion is covered with all manner of wetland types, and by law an applicant must identify water resources that might be compromised by its longwall operations. But despite the fact that the Pennsylvania Game Commission had repeatedly informed BMR that these wetlands were at risk, BMR issued the permit without making Consol identify them.

Streams dammed and dewatered by longwalling have few defenders. In Pennsylvania, for instance, coal seams occur in the southwestern part of the state where cold-water habitat is rare. The smallmouth fishing is fabulous, and while the trout fishing can be good, it's a springtime deal dependent on hatcheries. One can't blame Trout Unlimited for not raising hell because its mission is to protect and restore wild salmonids (although on June 17 the Pennsylvania council passed a motion opposing longwall permitting until proper safeguards are in place). And while one might suppose that some of the bass organizations would come to the defense of the self-sustaining smallmouths, I found no evidence of such an occurrence in my interviews or literature searches. Yet while sportsmen play Hester Prynne, the U.S. Fish and Wildlife Service for once is speaking up for fish and wildlife. It's nice to see a state field office that's earning its keep and that is neither staffed nor controlled by wimps.

Enlow Fork, separating Washington and Greene counties and wandering through old-growth forests bright with rare wildflowers (including the state-endangered Curtis' goldenrod found nowhere else in Pennsylvania), is one of the most beautiful smallmouth streams in the East. And it is—or was—one of the most productive, sustaining really large fish. What makes Enlow even more notable is that it's the only longwall-damaged stream in the nation where half decent data exists before and after mining. During the early 1970s the Fish and Wildlife Service led a successful crusade to prevent the old Soil Conservation

Service from flooding the valley for "flood-control." As part of its environmental impact study for its proposed dam SCS hired a consultant to survey fish and macroinvertebrates. In 125 feet of stream he found 2,500 fish representing twenty-three species, mostly base-of-the-food-chain stuff like minnows and darters. Then in 1998, after an eight-mile stretch had subsided due to longwalling, Consol Energy, the nation's largest underground coal producer, sought to expand the nation's largest underground mining operation—the Bailey complex under Enlow Fork. By sheer coincidence the consultant Consol hired to survey Enlow Fork sampled within a few hundred feet of the station checked by SCS's consultant more than two decades earlier, but now it had dropped about four feet into the earth. Despite the fact that the new study area was considerably larger (600 feet) electro-shocking gear turned up only thirty-six fish representing only ten species. The excuse offered by Consol was that SCS's consultant had sampled with rotenone, turning the belly of every last fish in the stretch sunward. When the Fish and Wildlife Service and the Raymond Proffitt Foundation observed that this was plainly and simply an untruth Consol claimed that SCS's consultant had been more thorough in his shocking.

When I asked Consol's manager of environmental permits, Jonathan Pachter, why the company's consultant had found more fish in the unsubsided sections in 1998 he said it could be coincidence and that "anything's possible when you're dealing with organisms that move all over the place."

Consol's PR staff said they knew why I was calling them. "There's a group of anti-mining organizations that have been contacting media of all types," Sandra Hamm informed me. "My guess would be that someone from the Raymond Proffitt Foundation contacted your magazine." (Actually, I had contacted the foundation.) When I asked her about the increased diversity of fish in unsubsided sections she said: "This comes up again and again and has been fed to journalists all over the country by the Fish and Wildlife Service. They [service personnel] come and protest at the hearings. They hold little media conferences downtown on their anti-longwall mining studies." But the Fish and Wildlife Service does no such thing.

Consol's Thomas Hoffman was even more direct. "I know what's happening here," he told me. "Certain groups [which he later narrowed down to the Raymond Proffitt Foundation] are working the media to generate as much publicity for their side of the story as they can. The Fish and Wildlife Service's whole case is based on an old study compared with a sample they think we have that shows this dramatic reduction in species and individuals at Enlow Fork. What they never tell you, because it's not in their interest to do that, is that the baseline study was done in the days when they'd take a long stretch and repeatedly shock until they virtually shocked every critter that was in the stream. ... Quite frankly, they don't know what they're talking about. They're comparing apples and oranges. We believe they know that that's what they're doing."

Longwall miners routinely damage perennial streams with impunity. In Pennsylvania all that DEP has required Consol to do on the eight subsided miles of Enlow Fork is make a stab at fixing 600 feet as a "mitigation experiment." According to the Fish and Wildlife Service, the experiment has failed spectacularly. Even the mining itself had been an experiment, permitted by DEP in the guise of a "low-cover study." Basically DEP told Consol, "Go ahead and grab the coal, and let's see if you ruin the stream." It did both. Because Enlow Fork is only about 400 feet above the coal seam DEP had major reservations about issuing the permit, but it just couldn't say no. Now eight miles of pools, riffles and runs have been converted to a series of stagnant impoundments that function as sediment traps. Boulders and cobbles that had provided superb habitat for smallmouth and a diverse community of macroinvertebrates have been smothered with silt. Where wading fishermen used to move with no trace they now leave fifty yard plumes of café au lait.

In a joint silt study the Fish and Wildlife Service and the EPA looked at three sites on Enlow, comparing them to an unsubsided reference stream with similar watershed characteristics. At the first Enlow site—downstream from the undermined area—18.2 percent of bottom composition was material less than two millimeters in diameter. At the next site upstream, in the subsided reach, the figure was 30.9 percent. And at the third site upstream, also in the subsided reach, it was 41.8 percent. By contrast, only 3.6 percent of the reference stream's bottom composition was material less than two millimeters in diameter. But according to Consol, the ponding is good. "The fish like cold, deep pools," says Sandra Hamm. "When the undermining first occurred there was a drought, so it was actually pretty good that there were pools because it gave the fish someplace to hide."

"A complete misrepresentation of data" is how the fish refugia line, oft repeated by Consol and its hirelings, strikes aquatic ecologist Lou Reynolds who has been contracted by the Raymond Proffitt Foundation to study the impacts of longwalling. "I think that when you get into these drought situations the fish pretty much stay where they are, and the habitat shrinks," he says. "It's not like the fish are actually seeking these pools out. On a density level there are fewer fish there than on the unsubsided reaches. I'm pretty concerned with what I see. Headwater streams are disappearing, and the coal companies know it. These impacts are happening from the headwaters all the way down to the larger streams. The coal companies say give the streams time and they'll correct themselves. Well, I don't think they're qualified to make those kinds of statements. They're not hydrologists."

Both the Raymond Proffitt Foundation and the Fish and Wildlife Service are also collecting other incriminating data. Of the 131 streams in southwest Pennsylvania that the service has evaluated, 26 have subsided sections and 38 others have reduced flows or, in some sections, no flows.

"The Fish and Wildlife Service," charges Consol's Hoffman, "has a point of view; they are in the minority among the agencies. They don't really have a role to play in the regulation of the industry." But the service does have a role; it is required by law to advise DEP and the Army Corps of Engineers on mining permits. Moreover, the service is not in the minority. In issuing the permit to mine under Enlow Fork DEP ignored the advice not just of the service but of the Pennsylvania Fish and Boat Commission and the Pennsylvania Game Commission. In fact, both commissions saw fit to sue DEP and Consol over the permit. As part of the settlement Consol agreed to do what it was already obligated to do—delineate wetlands and riparian zones over the mined areas 400 feet or less above.

DEP is required by law to send the Fish and Wildlife Service copies of mining permit applications on request. But such a request by the service's Pennsylvania field office sent DEP's Bureau of Mining and Reclamation director J. Scott Roberts into a state of high dudgeon. He fired off a blistering letter to the service's director Jamie Clark in Washington, D.C., informing her that if her Pennsylvania field office wished to see the applications it could get them itself, then wandering off into a long list of unrelated grievances such as a complaint that field office personnel "subrogate the scientific method" by "develop[ing] conclusions" and then conjuring supporting data. He further charged that: "In early July [2000] USFWS personnel held a press conference to publicize the preliminary findings. Neither DEP, nor the [federal] Office of Surface Mining, were given the courtesy of prior notice of this event." Apparently, the "press conference" Roberts referred to was a meeting in Waynesburg of the Fish and Boat Commission, Game Commission, U.S. Geological Survey, Natural Resources Conservation Service, Fish and Wildlife Service and concerned citizens who had requested information from these resource agencies. While two members of the press showed up, neither had been invited. The most telling part of Roberts' harangue was this proclamation: "At present, subsidence from longwall mining is the subject of spirited public debate in Pennsylvania. Little is known, either beneficial or adverse, about the 'pooling' impacts."

To this, David Densmore, who directs the Fish and Wildlife Service's Pennsylvania field office, responded to Roberts' boss as follows: "In fact, while there may be a 'spirited debate' about whether longwall mining should be permitted to cause subsidence under highways, buildings, utility lines, etc., there is little debate over whether streams have been impaired or, in some cases, existing uses eliminated, by either 'pooling' or flow reduction. Some streams, such as Laurel Run in southern Greene County, dried up entirely after being undermined."

Laurel Run had been a pretty little perennial stream full of crayfish and minnows, a support system for downstream smallmouth water before RAG Coal Holdings started longwalling the watershed two years ago. Murray and Laurine Williams who live beside the now-intermittent, fishless stream have spent 12 years restoring their 150-year-old farmhouse.

After they got it listed on the National Register of Historic Places RAG informed the National Park Service that, since it owned the coal under the house, it should have a say in the designation and that it didn't like the designation. The Park Service rolled over and delisted the house, but with the help of a smart, aggressive attorney named Dick Ehmann the Williamses got it re-listed. Now the spring that had supplied their water has dried up, and RAG's planned earth quake has badly damaged the house. "Every house on Laurel Run Road is damaged," declares Ehmann. "Walls have cracked. Doors don't open or won't close. On some of the houses you can set a marble on the floor and it will roll to one side. Water supplies have disappeared." Under a settlement forced by Ehmann RAG is restoring the Williams' farmhouse, but it can't do much about the missing spring and brook.

In 1966 the Pennsylvania legislature enacted a law that, reasonably enough, said that longwallers couldn't destroy people's homes. The industry challenged this "Subsidence Act" all the way to the U.S. Supreme Court and lost. Then, in 1996, coal moguls and beneficiaries serving as state legislators slipped through a law, written by the mining companies, that required longwallers to replace water supplies they destroyed but which also stipulated that it was okay for them to destroy property provided they pay to have it fixed later—in the case of water supplies, three years later. Few noticed the second part of the bill, and it sailed through without a single nay. So now King Coal can legally destroy private and public property, and, while it's supposed to pick up the tab for repairs, it frequently doesn't. Bob Ging, the attorney who has litigated every longwalling case in Pennsylvania so far, has been trying to get a water supply replaced since 1995. "If government agencies want to destroy your home, they have to compensate you first and then only after they go through eminent domain proceedings," he says. "So coal companies basically have more power than our government." You'd think the property-rights crowd would be screaming like rousted guinea fowl, but they've not uttered a peep.

The sad thing is that the damage to private property and the environment isn't necessary. Degrading perennial streams is illegal and wouldn't happen if DEP enforced the law. What's more, if coal companies would "backstow"—i.e., fill the cavities they create in the earth—most of the subsidence could be avoided. They can use their own longwall waste, dredge spoil, "overburden" from their strip mines which they currently dump onto headwater streams, and even the right kind of municipal trash. But backstowing costs money, and because it's not required in the U.S., longwallers don't do it here. European countries are not so permissive. In Germany, where backstowing is mandatory, Consol and RAG—both German firms—have no trouble with it.

America, whose executive branch of government is currently giving the green light to longwallers, has long preached energy self sufficiency. We decry the purchase of fossil fuel extracted from foreign nations. But we happily purchase it from energy companies based in those foreign nations after they have hacked it out of our own landscape sans environmental safeguards. We pay twice for longwalled coal, and the real costs of getting it out of the earth are borne not by the foreign energy companies but by American property owners, by American fish and wildlife, and by Americans who love fish and wildlife. That's something to remember next time you see an ad proclaiming that coal-fired electricity is cheap.

SPORTSMEN VS. THE NORTHERN FOREST

⤛⤜

Thinking sportsmen in the region were ecstatic. In December 1998 forest-products giant Champion International, having cut the guts out of 296,000 acres of what it aptly called "industrial forest" in northern New York, Vermont and New Hampshire, unloaded it to the public for $76.2 million. The deal—set up by The Conservation Fund, based in Arlington, Virginia, state and federal agencies and the sporting and environmental communities, showed what advocates of wildness can do when sufficiently frightened. It was a monumental coup for fish and wildlife. An opportunity like it may never come again; and part of the reason it may never come again is that thinking sportsmen are outnumbered by sportsmen who believe everything they heard from the last person who spoke to them.

The man who made this fabulous land purchase possible was developer Claude Rancourt, a.k.a. New Hampshire's "Trailer Park King." Ten years earlier he had scared the bejesus out of even the most environmentally insensitive citizens and politicians by acquiring options on 92,000 acres in Vermont and New Hampshire, including the beautiful and pristine Nash Stream watershed north of the White Mountain National Forest. Everyone had assumed that this land—owned by Diamond Occidental, another forest-products giant—was safe from the tacky development in which Rancourt specialized. But Diamond had fallen into the clutches of British corporate raider James Goldsmith, who had dissolved the company and was hawking its holdings. Easterners had learned to live with clearcuts. Hideous as they are, they eventually heal. Not so with trailer parks. With sportsmen and environmentalists screaming into the faces of their legislators, the U.S. Forest Service and the State of New Hampshire purchased 46,000 acres from Rancourt, leaving him with a 25 percent profit and gravel-mining rights along Nash Stream.

The Champion lands deal was better executed, but an emergency action also. Management plans could come later. In 1998 the land had to be saved from what the forest-products industry seriously calls "higher and better use" (HBU), i.e., commercial development. Remote trout water is a magnet for HBU. Suddenly, the yodeling of loons and the caroling of hermit thrushes are replaced by the bleating of boom boxes and the howling of ATVs. Wild trout vanish. The woods remain, but they are spiritless. It's the saddest death I know.

In the East the moniker "northern forest" refers to a specific biome—the 26 million acres draped across the shoulders of Yankeeland from Machias, Maine to Syracuse, New York. It's a zone of contrast and transition, rugged and delicate, where temperate hardwoods mingle with boreal conifers, where bobcats prowl with tabbies, and eagles pick off Peking ducks, where moose, at the southern fringe of their range, winter on north-facing slopes while, in valleys lit by the slouching sun, starving whitetails huddle under black growth at the northern fringe of their range. What makes the northern forest even more special for angler/naturalists is that it is America's last, best refuge for large, inland brook trout.

Our gaudy Yankee char—the "dweller of springs"—is an old-growth species, dependent on the shade of thick forest canopies. You cannot manage for it without also managing for thousands of other old-growth species from pine martens to spruce grouse to liverworts; and you manage for these organisms best by leaving their woods alone. That doesn't happen much in the Northeast.

In Vermont 133,000 acres of the Champion lands were protected from HBU development at a cost of $26.5 million through a joint investment by Essex Timber Company, the Freeman Foundation, the Mellon Foundation, the US Fish and Wildlife Service, the State of Vermont and small private donors. Of that $26.5 million, the state chipped in only $4.5 million, this for a public-access and sustainable-forestry easement on Essex Timber's 84,000 acres. A 22,000-acre Wildlife Management Area around West Mountain—containing an ecological reserve or "core area" that sustains wild brook trout and the rarest plants and animals in the state—was a gift to Vermonters from the Mellon Foundation and the federal government. The conservation easement, jointly held by The Nature Conservancy and the Vermont Housing and Conservation Board, guarantees use by anglers, hunters, trappers and even snowmobilers in the entire 22,000 acres, including the core area.

One of the deal's disappointments was that the precedent-setting easement on Essex Timber Company's 84,000 acres requires that the land be logged forever. Essex and all future owners will be in violation if they do not log. In the stump field that is northern Vermont the state had an opportunity to recover a rare and diverse ecosystem. Instead it elected to spin 84,000 acres back into industrial forestry. "It's absurd that we'd lock in an economic use that totally precludes alternatives," declares Tom Butler of the Wildlands Project. "It's as if a century ago a steam-engine factory was purchased with public funds on the condition that it produce steam engines for eternity. Now when I go to conferences I keep hearing the forest-products industry say: 'This is great. How can we get a forever-logging easement?'"

Another major disappointment was that the core area, where logging (but, again, not fishing, hunting, trapping or snowmobiling) would be prohibited, is only 12,500 acres. Wild brook trout simply cannot survive in industrial forests. Sometimes when I find myself in the northern forest I look for the flower-laced mountain rills where, in the distant days before beaver fever, I'd stoop to drink, scattering trout fry. In many of these places water and fish are gone, dried up and crushed by giant forest mowers called "feller-bunchers." Another sad death.

The ecologists assigned to study the former Champion land had wanted a core area of at least 40,000 acres. One of them—Jeff Parsons of Sterling College in Craftsbury—explains: "Ecosystems are hit regularly by natural disturbances—microbursts, hurricanes, insects, disease, ice storms. ... An ecological reserve needs to be bigger than the size of the average disturbance in the region (40,000 acres in this part of Vermont), otherwise there might not be adequate seed sources to regenerate the forest."

The West Mountain Wildlife Management Area is Vermont's only expression of true boreal forest. There are boreal trees such as black spruce and northern white cedar, boreal mammals such as rock voles, boreal birds such as gray jays, bay-breasted warblers and black-backed woodpeckers, boreal flowers such as bog aster and white-fringed orchid, boreal lichens, boreal sedges. Boreal bryophytes—mosses and liverworts—abound in unmatched diversity. Nowhere else in the state is there such a high concentration of bogs and fens. The area provided a reservoir of moose when they'd been extirpated everywhere else in the state. It is drained by "reference streams" so unpolluted the state uses them as a standard of what clean water should be. Remote ponds (rare in Vermont) provide refuge not just for brook trout but for lake-shore plant communities largely lost elsewhere. Ledges provide denning habitat for bobcats. Deer, severely winter stressed in northern Vermont, are limited by lack of thermal cover, not lack of browse. Before conifers reach a height where they can protect deer they're clearcut. What thinking hunter would want to perpetuate this cutting rotation?

I tracked down a thinking sportsman in Vermont—state Rep. David Deen (D-Westminster), the conservation conscience of the Vermont House, a leader in the fight to save the Champion lands from HBU and an Orvis-endorsed fly-fishing guide. Deen gets into the West Mountain Wildlife Management Area a good deal and knows its waters intimately. Paul Stream, partly in the core area, is a wild brook trout factory. "Every pool has a brookie in it," he told me. It's also one of the most productive nursery areas for Atlantic salmon fry in the entire Connecticut River watershed. But perhaps the most important function of this and other core-area brook trout streams is the icy, oxygenated water they pump into the Connecticut, providing summer refuge for the biggest trout in the region.

A decade ago Paul Stream lay in ruins, choked with silt bleeding from Champion roads and clearcuts. "Walking in places I used to fish was like slogging around in quicksand," Deen recalls. "It was an absolute disaster. Champion got up there with their chippers and took everything. There was nothing left to cut." But now, after ten spring runoffs have scoured its bed, Paul Stream is almost completely back. What thinking angler would want to re-open the core area to industrial forestry?

Despite the glaring flaws of the 133,000-acre Champion lands rescue in Vermont, maybe it was the best deal for fish and wildlife that state politics would allow. There wasn't lots of time for tweaking and negotiating, and the framers deserve hearty ovation for pulling it off. Instead, they're getting beaten up by sportsmen for banning logging on the little 12,500-acre core area. And now sportsmen are campaigning to do away with this reserve.

It started with seventy-four camp owners in the West Mountain Wildlife Management Area who had leased land from Champion. Under Champion, the leases expired after five years, although they were usually renewed if the holders behaved. When the public took possession of the management area the camp owners knew they'd have to clear out, but in a fit of benevolence the state granted them occupancy for life plus twenty years. Lifetime leases are unheard of in public land acquisitions. In New York, for example, camp owners who had leased land from Champion have been allowed to remain on what's now public land for just fifteen years; and that is more than generous. Still, the Vermont camp owners were not satisfied, and they demanded permanent leases. Governor Howard Dean and the legislature refused.

So at meetings of the Vermont Federation of Sportsmen's Clubs the camp owners proclaimed that The Nature Conservancy (TNC)— co-holder of the management area easement—had been taken over by anti-gun, anti-blood-sport, anti-Vermont flatlanders who had it in for the "traditional uses" of camp squatting, logging in the core area and ATV mud slinging on former Champion property (even though the state and Champion had long ago banned ATVs from all their lands). It was only a matter of time, pronounced the camp owners, before TNC did away with other traditional uses such as hunting, fishing and trapping, never mind that these uses had been guaranteed by the easement.

"There was this clause that said 'non-compatible uses' could be phased out of the core area," remarks avid hunter and angler Pat Berry, communications director of the Vermont Natural Resources Council. "The camp owners told sportsmen [untruthfully] that this meant hunting, fishing and trapping, and they believed it. So TNC said, 'Okay, fine,' and it took the clause out. Then the camp owners and the sportsmen they'd co-opted moved on to logging. This was 'a government land grab.' Hearings became crazy bullying sessions. I write a column for *Outdoors*

Magazine on conservation issues. And some of the guys are waging an all-out war against me. I'm 'not a sportsman' because I want a no-logging zone. They're actively supporting the legislators who cast the most damaging votes against water quality and wildlife habitat simply because they opposed the core area."

This past legislative session sportsmen and their allies hatched unsuccessful bills that would have allowed logging in the core area, that would have mandated that logging is, by definition, consistent with preserving natural resources, and that would have deleted language from the enabling legislation that protects wildlife habitat and identifies natural heritage sites.

Whipping the sporting masses to a froth of hysteria and paranoia is *Outdoors Magazine* editor James Ehlers, a "Music Man" figure who stomps and shouts and carries on about secret, government-financed, anti-sportsman conspiracies right here in River City. He preaches to his flock that the core area is a preemptive strike on the working class by "egocentric Chittenden County elitists," "narrow-minded misanthropic state officials" and the unholy Pooh-Bahs of the "shape shifter" Fish and Wildlife Department. "No cutting of trees means no habitat for [game] animals, which means no hunting." The Nature Conservancy is a "Goliath" but sportsmen (under Ehlers' leadership, of course) have brought it "to its knees after being ignored, excluded, patronized and prejudged." TNC is "saving the last great places on Earth for themselves." The Vermont Department of Fish and Wildlife is staffed by "disgruntled, coerced scientists." The Montpelier-based environmental group Forest Watch is a bunch of "emotional Bobos." Governor Howard Dean keeps "an ever thoughtful eye towards a wealthy America and discriminating microbrew drinkers." In the core area sportsmen can: "Come and watch healthy trees grow old, fall over and die. Come and watch the deer look for browse that is too high for them to reach. Watch them leave and die. ... Come and observe the underbrush wither and die because the large 'old growth' trees are blocking out the sunlight." "Biodiversity," warns Ehlers, "is the rallying cry of hell-bent preservationists everywhere. It is to the environmental community what rear-end revealing pants are to high-school kids today. ... The tweed academia even have a name for it—sacred ecology—and the Vermont Biodiversity Project zealots are on a crusade to control the social agenda, equating the constitutional rights of humans with the supposed rights of bugs." And so on and so on and so on.

"Why are you upset?" I asked Ehlers. "You can do anything you want in the core area."

"There won't be any management for game species," he responded.

"But doesn't game—brook trout, bobcats, deer and such—need old growth? Isn't restoring old growth management, too?"

"It is if all the cards are on the table."

Well, no. It's management with or without cards, with or without tables. When I asked Ehlers to explain how ecological reserves conflict with the interests of sportsmen he e-mailed me a list of "Open Land Species Threatened by Uniform Climax Forest Management" that included superabundant organisms proliferating in suburbia and industrial forests. Among them: Joe Pye weed, blackberry, black-eyed Susan, chokecherry, mourning dove and robin. He is serious, and so are the Vermont sportsmen who follow him in lock-step. Prevent ecological reserves! Save the Joe Pye weed!

After reading Ehlers' copious screeds and interviewing him for the better part of an hour, it became clear to me that of all the things for which he can be justly chided, failure to think is not among them. For example, he has figured out how to sell magazines, and he does it well. *Outdoors Magazine* is now the most influential sportsmen's publication in Vermont, and it has just gone regional, seeking circulation in Maine, New York, New Hampshire, Massachusetts and Connecticut. Tom Butler makes this observation: "There are state legislators who honestly believe that if you don't log every acre all the time, all the animals will die, that the only way to healthy wildlife populations is to have intensive forest management everywhere, that nature can't do anything right. There's an element in Vermont that is grossly ecologically ill-informed, and I think James Ehlers is savvy enough to goose it along."

"Ehlers loves to portray himself as representing the downtrodden, someone who waves a flag for hunters and anglers who get pushed around by modern society," says Steve Wright, who directed the Vermont

Department of Fish and Wildlife from 1985 to 1989 and now serves the National Wildlife Federation as its New England coordinator. "He's also a very ambitious businessman."

The stink raised by Ehlers attracted National Rifle Association (NRA) membership barkers who descended on Vermont like blowflies. "Dear Vermont NRA Member," read the January 29, 2002, missive. "As you know, the State of Vermont purchased the Champion lands, now known as the West Mountain Wildlife Management Area, for the purpose of preserving them for traditional uses, including hunting and trapping. Environmental activists are working hard to keep in place an easement that would allow them to close large areas of this parcel to these uses! They will tell you otherwise. Do not believe them. If we don't resolve this matter now, what will it mean for hunters, shooters, trappers, and fishermen? It means the environmental activists could, on a whim, end all of these activities on land that has been cherished by sportsmen for generation upon generation. It means you could be denied access to more than 20,000 acres paid for by your hard-earned tax dollars. They will tell you we should be happy because this land was a gift. When was the last time you paid $4.5 million for a gift?"

Actually, the state did not "purchase the Champion lands." Vermonters didn't pay a cent for the "more than 20,000 acres." The management area was, as I reported earlier, given to the state by the Mellon Foundation and the federal government. And, even if environmentalists wanted to (which they don't), they couldn't close one acre to fishing, hunting and trapping because these uses are legally guaranteed in perpetuity. Such is the NRA's commitment to truth.

Also scenting membership opportunities was the Ruffed Grouse Society, an outfit that would cheerfully sacrifice whole watersheds of brook trout for an imagined chance to fill one more grouse with chilled eights. It feigned outrage that the tiny core area would be preserved from the scalping delivered most everywhere else in northern New England, and it tub-thumped for a bill that would have done away with the ecological reserve or, as it chastely and deceitfully put it, "retain active timber management in the 'toolbox' of Fish and Wildlife managers for use on scientifically justified wildlife habitat enhancements."

Wise-use types puffed up and trilled like toads in rainwater. The Property Rights Foundation of America proclaimed that "the long-range goal" of the entire campaign to save the northern forest is to "eliminate forestry and other human use." The Northeast Regional Forest Foundation declared that "there is nothing preventing The Nature Conservancy from transferring or selling this easement to another, even more radical organization in the future."

Jim Northup, director of Forest Watch, makes this observation: "If the most shy and sensitive creatures we share this planet with are to survive over the long term, we absolutely must establish some wild places for them. The areas of the national forests that have the least logging have the most pristine waters and the healthiest fisheries. In a densely populated region like the Northeast the future is certainly more roads and more houses and more people. Many sportsmen here travel thousands of miles for high-quality hunting and fishing opportunities. And we have some chances to create those opportunities right here in the Northeast. Those chances won't happen accidentally." Nor will they happen if sportsmen keep trying to torpedo them.

By the time you read this Vermont will have a new governor, a new lieutenant governor, a new House and a new Senate. Instructed by Ehlers, most sportsmen are backing candidates who have it in for ecological reserves. With help from these politicians the Vermont Traditions Coalition—comprised of the camp owners, the Vermont Federation of Sportsmen's Clubs, clearcutters fronting as the Associated Industries of Vermont and the Vermont Forest Products Association, and property-rights groups—will have spawned (or will be preparing) legislation to get logging back into the core area. Even if they fail, they will have generated so much political heat that ecological reserves, desperately needed in the East and in all American forests, may no longer be politically feasible. And that's food for thought—or should be—for all sportsmen.

A PLAGUE ON ALL YOUR FORESTS

⊰⊱

If you want to locate the best fishing in our national forests, find the logging roads; then go somewhere else. Road building is the federal government's single most destructive land-management practice. Roads are mortality sinks for all manner of fish and wildlife. They fragment habitat; they cause landslides; they block fish migration with their frequently impassible culverts; they serve as delivery systems for silt bleeding off clearcuts and broken topsoil; they provide conduits for invasions of cowbirds and invasive exotic plants.

Consider Deer Creek in Idaho's Caribou-Targhee National Forest. Because it is in part of the forest that, until recently, was officially roadless Deer Creek runs cold and clear, and it ripples with big Yellowstone cutts— one of the most beautiful and ephemeral essences of the American West and recently petitioned for listing under the Endangered Species Act. So pristine was Deer Creek that, in August 2003, a Forest Service survey crew determined that it should be used as the standard of excellence— "a reference area for comparison to streams impacted by various land uses." The survey team went on to recommend "that activities not be allowed which would reduce the quality of fish and amphibian habitat in the drainage."

That recommendation certainly is in keeping with the Forest Service's stated fish mission for the 150,000 stream miles and 2.5 million lake acres we've entrusted it with: "World-class fishing depends on world-class habitats, and the USDA Forest Service together with other federal, state and local partners, is working hard to protect, restore and enhance your streams and lakes." Well, not really.

Deer Creek, along with other pristine trout streams in the Sage Creek Roadless Area, had been protected by President Clinton's roadless rule. In August 2005—two months after the Bush administration rescinded that rule—Deer Creek became the first victim of the administration's substitute, which relies on "local control" for roadless area management. In Idaho, dominated by timber and mining interests and with more roadless national forestland than any state other than Alaska, that's like asking two coons and a hen to vote on what to have for lunch. A major road was punched into the Deer Creek watershed for the benefit of J.R. Simplot Company which will now drill twenty-five exploration holes and, if it finds the phosphate its geologists say is there, will expand its open-pit strip mine for another 6.5 miles—through the Deer Creek drainage and the drainages of Manning, Wells Canyon, and upper Crow creeks, all prime cutthroat habitat.

"The Sage Creek Roadless Area, which protected the headwaters of what I consider some of the best cutthroat trout streams in the state, is no longer a roadless area," laments Pete Zimowsky in *The Idaho Statesman*. "It was a place where many big game hunters packed in on horseback to hunt trophy mulies and elk. It was a place where you could wander through groves of aspen on fall hikes and be amazed by the colors. ... Will [the area] be the same for my grandson, as it was for my kids? No, it won't."

How did we get from a "roadless rule" that protects trout streams to one that sacrifices them? The story starts in the late 1990s when a young, utterly aberrant bureaucrat was running the U.S. Forest Service. His background was not in timber extraction but in fishing, guiding, teaching, and fisheries biology. His name was Michael Dombeck, and he understood what no chief before or since has understood—that the most valuable resource produced by our national forests is water. Dombeck also understood that the best of that water comes from the healthiest woods, woods undefiled by roads, and that there aren't a lot of those kind left. If fact, only 58.5 million acres—two percent of the American landscape—were designated by his agency as "roadless," meaning they were greater than 5,000 acres and lacked the major, high-speed logging-truck highways taxpayers buy for timber companies. There were all kinds of smaller roads that allowed vehicular access by sportsmen.

If you just count major roads, the Forest Service has built or paid timber companies to build 383,000 miles worth—222,000 miles more than exist in all of our national highway system. You and I got to pay for these roads twice—first, with our fish, wildlife, plants, soil, and water; then with our tax dollars. And we're paying for them still because the Forest Service can't begin to maintain them and, as a result, they're sloughing into the lakes and streams it claims to be "working hard to protect." The road-maintenance backlog is now $10 billion. Meanwhile, we're paying for new national-forest roads. Roads are the main reason sales of the public's timber cost the public about $400 million a year.

Roadless areas are roadless for an excellent reason; they were the places Big Timber didn't want to go—the steep, infertile, icy, fragile, water-rich, trout-filled places. In fact, the national forests themselves were acquired because the timber industry didn't want them. Even today, after the industry has high-graded its own holdings, the national forests contribute less than 5 percent of the nation's lumber and pulp. If all national-forest logging ended tomorrow, our economy wouldn't flinch, and private-land operators would be spared subsidized timber sales that drive down fair-market value of their logs.

Dombeck, like every other thinking conservationist, concluded that the last thing our national forests need are more major roads, especially in areas greater than 5,000 acres where none exist. So in January 1999, as part of a modern "transportation policy" for his agency, he proposed an 18-month moratorium on road building on 130 national forests. The industry, accustomed to doing whatever it pleased on our national forestland, was apoplectic. In separate, ultimately unsuccessful, actions the State of Idaho and the Wyoming Timber Industry Association sued in federal district court.

In the most extensive and wide-ranging environmental review in the history of federal rule-making the Forest Service held 600 hearings in thirty-seven states and collected 2.5 million public comments, 96 percent supportive. A poll by Responsive Management of Harrisonburg, Virginia revealed that 84 percent of America's hunters and 86 percent of America's anglers favored keeping roads out of roadless areas. It was by far the most popular rule ever hatched by a federal resource agency.

On January 12, 2001, largely on the strength of that public commentary, President Clinton issued the Roadless Area Conservation Policy directive ending virtually all logging, roadbuilding, and coal, gas, oil, and other mineral leasing in 58 million acres of our last best forestland.

Then George W. Bush ascended to the Presidency. To run the Forest Service, as undersecretary of Agriculture, he selected Mark Rey who, as a timber-industry lobbyist and later as a staffer for forest subcommittee chair Sen. Larry Craig (R-ID), had dedicated himself to upping the cut on our national forests.

Immediate revocation of an initiative as popular as the roadless rule would have been politically costly. So the Bush administration set about administering daily drops of arsenic. First, it put the rule on hold for two months; then it refused to defend it in court. It even aided and abetted the plaintiffs by gushing about the timber industry's imagined woes—this despite the pledge to Congress by John Ashcroft, taken under oath during his confirmation hearings as attorney general, that he would defend the rule as the "law of the land."

In July 2001, in one of Rey's most cynically brilliant moves, the Forest Service issued an "interim directive" to local agency brass instructing them that the decision on whether or not roadless areas should be protected would now be in their hands. No longer would Forest Service officials committed to roadless protection be able to blame it on federal law; now they'd have to confront their neighbors, the powerful, well-connected timber executives who employed them, and the legislators who vote Forest Service appropriations and say: "Sorry, *I've* decided those trees are off limits." The directive also proclaimed that there would be no roadless protection for the Tongass and eleven other national forests. In September Rey proposed exempting major activities in roadless areas from the National Environmental Policy Act (NEPA). In December he issued a directive that relaxed standards for road-construction in roadless areas.

As Rey chipped away at Clinton's rule he launched concurrent attacks on the roadless areas themselves and on national forests in general. To circumvent the inconvenience of the Endangered Species Act, which requires federal agencies to consult with professional scientists of the Fish and Wildlife Service or NOAA Fisheries on projects that would destroy habitat of listed species—timber sales, for instance—the Bush administration now proposed "self-consultation" by agencies like the Forest Service, which, under Rey, functions as a wholly owned subsidiary of the timber industry. Rey did away with the wildlife liability regulations, implemented under President Reagan, which required the Forest Service to maintain viable populations of fish and wildlife across each planning unit. In its place he imposed a standard that requires managers merely to *think* about fish and wildlife sustainability. As part of the administration's "Healthy Forest Initiative," Rey tried (and is trying still) to categorically exclude timber sales and forest plans from environmental review and cut the public out of forest-management decision making.

The Bush administration officially killed the roadless rule on May 5, 2005, replacing it with a rule that gives Rey power to decide what roadless areas, if any, get protected but meanwhile invites the governors of each state to do the Forest Service's work for it—that is, commit to an expensive, tedious and perhaps ultimately pointless exercise in which state employees gather data, do inventories, dispense information, and hold public hearings. Forest supervisors and regional foresters have been quietly contacting governors and urging them to forget about making recommendations for roadless-area protection and just let the Forest Service deal with it in its planning process. "If you're not going to have a nationwide policy, why create a special process like this?" asks the Sierra Club's Sean Cosgrove." The answer, of course, is that it sounds better than just announcing you've killed the roadless rule.

Some states, however, understand that "local control" is a euphemism for business as usual. Local control, after all, is why our national forests are already sliced and diced with 383,000 miles of roads—enough to circle the globe fifteen times. The Attorneys General of California, New Mexico, and Oregon responded to Rey's subterfuge by suing the Bush administration, charging that by replacing the roadless rule with a state-by-state petition process the Forest Service violated NEPA. "When the 2005 Rule was announced, I made it clear that the federal government's actions placed an unfair and unnecessary burden on states that would amount to a price tag of millions of dollars and result in piecemeal management of federal forest land," declared Oregon governor, Ted Kulongoski. "The 2005 Rule turns back the clock on years of work, including public input and taxpayers' dollars, and the end result is greater uncertainty about the protection of our special roadless areas—not greater security." In November the Bush administration rejected Kulongoski's request for a rule amendment that would give states greater assurance that fish, wildlife, and clean water be protected in roadless parts of national forests.

New Mexico's attorney general Patricia Madrid said: "Our water supply comes from our forests and depends upon those forests remaining healthy. ... The federal government acknowledges that roadbuilding and timber harvest will result in decreased water quality, increased sediment and pollutants; yet they refuse to protect our state's few remaining pristine areas. They have also refused to follow federal law that requires them to look at the impacts of their actions on the environment. ... When the Bush Administration refuses to obey the law, we have no choice but to sue them."

"I am filing this lawsuit because the Bush Administration is putting at risk some of the last, most pristine portions of America's national forests," announced California's attorney general, Bill Lockyer.

On the other hand, Idaho's elected officials—most notably Sen. Larry Craig and Governor Dirk Kempthorne—are positively giddy about the demise of roadless protection. This seems odd because the state's 9,322,000 acres of roadless national forestland is keeping imperiled fish and wildlife vital to the state's economy on the planet and, at least in some cases, off the Endangered Species List. For example, Idaho's roadless areas contain 68 percent of the state's remaining bull-trout habitat, 74 percent of the Chinook salmon habitat, 74 percent of the steelhead habitat, 58 percent of the cutthroat habitat, and 48 percent of the redband habitat. And these areas produce the biggest and most elk and deer. After construction of new logging roads on the Targhee half of Idaho's Caribou-Targhee National Forest the Idaho Department of Fish and Game cut the elk rifle season from forty-four to five days.

Idaho is also home of the most tireless and pernicious of all roadless-protection opponents—a wise-use, timber-mining front called the BlueRibbon Coalition. Here's an example of how it operates: In 2004 the Forest Service asked for local input in preparing a new travel plan for the Caribou half of the Caribou-Targhee, as if locals owned the forest. Accordingly, Marv Hoyt, Idaho director of the Greater Yellowstone

Coalition, sat down with virtually all invested non-motorized user groups—such diverse outfits as the Backcountry Hunters and Anglers, the Eagle Rock Backcountry Horsemen, the Idaho Conservation League, the Southeast Idaho Recreation Alliance, the Western Watersheds Project, and the Southeast Idaho Mule Deer Foundation—and hashed out an eminently fair compromise over a period of about three months. "We had some fifty individuals and organizations," Hoyt recalls. "We went over the maps of the whole forest, and we put together a balanced alternative that left 50 percent of the routes open to motorized use. Everybody signed it, and we sent it to the Forest Service. The BlueRibbon Coalition went after and obtained the document via a Freedom of Information Act request, then mailed threatening letters to the organizations and individuals who had signed it, even boycotted businesses. They went after people in a really nasty way."

The BlueRibbon Coalition's letter, signed by its director, Clark Collins, read in part: "As representatives of recreation interest groups who enjoy the trails on the Caribou National Forest, we are offended by many of the recommendations you apparently support ... We would like to know what level of involvement you had with this document. We want to accurately represent your position to our readers. ... A lack of response on your part will leave us no choice but to assume that you are in total agreement with the document, and we will so inform our members."

The Forest Service responded to the alternative offered by the non-motorized users with a draft travel plan that completely blew them off and gave the motorheads all sorts of new ATV and snowmobile roads. "So the message is this," says Hoyt, "If you intimidate people and stymie public comments, you'll get rewarded."

With a few notable exceptions America's sportsmen have been strangely silent on roadless area protection, despite the fact that about 85 percent of them want it. Unfortunately many of these exceptions are among the 15 percent who *don't* want it. They include officials of make-believe conservation organizations such as the Ruffed Grouse Society (who obtain major financing from the timber lobby by whooping it up for roads and clearcuts at every opportunity) and outdoor writers who imagine that Clinton's rule was a conspiracy to separate their butts from their four-wheelers (despite the fact that roadless areas have plenty of off-road-vehicle access) and thereby allocate to predators the game they otherwise would have shot.

Burt Carey, president of Western Outdoor Writers and editor of *Rocky Mountain Game & Fish*, *California Game & Fish*, and *Washington-Oregon Game & Fish* magazines, complains about what he calls "the Clinton administration's thirst for creating wilderness and defacto wilderness (roadless areas) during Slick Willy's second term, and his zeal in repopulating the American West with wolves, lynx, grizzlies and other carnivores, and portions of the Southeast with wolves and panthers."

According to Jim Shepherd of *The Outdoor Wire*—which bills itself as "the Outdoor Sports Industry's Daily Transaction Newsletter"—the effort to limit roads on public land is really a plot by the antis. "To keep hunting alive in America," writes Shepherd, "it's critical that hunting become easier, rather than more challenging. Anti-hunting forces recognize that fact. They've already changed their tactics from their failed full-on assault on firearms to a 'kinder, gentler' approach to eliminating hunting: protecting the environment by increasing 'protected' wilderness areas. As more and more federal lands fall under the ever-broadening definitions of 'protected' areas, hunters and the hunting industry must recognize the fact that what some perceive to be diminished efforts to eliminate hunting is, in fact, a retrenching of the efforts to a more subtle—but equally fatal—outcome."

In a long, rambling harangue delivered to conferees of the Outdoor Writers Association of America in June 2004—a year before the Bush administration officially killed Clinton's roadless rule—Kayne Robinson, then president of the NRA and formerly GOP chairman of Iowa, railed against such imagined slights to sportsmen as their alleged eviction from roadless areas. "The Clinton administration closed millions of acres to hunting and shooting," Robinson proclaimed. "Every acre should be reexamined." Mike Dombeck, the architect of the roadless rule (which didn't close a single square foot of national forestland to hunting or fishing) happened to be sitting in the audience next to OWAA board member Tony Dean. Dombeck poked Dean in the ribs and asked him what the hell Robinson was talking about. (At a press conference later that day Robinson was unable to come up with a single example of land closed to sportsmen by Clinton's rule.) The following week Rich Landers of *The Spokane Spokesman-Review* offered this commentary: "The NRA's campaign to 'propel hunter rights into the public arena' stinks of opportunism. Robinson is trying to recruit uninformed hunters with the same big talk and promises a pimp uses to lure vulnerable girls into his realm. Some 12 million to 15 million American hunters are not NRA members, and this is no time for them to change their minds. Now, more than ever, a sportsman who is not an environmentalist is a fool."

In the early 1980s, when Bill Geer of the Theodore Roosevelt Conservation Partnership was directing the Utah Division of Wildlife Resources, he instructed his biologists to look for environmental factors that limited the size and number of deer. They found that the most important factor by far was road construction. "And in those days," he recalls, "we promoted as many roads as the Forest Service." So Geer had his agency do an about face and start *closing* roads. It proved to be the best thing he could have done for anglers and hunters.

I asked Geer why sportsmen keep working against their own interests—letting groups like the NRA and the Ruffed Grouse Society speak for them on roadless protection, voting in a president and legislators who cheerfully sacrifice fish and wildlife for the convenience of their campaign contributors. ... He couldn't answer the question, but I liked his response: "I've had this theory ever since I was director in Utah. You could tell hunters and anglers that 'tomorrow we're going to round you up and shoot you,' and they'd piss and moan about it all night long, and next morning they'd be lined up waiting to get shot."

PITS IN THE CROWN JEWELS

◄◄))►►

It was a day of superlatives in a place of superlatives. I had thought I threw a long line until I watched the guy fishing with me—Steve Rajeff, who can cast farther than any other man on the planet. Together we eased down the clean gravel of the river that sustains the world's biggest salmon runs—the Kvichak, 300 hundred yards from where it collects water from the biggest lake in Alaska. Now, in late September, the giant rainbows of Lake Iliamna were dropping down to snark the last eggs from the last moribund pink salmon. From twenty feet they'd chase down the Globugs Steve had tied that morning. We didn't have anything with which to weigh the fish that fried my reel, but it dwarfed the twelve-pound silver I'd caught two days earlier. Rajeff's photo of it hangs on my office wall. Anglers who haven't fished the Kvichak won't believe me when I tell them it's not a steelhead.

That's how I got hooked on the Bristol Bay area of southwest Alaska. No place on earth is wilder or more beautiful or offers finer salmonid fishing. In the Kvichak, for example, you can catch all five Pacific salmon, rainbows, dollies, char and grayling. The rivers, lakes, mountains, valleys, tundra and forests of Bristol Bay are aptly called "America's crown jewels." I cannot get enough of them. But the day may not be far off when you and I will get no more because, if a small Canadian mining company with no track record and backed by Middle Eastern money of unknown origin gets its way, they will be ruined.

Some of the fish and wildlife will, of course, survive. Many of the topographical features will remain intact. But the essence and magic of the place will be destroyed utterly and irrevocably. The Bristol Bay area will no longer be wild and remote. It will become a populated, easily accessed, industrial waste storage facility.

Even if the Vancouver-based Northern Dynasty Mines made a habit of keeping its word, its copious promises would mean nothing.

This is because its modus operandi is to find and stake deposits, then hawk them to larger companies who do whatever they please. Having never developed a mine, Northern Dynasty proposes to strip-mine what it describes as the nation's largest gold deposit and second-largest copper deposit near Upper Talarik Creek and the lower Koktuli river in the Nushagak and Kvichak river drainages, just south of Lake Clark National Park and Preserve and fifteen miles northwest of Lake Iliamna.

In addition to cyanide, with which gold is extracted from ore, the operation would release sulfuric acid, arsenic, lead, cadmium, zinc, mercury and sundry other toxins known to kill fish and wildlife, cause cancer and destroy nerve tissue. A witch's brew of these and other poisons would be held in a twenty-square-mile lagoon consisting of former wild-salmonid habitat in what is called the "Ring of Fire," a volatile seismic zone beset by major earthquakes (including one in the spring of 2005) at the base of Mt. Iliamna, an active volcano, and flanked by two other active volcanoes. In fact, all the past and present volcanism make the site one of the world's richest sulfide mineralization areas, meaning that production of acids and toxic heavy metals would be way higher than at other strip mines.

When the toxic-waste lagoons downslope from hard-rock mines fail, results are always catastrophic. So great is the threat to the Bristol Bay area that the D.C.-based environmental group American Rivers took the unusual step of including this land of many waters on its 2006 list of the nation's ten most endangered "rivers."

Northern Dynasty has yet to seek permits, but already it has established a long record of disturbing actions, deceptive and false statements, contradictions, and broken promises. For example, it assured the public that it wouldn't be using cyanide. Then—when the environmental community pressed, pointing out that extracting gold from this kind of ore isn't economically feasible without cyanide—the company allowed that it would use cyanide after all but only the "vat process" and not the more dangerous "heap-leach process." It publishes such outrageous untruths as: "Mercury in wild salmon comes from the ocean, not from mining or other land-use practices."

After promising to "stay out of the Upper Talarik Creek [watershed] because it is sensitive fish habitat" (as if the rest of the proposed site were not), it promptly began drilling test holes in the watershed. With that, it applied for water rights to Upper Talarick, the better to divert flow into the artificial lake where it will store toxic mine waste. Northern Dynasty's promise of "no net loss of fish" sounded alarmingly like a plan to festoon Bristol Bay with hatchery stock. But when anglers and enviros protested, the company quickly backed off and assured all hands that it wouldn't be flinging around any rubber salmonids. However, it offered no reasonable or cogent explanation of how it intended to duplicate Christ's fish miracle.

The Bristol Bay Times reports that Northern Dynasty's intense lobbying campaign includes paying all travel, lodging and food expenses for the local officials it fetches to Anchorage for its "community meetings" and then, on top of this, slipping each a cash-stuffed envelope ($600 for a three-day meeting). According to documents obtained by Alaskans for Responsible Mining, Northern Dynasty has hired as a lobbyist one Duane Gibson—former top aide to Jack Abramoff, the convicted felon who bilked his clients out of an estimated $66 million.

One of the few accurate statements I found in reams of company records is the following, from the 2004 Annual Report: "As Canadian citizens and residents certain of Northern Dynasty's directors and officers may not be subject themselves to U.S. legal proceedings, so that recovery on judgments issued by U.S. courts may be difficult or impossible." Not exactly an encouraging revelation when one considers that if these same Canadians get their way, they will severely damage American commercial and recreational salmon resources with respective values of $100 million and $77 million annually.

Even if the toxic waste could somehow be contained forever, the mine might still destroy Alaska's wild commercial salmon industry, whose image depends on a pristine Bristol Bay watershed. The mere suggestion of toxic contamination could make wild salmon uncompetitive with less expensive and non-seasonal farmed fish. In fact, salmon farmers can scarcely contain their glee over the impending damage to the Wild Alaska Salmon brand. Their industry association—Washington Fishgrowers—has even taken to plastering its Web site with banners announcing that "a massive open-pit gold mine, proposed upstream from Alaska's most productive sockeye salmon waters, could undercut the reputation for purity that has become wild salmon's key selling point."

Northern Dynasty, whose behavior is standard for the industry, is not the problem. The problem is that federal and state hardrock mining regulations (especially Alaska's) are lax and antiquated, designed for nineteenth century prospectors. It used to be that when you developed a mine in Alaska you had to put up a bond so that taxpayers wouldn't get stuck with the entire job of cleaning up your mess if you went bust. But two years ago the mining industry wrote a law for itself called the "corporate guarantee" which excuses companies from posting bond and instead requires a small token payment and a gentleman's agreement. Hardrock miners help themselves to the public resource basically for free, paying state royalties of less than one cent per dollar's worth of mineral extracted. (By contrast the oil industry must pay twenty cents on the dollar.) As a result Alaska's regulatory agencies are strapped for cash. But they've come up with a Mr. Bean-style solution: Allow the companies that require regulation to pay the state officials who regulate them, a cozy arrangement that has spawned the mine regulators' shibboleth of "Sure; go ahead." *Mother Jones* Magazine reports that Northern Dynasty has signed a legal memorandum pledging to contribute to the salaries of thirteen state employees who oversee the permitting process and that, by the time the mine is completed, it will have shelled out $700,000 to hire its own regulators. Then, to see if the mine meets federal muster, the U.S. Environmental Protection Agency will consult the state regulators paid by Northern Dynasty.

Most states allow "mixing zones" in which industrial and municipal waste can be dumped into lakes and rivers, provided the resulting cocktail doesn't get too potent. At this writing Alaska is a notable exception, but Governor Frank Murkowski and the mining industry are working feverishly to fix this. Indeed, the future of hardrock mining in the Bristol Bay area is largely dependent on mixing zones. Northern Dynasty promises that it will contain all its waste, but even if its word meant something and even if containment were possible in the Ring of Fire, the company that purchases the site won't be bound by any commitment mouthed by Northern Dynasty.

It is hard to imagine something more hideous than this proposal for the heart of America's holy water. The 2.5-mile-wide, 1,700-foot-deep crater would be the biggest open-pit mine on the continent. The twenty-square-mile toxic-waste lagoon would supposedly be contained by an artificial mountain, 750 feet high and half a mile wide at the base, wedged between two real ones. But Scott Brennan, campaign director for Alaskans for Responsible Mining, says the Pebble Mine could be just a subtle hint of things to come.

"The site only accounts for about ten percent of the mining claims that have been staked out there on state land," Brennan told me. "And around that land the U.S. Bureau of Land Management plans to open up millions of its acres currently closed to mining. In the long term, that's an even greater threat to the integrity of the fishery." At least eight other mining companies have staked claims in the Bristol Bay area, and they are intently watching what happens on the Pebble site. If Northern Dynasty gets a green light, they'll move in, too.

Former pro hockey player Brian Kraft, who owns the Alaska Sportsman's Lodge on the Kvichak River four miles down from the lake, is especially irked by the mantra from closet mine proponents that goes like this: "I'm waiting for the facts to come out in the Environmental Impact Statement before I make any judgments." "My question," says Kraft, "is what facts will come out that are going to show this project can be done in one of the most environmentally sensitive areas on earth? An EIS is a procedural process; it doesn't tell anyone if a mine will or won't contaminate. Water will have to be treated forever. There are right places and wrong places for mines, and this is the wrong place."

Tim Bristol, Trout Unlimited's Alaska program director who four years ago put me on some gorgeous Tongass National Forest steelhead, told me this: "One thing that hasn't been talked about is the influx of people. It's a sparsely populated country. The workers will hunt and fish; that puts a lot more pressure on the resource, too. And all the access concerns folks more than the mine itself—a 100-mile road from the west side of Cook Inlet, along the western shore of Lake Illiamna, to the

Pebble deposit. On the one hand Northern Dynasty is saying, 'Wait and see. We haven't applied for permits. You really need to reserve judgment.' But on the other, they're passing judgment themselves, proclaiming that there's never going to be any impact on fish. I think it's a two-way street when it comes to 'wait and see.' This is a bad place for a mine, especially this kind of a mine. Frankly, based on history of the mining industry, I don't want to wait and see."

Nor do I. We lack the space here for any comprehensive history of this sort of mining, but here are five typical examples:

Red Dog zinc and lead mine, northwest Alaska, still in operation. Zinc contamination reached 600 times the health standard. Operator Teck Cominco has been cited for 134 separate permit violations. Five years ago the National Park Service reported concentrations of toxic metals along the haul road as high as the most polluted industrial sites in Eastern Europe. Despite estimates that reclamation and water treatment will cost $100 million, the company has posted a bond of only $11 million.

Zortman-Landusky gold and silver mine, north-central Montana. Extensive surface and groundwater contamination. More than a dozen cyanide waste spills, including 52,000 gallons that poisoned drinking water supplies. (A mine employee reported the spill after he detected the smell of cyanide in his home tap water.) Serious acid drainage to aquatic habitat occurred when sulfide ores were extracted. In 1998 Zortman-Landusky Mines filed for bankruptcy, sticking taxpayers with $33 million in reclamation costs. Effluent treatment will be required in perpetuity.

Summitville gold mine, in the San Juan Mountains of south central Colorado. The company, Galactic Resources Limited, went bankrupt in 1992. Cyanide, heavy metals, and acid runoff from disturbed sulfide-bearing deposits of the sort that abound in Alaska's Ring of Fire caused a massive fish kill in Terrace Reservoir and sterilized seventeen miles of the Alamosa River of aquatic life. Cleanup of this Superfund site will cost taxpayers a minimum of $235 million.

Grouse Creek gold and silver mine, central Idaho adjacent to the largest wilderness complex in the contiguous U.S. In 1993, still in construction phase, it caused a major landslide, burying 100 yards of critical habitat for federally listed chinook salmon, steelhead and bull trout. Less than a year later the tailing impoundment sprang a leak. Operator, Hecla Mining, was cited for 250 toxic pollution violations. The Forest Service was obliged to post signs along Jordan Creek: "Caution, do not drink this water." In 1999, with a toxic lagoon breach imminent, the Forest Service issued a "time critical removal action." The bond posted by Hecla was $7 million, which has left taxpayers with a cleanup cost of $53 million for this Superfund site.

Gilt Edge gold and silver mine, west central South Dakota, in drainages of municipal water supplies for the Black Hills. Operated from 1988 to 1996 by Brohm Mining, the mine poisoned Strawberry and Bear Butte creeks with cyanide, and acid runoff wiped out fish in Ruby Gulch Creek. The $6 million reclamation bond didn't even cover a year's worth of reclamation and treatment costs for this Superfund site.

Maybe the best perspective on the Pebble Mine proposal comes from the most radical, anti-environmental, pro-development conservatives in America. Consider, for example, the recent spleen-venting by David Keene, chairman of the American Conservative Union, in *The Hill*, the newspaper for and about the U.S. Congress: "The so-called environmental movement has proved itself hostile to increased energy use or production, regardless of its source ... Instead, they tell us, we should scale back, give up our SUVs, abandon the suburbs and accept restrictions on our lifestyle ... To accomplish this, the do-gooders who run the movement have built themselves a multibillion-dollar empire of advocacy groups that rely on fear to raise money."

With all the standard invective and clichés, Keene goes on to pummel the vile and ubiquitous enviros for opposing oil drilling in the Arctic National Wildlife Refuge. And then he makes charges that, while also false, are utterly fascinating and revealing: "Meanwhile, they [the enviros] have largely ignored what could be a real threat to the Alaska they claim to be so dedicated to saving. The Alaska of our dreams may not be found on the mud flats that hide the oil we so desperately need, but it can be found in the Bristol Bay watershed, where streams flow into Lake Iliamna and provide the habitat in which some 40 percent of the state's Pacific salmon breed, where the world's largest moose and brown bears are to be found alongside streams harboring the largest and scrappiest trout on the continent. ... The environmental lobby hasn't gotten involved because it senses there is more money to be raised attacking our addiction to oil and SUVs and the people who run the oil companies than by taking on an obscure Canadian mining operation that may actually be putting the Alaska of our dreams at risk."

Then there are the admonitions of Sen. Ted Stevens (R-AK), one of the angriest and shrillest anti-environmentalists in Congress whose typical response to people questioning slap-dash development is to scream "Liar," and who, until now, never saw a mine he didn't like. Listen to Stevens, as quoted by Alaskan media: "If this was some essential commodity that we absolutely had to have to run our economy, it would be a different matter; and even then I would want to have a lot better attention being paid to the environmental process. But this one, I just don't like it. ... We really don't know what's happening with the reproductive capability of those streams out there ...

"I'm not going to change, and I hope people will listen to us. That resource is an enormous resource not just for the Native people but for the Bristol Bay run, and it ought not be tampered with by a gold mine. ... If that makes me a turncoat from being an extreme developer, so be it. ... They [Northern Dynasty] are hiring people from all over the place to criticize me, to fly back to Washington to talk to everybody about my opposition to this mine. ... My old friends in the mining industry ... are ready to put a red-hot poker to my throat."

Shortly before he died in 2005 Jay Hammond—former Alaska governor and scarcely a better friend to the environment than the current one—published this "clarification" in the *Kodiak Daily Mirror*: "I had said I could think of no place in Alaska where I'd less rather see the largest open pit mine in the world than at the headwaters of the Koktuli and Talarik Creek, two world-class fishing streams and wild salmon spawning areas. ... There is a location where I'd even less wish to see such a mine: right in the middle of our living room floor at Lake Clark."

Job-starved as they are, loud opposition issues from more than 70 percent of local residents and, in the form of strongly worded resolutions, from most municipalities and native corporations and councils.

All this bile from all these unlikely sources leaves me energized and hopeful. Finally, Scott Brennan, of Alaskans for Responsible Mining, makes an especially salient point: "This is anything but a done deal. To go forward the project would require enormous subsidies as well as permission to convert salmon habitat to industrial waste storage facilities. There's a tremendous opportunity for people who care about this part of the world to get involved. It's still early in the processes."

As Steve Rajeff and I slip-slid down the Kvichak, years before anyone had heard of the Pebble deposit, I remember telling him that "it will take them a long time to wreck all this." Maybe I was right.

ANN AND NANCY'S WAR

Until recently the tragically misguided effort to ban chemical piscicides rotenone and antimycin—led by Nancy Erman, a retired macroinvertebrate researcher from the University of California-Davis, and Ann McCampbell, of the Multiple Chemical Sensitivities Task Force of New Mexico (a group consisting, basically, of herself)—was only impeding restoration. Now, however, the two states where native fish populations are in most desperate need of these piscicides—the only tool for restoration—have, for all intents and purposes, banned them. Restoration in California and New Mexico has been stopped dead in its tracks; and the future of rotenone and antimycin, along with the native fish (not just trout) that can't be saved without them, is in jeopardy across America.

Facing possible extinction unless the bans are lifted are: the threatened Paiute cutthroat (the rarest trout in the world), the Gila trout (America's only inland salmonid listed as endangered), the Rio Grande cutthroat (New Mexico's state fish), the Lahontan cutthroat (once believed extinct), and the golden trout (California's state fish). In response, the Desert Fishes Council passed a resolution supporting piscicides at its November meeting in Tucson. In attendance was the world's foremost salmonid authority, Dr. Robert Behnke, who writes me as follows regarding the New Mexico Game Commission's August 18, 2004, decision to strip the Game and Fish Department of authority to use piscicides without commission consent: "Besides local chemophobes, a [non-practicing] medical doctor [McCampbell] raised nonsensical questions about contamination of groundwater-poisoning drinking water supplies. Her status as a 'medical authority' caused the commission to suspend treatment. Once this was accomplished, the chemophobe network notified the Lahontan Regional Water Quality Control Board, leading it to believe that credible risks for piscicides had been established, and the board blocked the Silver King Creek rotenone treatment [to recover Paiute cutts]."

McCampbell and Erman's stunning success this past year would not have been possible without major help from sportsmen and the media. The threat of genetic introgression tends not to register with anglers. And why should it? They've been conditioned by the management establishment to relish Frankenstein fish—pigment-impoverished mutants and weird hybrids that keep the hatchery bureaucracy in business because they have to be concocted from genetically twisted stock or from species so divergent they're likely to produce sterile offspring. It's expecting a lot of anglers who read the hype about "palamino trout," "centennial golden rainbows," "albino rainbows," "saugeyes," "splake," "tiger trout," "tiger muskies," and "wipers" to worry about rainbow genes showing up in Gilas or cutts.

But there's antipathy as well as apathy. To see it you need go no further than fly-fishing Internet forums. On *Fly Rod & Reel* magazine's conservation forum one fly-fishing instructor and former flyshop owner from Vermont writes this about the recently aborted rotenone treatment of California's Silver King Creek, which would have de-listed Paiute cutts, thereby opening a closed fishery: "I am a mongrel of sorts myself and delight in my diversity. … We Americans abhor those who seek human genetic purity! American military men and women have died and continue to die for the freedom of others oppressed by those who wish to impose the same limitations on man as you are seeking to impose on trout. One could argue that what you champion is an environmental form of 'ethnic cleansing' or the Nazi equivalent of racial purity. 'Purity.' I am uncomfortable with that word! 'Purity' is a word often used by racists, Nazi's and bigots. 'Purity'—that word is very much part of the argument to restore the Paiute cutthroat trout."

Two years ago the feds announced they would use antimycin to restore pure Colorado River cutts to Lake Pettingell on the west side of Rocky Mountain National Park. The lake is hardly a major angling destination-there's no trail, and it's a twelve-mile poke during which you climb 3,000 vertical feet, then slide down about 7,000 vertical feet to fish an eight-acre pond. Local anglers could have fished for the pure cutts, but they were sentimental about their mongrels and threw such a hissy fit that the Park Service backed off.

With few exceptions the media is fish-stupid and lazy. Rather than really investigate the issues of native-fish restoration, reporters collect a few quotes from someone like Behnke, then offer what they call "the other side" by interviewing some utterly uncredentialed crackpot. In one Associated Press piece about the proposed project to recover Paiute cutts the only alleged authority cited was one Patty Clary of Californians for Alternatives to Toxics, who was quoted as making this false statement: "Essentially what they're proposing is to kill everything—everything-in this stream." *High Country News* recycled wives' tales spun by a rancher (a heavy user of herbicides and insecticides) who claimed that his "pregnant ewes must have drunk some [antimycin] poisoned water [because] the following spring two lambs were born dead with kidneys that weighed four pounds. It was totally grotesque." More alleged evidence was provided in the form of quotes from the terrified owner of Paprika (a pregnant llama) who claimed to have "started studying antimycin" on the Internet where he found all manner of "disturbing" info. Finally, the piece reported that rotenone applied to California's pike-infested Lake Davis sent sixty-two people to the hospital. The truth was that sixty-two residents, having whipped themselves to hysteria with poppycock provided by McCampbell and others, went to the hospital because they wrongly supposed they'd been sickened by rotenone, a naturally occurring chemical that in seventy-five years of use by fish managers has never been known to harm a person. (To the credit of *High Country News*, it allowed me to set the record straight in "Writers on the Range"—a syndicated column it sends to major Western newspapers.)

Despite suffering from what she calls "multiple chemical sensitivity," McCampbell was in full cry in August 2004 at the New Mexico Game Commission meeting. Also in attendance were at least half a dozen of her acolytes, including Sam Hitt of Wild Watershed, who writes of her as follows: "Dr. Ann McCampbell, New Mexico's most effective advocate for a toxic-free environment, is a card-carrying outsider. Marginalized, ridiculed, ignored, she operates from the edge, without staff or budget, stitching together unlikely coalitions that win with the power of truth and little else. ... Today she advocates despite debilitating illness, forced to live from time to time in a relatively chemical-free 1983 Chevy. ... Dr. Ann slowly made her way from the back of the room to a table in front of the commissioners. After saying a sentence or two she would cover her nose and mouth with the respirator and take a deep breath."

McCampbell and her unlikely coalitions do win, but hardly with "the power of truth." She warns that the commercial formulation of antimycin-applied at less than twelve parts per billion-carries "a skull and crossbones warning" and "is fatal in humans if swallowed" directly from the bottle. All sorts of useful liquids also fall into this category, but not amtimycin. Because it's nontoxic to humans, EPA no longer requires the skull and crossbones on the label. At the commission meeting she and her troupe repeatedly called antimycin a "broad-spectrum poison"—this of a naturally occurring chemical with a half life of hours (unless it's exposed to direct sunlight, in which case, the half life is a few minutes) and that eradicates only fish, provided the treatment is successful. Further, she claimed that antimycin has been "banned in California … because, actually, California EPA has done the most updated review of this product."

First, it wasn't "banned;" it was just not re-registered because the new state pesticide regulations require rigorous testing that antimycin's manufacturer—Nick Romeo, who operates out of his house—can't afford, owing to his miniscule market. Second, California has not done a "review" of antimycin.

McCampbell told me there are plenty of alternatives to piscicides. When I asked her what these might be she said: "genetic swamping" (saturating mongrels with pure stock), "overfishing," and "netting" (none of which work), and "electro-fishing," which is horrendously labor intensive and works only on tiny streams.

Ilse Bleck, representing the 7,000-member Rio Grande Chapter of the Sierra Club, echoed McCampbell's untruths at the New Mexico Game Committee meetings that antimycin had been "banned in the state of California," recycled her misinformation about dangers to amphibians and macroinvertebrates, questioned whether the pure wild stock held in hatcheries could "adapt," and opined that saving Rio Grande cutthroats "does not outweigh the potential harm done to an otherwise healthy, self-sustaining ecosystem."

Lilly Rendt, another witness educated by McCampbell, likened piscicide formulations of antimycin and rotenone—which don't kill air-breathing organisms and are as close to silver bullets as chemical pesticides get—to DDT. And she said that, having seen the "eagles die," she didn't know "why we have to go through that again." As an alternative she suggested underwater TV cameras so managers could, well, kind of keep on eye on things.

However, there was much accurate testimony from state and federal fisheries managers and anglers, including TU's state chairman, William Schudlich, who passed out copies of my April 2004 *Fly Rod & Reel* magazine column "Environmentalists vs. Native Trout." Despite the histrionics of the McCampbell camp, sound science and good stewardship might have prevailed had it not been for the testimony of two respected outdoor writers from Silver City—Stephen Siegfried, outdoor editor of the *Silver City Daily Press*; and Dutch Salmon, author of seven outdoor books. "You're killing the threatened [Chiricahua leopard] frog," proclaimed Siegfried. (Adult frogs are unaffected and, if there's a frog or toad population in a project area, treatment is put off until tadpoles, which are usually unaffected anyway, have metamorphosed.) "What happens if an osprey has eaten a fish in the next drainage and flies over and drops the eggs? Do we poison the whole works again?" (Apparently, Siegfried is under the impression that unfertilized, digested fish eggs hatch.)

Both Siegfried and Salmon repeated most of McCampbell's misinformation, but their main contention (now part of McCampbell's standard harangue) was that introgressed fish are good enough if they're, say, 80 to 90 percent pure. As an alternative to poisoning mongrels they suggested the same non-solutions McCampbell endorses—electro-fishing and genetic swamping. They hadn't heard, didn't believe, or didn't care that subsequent cross breeding can increase alien genes.

Having assimilated all this testimony, the game commissioner who cast the deciding vote against piscicides, Peter Pino of the Zia Pueblo tribe, declared: "What if we came up with a poison that killed all the white people and left all the native people here? Would we like that? I think that's what we're talking about."

According to Sam Hitt, McCampbell was calling the meeting "a miracle in the making" before it even took place because she had been assured by Game Commission chairman Guy Riordan during one of her lobby sessions that he and "most of the board" agreed with her notions and found them "refreshing" and that, even before hearing a word of testimony, they "opposed" piscicides.

With this victory in hand, McCampbell and her network turned their attentions to Silver King Creek in California. Here they linked up with energetic ally Nancy Erman. The previous year Erman had single-handedly shut down Paiute restoration by convincing the Center for Biological Diversity to sue the U.S. Forest Service, thereby frightening away the California Department of Fish and Game, which has jurisdiction over native fauna and didn't need the Forest Service anyway. To her credit, Erman has great knowledge of and affection for insects, some of which do indeed die during piscicide treatments. But she is unwilling to concede that insects quickly recolonize from untreated water and that, when they do, they often fare better because they no longer have to cope with alien predators with which they did not evolve.

Like McCampbell, Erman plays fast and loose with the facts; and she cultivates a similar network of loud, aggressive, ignorant chemophobes. *Pisces*—the newsletter of the California-Nevada Chapter of the American Fisheries Society—allowed her to draw the old spurious connection between piscicides and DDT and to make the following false statements in its Winter 2004–05 issue: "Further poisoning is unnecessary for recovery of the Paiute cutthroat trout and may even threaten its future" and "many terrestrial mammals, birds, reptiles, amphibians … are put at risk from these projects." Perhaps the most dishonest statement in the piece, a mantra of Erman, McCampbell and their followers, was this: "'Management' that sacrifices other species and natural processes for the sake of one species is a betrayal of the public trust." To the general public, politicians and the media, that means piscicides "sacrifice species." They do no such thing; they occasionally "sacrifice" non-target individuals. The local population then recovers.

When it looked like Paiute restoration was going to get underway in the fall of 2003, TU volunteers helped the state and feds electro-shock as many mongrels as they could from Silver King Creek and evacuate them to nearby water in order to placate local anglers for whom "a trout is a trout." But in *Pisces* Erman falsely accused managers of dumping the mongrels into pure Lahontan cutthroat habitat: "CDFG, Trout Unlimited, and the U.S. Forest Service moved hybrid Paiute cutthroat/rainbows into other waters including Poison Lake. Poison Creek, the outlet of Poison Lake, had been a source for pure Lahontan cutthroat trout." I knew this to be false, and when I asked Erman where she'd gotten her information she hemmed and hawed and said: "Well, we found a reference that they had been using that stream for pure Lahontans." But the reference she produced talks about the Lahontan population introduced about a century ago to "Poison Flat Creek," a tributary of Poison Creek and isolated from it by a long series of impassable waterfalls.

Also testifying was Laurel Ames of the California Watershed Alliance. A month before the board meeting she had circulated an action alert entitled "Stop Poisoning of Sierra Nevada Creeks" that parroted Erman's and McCampbell's bogus claims: "It is well documented that non-chemical alternatives are available. ... We shouldn't poison wilderness streams and lakes for fishermen who want to catch a certain kind of fish. ... There is also new evidence that rotenone has long-lasting, possibly even permanent impacts on stream ecosystems." I pled with her to cease and desist, explaining that native fish restoration isn't "for fishermen" any more than condor restoration is "for birders," that there are no "long-lasting impacts," that she was jeopardizing the last best chance to save a beautiful and unique creature from extinction, and that, although native trout are rarely seen by non-anglers such a herself, they're a vital part of natural ecosystems. I might as well have been speaking Chinese.

In their attempt to treat a mere eleven miles of stream—thereby restoring Paiutes to their entire native range, something that has never been done in salmonid restoration—the agencies have been jumping through hoops for ten years. The recovery plan came out in 1985. On April 4, 2003, the project finally passed muster under a "biological opinion" prepared by the U.S. Fish and Wildlife Service. On April 10, 2003 it passed muster under the California Environmental Quality Act (CEQA). On May 5, 2004—after months of scoping sessions and public commentary—it passed muster under the National Environmental Policy Act (NEPA). With that, Erman filed an administrative appeal that went all the way to the chief of the Forest Service, who denied it. On July 8, 2004, the Lahontan Regional Water Quality Control Board (a strictly political entity) issued a tentative permit, so the agencies committed major funding to the project—which they now can't get back. On August 10, 2004, the Fish and Wildlife Service issued its final "Revised Recovery Plan." On August 27 the board recommended issuing a final pollution-discharge permit.

Then, at the September 8, 2004, board meeting, after the window for legal challenge had expired, all the same ancient red herrings were hauled out and flung around by Erman, McCampbell and their minions. Both CEQA and NEPA studies had determined that there were no mountain yellow-legged frogs or Yosemite toads in the project area, yet there was endless flap about "danger" to these species. Both CEQA and NEPA studies had determined that there would be no permanent damage to macroinvertebrates, but there was endless talk of "dangers to macroinvertebrates." Erman was supposed to get five minutes to testify, but she was allowed to go on for at least twenty minutes. Finally, the board voted to make no decision, thereby blocking restoration indefinitely. Since the Endangered Species Act requires federal agencies to do what's in their power to recover listed species, the board may be in violation of federal law.

"After all that work it just drove us nuts," declares Phil Pister, executive secretary of the Desert Fishes Council. "Nancy and all her buddies screamed so loud that the board was afraid to take action. It's going to get harder as time goes on."

Phister knows a thing or two about fish restoration. On August 18, 1969, he held the world's total population of Owens pupfish in two buckets. To save this fish he and his California Fish and Game colleagues had to build a refuge by damming a small stream and rotenoning out the largemouth bass, carp and bluegill. Today that would be politically impossible. Even back then he got a nasty letter from a snail fancier who fretted about snails getting poisoned from the two-acre impoundment. Since then anglers have continually slipped bass back into one of the refuges. They've done it "dozens of times," says Pister. "Each time Fish and Game removes most of the bass with electro-shockers and spear guns, since the impoundment is only about one acre. But it's extremely labor intensive. The local attitude is 'My granddaddy used to catch bass here and by Gawd I'm gonna do it, too.'"

Pister also helped save California's state fish, the golden trout, by poisoning browns that, in some places, outnumbered goldens two hundred to one. "Our job," he told me, "was to build a series of barriers, then introduce rotenone or antimycin. Luckily, this was before this big furor. We did run into some of it, though, with the animal-rights people." Millions of dollars have been invested in building these barriers, and now they're deteriorating. There are miles and miles of stream that need to be treated or re-treated, especially in the habitat of the threatened Little Kern golden trout. In the current climate that can't happen.

The turn-around has to begin with anglers who have acquired what nineteenth century sportsman and outdoor writer George Bird Grinnell called "a refined taste in natural objects," anglers who defend native fish not because they are fun to catch or good to eat or beautiful, not because they are anything, only because they are. Herewith, two important facts to pass on to those who remain unconvinced: 1) Piscicides can only be used on small headwater streams; no one is talking about or is capable of poisoning out, say, browns and rainbows from the Madison River. And, 2) With the home-field advantage native species tend to grow faster and bigger than non-natives. Witness the robust native greenback cutts, which—in arguably the most dramatic success story in the history of the Endangered Species Act—have replaced the scrawny, stunted browns, rainbows and brookies in and around Rocky Mountain National Park. Thanks to piscicides you can now fish for greenbacks.

The chemophobes can't be educated, but they can be outlobbied. And the public can be won over by people who have the facts and dare to speak the truth, and who understand that creatures like Gila trout, Owens pupfish, and all the vanishing cutthroats are every bit as precious to our nation as redwoods, timber wolves, bison or grizzlies.

A Vampire Story

◦—(·)◦—

Sea lampreys suck. Striking fast as cobras, these primitive, jawless, boneless fish latch onto their prey with tooth-studded disks, bore holes with raspy tongues, then imbibe bodily fluids. They can suck their way over wet dams and through rocky rapids. They hitch rides by sucking onto boats and humans. In the Great Lakes, Finger Lakes, and Lake Champlain a sea lamprey may kill forty pounds of salmonids during its eighteen-month adult phase. When one or several finish a trout or salmon it looks like Swiss cheese soaked in raspberry jam.

You can suppress sea lampreys by poisoning their mud-dwelling larvae, blocking their access to streams, and disrupting spawning with release of sterile males. But you'll never get them all; and if you don't keep at it, they'll bounce right back. The only sure way to protect game fish is to equip each with a wooden crucifix, at least according to columnist Dave Barry.

Consult most any credible source and you'll learn that sea lampreys are "alien invaders" from the Atlantic that gained access to Lake Ontario and the Finger Lakes through the Erie Canal and to Lake Champlain through the Champlain–Hudson canal. Now two comprehensive studies (unpublished at this writing) provide compelling evidence that this is not so, that sea lampreys are just as native to these waters as are landlocked salmon to Maine's West Grand, Green, Sebec, and Sebago lakes.

Dr. Kim Scribner, a fisheries professor at Michigan State University, supervised a project that compared the DNA of sea lampreys from Lake Champlain and Cayuga Lake with that of specimens from the Atlantic. "The genetics of the lake fish indicate long isolation," Scribner told me. "If colonization were a human-caused event, there should be certain genetic affinities between populations." There aren't.

Concurrently, independently and looking at different genetic markers, researchers at the Hudson River Foundation for Science and Environmental

Research have reached the same conclusion. "We found tremendous differences in mitochondrial DNA," declares the foundation's Dr. John Waldman. And he adds that because Champlain lampreys don't share DNA with Lake Ontario fish, they probably had a separate history of colonization. Certainly, there is nothing that would have prevented sea lampreys from entering Lake Ontario through the St. Lawrence River and Lake Champlain through the Richelieu River.

The notion that sea lampreys negotiated the Erie and Champlain–Hudson canals is a major stretch. Like other anadromous fish, lampreys require clean, well-oxygenated water, and the canals were filthy and stagnant. They were also choked with locks, and ripe lampreys need to spawn quickly because, like Pacific salmon, they undergo rapid decay. What's more, the sea lamprey (at least in freshwater) is one anadromous fish that doesn't home in on its natal river. Instead, it follows pheromones released by larval lampreys—the presence of larvae means there must be spawning habitat. If sea lampreys arrived from the Atlantic via man-made canals, there wouldn't have been larvae to attract them.

But why and how did sea lampreys negotiate the Welland Canal (which bypasses Niagara Falls) and enter the upper Great Lakes, where they are definitely not endemic? Slowly and in exceedingly small numbers. This relatively short (twenty-six-mile) canal was finished in 1829, but it wasn't until 1921 that sea lampreys showed up in Lake Erie. And apparently, not many lampreys made it through because Waldman and his colleagues found far less genetic diversity in Lake Superior specimens.

As recently the fall of 2003 the *Atlantic Salmon Journal* ran a piece in which a misinformed fish writer (one Ted Williams) reported that sea lampreys were probably not native to Lake Champlain and Lake Ontario because "not one of the historical accounts of salmon or lake trout catches mentions a fish bearing a circular wound." But native silver lampreys had been present in both drainages and would have wounded fish, an indication that lack of public commentary on scarring doesn't mean much.

How could Atlantic salmon and lake trout have thrived in the Finger Lakes, and Lakes Champlain and Ontario if sea lampreys had been present? Other documents (such as my master's thesis) contend that lampreys wiped out lake trout in Lake Ontario. But a newly released fifteen-year study by federal agencies and North American universities offers convincing evidence that by the 1940s the lake was sufficiently contaminated with dioxin to kill virtually all young trout. Lake Ontario's prolific Atlantic salmon were extirpated in the late nineteenth century by dams, which also would have knocked down sea lampreys. But a few lampreys survived, and the species exploded when the dams fell into disrepair and when humans replenished the lake with lamprey prey.

Could it have been that the extinct native races of lake trout and Atlantic salmon in Lakes Ontario and Champlain had adapted to sea lampreys? If this were the case, you'd expect the extant native trout from Seneca Lake (one of the Finger Lakes) to be resistant to lamprey attack. Indeed they are—so resistant, in fact, that managers stock them in the Great Lakes where they survive much better than the Lake Superior strain. Perhaps it's a behavioral thing or perhaps, because Seneca Lake is very deep, its lake trout prefer water too deep for lampreys.

So all this means that we should desist from controlling freshwater sea lampreys and kiss them Jimmy Houston style, right? Well, no. First, if it were possible to extirpate them from habitat they seem to have evolved in, we shouldn't; but it's not possible. Second, they aren't native to the upper Great Lakes; and, although it's not possible to extirpate them there either, it would be nice to. And third, the lamprey problem in lakes Ontario and Champlain is indeed the result of alien introductions—but the aliens are stocked salmonids, not (apparently) the sea lampreys with which they can't cope. The only solution is aggressive lamprey control.

Before the lamprey invasion, the United States and Canada annually harvested about 15 million pounds of lake trout from the upper Great Lakes. Then, between 1937 and 1947 the Lake Huron catch dropped from 3.4 million pounds to about nothing. Between 1946 and 1953 the Lake Michigan catch fell from 5.5 million pounds to 402.

Managers started work on the problem in 1946 when a team led by Michigan biologist Vernon Applegate began interdicting lampreys with barriers. But the researchers quickly realized they'd also need a selective poison, and there'd never been such a thing for any pest, let alone fish. Still, three years later Applegate (now with the U.S. Fish and Wildlife Service) began what he called "a six-year sentence of unmitigated boredom," testing about 6,000 chemicals by dumping them into ten-liter glass battery jars that contained a rainbow trout, a bluegill and a larval lamprey.

Finally in 1955 lab chief John Howell found one jar in which the lamprey was dead and the trout and bluegill "alive and happy." At first he thought something had gone wrong. But when he tried again he got the same result. Unfortunately, the chemical—3-bromo-4 nitrophenol—was expensive and almost impossible to synthesize. So Applegate turned to Dow Chemical Co. for help. Dow suggested testing close chemical relatives, then concocted some soluble formulations. The winner was 3-trifluoromethyl-4 nitrophenol (TFM), still used today and as close to a silver bullet as chemical pesticides get. Non-target mortality is almost nil. Occasionally, when dosages are off, young mudpuppies (large aquatic salamanders) are killed. But numbers swiftly rebound, and in roughly 3,000 TFM treatments over the last forty years not one population is known to have been lost.

No lamprey control was more effective than water pollution. For example, the St. Marys River, which runs from Lake Superior into Lake Huron, produced few lampreys before it was brought back to life by the Clean Water Act. At twenty-five times the size of the biggest river ever treated with TFM, there had been nothing managers could do but watch the cleaned-up St. Marys pump vampires back into Lake Huron.

But in 1998 the Great Lakes Fishery Commission tried a new selective lampricide called granular Bayluscide. Grains of sand are coated with the poison, then coated again with a time-release substance. Applied to hot spots by helicopter, the lampricide sinks and spreads over the bottom, allowing non-target fish to swim up or away. After Bayluscide treatments on the St. Marys, and release of sterile males that tie up multiple females in unproductive spawning, scarring of Huron lake trout declined by 50 percent. There are still problem areas in the Great Lakes (upper Lake Michigan, for instance), but the sea lamprey is the one alien invader (out of 165) that managers have learned how to control. Today Great Lakes sea lampreys are down 90 percent from their 1961 peak. The control program costs about $12 million a year and produces income—from sportfishing—of between $4 and $6 billion a year.

Lamprey control is forever. But without it, says the commission's Marc Gaden, "Endangered species would be wiped out, and we'd have no fishery to speak of, just a cesspool of exotic organisms that have infested our waters." In Europe, where sea lampreys fetch as much as $25 per pound, they've traditionally been relished as gourmet food. Crazed with gluttony, King Henry I of England is said to have killed himself with a "surfeit of lamprey." We plunder our dogfish for the Brits; why not plunder our lampreys for them and get paid for it? But when I put the question to Gaden, he said the commission needs every male lamprey it can get its hands on for its sterile-release program. "The last thing we want is to be competing with commercial fishermen." The commission traps lampreys, kills the females (which are fat with eggs and lack the spinal ridge), then runs the males through a machine that weighs them, figures out the right dosage of sterilant, shoots it into them, then dumps them into a holding tank.

In 1990 Vermont, New York, and the US Fish and Wildlife Service (having finished a five-year, 997-page Environmental Impact Statement (EIS) that restudied everything the lake states and Canada had learned about TFM since the 1950s) finally got around to using TFM in Lake Champlain's tributaries. The results on the Atlantic salmon fishery were spectacular. "Some of the guys were fishing the Ausable, Boquet and Saranac instead of going up to the Gaspé," reports Larry Nashett of the New York Department of Environmental Conservation. "Up there they might spend a lot of time and money and catch one fish. Here, on good days, they were taking three-fish limits." The better salmon were seven or eight pounds. There was even some natural reproduction.

But when the EIS expired in 1997, it seemed as if Vermonters had never heard of TFM; the stuff terrified them. At this point Vermont, New York and the US Fish and Wildlife Service undertook a two-year, 579-page "comprehensive evaluation" of the eight-year program and-when this was hatched-a two-year, 562-page supplemental EIS, in which they restudied everything they'd restudied in the first EIS.

Since the end of all the studies in 2001, New York has been knocking the bejesus out of lampreys on its side of the lake. But because of low water in 2001 along with public chemophobia and ongoing timidity among health officials, there has been only one TFM treatment in Vermont—on Lewis Creek in 2002. Meanwhile, the salmon fishing in 2003 was the worst in recent memory, according to district fisheries biologist Brian Chipman.

On the Poultney River—one of three large Vermont streams that desperately require TFM treatments—The Nature Conservancy has talked the state and feds into a five-year moratorium while everyone chats about non-chemical "alternatives" that don't exist. *Fly Rod & Reel's* editor, Paul Guernsey, describees TNC as "arguably the world's most effective environmental organization." This is correct, and that's why I was so surprised and distressed to read TNC's commentary on the supplemental EIS. It was pure gobbledygook, rambling on about lampriciding being ill-advised because, having no "endpoint," it didn't contribute "toward the goal of having the system 'manage itself,'" as if this were ever anyone's goal or even a possible goal. By this logic we should write off 80 percent of the Yellowstone cutthroats on earth and forget about perpetual alien lake trout control in Yellowstone Lake; and we should abandon perpetual lamprey control in Lake Superior, a program that has allowed native lake trout, the top predators in that vast ecosystem, to recover to the point that they're self-sustaining. The supplemental EIS ignores the "likely detriment" to existing fish that would result from stocking salmon and lake trout "strains of a different origin and different genetics than the populations that were lost," continued TNC. By this logic the United States should never have introduced tundra and Canadian anatum peregrine falcons after our eastern peregrine was lost.

Such statements provide ordnance to a minority of hothead sportsmen and property-rights types who, at least in Vermont, seem to make a majority of the noise. I scarcely dare imagine what else they're saying about TNC after reading their comments on *Fly Rod & Reel's* internet bulletin board regarding a column in which I'd merely mentioned TNC's role in land preservation. For example: "Dear Ted Williams ... TNC appears to delight in crushing the will of local people. ... Where is your article on the need for lamprey control in Lake Champlain? Your buddies are interested in protecting the sea lamprey, mudpuppy, etc. ... These organizations are sucking blood money out of the restoration effort. ...

Go ahead change the name to *Sea Lamprey & Mudpuppy Magazine* and see how well it is received by fly fishermen!"

To its credit, TNC chose to respond calmly and rationally to this and other tantrums and to engage the state and feds in dialogue rather than court action. The Vermont Public Interest Research Group (VPIRG) and Audubon Vermont, on the other hand, sued.

What I find so frustrating about the environmental community, not just in Vermont but nationwide, is its frequent inability to see native fish as part of ecosystems, even when these natives are apex predators. In announcing its lawsuit, VPIRG advanced the argument that Atlantic salmon and lake trout recovery was "strictly for sport fishing." It then proclaimed that TFM has "potentially far-ranging and largely unknown effects on non-target organisms." This is an untruth. There are no "far-ranging" effects; no piscicide is safer for non-targets; and no pesticide, with the possible exception of rotenone, has been better studied. During the 2002 treatment of Lewis Creek, managers placed mudpuppies in wire cages to see what would happen to them. Not one was harmed.

The supplemental EIS commentary of VPIRG and Vermont Audubon, whose lawsuit failed, made no more sense than TNC's: "The benefit of catching fish without visible scars accrues to a tiny segment of the population while the potential damage to the environment from lampricide treatments must be borne by all Vermonters," declared VPIRG, as if scarring were the issue or had something to do with rebuilding Lake Champlain's native ecosystem, or as if Vermonters were in any way threatened by quick, localized, EPA approved applications of TFM at less than five parts per million. "The intent of the program is to produce more and larger individuals of three species of game fish," remarked Audubon Vermont, as if Atlantic salmon, lake trout and walleyes were of no value in and of themselves and played no role in the lake's native ecosystem.

If Vermont finally commits to aggressive chemical control, Champlain's sea lampreys will probably be reduced to something like their natural level back when native salmonids had the ability to avoid them. But what role should the saltwater race of sea lampreys be allowed to play in the

Atlantic Ocean and in the rivers it collects? With one hand Vermont and the feds are killing lampreys that are apparently native to Lake Champlain and, with the other—a few miles away, over a low mountain range— they're rehabilitating native lampreys in the Connecticut River.

In the spring of 2003 the feds and the watershed states passed 8,063 lampreys over the fishway at Vernon, Vermont. Downstream, at Holoyoke, Massachusetts, they passed 53,030. Isn't this schizoid, not to mention dangerous and irresponsible? Yes, according to some fish pundits. For example, *The Lawrence* (Massachusetts) *Eagle-Tribune's* respected outdoor columnist, Roger Aziz, scolds managers for allowing sea "lamprey eels [which] literally suck the life out of their host fish" through fish-passage facilities: "The fish ladders ought to be used to diminish the lamprey and prevent it from entering into the lakes and streams of New Hampshire."

But in the marine ecosystem saltwater lampreys limit no species; they are incapable of feeding when they enter freshwater; and they all die after spawning. The danger to freshwater fish is "zero to none," to quote Fred Kircheis, former director of Maine's Atlantic Salmon Commission who, contracted by the National Fish and Wildlife Foundation, has just finished a white paper recommending policy for saltwater sea lamprey management. When you try to acclimate a saltwater lamprey to freshwater it dies, he explains.

With their carcasses, feces, eggs, milt, and young, saltwater lampreys bring a feast of nutrients to sterile, glaciated feeder streams. Spawners clear sediments and pebbles with their sucker mouths, creating clean areas that attract spawning salmon. Lamprey carcasses are gorged on by the caddis larvae that trout and young salmon eat. Larval lampreys bury in the bottom, thereby preventing a prime impediment to successful salmonid reproduction: stream embeddedness. Lampreys feed eagles, ospreys, herons, vultures, turtles, minks, otters, crayfish and dozens of other native predators and scavengers. "It wasn't until I started talking to some birders that I realized owls prey heavily on lampreys when they come up in the shallows at night," says Steve Gephard, Connecticut's anadromous fish chief. "Sea lampreys have played a very important role in this watershed for a lot longer than any other species. We don't begin to recognize the benefits."

It's hard to blame sportsmen and outdoor writers for not grasping the value of native saltwater lampreys when some managers are just as ignorant. In Maine the Department of Inland Fisheries and Wildlife and the Division of Marine Resources interdict spawning lampreys west of the Penobscot River and let them go to the east (where there are essentially no dams for interdiction). "Why?" Gephard keeps asking.

When I repeated the question to Fred Kircheis he said: "Uninformed bias." The superstition that saltwater lampreys are somehow "bad" started in the 1960s when a few "transformers" (newly metamorphosed larvae trying to get to sea) left scars on landlocked salmon in Sheepscot Lake. Usually transformers are just hitchhiking, but if they do feed (because low water temporarily blocks seaward migration), they're so small they apparently don't kill their hosts.

Because Maine Atlantic salmon and other native anadromous fish evolved with sea lampreys and need them, the state's anti-lamprey bias has long infuriated TU's New England conservation director, Jeff Reardon. Currently, he is trying to solve a fish passage problem on the Sheepscot River where dam removal is an option. "I thought we were ready to move on this a year ago," he told me. "Then there was a huge blowup about lampreys. The Maine agencies wanted to use the dam as a lamprey barrier. The National Fish and Wildlife Foundation and NOAA (National Oceanographic and Atmospheric Administration), which would be providing funding to remove the dam or build a fishway, have been telling the state agencies, 'Look, if there's a reason to exclude lampreys, tell us what it is.'" They can't because there isn't one.

Thoughtful anglers who notice and appreciate the natural world need to carefully consider sea lampreys in all waters, fresh and salt. Lampreys may suck. But, then, so do bonefish, humming birds, butterflies, and human infants. Sea lampreys everywhere teach us that, in nature, "ugliness" is a word that applies only to ecological messes—messes that, without exception, are made by humans when they destroy beautiful and complex machinery or toss parts where they don't belong.

MOTORIZING PUBLIC LAND

November 27, 1999, found me at the "spring hole" in my twelve-foot fishing scow in the warm, misty finish of a New Hampshire squall. I had come here with brothers-in-law Wiz and Barry to escape sundry irritations, including a fifth meal of turkey. Propelled by our bowed rods, fat, gaudy yellow perch shot over the low gunwales. Gear down and wings set, Canada geese sailed across the north end of our island and spiraled into Schneider's Cove. Now lake and forest were still, save for the splashing of hooked fish, the mutterings of mergansers, and the distant whistle of goldeneye wings. Then half a dozen all-terrain vehicles (ATVs) appeared on the mainland shore, roaring and racing, rousting the waterfowl. They sashayed through the swamp and hurled mud and vegetation thirty feet into the air. Finally, one got stuck.

In winter, when I do my serious perch fishing, snowmobilers race over the frozen lake and across the spring hole, which never freezes, because they like to see how far their craft can carry them on open water. No longer do I attempt to kick them off our island—a posted, 280-acre wildlife sanctuary. While they stress the wildlife and make it unsafe for us to ski or hike on the narrow trails, they are quieter than they were twenty years ago and easier on ground cover than the ATVs.

I am not anti-internal combustion. In fact, I agree with Forest Service Chief Mike Dombeck, who proclaims that off-road vehicles (ORVs)—which include ATVs, snowmobiles, and motorized dirt bikes–are "the only way many people can realistically enjoy our public lands" and that "as baby boomers age and society continues to urbanize, more and more people may turn to off-road vehicles as their primary way of enjoying the great outdoors." Mounted on my fishing scow is a six-horse, two-stroke outboard because a four-stroke, though far quieter and cleaner, would sink it. Two-stroke engines—which power most outboard boats and ORVs—are crude, filthy devices. At least a quarter of the fuel they "consume" enters the environment unburned, via the exhaust.

But there's a difference between outboards and ORVs. My motor gets me to the spring hole, then I shut it off. Riding ORVs, on the other hand, has become recreation unto itself; mainly they are used to provide thrills, not transportation. What moves and inspires most ORV operators is different from what moves and inspires most other people who gravitate toward wild land. For example, my outboard–which bears no model name other than "6MSHY"—is manufactured by Yamaha, a company that also offers a line of ATVs named, it would seem, for the noise they make (Banshee and Blaster) or the predators they displace (Grizzly, Kodiak, Wolverine, Timberwolf, Big Bear, and Badger).

I can and do live with ORVs. But where should I go for quietude and wildness: to hear the sigh of wind through canyons and forest canopies, the music of flowing water, the hum and clatter of insects, the songs of birds, the silence of winter? A national park? BLM land? Perhaps. But last winter nearly 200,000 snowmobiles were allowed to enter thirty-eight national park units, and about 90 percent of Bureau of Land Management lands have areas open to snowmobiles, dirt bikes, and ATVs. They regularly trespass on wilderness, and the Forest Service even allows them in wilderness study areas. Moreover, they are not among the environmental menaces the Clinton administration is trying to remove from roadless areas. After promoting ORVs for thirty years, the agencies that administer public land are suddenly wishing that they hadn't.

In the 1980s snowmobiles were basically restricted by their own design to groomed trails, and until 1990—when the ORV lobby got the Forest Service to cancel its ban on off-road vehicles wider than forty inches— ATVs were effectively prohibited from national forests. Now, with wider bases and more powerful engines, ORVs of all sorts engage in "high pointing" contests, in which the object is to see how steep a slope you can negotiate without tipping over. The new snowmobiles can exceed 110 miles per hour. Are they appropriate in our wildest and best public land—Yellowstone National Park, for instance?

From mid-December to mid-March, Yellowstone bans cars from most of the park, but it welcomes snowmobiles on 189 miles of snow-covered roads. One of these machines can emit as many hydrocarbons as 1,000 cars and as much carbon monoxide as 250 cars—and there are about 80,000 snowmobiles in the park each season. Park employees complain of headaches, nausea, and throat irritation from the pollution, and fresh air has to be pumped into the entrance booths. The Bluewater Network, leader of the national campaign to keep snowmobiles out of the park, calculates that in addition to befouling the air, two-stroke snowmobile engines dump 180,000 to 210,000 gallons of unburned gasoline and motor oil on Yellowstone's ecosystems each season.

"We believe that the mode of winter transportation, primarily snowmobiles, tends to overwhelm the experience of visiting the park," comments John Sacklin, Yellowstone's chief planner. That's why there are laws against it. By allowing snowmobile use in Yellowstone, the Park Service has flouted not only the Clean Air Act but its own Organic Act, which mandates that public enjoyment of a park leave it "unimpaired for the enjoyment of future generations," and President Nixon's Executive Order 11644 (later reinforced by Jimmy Carter), which forbids federal land-management agencies from permitting ORV use unless they demonstrate that doing so won't compromise natural values. As Yellowstone's superintendent, Michael Finley, puts it in his current bid to limit snowmobiles, "We are not debating some abstract scientific interpretation here. We are deciding if we are going to pass Yellowstone on to our children in good condition."

Finley's life would be easier and his park quieter and cleaner had the Park Service traditionally been less infatuated with snowmobiles. In 1973, when there were already 30,000 of them in Yellowstone each winter, Superintendent Jack Anderson received the International Award of Merit from the International Snowmobile Industry Association for showing "enlightened leadership and sincere dedication to the improvement and advancement of snowmobiling in the United States." The following year he designated most of Yellowstone's primary roads as snowmobile routes. In 1977, two years after he retired, he called snowmobiling "a great experience and a great sport, one of the cleanest types of recreation I know" and prescribed earplugs for those offended by the noise. John Townsley, who took over for Anderson in 1975, successfully defended snowmobiling against none other than Secretary of the Interior James Watt—an effort for which he, too, won the snowmobile industry's International Award of Merit.

When Robert Barbee replaced Townsley in 1983, he attempted to get a line on the problem, but by then it was like hooking a submarine. Now that Barbee is running the national parks in Alaska, he's trying to remove snowmobiles permanently from about a third of Denali National Park and Preserve. "We don't want Denali to become another Yellowstone," he says.

On the rest of our public land—basically that tended by the BLM and the Forest Service—the situation is even worse. And any manager who tries to control ORVs gets to eat their dust. Last summer members of the Montana Wildlife Federation helped the Forest Service gate and post critical wildlife habitat in the Helena National Forest. In exchange, ORV users were granted new access to a different area. The deal was a model of multiple use in action, but in November malcontents tore down the signs, sawed off the posts, and pulled up the gates, doing several thousand dollars' worth of damage.

The BLM and the Forest Service actually permit ORV races. There are, however, certain basic rules. For instance, on the Owyhee Front, across the Snake River from Boise, Idaho, the BLM proscribes "bomb-run starts," in which 100 or so dirt bikes line up, pop wheelies, and send ground cover into orbit. On May 20, 1998, the BLM's Owyhee field manager, Daryl Albiston, sent a letter to an off-road-motorcycle club called Dirt, Inc., advising it that its races on March 21 and 22 had been in violation because: bikers traversed the course "as many times as possible for a two-hour period" instead of just once; "an unauthorized new trail was developed"; racers ventured "off trail"; and "spectators on motorcycles, all-terrain vehicles, and in trucks were allowed to drive off the existing road and trail network." Dirt, Inc., was instructed in writing to rehabilitate the area with fencing and native seeds, but it refused to do so. When it was reminded in writing, it refused again.

The upshot was that the BLM allowed Dirt, Inc., to race on September 26, 1998. Later Albiston sent the group a letter advising it that it again had violated regulations by: not marking "the passing zone for sensitive plants"; "rerouting" a part of the course without authorization; creating "a new connector trail"; and allowing spectator vehicles to "travel off of the established roads." Still, Dirt, Inc., was permitted to race again on May 23, 1999. This time the violations chronicled by Albiston included: a bomb-run start; failure to stay on "the designated trail," which resulted in the destruction of "many shrubs"; allowing spectators "on motorcycles, ATVs, and trucks" to drive over vegetated land; and leaving flags, posts, and signs on public land. Dirt, Inc., plans to race next on April 2. Albiston won't tell me if he's going to authorize yet another race but says I "can probably guess what's going to happen." Indeed I can.

In 1995 the General Accounting Office investigated ORV management on BLM and Forest Service land to see if Nixon's and Carter's executive orders were being obeyed. They weren't. "At all locations," reads the report, "off-highway vehicle use was being monitored casually rather than systematically; adverse effects were seldom being documented."

Under Dombeck the Forest Service is at least doing better than the BLM. All 155 national forests are drafting traffic-management plans that include ORVs. The agency is struggling to decide how to manage at least 60,000 miles of "ghost roads"—illegal routes created by ORV use. "Our position is that no policy of the Forest Service should encourage the creation of illegal roads and trails," Dombeck's chief of staff, Chris Wood, told me. "But the fact is that a lot of them already exist. Sticking your head in the sand and saying, 'We didn't authorize them, so we're going to close them' is kind of an untenable approach."

Maybe so. And now that Dombeck is changing the mission of the Forest Service from resource extraction to resource stewardship with such measures as his recently proposed protection of roadless areas from logging, road construction, and mining, he's catching hell from a cabal of timber, mineral, and ORV interests. "We've got the sledgehammer out on a number of issues right now," says Wood. "This is one that requires a little bit more finesse at a more local level."

Yet studying each illegal road that has been or will be created to see if it's ORV-worthy is going to cost manpower and resources the agency does not have, and regulations don't matter anyway, because it can't provide enforcement. An internal monitoring report from the Wayne

National Forest in Ohio reads as follows: "Whether we look at the designated trail system or the non-ORV management areas, we have no control over off-road-vehicle use. We install signs and they are ripped out. We erect barriers and they are removed or ridden around. We rehab areas and they are violated again and again. We provide virtually no law-enforcement presence on the Forest when use is highest. Whether it is the Wayne or any other Forest, the concept of 'off-road vehicle' is contrary to the mission of the National Forests. We cannot, regardless of dollars, maintain trails that will not erode into our streams. And we cannot control users equipped with vehicles designed to go on all types of terrain."

In October the BLM and the Forest Service published a joint environmental-impact statement for Montana, North Dakota, and parts of South Dakota in which assessing ghost roads for ORV use is the preferred alternative. "The EIS is horrible," says Montana Fish, Wildlife and Parks biologist Gayle Joslin, who led a drive in which the Montana Wildlife Society raised $73,700 to prepare a report on the ways ORVs hurt wildlife. "The agencies put together a committee to define trails; it took them eighteen months. The definition of an ORV trail they came up with—and I kid you not—is one that has been used by a motorized vehicle. This even includes game trails!"

Greg Munther, who retired as the Lolo National Forest's Nine-Mile District Ranger after thirty-one years with the Forest Service, had this to say: "The Forest Service and BLM chose out of political convenience not to take on these illegal roads. They told us professionals for years that the only way to have a legitimate road was to properly design it with respect to grade and drainage. Now they've accepted these ghost roads for years while they go through this endless analysis."

Carrying the ORV industry's gas—and venting it—is the BlueRibbon Coalition, one of the original signatories to the Wise Use Agenda, an official platform hatched by Seattle-area propagandist Ron Arnold and convicted tax-fraud felon Alan M. Gottlieb that advocates the sale and development of public land as well as the suspension of federal statutory protection for "non-adaptive species." The coalition is jointly funded by Yamaha, Honda, Polaris, Ski-doo, and Horizon, and lists among its members scores of motor-head clubs with names like the Missouri Mudders, and such firms and cartels as the Western States Petroleum Association, American Forest & Paper Association, Boise Cascade, Idaho Cattle Association, Committee for Public Access to Public Lands, Idaho Mining Association, and Northwest Mining Association. Cofounder and director Clark Collins defines Forest Service Chief Dombeck's temporary moratorium on new logging roads as a wilderness-expansion plot by the "GAGs" (green advocacy groups, which he has also referred to as "hate groups" and "nature Nazis"). And in late August he launched the Wilderness Act Reform Coalition, to gut the statute that the ORV-timber-mining axis most loves to hate.

But in addition to spewing rhetoric and fumes, the BlueRibbon Coalition gets things done. In 1999 it prevailed on Congress to fund the lapsed National Recreational Trails program, thereby providing the states with $270 million over six years, at least a third of which will be used to build and improve ORV trails on public land. And it manipulates hunters and fishers with remarkable success.

One of the coalition's six "industry supporters" is the Outdoor Channel, the first full-time cable network with a programming focus on hunting and fishing and which reaches 11 million homes across the nation. It includes the coalition on its website links to "conservation" organizations and gives it plenty of airtime to tub-thump for motorization and privatization of public land. Jake Hartwick, the Outdoor Channel's executive vice-president, advises me that "wise-use groups are defending the very foundation of our system" and that "environmental groups are advocating the complete abolition of private-property rights." He warns that "the Forest Service is locking up roads at an alarming rate."

But not all sportsmen are so easily seduced, and when you strip away the mirrors, gongs, water, and dry ice, Clark Collins becomes a little man in a Wizard of Oz suit. In the BlueRibbon Coalition's home state of Idaho—domain of its effusive champion, Rep. Helen Chenoweth—the state Fish and Game Department reports that at least 86 percent of elk hunters find that encounters with motorized vehicles detract from their outdoor experience. Less than 5 percent of the 8,500 members of the Montana Wildlife Federation (composed basically of hunters and anglers) own ORVs, and the group is asking the Forest Service to close all roads that don't service full-size vehicles. Declares Jim Posewitz, director of the Montana-based sportsmen's support group Orion, The Hunter's Institute: "The presence of ATVs on public hunting grounds will probably be one of the largest contributors to loss of hunting opportunity that we've yet experienced. It puts the animals at a disadvantage. It violates the security that wildlife once had in difficult terrain. The Forest Service and BLM have decided to disenfranchise the people who have followed the law and empower those who have violated it. We're battling this terrible EIS tooth and claw. Those of us who have participated in nonmotorized use have no way to stake a comparable claim."

Clark Collins blames the unpopularity of ORVs on the behavior of "bad apples," and maybe he's right. But because the new machines can go where there is no enforcement, bad apples proliferate. Evaluating the "600cc mountain line" snowmobiles for *SnoWest* magazine, Steve Janes of the *SnoWest* test crew filed this report in the magazine's October 1999 issue: "In the four days of riding in Quebec, we estimate that we violated around 652 laws or regulations. But since our crew's motto was 'If you can't break parts, break laws,' we acted naive and 'wandered' off the groomed trails in search of test areas."

The 500 combat missions flown by Colonel George Buchner over Vietnam didn't prepare him for ORV combat in Michigan, where the machines had done an estimated $1 billion worth of damage, tearing up ground cover so badly that utility poles were falling over. Where Lake Huron collects the Au Sable River system, Buchner found trespassing ATV operators popping wheelies in his private trout stream. When he demanded their names, one rider dismounted and attacked him, breaking his nose. When he fenced his posted stream and property, ORV operators cut the wire and pulled the stakes. When he reinforced the stakes with cement, they knocked them down. When he and the Michigan United Conservation Clubs successfully pushed for a state ORV policy of "closed unless posted open," he received death threats, his streetlights were shot out, his mailbox smashed, his driveway seeded with broken glass, the eight-strand fence on his Christmas tree farm cut in eighty-eight places, and his wife run over. "Robin was screaming," he said, "and the guy calmly cranked up his machine and finished running over her. He'd come through multiple barriers, multiple posted signs, three fences, and a gate. She had a hematoma extending the length of her leg." In July 1996 Buchner confronted two trespassing ATV operators, one of whom knocked him down. "Basically, ORVs ran me out of Michigan," Buchner told me from his Arizona home.

But in the end the problem comes down not so much to the nature of ORV users as to the nature of ORVs. They are designed to go "off road," where motorized vehicles don't belong. Their noise is undemocratic—like second-hand smoke. They need to be removed from our wildest and best public land—not because regulations can't control them (although they can't), not because most people hate them (although they do), but because they intrude and usurp. Snowmobile din now penetrates five miles into the backcountry of our first national park. Winter visitors are having trouble hearing the geysers, and winter-stressed elk and bison are being driven from the forage of open meadows and the shallow snow of thermal areas, which they desperately require. In order for ORV operators to do their thing, everyone else, including wildlife, must cease doing theirs—at least in part.

ORVs have their place, and, as Chief Dombeck notes, many people can't enjoy our public lands without them. But when there's no escape from ORVs, the rest of us can't enjoy our public lands either.

SAVE THE REDWOODS: KILL EVERYONE

⤌⤍

The coast redwood is the fastest growing, most easily renewed softwood in the United States. Cut it any time of year and three weeks later it will be sprouting from stumps and root crowns. It can be harvested on a sustained-yield basis with little damage to publicly owned forest resources such as salmon and steelhead. It doesn't have to be strip-mined; in fact, if regeneration is a goal, large clearcuts should be avoided. Logs don't have to be transported on roads that are hacked into unstable slopes; in fact, if regeneration is a goal, haul roads should be well engineered. But for the average timber company CEO, who's in office for about five years, regeneration is basically irrelevant. He's not thinking about what happens half a century in the future when he and his stockholders are dead; he's thinking about dividends and quarterly performance. So soil sloughs into rivers, and salmonids flicker out.

Take northern California's Garcia River, once famous for enormous coho runs and giant chinooks (and still famous for wild steelhead, a resilient species that finds refuge in undefiled headwaters). Chinooks are main stem spawners, and main stems degrade first. So now the Garcia chinooks are extinct. Cohos spawn in main stems, too, but also in low-gradient tributaries whose banks are easily roaded and whose channels have provided handy conduits for skidding logs. So now Garcia cohos are almost extinct.

But in free-flowing rivers blighted only by cut-out-and-get-out logging, healthy salmonid runs can be rebuilt from a few wild genes by controlling sediment, replacing hanging culverts with bridges and restoring large, woody debris. So in June 1998, as Mendocino Redwood Co. (MRC) was signing off on a deal to purchase the Garcia's watershed along with almost 235,000 acres of coastal California rainforest, Trout Unlimited's state policy coordinator Steve Trafton approached the company's CEO, Sandy Dean, with a proposal to do restoration work. Trafton told him how, on Lagunitas Creek near San Francisco, TU had rekindled the last spark of a coho population to a stable run of 500 wild spawners. Dean gave every appearance of being genuinely enthusiastic. He kicked in $150,000. About $90,000 more was provided by the National Fish and Wildlife Foundation, $200,000 by the California Department of Fish and Game, $25,000 by the Mendocino Resource Conservation District and $5,000 by TU.

Trout Unlimited hired professional stream restorer Craig Bell, who asked Dean if it would be OK to train MRC employees in the classroom and in the woods. Fine, said Dean; then he insisted that the company's independent contractors receive the same instruction. Because TU's resources were fully committed, MRC struck off on restoration of its own on the Albion and Navarro rivers, using TU's Garcia formula as a model. In its first year of existence MRC spent $3 million moving and stabilizing fish-killing roads, then committed $4 million for fiscal 2000.

MRC gave TU unlimited access, handing over all maps, all road-maintenance data, all fish records, all temperature records, all sediment-assessment records. I asked Bell how that compared to the cooperation he'd received from the previous owner, Louisiana-Pacific, when he had worked on the Garcia and other streams. He said he had gotten no access to uplands, roads, data or documents, no encouragement, not even a kind word, just "a stern lecture at the gate to stay in the streams." Total cash commitment over ten years amounted to about $200 for redwood seedlings to be planted by TU volunteers.

The motives of the investors who set up MRC—the Donald Fisher family of San Francisco—seem innocent enough. The Fishers run the 2,300 outlets of The Gap, Banana Republic and Old Navy clothing stores. Gap division president Robert Fisher sits on the board of the tough, effective Natural Resources Defense Council. He and father Donald, Gap's chairman and founder, have insisted on energy-efficient stores built with lumber purchased from the few timber companies certified as environmentally responsible by a demanding independent auditor called the Forest Stewardship Council. And Dean sounded sincere when he told me that he and the Fishers want to prove that it is possible—indeed, profitable—"to manage a large block of productive forestland utilizing high standards of environmental stewardship." If MRC could do that, he remarked, other companies might attempt this radical new strategy. Along with the good words there have been some good deeds. Dean has ended traditional clearcutting and embarked on progressive, earth-friendly silvicultural practices.

But a large element of the environmental community remains unimpressed. For instance, the Redwood Coast Watersheds Alliance, which represents thirteen watershed associations in Mendocino County, is leading a national assault on MRC in court, in the press and on the Internet. According to president Mary Pjerrou, all the forest's owners past and present and all regulatory personnel past and present are liars: "The lies of the California Department of Forestry, the lies of foresters in timber harvest plans, the lies of Louisiana-Pacific and the Board of Forestry and Terry Gorton, are why the redwood forests are in their present condition." And what about MRC and the Fishers? "Might even be considered worse." Pjerrou disses Donald Fisher as an "aging monarch" and a "contributor to rightwing causes." She'd heard about TU's work on the Garcia but didn't know anything about the National Fish and Wildlife Foundation—which has proved itself to be the most effective force for aquatic and terrestrial habitat restoration in North America. "I looked at their brochure on grants," she said, "and I had the impression that it was industry-funded. A few alarm bells went off."

Pjerrou also serves as general coordinator of Gap Picket, and her group is part of a national effort by environmentalists called Save the Redwoods/Boycott The Gap Campaign. On November 27, 1998, environmentalists staged a bagpipe-and-drum march down San Francisco's Powell St. to The Gap's flagship store. "We made the front page of *The San Francisco Examiner*," crows Boycott The Gap, "with a wonderful color photo of the parade, including the Art and Revolution giant Fisher puppet wearing the sign 'Fishers: G-reed A-nd P-rofit,' giant redwoods on stilts, marbled murrelets on 15-foot bamboo poles, and more!"

That day there were similar protests at Gap stores in forty U.S. cities. On March 6, 1999, 18 of 300 protesters, again demonstrating at The Gap's flagship store in San Francisco, were cited by police for disorderly conduct. On June 14 "Redwood Mary" of Mendocino led a protest at the Sixth Avenue Gap store in New York City, in which she and others held the doors shut. On December 10, 1997 (before MRC even existed), Julia Hill, an Arkansas woman who calls herself "Butterfly," climbed into a tree house in a redwood that she named "Luna," near Stafford, California, and lived there until Dec. 18, 1999, eating only fruits and vegetables supplied by fellow activists who stuffed them into the bag she lowered on a string. From her tree house Butterfly granted interviews by cell phone, composed poems on recycled paper, and protested all sorts of alleged outrages, including the alleged rapaciousness of the Fishers.

Environmentalists demonstrated at MRC logging operations, too. Beginning in April 1999, they held rallies at the scene of a planned selection cut in the Albion River watershed, playing a song entitled "Chocolate Albion," ensconcing themselves Julia-Butterfly-style in redwoods for almost two months, throwing a cargo net over five trees (four of which weren't marked for harvest), and getting cited for disorderly conduct. These kinds of timber-harvest plans get approved, explains Save the Redwoods/Boycott The Gap Campaign, because of "our corrupt and useless regulatory agencies, the California Department of Forestry and the US Fish and Wildlife Service."

"There are many other reasons people don't like Donald Fisher," reveals Mary Bull, national coordinator of Boycott The Gap and a pooh-bah of Guardians of Elk Creek Old Growth, the group that spawned it. "He's very big in the World Trade Organization; he's privatizing public schools; he's engaged in sweetheart deals with the City of San Francisco. The list goes on."

Speaking more softly is Linda Perkins, president of the Albion River Watershed Protection Association. "MRC's practices in and by themselves might not be considered too horrible," she avers. "But the point is the lands are blasted, so anything you do is bad. Sandy Dean wants to cut 40 million board feet a year, and that's too high. Everyone has said the maximum should be 20 million."

Maybe Perkins has it right, yet when you get down to haggling between 40 million and 20 million board feet a year from 235,000 acres you're basically in the same camp. Forty million board feet a year is two percent of MRC's standing inventory, 30 percent less than the long-term harvest planned by Louisiana-Pacific, and 66 percent of current annual growth. Not only is it sustainable, it is a prescription for forest revitalization.

Yet, with no data, groups like the Medocino Watersheds Alliance, the Greenwood Watershed Association, Guardians of Elk Creek Old Growth and Save the Redwoods/Boycott The Gap chant the mantra that MRC's planned cut is nonsustainable. "Last summer," declares Mary Bull, "MRC was denied certification by the Forest Stewardship Council." In this Bull speaks the truth.

But what interests me more than MRC's failure to win certification on its first try is the fact that it wanted it. Other timber companies don't. MRC is the largest forestland owner in the nation that has made a run at certification and, west of the Cascades, the only large industrial landowner to do so. Green certification by an independent, non-profit third party is an idea that originated in Europe, where consumers worry about how their wood is procured. It has been an enormous success there. In Sweden, for instance, 60 percent of the industrial land base is certified. But in the U.S., where less than one percent is certified, companies resist. Their trade group—the American Forest and Paper Association, which seeks the lowest common denominator in order to keep the bottom feeders in the fold—sees genuine certification as a threat. So, as a countermeasure, it has devised the "Sustainable Forestry Initiative," a make-believe certification process with no possibility of public review and based entirely on vague promises. More than 99 percent of AF&PA's members—owning 80 percent of the nation's industrial land base—were quickly certified under this handy arrangement.

MRC wanted the real thing, and it flunked. Robert Hrubes, of the Oakland-based Natural Resource Association and co-leader of the auditing team contracted by the Forest Stewardship Council, reports that MRC is clearly moving in a new and better direction and that he was "impressed" by the effort. Real certification has to be "transparent," he explained, but only after the fact. That is, when the company begins trading on its green certification, consumers need to be able to see that the process isn't an AF&PA-style fake. If the council's contractors went around airing dirty laundry before certification, they wouldn't have many customers. That's why Hrubes declined to tell me about the problems he found.

But MRC's chief forester, Mike Jani, didn't hesitate. "We need to put together a management plan for the 235,000 acres that not only deals with sustainability of the timber but also the issues of wildlife, fisheries and biological components. We know our forest is going to get better. But we don't know where, over the next fifty years, we're going to go to do our harvesting. The other issue was that our interim policy about old growth [no cutting of trees over forty-eight inches in diameter] needed an element to assess biological value."

Maybe he was lying. Maybe Dean and the Fishers were lying. Maybe MRC was a wolf in granny drag. I needed a third-party observer more talkative than Hrubes, so I contacted Greg Giusti, Extension Service forest advisor for the Univiversity of California. I asked him to compare the forest practices of Louisiana-Pacific with MRC's and please to be blunt. "OK," he said. "L-P didn't give a shit about the land; they wanted their quarterly dividends. They hired fisheries and wildlife biologists, but it was window dressing. Those guys told me that it was a fight to get every possible inch of protection for the stream corridors. I had a lot of respect for them because I knew what they were up against—real hardcore timber-beast mentality."

MRC hasn't made Giusti a believer yet. But he calls it a "breath of fresh air," explaining that virtually all the other big industrial tracts are managed by absentee owners headquartered in other states. "Because MRC is based in San Francisco the owners have the ability to jump in a car and go see their property. There is much more open and honest dialogue now between the landowner and the public." His theory is that Dean—a brilliant, thirty-five-year-old graduate of Stanford Business School—hadn't fully understood what certification involved and perhaps had sought it too early. But Giusti says this: "MRC has established certification as a goal. Are they there yet? No. Can they get there? Well, they've got the guy who can get them there. His name is Mike Jani. He walks the walk; he is the best of the best." Other independent forest professionals agree. They say that, as chief forester for Big Creek Lumber in Santa Cruz, Jani established the company as one of the most exemplary forest managers anywhere and won certification from the Forest Stewardship Council.

What dark motive could MRC have had in hiring someone like that? I couldn't think of one. But Mary Bull explained that Jani is a charlatan—"not green in the least"—and Mary Pjerrou proclaimed that he "is fooling himself." Jani told me he thought he was making progress with both women. But when I asked Pjerrou if MRC was possibly doing a little better with Jani running its forest she gave me an emphatic "no." When I asked Bull the same question I got another emphatic "no." But then, almost in the same breath, she intoned: "We just got some concessions on a plan on Greenwood Creek that we made a huge brouhaha over; in the last week they've caved in and are retaining all the old growth." Jani says he's going to keep up a dialogue with any environmental group that behaves in a civil manner.

His definition of "civil" is, well, generous. For example, you log on to Save the Redwoods/Boycott The Gap's Web site (created by Mary Bull's Guardians of Elk Creek Old Growth and shared with the Greenwood Watershed Association) by punching in "Gapsucks.org." After that you don't expect or get much text that is civil or even interesting, and you read nothing about the genuine reforms MRC has implemented. Still, that's not to say that in its first year and a half of business MRC hasn't made mistakes. For one thing, the company went forward with some controversial L-P timber-harvest plans. Looking to display its inventory to prospective land buyers, L-P had applied for a large number of plans before it put its forest on the auction block. Some were too controversial even for L-P, a fact that Dean and the Fishers may not have known. When MRC began implementing some of the L-P plans it got eaten alive by the enviros. Maybe it should have moved slower.

On the other hand, there weren't lots of choices. MRC inherited about nine months worth of state-approved plans. Basically, it had two options: shut down its mills and lay off its workers or proceed with logging. It chose the latter. Since then it has moved ahead with superb plans of its own and has substantially amended L-P's. But don't expect to read about that by connecting to the Internet and typing in "Gapsucks.org."

What you can read about on the Save the Redwoods/Boycott The Gap's website and in the rambling harangues issuing from the Mendocino

Watersheds Alliance and its members is the fact that MRC, like L-P, uses herbicides. The Fishers, Mary Pjerrou informed *The San Francisco Bay Guardian*, "are going to gas us and take our trees. They are going to poison our children, send the coho salmon to extinction." Actually, MRC uses a relatively benign herbicide (Garlon), delivering it entirely by hand on the ground and protecting fish-bearing streams with 100-foot buffers. When you clearcut old growth, as did L-P and previous owners, brushy species like tanoak take over. "To be profitable they've got to turn those lands back to conifers," says the Extension Service's Giusti. "Over time, I would hope that their silvicultural practices would be such that chemical treatments would cease. Maintain enough canopy and these weedy species will be held in check. Right now they're doing a lot of cleanup."

As the Santa Rosa *Press Democrat* editorialized back on November 20, 1998: "One would have expected North Coast activists to welcome the Fisher family of San Francisco. … And the Fishers arrived with a demonstrated record of environmental commitment. Here was a family that gave millions of dollars to environmental causes. … Surely, people committed to environmental protection would give the new company, Mendocino Redwoods, time to prove its stewardship. Six months later, activists are mounting attacks on the Fishers' business holdings. … This is the dogma: Don't bother us with the complexities of timber economics. Don't permit a fair hearing or adequate time to demonstrate commitment. All timber companies are bad. If the Fisher family takes this kind of public pounding, the next prospective investor will ask, what are the chances that I will get a fair shake?"

I asked Mary Bull and Mary Pjerrou what they thought the Fishers should do with their redwoods, virtually all of which are second growth. The answer was: cut none of them—i.e., let them become old growth. In Pjerrou's words: "I think they should set them all aside and invest money in restoration work, particularly to employ out-of-work fishermen and timber workers. I don't think they should cut anymore. We're talking about people who have an eleven-billion-dollar fortune. They're in the Rockefeller class. They could do this."

Indeed they could. But that's not how the real world works, and that's not how businesses work. Moreover, they wouldn't be accomplishing much for fish and wildlife. When you take an industrial forest out of production, you put that much more pressure on other industrial forests. And there aren't enough rich philanthropists to buy up and protect significant chunks of commercial forestland. Sandy Dean and the Fishers can do far more for trout, salmon and other forest resources by setting an example for the world.

Meanwhile, environmental groups in California and elsewhere should remember that it's OK to train your people to be watchdogs and even attack dogs. Once trained, it's OK for them to watch everyone. But it's not OK for them to attack everyone. What makes an effective environmentalist is what makes an effective forester—selectivity.

COAL-COUNTRY TROUT

—‹‹- ›–›—

On the morning of February 16, 2004, I stood beside a misty pool, the first of three that feed an icy rill collected by the Cheat River in northern West Virginia. A song sparrow trilled; corn snow crunched beneath my boots; a breeze rolled off a frozen peak; and the mist enveloped me, burning my eyes and sinuses and causing me to leap backwards. I had just inhaled anhydrous ammonia.

The chemical is being injected by the state Department of Environmental Protection into the acidified orange outflow from the old T&T mine. Color and acidity come not from coal but the pyrite associated with it. When pyrite is exposed to water and air it forms sulfuric acid and iron hydroxide. The pH of water entering this treatment facility is 2.5; leaving it's 8.5. As alkalinity increases, the iron hydroxide and other toxic metals in acid mine drainage, many of which magnify in food chains, settle out as sludge or "yellow boy." Here the yellow boy is collected from the settling ponds and pumped 2.5 miles back up the mountain where it's dropped into an old mine shaft.

The system can handle 600 gallons of acid drainage a minute; but the outfall from the mine portal can exceed 2,000 gallons a minute. So it frequently runs directly into Muddy Creek, and thence into the Cheat where, as it's diluted and partially neutralized, it dumps its yellow boy, smothering benthic life. Only three miles upcurrent from the mine Muddy Creek sustains wild brook trout. In the Cheat, watershed mine drainage has impaired 100 miles of habitat on fifty-three streams; 73 of these miles once supported wild brook trout and, with the proper investment, could do so again. All told, acid mine drainage has destroyed or severely damaged about 12,000 miles of fish habitat in West Virginia, Pennsylvania, Ohio, Kentucky, Maryland, Indiana, Illinois, Oklahoma, Iowa, Missouri, Kansas, Tennessee, Virginia, Alabama and Georgia.

The former owner of the T&T mine, Paul Thomas, had been required by the 1977 Surface Mining Control and Reclamation Act to post a bond that supposedly would allow the state to clean up any pollution or repair any wound he might create. But, like all coal bonds, this one had been ridiculously low, and now the state is stuck with the enormous expense of perpetual ammonia treatment. Until very recently, it was standard practice for an operator to go out of business and walk away from one mess, then start a new company and make a new mess. On the Cheat watershed alone there are seventy-four other forfeited sites, all belching acid. "The bonding system made a lot of bad people out of good people," said Trout Unlimited activist Bill Thorne, with me on that morning.

Not that Thomas was all that "good." In an effort to avoid treatment costs, he sealed up his mine, secretly cut a hole into an adjoining one, and began pumping in his effluent. But he'd miscalculated; the hole was too small, and pressure built up. On April 8, 1994, the wastewater blew a hole in the mountain and poured into the Cheat, staining it orange for miles, killing fish and other aquatic life, poisoning riparian habitat, burning the eyes and skin of rafters and boaters and devastating the local economy, which hasn't fully recovered to this day.

Randy Robinson, a filmmaker who happened by just after the spill had started, recorded the disaster. His footage, aired by local and national TV stations, galvanized the public and helped convict Thomas for violating the Clean Water Act. Robinson, Thorne and others then helped build a support group called Friends of the Cheat.

In addition to fish, wildlife, rivers, mountains and forests, waste products of the coal industry include people. Also accompanying me was Friends' director, Keith Pitzer. "We looked at the lowest income census block groups in Preston County," he said. "And the first thing I noticed was that a lot were heavily mined. I contacted the public service district to see where their water lines were or were planned, and there was a distinct overlap because mined areas need public water. If you drill a well, you get orange, metal-contaminated acid. These are very low-value homes, not likely to be upgraded or sold."

Three weeks earlier Dr. Ben Stout of Wheeling Jesuit University in Wheeling, West Virginia, one of the nation's leading researchers on acid mine drainage and its costs, had told me this: "Kids come into this school thinking you can treat any kind of water and make it drinkable. 'Who taught you that?' I ask them. You can't get manganese out of water without just torturing it. You've got to take it way up in pH, treat the hell out of it, take it way back down in pH, settle it out, and by the time you've done all that you've introduced so many other things that you can't drink it."

Stout pays special attention to aquatic insects because they're indicators of ecosystem health; and in coal country he's chronicled a 50 percent reduction in both numbers and species. Many of his check stations are on headwater streams, which lawmakers assume don't count and therefore can legally be buried and/or polluted by the coal industry. But he has found that these streams are the "linkages" by which leaves and twigs are converted by insects to fats and proteins, very rare commodities in forests. These insects take to the air and float downstream, sustaining fish, salamanders, frogs, turtles, birds and mammals, jumpstarting energy flow in the whole forest ecosystem. Now the Bush administration is attempting to do away with the regulation that prevents mining activity within 100 feet of perennial streams.

Upstream from Muddy Creek, Thorne and Pitzer showed me four lifeless streams running orange over slimy carpets of yellow boy—Lick Run, Pringle Run, Heather Run, and Morgan Run. They used to ripple with wild brook trout. Now they're known as the Four Dirty Sisters. In the last decade the big change hasn't come in their water quality but in how that water quality is perceived by the public. These days it's no longer "okay" that they're the Four Dirty Sisters. Here and in other acidified watersheds around the state groups like Friends of the Cheat, Trout Unlimited, West Virginia Rivers Coalition, the West Virginia Highlands Conservancy, the Citizens Coal Council, Friends of Blackwater (who look after one of the Cheat's two biggest tributaries), and at least twenty-five local watershed groups have a firm grasp on the lapels of elected officials and are shouting into their faces.

The Corps of Engineers is about to install a "passive treatment" facility on Lick Run. Passive treatment (as opposed to active treatment— the sort I'd seen at the old T&T mine) requires no daily maintenance.

The hollow is very narrow, with two mine portals on opposite sides and about 100 feet from the stream. The Army will put in a limestone-lined pool at each outfall and, below one, install a limestone channel half a mile long. On the other side it will use the stream itself, lining a half-mile with limestone boulders.

At Morgan Run we hiked up to another type of treatment facility. Perched over the mine outflow was a green "Aquafix" silo inside of which a buffering agent such as crushed limestone or cement-kiln dust is pulled down by a wheel powered by the water itself and at a rate appropriate to and determined by the flow-the more water, the faster the wheel spins; and the faster the wheel spins, the more buffering agent is dispensed. The device seemed sufficiently ingenious to have been invented in Japan. But no. "By two local miners," said Pitzer. "Milford Jenkins and his son Mike." After passing under the Aquafix the mine drainage goes through two settling ponds. All DEP has to do is show up every few months to fill up the silo and haul off the yellow boy. The whole project, including excavation, cost $251,000—which sounds like a lot until you consider that the West Virginia Division of Natural Resources has determined that a mile of trout stream contributes $40,000 to the state's economy each year. Morgan Run needs many more treatment facilities before it can support fish again.

No less nasty is Greens Run, which enters the Cheat across the canyon from Muddy Creek. But its North Fork is marginal, and, with three new passive treatment systems, including an Aquafix, it may soon be suitable for a transplant of wild brook trout. I inspected one of these systems, installed last fall by Friends of the Cheat with funds from EPA and the Department of Interior's Office of Surface Mining. Carved into an embankment thirty yards above a dirt road was a foot-deep, limestone-lined pool that catches mine drainage and brings the pH up, but not too far or too fast. The trick is to get it almost but not quite to the point where the metals drop out of suspension; otherwise the pool would fill up with yellow boy. From the pool the drainage tumbled down 800 feet of limestone-lined channel curled through mixed hardwoods as if it had always been there. "We're very happy about the way the contractor minimized his footprint," said Pitzer. "I don't think he took out any tree bigger than ten inches in diameter. He just picked his way through the woods."

The North Fork's new trout population, however, will be cut off from the rest of the Greens Run drainage. Isolation is a problem with much of Appalachia's brook trout water and an enormous challenge for Friends, TU and their allies. Still, they're making headway. Pitzer rolled out a county map on which grossly acidified streams were colored red. The Big Sandy watershed showed as scarlet spaghetti, but the map was ten years old. "That wouldn't be colored red today," he said. "There's been a lot of passive treatment. We put in two sites on Beaver Creek, and we have one more to go; but above that—in four of the seven miles—we've introduced brook trout, and they're spawning. Once we put in the third site, we'll have a connection [for the trout] to Little Sandy." In 1989 the state Division of Natural Resources found no fish in a survey of Little Sandy. In 2001, at the same sampling site it found fourteen species, including brook trout.

Like stream-bred brookies most everywhere, Appalachia's aren't giants; but, using dry flies only, Thorne exercises many ten-inchers and a few twelve-inchers. "Few people realize how good our wild trout fishing is," he said. "Lots of woodland streams have gotten no mine runoff." What's more, the fishing is getting better fast. Thorne showed me a photo of a thirteen-inch male in spawning colors taken in the Red Run of Dry Fork, dead five years ago from acid rain. Here, and in other streams acidified by precipitation or mine drainage, a new and especially effective passive treatment is in use-dumping limestone sand directly into the stream each year. There's a formula that factors in pH and watershed acreage, but you can't get in trouble by using too much. At first biologists thought the lime would cement the bottom, but it doesn't. Frequently, trout hover over it.

In Charleston I stopped at the office of Friends of Blackwater, where director Judy Rodd and North Fork project leader Emily Samargo loaded me with documents, including an account in *Harper's New Monthly Magazine* by David Hunter Strother who, on a brook-trout quest in 1851, led the first Caucasians into the Blackwater country. Armed to the teeth with the fanciest tackle, much of which they smashed or dropped in the river, they killed fish like a reclamation crew. For example: "Conway ... who had gone over to Blackwater, returned with about a hundred and fifty fine trout. This lucky forage afforded the company a couple of hearty meals."

The fishery didn't last long after that, but overharvest wasn't an important factor. Clearcutting weakened it, and coal mining killed it. Below Beaver Creek (not the one restored by Friends of the Cheat), the Blackwater was essentially dead until 1994. But then the state installed four perforated, hopper-fed drums which the current turns, grinding the limestone within and pulling out the particles in quantity proportional to the flow. This has restored excellent fishing on about 4.5 miles until the Blackwater collects its grossly acidified North Fork. Five years after the liming station went in, fish biomass in the spectacular Blackwater Canyon above the North Fork had increased from 15 pounds per acre to 42.3; and there has been steady improvement since.

The state now has a catch-and-release area in the canyon's first 3.5 miles. "It has turned out extremely well," says Mike Shingleton, in charge of the DNR's trout program. "In spring we stock catchable rainbows. In fall we put in fingerling browns. There's even limited brown trout reproduction." Fishing schools and guiding services are springing up. Darrell Hensley offers this description of canyon fishing in *Fly Fish America*: "Awesome waterfalls from countless feeder streams plunge into the river and the late afternoon sun causes the sandstone cliffs at the canyon's rim to glow a vibrant orange. During June and July the aroma and pinkish white blossoms of mountain laurel and rhododendron are throughout the canyon. ... fishing these runs is fast and furious— lightning quick strikes will surprise you."

This restoration and the kind of work I'd seen on smaller tributaries, has dramatically improved the Cheat River for eighteen miles. In 1973 survey crews turned up twenty-four smallmouth bass per acre at Seven Islands between St. George and Rowlesburg. In 1999 they found 289.

No major river in the United States has been made sicker by acid mine drainage than the Susquehanna's West Branch in Pennsylvania. Seventy-two percent of its 6,992 square-mile watershed has been damaged, and at least 150 miles of main stem and 500 miles of coldwater feeder streams have been essentially sterilized of aquatic life. Rehabilitation will cost something like $500 million, not counting operation and maintenance of treatment facilities; but that hasn't prevented Trout Unlimited, six state agencies, four federal agencies and ten other partners from making impressive headway.

Five years ago TU launched an initiative to restore the lower section of Kettle Creek—a major West Branch tributary which, in its upper reaches, is one of the most productive trout streams in the East and, along with its tributaries, offers about seventy miles of Class A wild trout water. The last 6.5 miles of the mainstem, however, is severely acidified, and two miles before it merges with the Susquehanna's West Branch, and after it picks up Twomile Run, it's lifeless.

TU wrote a science-based restoration plan for the lower watershed. And, with the Kettle Creek Watershed Association, it helped the state DEP plan a large passive treatment facility, now complete, on a tributary of Twomile Run. On that same tributary TU is in the process of reclaiming a fifty-seven-acre strip mine, regrading, planting vegetation (of the sort favored by the local elk population), and thereby preventing a good deal of precipitation from reaching acid-forming pyrite. On another Twomile Run tributary it will have started work on four passive-treatment sites by the time you read this. Total cost for restoring the lower section of Kettle Creek: $10 million.

In the long run, eliminating instead of treating acid mine drainage is probably cheaper and definitely more effective. You do it by reclaiming (as defined by biologists, not industry) strip mines and mountaintop-removal sites. And you do it by filling up or sealing off deep mines so that water and air can't mix with pyrite. This takes a major financial commitment of the sort America hasn't yet been willing to make. Currently there's a political battle between Western and Eastern coal producers over the Abandoned Mine Land (AML) Trust Fund, into which coal companies must pay thirty-five cents per ton for surface-mined coal and fifteen cents per ton for deep-mined coal. Some of the money is supposed to go to the states for restoration of water and land damaged by mines before the August 3, 1977, enactment of the Surface Mining Control and Reclamation Act; but $1.5 billion sits unused, except to help offset the federal deficit. AML funds are crucial to rivers like the Cheat, which gets 80 percent of its acid from mines that went in before 1977.

It used to be that Appalachia was the biggest coal producer; now it's just the biggest acid producer. These days the largest coal producer by far is Wyoming; but Western coal deposits contain little pyrite and there's not much water to form sulfuric acid anyway. Western companies argue that they shouldn't have to help fix messes in Appalachia. Eastern companies, on the other hand, argue—and logically—that their dirty coal helped the country win World War II, got it industrialized in the 1950s and 1960s, and that Western coal producers are getting fat off that public service and therefore owe them big time.

Meanwhile, the politicians are posturing like tom turkeys on the strutting ground. Without renewal by Congress the AML fund will expire on September 30, 2004, and the $1.5 billion will get gobbled up for general expenses. For a while, the renewal was tacked onto Bush's energy bill, which was so dreadful that no legislator with an environmental conscience could vote for it, even to save the AML fund. Different bills are being hatched to save the fund, but it's not clear how much, if any, of a renewed fund would go to acid remediation.

Controlling what politicians do with AML money is infinitely easier than controlling how they aid and abet the coal industry in ducking cleanup responsibilities. The problem is that where coal is king most legislators are courtiers. Consider the current effort to do away with West Virginia's "Tier 2.5" designation for water quality. Tier 2.5 means streams in which brook trout are self-sustaining; and, while it offers modest protections, it exempts non-point pollution sources such as agriculture and logging. But, whipped up by the coal industry and the politicians who front for it, property-rights advocates and Farm Bureau and chamber of commerce pooh-bahs imagine that it contravenes the Fifth Amendment. Recently the legislature passed a law that lets a property owner petition the DEP to delist a Tier 2.5 stream. So now wild trout habitat can be defined by public opinion.

Last year State Senator Sarah Minear (R-Tucker County) got an amendment accepted by the legislature's joint Interim Rulemaking Committee to remove the current trout stream list from the water-quality rule. Had it been enacted, West Virginia would now—at least officially—

contain no trout habitat. Such is the opposition faced by those who love things wild and beautiful, and not just in West Virginia.

"What kind of person owns land with a brook trout stream running through it and doesn't want it protected?" said Pitzer.

"A coal mogul or property-rights zealot?" I asked.

But, as Pitzer and Thorne had reminded me, there are other voices; and, even in coal country, they're starting to be heard. With the public's new ability to petition for delisting Tier 2.5 water comes the ability to nominate it. Available for saving are all the trout streams never surveyed and all the trout streams that keep surging back to life.

TIME BOMB IN THE EARTH

◄-(- -)-►

Selenium, a naturally occurring element, performs all manner of useful functions, not the least of which is teaching us that if a little is good, a lot isn't necessarily better. In varying quantities and applications it can make you healthy, wealthy and dead. It's great for vulcanizing rubber, tinting glass, bluing gun barrels, controling dandruff and curing eczema. Farmers add it to livestock feed because if mammals don't ingest enough, they acquire debilitating calcium deposits, contract white muscle disease, and abort fetuses.

But there's a threshold after which selenium morphs into a poison at least five times more toxic than arsenic and that, like DDT, bioaccumulates as it ascends the food chain. Exposure to high concentrations can eliminate populations by causing reproductive failure and embryonic deformities, short-circuiting nervous systems, and blowing out kidneys and livers. Such concentrations are unnatural. They occur when rock- and earth-bound selenium is unleashed into the environment by such human disturbances as oil refining, coal-fired electrical generation, agricultural irrigation, mountain top-removal coal extraction and strip-mining of sulfide minerals—especially phosphate, used mainly to make fertilizer and phosphoric acid.

Forty percent of the nation's phosphate reserve lies hundreds of feet below the earth's surface in Idaho, Wyoming, Montana and Utah, bound up in rock formations. When phosphate ore is extracted selenium is cast to the four winds and carried away in runoff. Plants and microbes quickly assimilate it and are consumed by larger and more complex organisms which, in turn, are consumed by still larger and more complex organisms. By the time the selenium reaches fish and mammals, concentrations can be deadly. Hundreds of sheep and dozens of horses have been killed, and we can only guess at the number of birds, fish and wild animals because no one is watching or counting in this isolated and forgotten land.

Selenium pollution threatens to extirpate the Yellowstone cutthroat trout (now found in just 10 percent of its natural range) from two of its few remaining strongholds—the Blackfoot and Salt river drainages in southeast Idaho. Four permitted phosphate strip mines are belching selenium into these systems. Yet the J.R. Simplot Co., one of three current operators (the others being Nu-West, Inc., and Monsanto), wants to expand its Smoky Canyon Mine into the Caribou-Targhee National Forest. And the Bush administration's scuttling of the roadless area protection rule has allowed Simplot to hack roads into the Deer Creek watershed for test drilling. In addition to the four permitted phosphate strip mines, southeast Idaho has seventeen abandoned strip mines—all Superfund sites because they, too, are belching selenium.

Simplot vows to use the best technology available, but still admits that the creeks coming out of its mine expansion will be at or just below the current selenium standard of five parts per billion. And that's only if the cleanup of its existing mine (a Superfund site) turns out to be successful.

A section of Crow Creek (a tributary of the Salt River) flows through a ranch bought nine years ago by Pete and Judy Riede when they retired from General Motors to go fishing. "The average fish is twelve to fourteen inches, and I've caught them significantly over twenty," says Pete. "A section of Deer Creek (a tributary of the Crow that the mine will pollute) flows through the ranch, too; its trout are generally smaller, but there are beaver ponds that produce some tremendous fish."

So pristine was Deer Creek that, in August 2003, a Forest Service survey crew determined that it should be used as the standard of excellence— "a reference area for comparison to streams impacted by various land uses." The survey team went on to recommend "that activities not be allowed which would reduce the quality of fish and amphibian habitat in the drainage." Angler, author and communications director for Trout Unlimited's Public Lands Initiative, Chris Hunt, tells me this: "These fish are truly special; they move up out of the Blackfoot Reservoir—twenty two- to twenty-four-inch cutts that, come August, will charge up from under a cutbank and nail a grasshopper pattern. It's unbelievable in small stream settings like this. As a fisherman, I can see the writing on the wall.

These streams profiled in my guidebook [*A Fly Fisher's Guide to Eastern Idaho's Small Water*] are eventually doomed. I know that sounds drastic, but armed with the information I have now, I don't see a very bright future for the Yellowstone cutts and the non-native trout in the Caribou Highlands."

Nor do I, given the blasé attitudes of state and federal bureaucrats. On February 21, 2006, the Fish and Wildlife Service published the following statement in *The Federal Register*: "[US Forest Service selenium expert Dr. Dennis] Lemly (1999) described a particularly threatening scenario in the Blackfoot River drainage of Idaho where very high selenium concentrations were first discovered. A preliminary hazard assessment indicated that waterborne selenium concentrations in the Blackfoot River and 14 of its tributaries met or exceeded toxic thresholds for fish. The selenium problem centers on surface disposal of mine spoils. Compounding this problem is the presence of historic tailings dumps, many of which are large (greater than 353 million cubic feet) and contain a tremendous reservoir of selenium that has the potential to be mobilized and introduced into aquatic habitats (Lemly 1999). Continued expansion of phosphate mining is anticipated in these watersheds, and large mineral leases are awaiting development both on and off National Forest lands (Lemly 1999, Christensen 2005)."

That disheartening assessment accompanied a long string of similar disheartening assessments (all appended with "but," "however" or "nevertheless" clauses) as part of a denial of a petition to list the Yellowstone cutthroat trout as threatened. Identifying imperiled organisms and then protecting and recovering them as required by the Endangered Species Act is something our federal government just doesn't do anymore on its own volition. The administration of George H. W. Bush listed an average of fifty-eight species per year. The Clinton administration listed an average of sixty-five per year—this despite a one-year listing moratorium sponsored by Sen. Kay Bailey Hutchison (R-TX). The George W. Bush administration has listed an average of eight for a total of forty. Thirty-eight of these listings were in response to court action, one in response to threatened court action, and one in response to a citizens' petition.

Because selenium bioaccumulates, a one percent increase in the water column can translate to a 1,000-percent increase in fish flesh. At elevated but sublethal levels adult trout appear perfectly healthy, but their deformed fry perish in the swim-up stage or are quickly nailed by predators. Populations can wink out before biologists have a clue that there's a problem.

"It doesn't matter how little selenium may get into a stream; in some cases it's too damn much," declares Marv Hoyt, Idaho director of the Greater Yellowstone Coalition. "We've sampled these streams and found selenium in water below detectable limits, but levels in fish, insects and aquatic plants were 10 to 15 parts per million. Those concentrations cause reproductive failure in fish. Increasing selenium in streams by phosphate mining is just plain unacceptable. The Blackfoot and Crow cutthroat populations are really critical—two of the most important left in Idaho, and we're poisoning them."

From 1997 to 2001 the Idaho Department of Environmental Quality whitewashed the selenium hazard in what it called a "Human Health and Ecological Risk Assessment." According to this bogus document "regional human health and population-level ecological risks are unlikely to occur in the overall [phosphate mining area] based on observed conditions." But the department watered down the risks by distributing them over the entire mining area instead of impacted areas. When the Greater Yellowstone Coalition did its own analysis on seven streams in the Blackfoot and Salt River drainages it found that all fish sampled had elevated selenium levels dangerous not just to the fish but to humans who might eat them. In some cases the levels were four times the much laxer health standard now proposed by the Bush administration. The department had already posted a health advisory for consuming fish from East Mill Creek, where selenium levels are lower than in the seven streams sampled by the coalition.

Even more disturbing is the draft environmental impact statement (DEIS) for J.R. Simplot's Smoky Canyon Mine expansion into the Deer Creek watershed, released December 29, 2005, by the Bureau of Land Management and the Forest Service. The conclusion—full speed ahead—is based on misinterpretation of data, much of it obsolete and discredited anyway. The document isn't just grossly deficient; it is slovenly to the point of mocking the National Environmental Policy Act (NEPA). There is, for example, no mention that the entire length of Sage Creek, including the Pole Canyon drainage, has been added to the list of selenium-impaired streams. The authors evince scant comprehension of the bioaccumulation process, and they appear not to grasp the meaning of "mitigation," defining it as "actions to avoid, minimize, reduce, eliminate, replace, or rectify the impact of a management practice." As one reviewer—Dr. Patrick C. Trotter, a consulting fisheries scientist commissioned by the Greater Yellowstone Coalition—puts it: "I have had considerable experience working on teams that have prepared EIS documents for the NEPA process, and I recall quite a different set of guidances for applying the term 'mitigation' than appear to be used here. Careful design, careful construction, careful operation, and the application of best management practices were things that were expected would be done to prevent or avoid the occurrence of environmental impacts. Prevention and avoidance measures were not credited as mitigation. Mitigation meant measures taken to make right any environmental damage that could not be prevented or avoided despite best management practices or other best efforts."

For most of my career as a fish and wildlife journalist the Greater Yellowstone Coalition has provided me with information that has proved unimpeachable. Still, it's an environmental advocacy group, and for at least some readers its credibility is therefore suspect. So I went straight to the U.S. Forest Service—which co-authored the DEIS and invited J.R. Simplot to cut roads and do test drilling, thereby making the Sage Creek Roadless Area the first casualty under the Bush administration's new roadless policy. The agency's resident selenium expert is Dr. Dennis Lemly, a senior scientist at the Southern Research Station in Blacksburg, Virginia, and one of my main sources in the early 1990s when he was with the U.S. Fish and Wildlife Service and I was reporting on selenium poisoning of fish and wildlife at the Kesterson National Wildlife Refuge.

Kesterson is in California's Central Valley where selenium has always been present. The prolific wildflowers encountered by John Muir when he hiked down from the Coastal Range were taking selenium in precisely the proper dosage. But as agriculture swept into the area, unhealthy levels were pumped from the earth with groundwater. By the 1980s hundreds of thousands of eggs, hatchlings and adults of at least twenty species of aquatic birds were being fatally deformed or poisoned to death in gross violation of the Migratory Bird Treaty Act. The federal government's response was to whitewash the problem and punish the people who discovered it.

Dr. Lemly was calling selenium a "time bomb" back then; and he calls it one today. I asked him if, as a nation, we were doing better at defusing the selenium threat now than when he and I had talked fifteen years ago. "Same issue, same problem, different place, different time," he said. "The damage used to be associated with irrigation drainage; now it's associated with mining. The bottom line is that when you start disturbing soils and geological formations containing selenium they're going to leach selenium."

Can phosphate be strip-mined in the Blackfoot and Salt river drainages without hurting Yellowstone cutthroat trout? Dr. Lemly thinks not. "These ecosystems cannot spare any more selenium input," he told me. "They're already at the threshold. We need to look at this in terms of the long-term health of the fish, but the secretaries [of Agriculture and Interior] are going to weigh jobs. So it's the age-old question of pitting environment against development. It's no different there than at Kesterson, but now it's the Mining Association doing the pushing instead of the farmers." According to Dr. Lemly, the NEPA process "is broken with respect for having a procedure in place to identify selenium threats." For the past five years he's been working out a five-step process that considers all sorts of biological, geological and hydrological conditions to figure a TMDL (Total Maximum Daily Load); and he is urging his agency to adopt it.

"Is there a safe TMDL for the Smoky Canyon Mine expansion?" I asked him.

"Probably not," he said. "But the agencies haven't gone through the process to determine that." In his review of the DEIS, he observes that, because it ignores and misinterprets data, it "seriously underestimates selenium threats." For example, he quotes the document's repeated claim that "Hardy (2003) showed that cutthroat trout grown for 44 weeks ... showed no signs of toxicity." This statement, writes Dr. Lemly, "is absolutely not true," and he goes on to extensively quote Hardy's findings that link selenium with potentially fatal fry deformities. "From a fish-health perspective," Dr. Lemly continues, "it is irresponsible for the Agency Preferred Alternative [mine expansion] to be implemented. ... This ecosystem is a tinder box, and allowing additional selenium discharges will likely start a cascade of irreversible events, culminating in severe toxic impacts to fish and aquatic life for many years to come. ... The [secretaries] should not permit a process that could cause residual toxicity and place trust resources (and future land managers) in jeopardy for 100-plus years."

Despite the gross deficiencies of the DEIS, it contains three statements with which Dr. Lemly "strongly agrees": 1) "Impacts related to selenium bioaccumulation would be unavoidable." 2) "Indirect impacts to native fishes of the Study Area from further selenium accumulation, if they occurred, could be long-term and moderate to major." And, 3) "Specifically, long-term productivity effects related to cutthroat trout and other native fishes may be sacrificed through the bioaccumulation of selenium in Project Area streams (and eventually, the potential loss of reproductive function in resident fish)."

The Bush administration has reacted to America's selenium crisis by proposing relaxed standards. The current standard, which is causing so many problems with bioaccumulation, sets the limit for waterborne selenium at 5 parts per billion. The far laxer proposed standard—which EPA has offered in the wake of intense lobbying by mining, agribusiness and the electrical power industry—does away with a waterborne standard, replacing it with a fish-borne standard of 7.91 parts per million.

So that I might better understand the biological implications of the proposed standard I sought out the Department of Interior's resident selenium expert, Dr. Joseph Skorupa of the U.S. Fish and Wildlife Service, who provided this assessment: "Nothing short of reckless." And he said: "The tissue standard would mean 50- to 90-percent mortality for cutthroat trout. And one commonality that everyone, including the corporate sector, agrees on is that, if EPA is going to switch to tissue-based standard, it needs to develop guidelines on how regulators can use that because it's not fish that come out of discharge pipes; it's water. You have to relate that tissue standard to what goes into the environment."

I'd first met Dr. Skorupa in 1993, shortly after he'd been disciplined for discovering and disseminating information about selenium—namely that it was wiping out Central Valley wildlife, including endangered species. "Basically," he told me at the time, "I was locked into a windowless office, not allowed to take phone calls, not allowed to talk to anybody, not allowed to say 'hello' to the person in the next office." He was forbidden to pursue further selenium study, and when he procured an $800,000 grant from the California Department of Water Resources he was ordered to give it back. Finally, he was forbidden to seek outside funding for selenium work, although he was free to pursue other grants.

Since then Dr. Skorupa has been high-profile enough that bureaucrats fear him. Still, he says this: "Any time the selenium issue gets near the energy sector I still get clamped down on really tightly." For example, shortly after selenium became a potential impediment to mountaintop-removal coal extraction he was invited to speak at a U.S. Geological Survey symposium. The Department of the Interior heard about the title of his paper: "Fatal Flaws in EPA's Proposed Selenium Criteria" and informed USGS that the conference would be cancelled unless the title was changed. "I got this meek call from USGS begging me to let them change it," he reports. "I said fine, they could call it 'Bambi Meets SpongeBob,' but I wasn't going to change the content." Nor did he under the new title of "A Technical Review of EPA's Proposed Selenium Criteria."

Recently California irrigators served by the federal Central Valley Project have taken to citing the draft 7.91 parts per million tissue-based criterion as "scientific" support for relaxed environmental standards for their twenty-five-year water contract renewals.

Rather than hacking new phosphate strip mines into the habitat of vanishing species, it strikes me that we should be cleaning up all twenty one abandoned and permitted phosphate strip mines that are already poisoning Idaho's earth and water. By no means is the nation starving for phosphate. We have more than enough in places where it can be extracted without further compromising threatened and endangered species and creating new ones.

Under the current setup the public gets to pay for selenium cleanup twice—once with its fish and wildlife, and (provided the states and feds get around to doing something) once with its money. In the past, mining companies just walked away from their messes, and they aren't doing a whole lot better today. In no case is the damage by active or abandoned mines to fish, wildlife, water quality and public health being adequately remediated or even assessed.

Recently, mining companies have been required to set aside cleanup and reclamation bonds of $2,500 per affected acre, but this doesn't begin to cover the expense. Finally, "reclamation" in sensitive watersheds is a will-of-the-wisp goal that has never been achieved and may well be impossible. And, if it is impossible or if mining companies can't afford to do effective reclamation in sensitive watersheds (and elsewhere), the public cannot afford to allow them access to public resources on public lands.

UNDER THE INFLUENCE OF ETHANOL

-<-(- -)->-

Ethanol is even more popular now than when Americans made it to fuel themselves rather than their cars, and some of the behavior it generates is no less silly. The cornbelt, Congress, and the departments of Energy and Agriculture are hawking the stuff as if it were Dr. Kickapoo's Elixir for Rheum, Ague, Blindness and Insanity. Bill Gates has invested $84 million in it. In the last five years the amount of corn poured into ethanol distilleries has tripled to 55 million tons. At this writing, projections by the Department of Agriculture have world grain use growing by 20 million tons in 2006, six million tons of which will be consumed by the world's rapidly proliferating and hungry human beings, 14 million tons of which will be consumed by America's proliferating and gas-guzzling cars. Eighteen percent of all the corn we grow goes into ethanol production, and goals mandated by Congress will sharply increase that percentage.

It all started in 1990 with amendments to the Clean Air Act, revolutionary in that they regulated not just how we burn gasoline but how we make it. In areas out of compliance with air-pollution standards, gasoline had to include at least two percent oxygen-containing chemicals (oxygenates), the better to combust carbon monoxide, toxic hydrocarbons, and smog-producing volatile organic compounds. There were only two choices—ethanol and the petroleum-based methyl tertiary butyl ether (MTBE). This was precisely what the cornbelt had fantasized about and lobbied for. Suddenly the moribund ethanol industry had a future. City air would become breathable. We'd have plenty of fuel. It was going to be a win-win-win.

Instead of cleaning up America, ethanol has added to the mess we're making out of our water and air. Now the Bush Administration has decreed that ethanol replace the far more efficient MTBE as an oxygenate. But with current refining technologies and anti-pollution paraphernalia on motor vehicles there's no need for *any* oxygenate, a fact the powerful agribusiness lobby doesn't want you to know. Under its withering pressure, Congress and the executive branch have committed the nation to ethanol as both oxygenate and fuel.

The Energy Policy Act of 2005 requires that U.S. gasoline contain 7.5 billion gallons of ethanol by 2012, up from four billion. One hundred and one ethanol plants are online, and forty-four are under construction. Eighty million U.S. acres were planted to corn in 2006; and the ethanol boom will require ten million more just in 2007. Ethanol, we are being told, is going to "reduce our dependence on foreign oil" and "lead us to energy independence." "Live Green, Go Yellow," effuses General Motors, one of the major roadblocks to fuel-efficiency standards. "Fill Up, Feel Good," gushes the Ethanol Promotion and Information Council, a front for agribusiness.

How will ethanol affect your fishing, apart from possibly ruining your outboard motor? (Ethanol does this in lots of ways. Just ask David Blinken, the famous Montauk fly-fishing guide, who recently spent $25,000 pulling his deck, replacing his fuel lines and tank, extracting aluminum-oxide gum from his carburetors, and basically rebuilding his twin 100-horse Yamahas.) First, no crop grown in the United States consumes and pollutes more water than corn. No method of agriculture uses more insecticides, more herbicides, more nitrogen fertilizer. Needed for the production of one gallon of ethanol are 1,700 gallons of water, mostly in the form of irrigation taken from streams either directly or by snatching the water table out from underneath them. And each gallon of ethanol produces twelve gallons of sewage-like effluent.

Ethanol plants are gross polluters of air and water, and because of the exorbitant price of natural gas some of the new ones will be coal-fired, adding to the already dangerous mercury content of fish. The response of the Bush administration has been a proposal to relax pollution standards for ethanol production. Under the conservation programs of the 1985 Farm Bill and its successors, some farmers are bootstrapping their way toward sustainable agriculture, but corn production still erodes topsoil about ten times faster than it can accrete.

The toxic, oxygen-swilling stew of nitrates, chemical poisons, and dirt excreted from the corn monocultures of our Midwest pollutes the Mississippi River and its tributaries, limiting fish all the way to the Gulf where it creates a bacteria-infested, algae-clogged, anaerobic "Dead

Zone" lethal to fish, crustaceans, mollusks, and virtually all gill breathers. In some years, depending on seasonal heat and water conditions, the Dead Zone can cover 8,000 square miles. And it's expanding.

No habitat is more important to fish and wildlife than wetlands. They filter out pesticides and sediments, and they consume phosphates and nitrates. At least 70 percent of the wetlands in the cornbelt have already been lost. But, in order to produce surplus corn for ethanol, remaining cornbelt wetlands are being drained. In some areas—Nebraska, for instance—corn has to be irrigated by pumps that suck water from the ground faster than it percolates back in. Both pumps and the ethanol plants themselves are powered by natural gas, the frenzied production of which is creating horrendous problems for fish and wildlife in the West.

Where is the land to grow all the extra corn needed for ethanol supposed to come from? Well, the Bush administration has an idea: In testimony to Congress, the USDA's chief economist, Keith Collins, has raised the possibility of using land enrolled under the Farm Bill's Conservation Reserve Program (CRP). Not so coincidentally, it happens that this is precisely the idea that the corn lobby had come up with. In an op-ed in the December 6, 2006, *Des Moines Register* Bruce Rastetter, CEO of Hawkeye Renewables, Iowa's largest ethanol producer, writes: "First, the government should immediately release some of the 37 million acres that now sit idle in the U.S. Department of Agriculture's Conservation Resources [sic] Program."

"We're hearing rumors every day that the [USDA's] Farm Services Agency is on the verge of announcing they're going to allow people to liquidate CRP contracts to grow more corn for ethanol," says Julie Sibbing, point person for the National Wildlife Federation's agriculture and wetlands program. "That's a huge concern. They've been studying CRP to see if there's land they can pull out to grow more corn. We're hearing from folks up in the plains that farmers are going in and breaking up virgin prairie. It's lousy land for agriculture, but they're planting it because of the high price of corn brought on by this ethanol boom. It's scary. And there are huge water requirements. People are building these ethanol plants anywhere, paying no attention to the water needs. We're worried about instream flows."

CRP—originally conceived not for the benefit of fish, wildlife or soil but simply to reduce surplus, government-subsidized corn—has restored two million acres of wetlands and adjacent buffers, produced 7.1 million acres of new native grasses, protected 170,000 miles of streams, restored 1.2 million acres of rare and declining wildlife habitat, and saved 450 million tons of soil (enough to fill 37.5 million dump trucks). What's more, CRP annually produces 15 million pheasants and 2.2 million ducks and sequesters 48 million tons of carbon dioxide. It is absurd to suggest we can't afford CRP. The increased soil productivity it has provided is worth $162 million a year, increased waterfowl hunting $122 million, increased wildlife viewing $629 million, and runoff reduction $392 million.

Thanks to CRP and other Farm Bill conservation programs, Iowa— the corn capital of the nation—is suddenly teeming with smallmouth bass and, in the state's northeast hill country, wild trout. Yes, *wild trout.* "Our trout fishery is one of the best kept secrets in the country," declares Rich Patterson, who directs the Indian Creek Nature Center in Cedar Rapids and serves on the Circle of Chiefs of the Outdoor Writers Association of America. "When I first came here twenty-eight years ago it was all put-and-take, guys tossing corn to stupid hatchery trout. I'm catching incredible wild trout in streams that were mucky in the 1980s. And there has been a tremendous turnaround on smallmouths. They're sight feeders, and with clearing water they're increasing like crazy."

Marion Conover, chief of fisheries for the Iowa Fish and Wildlife Division, confirms Patterson's assessment. "The smallmouths are a reflection of improved clarity in our streams because of buffer strips and best management practices funded through the Farm Bill's conservation title," he says. "We manage four stream segments as catch-and-release for smallmouth—on the upper Iowa, Cedar River, Middle Raccoon, and Maquoketa. These are higher-quality streams, but we've seen smallmouths improve in places like the Mississippi River, parts of the Des Moines River, and the Missouri River in the Sioux City area of all places. It's simply a function of less dirt in the water. But there's a concern among the whole environmental community about what bodes for the future, what our landscape is going to look like next year or five years from now."

The Iowa brookies are a national treasure, genetically distinct from Yankee brook trout, Appalachian brook trout and even fish from Wisconsin and Minnesota. In 1980 only one of the state's streams had native brook trout reproduction, and only four had brown trout reproduction. Today there are at least twenty-three with self-sustaining browns and six with self-sustaining native brookies. The division's northeast fisheries supervisor, Bill Kalishek, expects that by the time you read this, new survey results will have significantly increased these numbers. And if farm bill programs remain intact, streams where there is now only sporadic reproduction will become self-sustaining. The brookies are small, but the browns are huge in relation to the little spring creeks in which they abide. Kalishek reports that fifteen- to twenty-inchers are not unusual, and he's seen them up to twenty-eight inches. "The unglaciated terrain here in northeast Iowa is highly erodible," he told me. "So cropland is very eligible for CRP. That program has taken a lot of the most highly erodible land out of row-crop production and reduced the amount of sediment getting washed into the streams. Not only has the water quality improved, so has the substrate quality for spawning."

But America's ethanol orgy frightens Kalishek and his colleagues. "I've seen some of the results already," he says. "The bulldozers are out there on the little corners of cornfields that used to be brushy draws or old fence lines so farmers can grow more corn. A lot of our general signup CRP enrollments—where whole, erodible fields were taken out of production—are expiring in the next two or three years. And I'm worried that with this increase in corn production we're going to take a big step backwards in water quality and stream habitat and in our trout populations."

Well, as we so frequently tell ourselves and are told by our federal government, we all have to make sacrifices for energy self-sufficiency. But the sacrifices fish-and-wildlife advocates and taxpayers are being asked to make for ethanol do not and cannot decrease our dependency on foreign oil. In fact, they do just the opposite. This is because it takes more energy in the form of fossil fuels to make corn-based ethanol that we get from it.

Some researchers dispute this, but almost without exception they are directly or indirectly funded by or otherwise allied to agribusiness or the USDA (a wholly owned subsidiary of agribusiness). The credible stats issue from independent researchers whose studies have been published in peer-reviewed scientific journals and who have no irons in the fire.

Two of the more notable ones are Dr. Tad W. Patzek, a chemical engineer from the University of California at Berkeley, and Cornell University's Dr. David Pimentel.

Pimentel, author of twenty-four books and nearly 600 scientific papers and selected by the Department of Energy to chair two scientific panels on ethanol production, told me this: "Ethanol is a boondoggle. Optimistically, using Department of Energy numbers, it amounts to one percent of our petroleum use. Ethanol requires almost 40 percent more energy to produce than you get out of it; we're having to import oil to make this stuff. And, of course, the environmental impacts to water, air and soil are enormous. During the fermentation process, when yeast is working on the starches and sugars, large quantities of carbon dioxide are released. In fact, some plants collect it and sell it to beverage companies. So it's a double whammy for global warming—not only burning fossil fuel but carbon dioxide production."

Pimentel reports that ethanol, which yields only two-thirds the energy of gasoline, gets forty-five times more federal subsidy per gallon than gasoline. "That's what's attracting all the flies," he says. All told, you and I are spending at least $3 per gallon on ethanol subsidies for a total of $6 billion per year. Without all this gravytrain, Pimentel has calculated that the cost for 1.33 gallons of ethanol (the equivalent in energy yield to a gallon of gasoline) would be $7.12.

The subsidies aren't going to family farms but to bloated, effluent-spewing agribusiness giants which get hungrier and dirtier with each feeding. According to one estimate—by financial analyst James Bovard of the Cato Institute—every dollar in profits earned by the nation's largest ethanol producer, Archer Daniels Midland (ADM), costs taxpayers $30.

In February 2006 Energy Secretary, Sam Bodman, showed up at ADM's Decatur, Illinois headquarters to pose with CEO Allen Andreas and announce that the Department of Energy would offer $160 million for the construction of three biorefineries for ethanol production. "This funding will support a much-needed step in the development of biofuels and renewable energy programs," declared Bodman. "Partnerships with industry like these will lead to new innovation and discovery that will usher in an era of reduced dependence on foreign sources of oil, while strengthening our economy at home."

This is the same ADM that made it to number ten on the University of Massachusetts' Political Economy Research Institute's "Toxic 100" list of America's worst corporate polluters, the same ADM that in 2003 was assessed $351 million in fines by the EPA for Clean Air Act violations at fifty-two plants in sixteen states, the same ADM currently slugging it out with the state and feds in twenty-five judicial and administrative proceedings regarding its contamination of air, soil and water.

ADM is just one of many offenders. Another example: in June 2006 Ace Ethanol LLC of Stanley, Wisconsin and John S. Olynick, Inc., of Gilman, Wisconsin, (an excavating company) agreed to pay $61,000 after they'd been cited for filling wetlands adjacent to a tributary of the Wolf River. And Ace has been ordered by Wisconsin's attorney general to pay $300,000 in fines for Clean Air Act violations.

"I've been following this ethanol development very closely," says Iowa Fish and Wildlife's Kalishek. "And I have one hope—biomass ethanol. If we can get plants shifted over to biomass [cellulosic ethanol derived from wood chips, straw, hemp, crop stalks, etc.], we could have farmers growing something like switchgrass [one of the native prairie covers approved for CRP enrollment]. Then we wouldn't have to worry about erresion. There'd be many benefits for fish and wildlife and water quality. But it looks like the demand for corn for ethanol is going to continue to increase. Every prediction I've seen, and the most recent one came out of Iowa State University, is that demand for corn is going to outstrip Iowa's ability to produce corn. If you've every driven across our state, you'd scratch your head and say, 'Huh? All that corn is not going to be enough to feed the ethanol plants?'"

The National Wildlife Federation shares Kalishek's hopes and fears. "We're working on a program for the next farm bill that would try to advance the whole next generation of technologies like switchgrass ethanol," says Sibbing. "A couple [cellulosic] plants are being built now— one in Iowa and one on Idaho. If we get to cellulosic ethanol, we can produce something like five times more per acre. It would be a lot better for land and water and a produce a lot more bang for the buck."

Switchgrass is certainly attractive to burn directly as a biomass fuel; and one day, perhaps, it will be an ethanol source. Because it is harvested in early spring or late summer or fall, declining ground-nesters such as quail and bob-o-link that fledge their broods in late spring would benefit. Switchgrass requires essentially no fertilization; and it's a perennial, which means there's no tilling, reseeding or erosion.

But, warns Cornell's Pimentel, cellulosic ethanol is far more difficult to produce than corn-based ethanol, which itself isn't practical or economical. "There are only about half as many starches and sugars in woody material and straw as in corn," he explains. "There are also extra steps. You have to use an acid or enzyme to release the cellulose from the lignin—the stuff that holds the plants up straight. If you use acid, you have to stop the acidity process with an alkali. So that's another step. You hear stories from pro-ethanol people that the lignin (about 25 percent of the wood) can be used to for fuel, but that's if it's dry. It's dissolved in water, and to dry it takes a good deal of energy."

Ethanol rendered from crop stalks is no less problematical. And any major commitment to that source could be even more environmentally hurtful than corn-based ethanol by spiking already gross erosion rates.

So, until we figure out how to make ethanol cheaply and efficiently from native prairie perennials like switchgrass, where are we going to find the fuel to run our cars? Berkeley's Dr. Tad Patzek makes the point that corn is merely one way of converting solar energy to fuel. Solar cells, far more efficient, could make hydrogen fuel. That's where the subsidies need to go, he contends. But technology for practical, affordable hydrogen fuel, like technology for practical, affordable ethanol fuel, doesn't exist yet.

We do, however, possess the technology to build fuel-efficient automobiles. In the current charade designed by and for agribusiness we're allocating 18 percent of the corn we grow to ethanol, thereby cutting our petroleum consumption by one percent. But Patzek has calculated that if we doubled automobile fuel-efficiency, we'd cut petroleum consumption by 33 percent or, put another way, we'd increase our petroleum supply by a third. It's a revolutionary concept that America has never tried. Fish-and-wildlife advocates are calling it *conservation*.

CREDITS

—‹‹· ··››—

Essence of Patagonia, *Gray's Sporting Journal*, Feb. 1997 • Role Reversal on the Colorado, *Fly Rod & Reel*, April 2003 • Dixie Trout, *Blue Ridge Press*, March 2002 • Bringing Back the Giants, *Fly Rod & Reel*, March 2006 • Twilight of the Yankee Trout, *Trout* magazine, Autumn 1993 • Environmentalists vs. Native Trout, *Fly Rod & Reel*, April 2004 • Trout are Wildlife, Too, *Audubon*, March 2003 • Western Water Cure, *Fly Rod & Reel*, January 2002 • Bluefin Summer, *Fly Rod & Reel*, July 2006 • How It Is at South Andros, *Saltwater Fly Fishing*, August 2004 • The Exhausted Sea, *Audubon*, Sept, 2003 • Striper Recovery Not, *Fly Rod & Reel*, Jan. 2005 • Why Should Anyone Listen to Striper Anglers, *Fly Rod & Reel*, Jan. 2007 • Shark Attack, *Audubon*, July 1996 • Marketing MPAs, *Fly Rod & Reel*, Nov. 2002 • Do We Need Saltwater Licenses?, *Fly Rod & Reel*, April 2005 • The Highlander Hatch, *Fly Rod & Reel*, March 1992 • Everything But Salmon, *Patagonia Catalogue*, Winter 2003 • Salmon Stakes, *Audubon*, March 2003 • Have Salmon Endangered Maine?, *Fly Rod & Reel*, June 2005 • Salmon of the St. Lawrence Lakes, *Atlantic Salmon Journal*, Autumn 2003 • As Maine Goes So Go the Salmon, *Fly Rod & Reel*, Sept. 1999 • Salmon Shell Game, *Fly Rod & Reel*, Nov. 2004 • Something's Fishy, *Audubon*, June 2005 • Getting Past Hatcheries, *Fly Rod & Reel*, Sept. 2000 • Want Another Carp?, *Fly Rod & Reel*, June 2001 • Fish-Poison Politics, *Fly Rod & Reel*, March 2001 • Big Water Blues, *Audubon*, July 2001 • Damn the Tax Payers, Full Speed Ahead, *Audubon*, July 2000 • Dam Removal, *Fly Rod & Reel*, April 2002 • Where Baitfish Don't Belong, *Fly Rod & Reel*, July 2007 • Management by Politician, *Fly Rod & Reel*, June 2002 • Robbed by RATs, *Fly Rod & Reel*, June 2007 • Saving the North Woods, *FlyRod & Reel*, Dec. 2003 • Sludge Slinging, *Audubon*, May 2004 • Sagging Streams, *Fly Rod & Reel*, Nov. 2001 • Sportsmen vs. the Northern Forest, *Fly Rod & Reel*, Jan. 2003 • A Plague on All Your Forests, *Fly Rod & Reel*,

April 2006 • Pits in the Crown Jewels, *Fly Rod & Reel*, Nov. 2006 • Ann and Nancy's War, *Fly Rod & Reel*, July 2005 • A Vampire Story, *Fly Rod & Reel*, June 2004 • Motorizing Public Land, *Audubon*, March 2000 • Save the Redwoods: Kill Everyone, *Fly Rod & Reel*, May 2000 • Coal-Country Trout, *Fly Rod & Reel*, July 2004 • Time Bomb in the Earth, *Fly Rod & Reel*, July 2006 • Under the Influence of Ethanol, *Fly Rod & Reel*, April 2007.